A LIFESTYLE OF WORSHIP

Living in the Awareness of God's Presence

WILLIAM F. HOLLAND JR.

Copyright © 2015 by WILLIAM F. HOLLAND JR.

A LIFESTYLE OF WORSHIP
Living in the Awareness of God's Presence
by WILLIAM F. HOLLAND JR.

Printed in the United States of America

ISBN 9781498433815

All rights reserved solely by the author. The author guarantees all contents are original and do not infringe upon the legal rights of any other person or work. No part of this book may be reproduced in any form without the permission of the author. The views expressed in this book are not necessarily those of the publisher.

Unless otherwise indicated, scripture quotations are taken from The King James Version (KJV).

www.xulonpress.com

Lord, we ask for wisdom

A revelation of love we pray

From your blueprint we will build

With single vision to obey

Sowers of truth in fields prepared

Sharing the suffering cost

Proclaiming Jesus the Holy Ransom

Who seeks to save the lost

CONTENTS

Acknowledgements ix
Introduction xi

Part I: The Awareness Of His Holiness 17
1. *Repentance Before Adoration* 19
2. *The Corporate Assembly* 25
3. *Infectious Enthusiasm* 31
4. *Being Altered* 34
5. *Godly Sorrow* 40
6. *From Faces To Fingerprints* 47
7. *The Windows Of Heaven* 55

Part II: The Awareness Of His Truth 59
8. *An Acceptable Offering* 61
9. *Plowing The Fields* 72
10. *In His Presence* 75
11. *The Default And The Divine* 83
12. *A Sweet Smelling Fragrance* 90
13. *Every Knee Shall Bow* 96
14. *Seeking After A Sign* 98

Part III: The Awareness Of His Love 107
15. *Constant Awareness* 109
16. *More Than Music* 115
17. *The Leader Of Songs* 122
18. *Learning To Let Go* 129
19. *Holy Ground* 132

20. The Bridal Procession 136
21. Spiritual Intimacy 149

Part IV: The Awareness Of His Majesty 157
22. The Anointing 159
23. Reverential Fear 171
24. Crying In The Wilderness 177
25. The Levites: Pioneers Of Praise 182
26. The Agony Of Disrespect 185
27. The Mantle Of Leadership 197
28. A Little Leaven 202

Part V: The Awareness Of His Intent 207
29. Refiner's Fire 209
30. Guarding Our Joy 215
31. Burned Out Or Back Slidden? 224
32. The Religious Spectator 229
33. God's Tangible Presence 233
34. A Still Small Voice 237
35. The Psalmist 241

Part VI: The Awareness Of His Mercy 251
36. Intentions Of The Heart 253
37. The Secret Place 259
38. Making The Investment 268
39. The Anticipation Of His Glory 278
40. Worthy Is The Lamb 284
41. God Calling 289
42. The Power Of Praise 298

Part VII: The Awareness Of His Glory 305
43. The Beauty Of Descending 307
44. Downward Mobility 313
45. The Overcomers 322
46. Discerning The Seasons 330
47. The Upper Room 337
48. Be Still And Know 344
49. An Audience Of One 350
Final Thoughts 357

ACKNOWLEDGEMENTS

I am grateful to my wife, Cheryl, who has been a constant source of encouragement and support throughout the years. She does not just go along with my ideas; she has a mind of her own and is not afraid to express her keen sense of spiritual discernment which has brought much needed balance in my life. I love you and thank you for this wonderful journey we have shared together.

It is a privilege to know God and receive His mercy. He is patient with me, as I am just another example of His long-suffering. I am not a scholar of worship; neither am I a world renowned theologian. I am simply a thankful seeker that is not only trying to understand His truth – but to become determined to live it.

INTRODUCTION

"Give unto the Lord, O ye kindreds of the people, give unto the Lord glory and strength. Give unto the Lord the glory due unto His Name: bring an offering, and come into His courts. O worship The Lord in the beauty of holiness: fear before Him, all the earth" (Psalm 96:7-9).

This book is not just for those who are involved with spiritual music; it is about ALL of God's children that long to live within a constant worship *service* of His presence. Our concept of exalting the Lord is usually built around the idea of music, but we are discovering that expressing our love to Him goes far beyond singing songs; it is how we live each moment. When adoration and thanksgiving become a *state of mind,* we will begin to abandon our thoughts and be more connected with His will. Embracing this level of personal intimacy with the Creator establishes a beautiful communication exchange which evolves into an awareness of loving Him with all of our soul, mind, and strength. This revelation may be sudden, but learning how to develop a lifestyle of worship will take a lifetime of training our minds to concentrate on God.

Every song that has ever been sung and every book that has been written can only scratch the surface in describing His endless mercy and glorious Majesty and how worthy He is of our worship. Brother Lawrence, whose 17th century work, *The Practice of the Presence of God*, details his determination to *re-train* his conscience to become so discerning that he considered everything as an opportunity to serve

Christ. By allowing this concept of perception to transform who we are, we not only have a wonderful opportunity, but a responsibility to mature into a higher level of spiritual sensitivity. We are learning that the Christian lifestyle is about establishing and maintaining a bond of holy devotion with Christ, as we allow our conscience to be changed into a reflection of His image. It is not about the world watching us worship Jesus; it is about them sensing God's presence in our lives. People are tired of talk; they want to witness the love of heaven, as it is true that the most powerful sermons are without words.

If you want more of God, you must choose to deliberately pursue Him! As we become more intense in this love relationship, worshipping who He is will become as natural as breathing. Spending time with Him is how we get to know Him, and this is exactly what He desires from us. It is enlightening to discover that bringing our sacrifice of praise to God is not limited to an act, but the more He is on our minds the more our lives become the living sacrifice. When all is said and done, and we stand before His throne, the amount of our conscience we allowed Him to occupy will reveal what meant the most to us. Jesus can be the Lord of our hearts when we remove our carnality and allow Him to sit on the throne of our hearts, and this is when worshipping in Spirit and Truth becomes a *lifestyle*.

Within these pages I am not trying to imply that I have cornered the market on understanding worship or the mysteries and secrets of heaven; this is just a collection of my thoughts and experiences along with God's Word that I hope will bring encouragement and a fresh purpose-driven insight into what a privilege it is to worship Jesus Christ. I do not believe we can necessarily train people how to worship God because we must avoid drifting into a legalistic ritual. However, concepts and illustrations about Christian living can reveal spiritual principles and components that can help us develop a more meaningful personal relationship with Christ. Each person has the free-will to experience the depths of His presence, and for those who are longing to go to heaven after this life is over, it would go without saying that we are also looking forward to the glorious worship around His throne for all eternity. It is true that many are not taking their spiritual life seriously, neither have they obtained the revelation that God is giving us the opportunity to take advantage of this life as a temporary *worship practice* so that when we enter into the gates of eternal life we will blend into the most powerful worship service time has ever known. I realize it is awkward to worship someone we cannot see, but that is the point of living by faith. The covenant life is all about having a passionate desire to be with Jesus in the secret place of our hearts, and as we draw nearer to Him, He will open the eyes of our spirits so that we can see and know Him more personally. These lines and precepts of spiritual levels expose the vast difference between living a default religious existence and becoming a remnant disciple of our living Lord and Savior.

God is calling us today to spend more time with Him and fall in love with Him so deeply that nothing in this world can interfere with this bond of holy intimacy. Is this what you want today? Do you long to be loved with the most fervent affection in heaven and earth? We can be as close to God as we want and be filled with His Spirit with a constant awareness of His presence IF we allow Him to become our highest priority. If this is what you are seeking today, then you have found the meaning of life! There is only one thing that can prevent you from becoming what Jesus died for you to be – your will. When we are truly in love with someone, nothing can keep us from them. *"O God, thou art my God; early will I seek thee: my soul thirsteth for thee, my flesh longeth for thee in a dry and thirsty land, where no water is; to see thy power and thy glory, so as I have seen thee in the sanctuary. Because thy loving-kindness is better than life, my lips shall praise thee. Thus will I bless thee while I live: I will lift up my hands in thy name. My soul shall be satisfied as with marrow and fatness; and my mouth shall praise thee with joyful lips"* (Psalm 63:1-5).

Worship is a unique and widely misunderstood term that humans seem to avoid thinking about, yet actually practice it constantly. Our fallen nature shrinks away from thinking about or openly praising God but boldly exalts the other idols in our life. It is amazing how many people focus their attention toward a special interest but would never consider worship as the simple act of personal adoration. There is an old saying *"Everybody serves somebody,"* and I believe we can conclude that whatever has captured our imagination receives our highest worship. Of course, the human race comes fully equipped with this ability to be infatuated and controlled within the free-will of the conscience and is more than willing to *bow down* to whatever we love. We deny that many times we have actually crowned ourselves as lord and king, which explains why human nature rarely considers the fact that idolatry has more to do with the one we see in the mirror than an outside influence or temptation. The gospel summarizes the concept of worship as either going through life in the default mode of serving our own wills or making the decision to be spiritually re-born to serve and worship God in His divine reality. Let it be said that He will compel but does not force anyone to worship Him; and according to His spiritual principles, the dark side also abides by the same law. In other words, you and I are constantly being influenced and choosing whom we will serve and obey.

Together let us take a serious look at the definition of worship: *"A homage or reverence paid to a thing or person; the acts, rites, or ceremonies of worship; adoration or devotion comparable to religious homage shown toward a person or principle (like the worship of wealth), honor, respect, veneration, reverence, esteem, exaltation, admiration, to extol, admire, glorify, magnify, and praise"* (*The Oxford Dictionary* – American Edition). Our hymns and worship songs are filled with appreciation as we attempt to relay our deepest love and devotion to the God of the universe but in our limited human ability to understand, many times we are left speechless in glory of His presence. He draws us with His love, and we respond with gratitude and reverential awe. ***"I will sing unto the Lord as long as I live: I will sing praise to my God while I have being. My meditation of Him shall be sweet; I will be glad in the Lord"*** *(Psalm 104:33-34).*

The school of Christian living is our daily classroom and within our daily prayers should be the request to understand what we are learning. Without wisdom, knowledge is just a beautiful collection of facts, and in the Christian life it is not how much we know - but how much we apply. God views our spiritual voyage not as a religious parade that is filled with programs and ceremonies but as a holy *communion* that nurtures a covenant relationship that includes a continual exchange of thoughts and expressions. We worship Him not because of what He can do or how much He will give, but simply because we are infatuated with His person. Our joy overflows when we weep at His altar as our broken and contrite hearts release a sweet-smelling aroma around His throne and in the secret place of His presence. It is with trusting innocence that we can snuggle into the lap of a loving Father and allow Him to put His arms around us as He gently rocks us to sleep in His peace that passes all understanding. In the essence of His glory we become supernaturally entwined with the ruler of the universe, who longs to mold us as soft clay on the potter's wheel. This miracle begins to happen when we abandon our old nature and embrace Him

Introduction

as the Master of our destiny. Only then can our lives finally begin their humble descent so that Christ can be formed and displayed within us. When He becomes the meaning of our lives, His presence will become as natural as breathing. To know Him is the purpose of living, to love Him is our most precious gift, and to worship Him is our greatest honor and privilege.

Wherever you are in this journey, God desires to fill you with His love and teach you everything you will need to know concerning the divine realities of His abundant life. I sincerely invite you to travel with us as we continue on this pilgrimage together. This is not another seeker sensitive compilation of religious ideas; it is simply a collection of teachings for those who are serious about becoming more vehement in their relationship with Jesus. May you receive the illumination of God's Word as a vital stepping stone in your pathway toward knowing Him more intimately, and I pray that you will continue to be filled with the joys of worshipping Him as your Lord and Redeemer - The King of glory.

"I am sorry Lord for all of the times I was too busy trying to blaze a trail for you without stopping to smell the flowers. You were there all along, and I was just too distracted to see you. Thank you for speaking to my heart with your kindness and mercy. It is so easy for us to become confused with deception, and I pray for all who are asking, knocking, and seeking your truth. Stir my heart Lord that I might understand how important it is to spend time with you. We do not know it all, and when we think we do, we are already caught in a snare trap of deception and denial. I repent of my sins today, and ask you to cleanse me and purify me with your holy refining fire. Teach me how to love you and how to worship you with all of my heart, soul, mind, and strength. Take me DEEPER and HIGHER into your ways and your thoughts. Thank you for provoking me, inspiring me, and encouraging my heart as I am now determined to deliberately pursue you. Prepare and plow my heart that I may receive the engrafted Word that is able to save my soul. I am hungry and thirsty for your presence. Have mercy on me O God; I am desperately needy for you, I love you, I worship you. Amen."

"O come, let us worship and bow down: let us kneel before the Lord our maker" *(Psalm 95:6).*

PART I
THE AWARENESS OF HIS HOLINESS

Chapter 1

REPENTANCE BEFORE ADORATION

"The hills melted like wax at the presence of the Lord, at the presence of the Lord of the whole earth. The heavens declare His righteousness, and all the people see His glory" (Psalm 97:5-6).

B eing in God's presence is the highest place of spiritual joy and peace that is attainable in any existence. When we step from this realm into the next dimension, those who are born of God's Spirit and have followed the Lord of creation will have the ultimate privilege to worship and adore Him for all eternity. For His children, the joys of His truth reveal that we need not wait to enter into His gates and courts of glory, but we can abide in this divine reality here and now!

Worship is idolizing our most valuable treasure, and those who adore the Savior of the world cannot fathom the awesome, majestic wonders that are waiting for them in the life to come. His *"good news"* contains the mysteries of His truth. His children need not wait until they leave this earth to enter into His gates, but have been invited to abide in this divine reality with Him now! Though our journey is taking place in a harsh environment of darkness, and we constantly struggle in the war against our flesh and the devil, the occasional glimpse into the province of God's holiness and revelational truth is enough to excite and cause us to reach heavenward with fervent anticipation. It is with passionate expectation that I place my hope in His Word and completely trust my life to the Alpha and Omega, the Great I Am. We can look forward to dancing and singing and shouting praises to the King of Kings and Lord of Lords forever as we will never grow tired of repeating holy, holy, holy is the Lord God Almighty who was and is and is to come. Let us continue our journey together as we learn more about who He is, which will cause us to fall deeper in love with Him. May we understand how to deny our flesh so that our own carnal natures will not prevent us from living the life He died for us to live. It is my prayer that everyone will continue allowing Jesus to be not only their Savior but also their Lord, which includes submitting to His authority in the beauty of His holiness. May you enjoy the abundant spiritual life that He has provided, and may this book inspire you to give Him the reverence and honor He is so worthy to receive.

With so many different religious worldviews and expressions of spirituality in the world, I am sure there are many questions pertaining to the reasons and rituals of worship. It is difficult not to offend the masses when teaching dogmatically about giving our hearts to a particular religious deity, especially when people believe they are communicating with their divine *higher power* the best way they know how. My intention with this resource is not to explain about the kaleidoscope of world religions or the Biblical reasons why there cannot be thousands of philosophic paths to heaven. These writings about worship are not intended to condemn other belief systems that are devoted to other doctrines that capture the imagination of the human mind, but rather my particular concentration is the Christian view that is centered on the triune God of the Bible. Even as we increase our focus on this narrow way of spiritual interpretations, we find there are still many different styles and convictions within the umbrella of the Christian faith. With this in mind, I hope to build a sense of unity with those who seek to go deeper with God instead of helping to build more walls that hinder and separate our mutual adoration for the Master of the universe. I believe the Father sent His Son Jesus to shed His blood and die on the cross so that we might be saved, redeemed, ransomed, and restored into His royal family and that it is His desire that we be intertwined together into covenant relationships with each other. As we receive Christ into our hearts by faith, we become born again into Him, and with this holy and intimate connection between God and humans, we are drawn and compelled by the Holy Spirit to bow down and worship the Father for His endless love and grace. This is a very compact illustration of the

Christian life I am referring to, and it is in this view that I convey my intentions and sentiments throughout this work.

In this first chapter we are establishing the realities of how God will not be enthused or obligated to accept any type of attitude, offering, or imagination that is tainted with the corruption of carnality. He is holy and is long-suffering toward the blind and ignorant, but He likewise has no pleasure listening to the babbling of religious hypocrites or clever spectators that intentionally try to play games, manipulate, or make business deals with point systems or grades. **"For there is no respect of persons with God. For as many as have sinned without** [apart from] **the law shall also perish without the law: and as many as have sinned in the law shall be judged by the law"** *(Romans 2:11-12)*. The Lord loves our offerings and sacrifices, but they must be pure and given in the spirit of brokenness and humility. Worship is a passionate practice to those who realize the importance of prayer, love, honesty, and growing in wisdom and sanctification that stabilizes the foundation of responsibility to abide in His presence. Worship is not something we do as an occasional *high- five* when life is going good, but rather it is a result of a heart that continually walks with God in a balanced state of spiritual discernment whether in comfort or crisis. As being sensitive to His still small voice becomes a normal way of living, we allow His Lordship to teach us how important it is to have a disciplined conscience. We cannot comprehend who God is and what He has done without also coming into the knowledge of who we are in Him. The heart that appreciates His love and is grateful for His truth will respond to Him with praise, thanksgiving, reverence, and honor, but the fulfillment of worship comes within the revelation that we have taken a holy wedding vow that seals our intimate relationship with Him as the Lord of our lives.

Purity is NOT an option. We pray before we begin the journey into God's presence just like the priest that presided over the tabernacle in the wilderness. As we worship the King of Kings, it is crucial to become transparent and ask Him to forgive us all sin and inferior attitudes and thoughts—not because it seems to be the religious thing to do but rather to invite His holy refiner's fire that burns away any impurities and that can present us to Him as spotless. We will not desire to approach Him or interact with Him if we have darkness within our conscience because sin makes us want to avoid God's perfect judgment. Realizing that we must be clean before going into His holy of Holies is developing a reverential fear of who He is. God's holiness is poured out through pure vessels. This revelation melts our arrogance and is cast into a mold of humility in order to reveal our gratefulness for His mercy and love. Our genuine freedom from sin releases us to have confidence as we openly and boldly profess our passion! Let us pray that our lives become an open worship service that will inspire others to celebrate with us.

As a matter of fact I have three phases of the worship experience that I have learned from the Lord and believe are crucial to bringing everyone into one accord. They are REPENTENCE, PRAISE, and WORSHIP. This is not a religious format but rather follows a divine order that allows us to proceed correctly. We ask Him to forgive us and wash us clean; we thank Him for all that He has done for us; and then we proceed into expressing our love to Him. Each one of these steps is a progression toward His holy of holies. You see, many people stagger into the church service on Sunday spiritually distant from the Lord, especially if they have not spent any personal time with the Lord throughout the week. I realize it seems strange that Christians would not feel the need to pray or repent daily, but evidence reveals this is the case. It is little wonder when they come into the corporate meeting why they feel the weight of guilt and sin and this automatically causes them to sense that God is far away. This produces an awkward tension between them and Jesus. No wonder they can hardly raise their eyes or open their mouths to sing. Again, this is why it is crucial for God's people to spend time with Him BEFORE they come into the sanctuary in order to experience a smooth and rewarding transition.

Those who spend much of their time on the stage must come into the realization about this revelation and be committed to leading the entire assembly into an honest prayer of repentance. To presume that everyone is on fire and overflowing with The Holy Spirit is a perfect example of not being spiritually discerning and only concerned with presenting a religious program. We must tear down the walls that are isolating us, and we must face our sins and deal with them before we can be restored! This barrier of hardness and rebellion will close our ears and diminish the amount of the message we may hear which is one of the most important purposes of our gathering together. The calloused heart is not as receptive, and our separation from God's presence hinders our conviction if we do not ask the Lord to help us. It only makes sense that His children would not want to crawl into God's lap and lay their heads on His chest if they are saturated with bad thoughts and wrong attitudes. It is SIN that quenches the desire to worship, and causes the heart to feel numb and cold. When the *temple* has been defiled (whether the church or an individual), the Lord is disappointed. There is even such a drastic measure where He will remove the candlestick from certain assemblies because of their refusal to deal with sin! Those who consider themselves spiritual enough to recognize this problem should intercede day and night for each member and the atmosphere before anyone enters the sanctuary. When the people repent and draw near to Him, He will listen and respond and re-light the environment with the fire of His presence. You see, we do not go to VISIT God at His house. We bring Him with us! We do not give Him an hour - we give Him our lives! The church is God's people, and where they meet is only a building. The beauty is being gathered together in His Name and Him being with us.

A highly successful minister was compelled one day to share his thoughts on why his church was so filled with God's power and what was the secret as to the number of souls that were being saved and healed. He asked them to follow him, and as they came to the basement door, he opened it and revealed a large group of saints who were on their knees crying out to God in fervent prayer. He humbly said, *"It is not me - but the power of intercession."* Can you imagine the raging fire and mighty wind of revival that could sweep around the world if every church would begin to passionately fast and pray? An assembly of believers filled with God's Spirit is a group of disciples that have surrendered their wills and taken up their crosses. God's remnant disciples should pray for the body of Christ every day, the pastors, the leaders, and each member of the flock. What a difference it would make if Christians would pray in the Spirit on the way to the gathering and not stop even when they sit down in the sanctuary. This focus and commitment would not only make a difference in the local assembly experience but also in the big picture of everything God wants to do everywhere. This is revival thinking! This is a Holy Ghost stirring of excitement! Through prayer, God's power can be explosive and many hearts can be changed every time we meet together! Do we want the floodgates of His presence to fill our times of worship? Do we have a burden for lost souls and want to see people saved and re-ignited for God's service? Do we desire to see His miracle power, anointing, salvation, and healing compassion being poured out to those who need His touch? Is this what we are seeking when we assemble together?

How many failures will it take for us to realize that without repenting before we go on stage, our praise service will continue to be just another talent show? Just as we examine ourselves before we take communion, we must also deal with our sin and allow Him to purify us with His blood. The Christian life is a process of being sharpened, cleansed, purged, and grinded, sanded, washed, and renewed and is what yielding our will to Him and willingly lying on His sacrificial altar is all about. Just like the Old Testament Priest that was very careful to enter with a pure heart, we too must keep a check on our thoughts and attitudes. If there is any garbage between us and the Lord, we will not really want to take that corruption into His presence. This is why we ask God to forgive us each time we worship. We are openly professing that we realize our need to constantly *take out the trash* and that purity in the spirit of meekness invites Him to draw near to us.

When we come before His throne it is good to prepare our hearts for the bright, penetrating light of His holiness to shine into our consciences and flood our senses with His Glory. The same reason we clean our houses when we know company is coming is a practical illustration that helps us understand why we want to have a pure conscience in the presence of God. The image of Christ is to be reflected from us to all people, but how can His perfect purity come from within or be reflected from dirty vessels? This is why repentance is such a crucial part of our lives. He cleanses our hearts and washes us clean so that He can use us. We do not step on the stage with an agenda to manipulate or perform a rock show, but we draw near and reach out to Him because we love who He is and are hungry and thirsty for His presence. God cannot and will not be contained or controlled by our religious programs or made to fit into our ministry schedule. As soon as we create a system or a formula and think we have it all figured out, we miss Him. We cannot demand or command Him; we cannot manipulate Him or bargain with Him. It is true that personality is an important part of the effectiveness, but let us remember even this is a part of the divine spiritual calling that He has included in our ministry toolbox. We are anointed to do what God has destined for us to accomplish! Our ability is not as important as our availability, and being prepared spiritually is more important than our instrument being in tune, our voice clear, or even knowing the melody of the song.

Chapter 2

THE CORPORATE ASSEMBLY

Since most people associate worship with church, it would only be natural to include the corporate assembly within our thoughts on the subject of worship. The church is a collection of individuals that contain God within the temple of their bodies. Though spiritually they are a *lively stone,* the church of God is NOT made of natural brick. The local visible church is made up of groups of Christians that fellowship together; the body of Christ consists of every member of God's family, and this is THE church of Jesus Christ! However, it seems the masses have still not received this revelation. Most people continue to believe that they go to church, and their particular flavor is also God's favorite, which has caused much of the confusion we have today. I have studied the church for many years and have drawn the conclusion that its problems are rooted in man's pride and carnality; nonetheless we must continue in our mission to have a positive attitude and preach the full gospel with all diligence. *What does this have to do with worship?* In our intimate relationship with God, there is nothing more important than having a clean heart, but when we are infected with being haughty, there is nothing more destructive. We can be convinced that we have pride under control and believe that our self-discipline keeps the darkness from crossing the borders into our sincerity, but deception is the silent but deadly killer that can hold us captive within our minds, without us even recognizing it.

Unfortunately, this character trait of our old carnal nature is usually noticeable to everyone except the one that is blind and is especially common in those who are knowledgeable about their favorite subject and have spent much time becoming supposedly more informed than everyone else. Many have become lofty in their arrogance and could be doing great things for God's Kingdom, but haughtiness has contaminated their spiritual growth, and now they have a very difficult time listening and accepting instruction from anyone that has fresh insight or wise counsel. Many times even though we are highly persuaded in our conclusions things are not always the way they seem. It is no secret that all humans are like this to a certain point, but the difference between those who continue learning God's wisdom and those who are hindered by a rebellious attitude comes down to seeking truth no matter how uncomfortable, and simply listening to God's still small voice. He does not want us to compromise, but rather to follow the landmarks and road signs that are included in His specific will. Everyone needs a mentor and wise counsel where God can use others to speak into our lives and help us see His truth more clearly. I realize that creative people are called to blaze their own unique trail, but there are many precepts associated with having the *green light* to proceed, and one is to be quick to hear and slow to speak.

It is a revelation to eventually realize that pride can block the arteries of our souls and is responsible for spiritual heart disease that can bind us as slaves to ignorance and blindness. Arrogance will produce a calloused conscience and even resentment where we spend more time criticizing the way everyone else lives instead of having compassion and demonstrating how Jesus wants to live in US! How close we are to Him depends on how pure we choose to be, and the amount of my mind that I allow God to transform will determine the level of worship I will release back to Him. There is much revelation to absorb about worship as we strive to understand that it is more than what we thought it was. Like most people, my studies and experiences have influenced my theological views and molded my convictions into what I believe. In my quest to find the mysteries and wonders of God's glory on earth, I have seen bits and pieces of His super-natural power, and on these rare occasions my faith has been strengthened. I am convinced that we must have a spiritual vision of purpose, which is an internal clarity of God's will that is given through the intimacy of seeking Him personally. Religion is a neatly arranged *container* of man's thoughts, but if we desire to maintain the fervency and zeal of God's Word, we must think "outside" of this box. This will require levels of courage and faith that can be found only in Jesus Christ. In my spiritual travels, the assembly has repeatedly been a place of hurt, misunderstanding, rejection, and disappointment; however this does not mean that God is not blessing His people, all over the world, that are seeking His face. There are pockets of disciples that have made the CHOICE to be remnant warriors and are accomplishing His will and manifesting His glory. Amen! The body of Christ is a living organism much more than it is an organization, and He will NOT allow it to fail! Rest assured – God has a place for you. The King of glory is in total control, and everything is going according to His plans!

The message of the hour is the same as it has always been, which is for God's people to abandon their wills, take up their crosses, and follow Him. If we allow Him to change us, He will use our investment to change others. I have always thought I had no shortage of enthusiasm or willingness to be involved, but it has been my perception of how things *should be* that has frustrated me and hindered my spiritual development. We all believe we are right and want to control what we are involved with, but if this selfish audacity is not surrendered through conviction from the Holy Spirit, we will win the devil's gold medal for being a champion of discord and strife. Instead of being a blessing for the Lord Almighty, we can actually become the leaven that He is trying to protect His people from. It is common for the average assembly to have these difficulties, but there is no excuse for the lack of discernment about our own carnality. Within our hearts we must become less while allowing Him to become more, or we will continue living as our own worst enemy.

Though the core of God's faithful saints are alive and well, we must realize that the majority of the religious masses are still in the playpen spiritually speaking because they have not made a decision to surrender their wills. Seeing this revelation, we can understand why the mighty rushing wind does not blow through the buildings, and the services are consistently dry and stagnant. My disappointment of not seeing the power and presence of God in the assemblies is now put in the perspective that the general church population is NOT living a consecrated life and thus is NOT able to participate in God's required level of spirituality. It is sad, but this *normal* way of lukewarm living is common, and in order for the manifestations of God's glory to be revealed, there must be a desperate seeking of His presence within the life of the believer. When will we realize that the corporate assembly is a direct reflection of the passion for God in the life of the individual?

Please do not misunderstand me. I am not saying that God's power being manifested in the corporate services cannot happen; I am saying that it must happen in the heart first! We cannot put the cart before the horse by expecting to lie around on the couch all through the week watching TV and automatically be overwhelmed with the glory of God's presence on Sunday mornings (or any time). Amen or oh my!

As a divine principle, there must be sowing before the harvest and there MUST be an investment before we can reap a return! If we are waiting for the Shekinah clouds with lightning and thunder from God's majesty to fill the sanctuary - we are probably going to be disappointed. Again, I am NOT losing my faith or compromising but just trying to see the "big picture" of what the glorious church is all about. Yes, the Lord desires to move mightily when His children meet together, but He cannot manifest the literal glory of His throne when the majority of the members do not believe it and do not even want it! Since we are the temple of the Holy Ghost, why aren't we more enthused about having a fiery revival *within us* instead of just wanting to see it in a building? I believe this mystery is being revealed unto those seekers that have become determined to give their entire lives to God and know His absolute truth. Even if the traditional local assembly ends up meeting in the isolation of homes because of persecution, the power and presence of God will still have the same endless possibilities as it ever did. When God's people begin to love others as they love themselves, there will be no limit of the amount of His glory that will be revealed to the world. *John 3:16* talks about *"whosoever will,"* but they are NOT experiencing Christ behind the four walls of a church service because they are not there! Our mission is to go into the highways and byways and allow the lost to SEE the light of Jesus everywhere we go and in every word we say! This is why we are called to demonstrate worship at the ballpark and the grocery store. Where else are they going to see it? Our heavenly Father desires for us to worship Him in Spirit and truth and to manifest miraculous healings and miracles in our daily walk because He loves the world and wants to encourage people's faith. He longs for men and women to release their gifts into the body AND the world so all might be edified and excited; however, foundations must be laid before the house is built. If we do not study to show ourselves approved and learn how to be prepared for divine appointments, we will miss the point of our Christianity. If our corporate meeting preparation is donuts and coffee instead of intercessory prayer, then sadly we have received the dividends from our investment.

As a worship pastor, I have burned the midnight oil practicing and looking forward to leading the people to God's throne. Before services I have been like an expectant father pacing the floor, praying and excited because I just knew that something amazing was going to happen, and it did; we were given the opportunity to become wonderfully saturated in His presence! However, as I still have this exciting anticipation, I now realize that I was so focused on the phenomena that I missed the fundamentals of personally caring about people. I thought I was being sincere because I really wanted everyone to see God's glory but was failing to have a pastor's heart. I was not being sensitive that many were in need of a friend, a prayer, or just someone who cared. I was like Moses who asked the Lord to please show him His glory, and there is nothing wrong with this until we begin to decide how and why we want to see Him and then enthusiastically build an elaborate agenda around it. It is true, He desires to show us His intoxicating splendor, but He wants to develop a balance within us where we can see the big picture of what HE is trying to do. He desires to be our Master where He possesses our minds! He is calling for us to yield our wills and allow Him to rule on the throne of our hearts as LORD - not to develop another entertaining program! When we learn that PRAYER will cause us to see others as God sees them, and then become determined to make this a constant awareness within our consciences, we will truly walk in the power of His Spirit with confidence and victory. It will not matter if there are ten or ten thousand people, we will know that our labors are not just bringing people into God's presence, but we are doing it because we love them as much as we love ourselves! To lead and not connect is the wrong idea. If we are failing to build relationships, we are more of a sheep herder than a true shepherd. When His highest law of love becomes the center of our focus, we will abide in the FULLNESS of His heavenly peace and joy. We will not fully appreciate the blessing until we have willingly made the sacrifice. He that has an ear let him hear.

It is true, we are to believe in the full gospel that is the New Testament representation of His Kingdom with an unlimited supply of spiritual gifts, but please hear my message; the most valuable treasures of wisdom are learning how to demonstrate the fruits of His character! Maybe the reason we have not witnessed the manifestations like we have dreamed is because we believed the gifts were *evidence* of being filled with His Spirit, and in this confusion the gifts became more important to us than being transformed into His image. What good would it be to demonstrate the gifts of the Spirit but not have love? God is not a faucet handle that we can turn on and off, or a cosmic vending machine, but He demands holiness and humility and in His sovereignty moves according to His divine order. May we also remember that most of the time He can only intervene according to the conditions of faith and obedience. Whatever the situation, it is our responsibility to ABIDE in Him as His ambassadors and representatives of His Kingdom, and hopefully others will be convicted and inspired to seek Him. What else can we do? Yes, God's people will be filled with His power and with signs and wonders following, but the beauty of holiness and the perfection of His endless love must become the REAL demonstration of His church! The Father longs to reveal His wonders to those who desire to see heaven on earth, but it will not be within hearts that have decided to lead their own ministry.

Chapter 3

INFECTIOUS ENTHUSIASM

When we think of enthusiasm, words like passion, zeal, energy, commitment, and devotion come to mind, and we can agree that the Christian life needs to be filled with this type of wholehearted dedication. When we look in the mirror, we notice there are days when we feel positive, and everything seems bright and filled with hope, and other days when we have feelings of doubt and concern. In the views of many, life seems simple, but for those who search below the surface, we discover a war between our flesh and spirit along with a divine order that God has implemented within the fabric of our being. This order is based on principles that are based on His absolute truth and is recognized as the divine foundation of the highest wisdom. When we abandon our trust in mortal intelligence and allow Christ to fill us with His divine reality, the world will be able to see our enthusiasm for Him more clearly. Those who like the idea of being blessed but are not interested in being a soldier are failing in their responsibility to walk in spiritual victory. Since every Christian has been called to go through a lifetime of training in order to develop into a faithful warrior for Christ, our enthusiasm becomes a vital part of armor. In fact, it has everything to do with what level of Christianity we choose to live in.

Whether we are leading worship or have just come to praise Him, we must be aware that we might be tested in our feelings. Maybe we should be more blunt; we will be tried and tested, and how we react has a whole lot to do with who is in control of whom. In cases of anxiety, it is crucial to learn how to control breathing and to not allow the breathing to control you. The same is true with our emotions.

Developing an awareness to when we are being challenged is good, but knowing how to be victorious in these confrontations will require much training. Our flesh does not want to give God praise, and our will is convinced that it has its rights, and on top of all of this the enemy does NOT want to see us be blessed or anointed in our assignments. Whatever attitude we bring in with us, the people will see it and be affected by it whether it be positive or negative. If we have prayed and are filled with joy, it is such an encouragement and generates an excitement that is very contagious. If we hold on to the weights that are causing us to be miserable, our spirits cannot enter into the holy of holies, and we could possibly hinder the spiritual atmosphere for everyone. Yes, of course there are times when we are facing adversity and are feeling the stress of a crisis, but it is how we project the mixture of our feelings into the environment. If we are leading in some type of ministry, we should pray through the situation or allow someone else to take our place until we can gain composure. If we are falling apart in front of everyone, we can bring more sorrow and discouragement to others that are struggling. I have witnessed members of the band that came in upset, and it seemed as if they were carrying a dark cloud of frustration and hopelessness into the camp. Many have never realized that oppression can be emitted into the atmosphere, and these out of control emotional storms can hinder and distract the service. I was visiting a church one evening, and they were having a pot-luck dinner in their recreation building. I was standing in line and could not help but hear a conversation that was going on behind me. A young adult was talking to an older member about how dark and depressing her life has been and how it was a struggle to even get out of bed in the mornings. She went on and on about her problems and how she seemed to live in a fog of sadness and felt that her future was hopeless. The older member was trying to make light of the conversation by reassuring her that things would get better. The interesting and disturbing discovery about this story is that as I finally turned around and introduced myself, this young person was the worship leader. I had already been informed that the church was struggling in this area, and the main complaint was that it seemed sleepy, without enthusiasm, and spiritually dry. It did not take a rocket scientist to realize where the problem was coming from.

    To say the least, it is very important to check our hearts at the door if we are going to demonstrate leadership ministry. Being in the right frame of mind along with a clean conscience and of course being prepared makes a huge difference. If we are not ready to be used, we need to just fall on our knees right there and repent so that He can take over the service, which is what Jesus wants to do anyway. And if there are others that are struggling, and we know about it, we must have the courage and boldness to advise that they sit this one out until they can deal with whatever is coming against them. Enthusiasm is infectious, but so is depression, and it is essential to be sensitive as to what kind of influence we are projecting. Let us not forget that the devil is trying to attack all of God's people, and he especially loves to turn up the heat right before we go to church. How many times have husbands and wives become involved with an argument on the way to church, and it ruined the occasion for both of them. This is exactly what Satan is trying to do, not just with the ones involved but to bring static and chaos to the entire congregation in order to quench the atmosphere which could interfere and deflate the meeting. Stand guard and keep a close watch on your enthusiasm because it is directly connected to your joy. God will help us maintain enthusiasm for Him if we just ask Him, the same as He helps us overcome all tragedies, sorrows and heartaches. We have much to be enthused about! Jesus has given us the victory and we are filled with His presence! Enthusiasm makes life exciting and creative because we are living by faith and expectation that He is accomplishing His perfect will all around us! ***"Looking for that blessed hope, and the glorious appearing of the great God and our Savior Jesus Christ. Who gave Himself for us, that He might redeem us from all iniquity, and purify unto Himself a peculiar people, zealous of good works"*** *(Titus 2:13-14).*

Chapter 4

BEING ALTERED

M any people know that altars in the church are a familiar part of the *furniture* of the sanctuary as much as the pulpit, pews, and baptismal, but they can be anywhere we designate as the secret place of prayer and fellowship with God. The altar was created to offer sacrifice to God as a form of worship. Falling on His altar is a sense of becoming totally transparent and consumed as we yield our minds and hearts to complete obedience. It should be our hope and prayer that we will allow God to ALTER us and that we never develop such a familiarity with the beauty of consecration that we forget why God is calling us to live in this place of abandoning our own will. The physical structure itself is just a symbol that represents a consecrated meeting place with God while the conscious altar is within the holy sanctuary of our hearts where we stay alert and focused on our thoughts and behavior and His constant presence. Those who have a serious personal relationship with the Lord have learned that staying on His altar is walking in His Spirit and the only way to live the abundant VICTORIOUS life! In simple, straight to the point language, we as disciples of Jesus Christ need to spend more time being engaged with Him! In the midst of the church services and in any situation where souls need to be saved, we as Christians should have this at the top of our prayer list. If we are in the corporate assembly, we should be praying that everything that is done in the service will be used by God to touch the hearts of the listeners. We should be interceding for the music and that each word of every song would be a divine appointment to every heart. We should pray through the week that God's message would be filled with the conviction of the

Holy Spirit and that individuals will respond to God's voice. When I lead worship or teach the Word, I trust that God's power is touching every person and increasing faith so that all can receive the miracle they need. It is a blessing to witness the people being stirred and challenged by God and then see them have the courage to find their way to a place of prayer. It is awesome when hearts break from the weight of sin and miracles are being released to those who need healing and restoration. Can all of these miracles happen in the worship service? Absolutely! I have been in services where the power of God fell so heavily that the entire service was nothing but worship and praying. This is the beauty of being in a church body that is committed to ALLOWING the Holy Spirit to be in complete control. For a world that is craving for sin – we need a church that is craving to pray!

I realize that in most churches there are time restrictions and children's ministries that need to be released at certain intervals. And I understand that many people are set in their routines and do not like anything weird or different when it comes to their church programs. However, it is noteworthy to mention that our time to assemble has been called by God and is in accordance to HIS affairs - not ours. If we truly have every intention to follow Him in everything and we are convinced that our life and ministry should be controlled by Him, why would we think that it is strange if He wanted to do something that was not a part of our agenda? Actually it is difficult to understand why the churches proclaim they would love to see revival and a move of God to revitalize and set their hearts on fire, yet the first time something happens that seems odd or out of order everyone becomes uneasy. I have been in churches where everything was on a timer and other places where they threw the clock out the window. Without siding with traditional rituals or emotional substitutes for God's presence, I believe we can become legalistic in both extremes. It seems more like we want Him to bless our ideas and our programs exactly the way they are, without Him modifying them or making suggestions. I would hope that everyone would agree that our worship services have wonderful potential to uplift and encourage the entire body, but we must realize that it will take more than suits and ties or fancy decorations - it will take prayer. Yes, hands can be laid on those who are hurting and seeking, we can anoint with oil and prayers of hope and inspiration can be spoken over those wanting more of His Spirit and a deeper dedication to Him, but there is no substitute for the sincerity of an individual bowing before

God in total surrender. It does not matter if Jesus wants to have a 30 minute service or a 3 day service; we should be prepared and willing to humbly follow Him.

Altars can be traced to the beginning of civilization as places of sacrifice along with the concept of pledging allegiance to the one you trust with your soul. So how does the modern prayer altar in the church sanctuary connect with the Old and New Testament references to surrender and self-denial? The first thing is obvious with both of them; they represent *death*. We know that altars were used in the Old Testament as places where blood was shed to cover sin and where animal sacrifices and incense were burned. Our minds think of blood-drenched boulders or pits filled with burning coals of fire which can bring intimidation, but these were an external illustration of the internal work that pointed to Jesus that forgives us and transforms us into His image. In the book of Exodus we see a treasure of spiritual blueprints and mysteries that explain God's design of salvation and understanding; our faith recognizes the cross is not only the foundation of our righteousness but a divine predestined altar that held the ultimate sacrifice of all eternity.

Let us be clear in our presentation of the gospel to the lost; God does not desire to kill us or burn our fleshly bodies, but He is dead serious about transforming our spirits, minds, hearts, and consciences. He knows the only way any of His children can walk in His power and under the control of His Spirit is to cast down the authority and influence of our old natures. An altar can simply be any place where we crawl into Father's lap and rest our heads on His shoulder. It is a secret location of trust and security, where we can pour out our problems, confess our sins, ask for forgiveness, seek His face, listen for His answers, and feel His presence. Whether sitting in the woods, walking along the beach, or kneeling in church, our secret place with Him is an awareness where we connect with Him. We can bow before Him as a way of humbly submitting to His will; we can weep and seek His face, worship, praise, shout, and dance in the glory of His holiness. Whether the altar is literal or a vision within our hearts, the point is that we desperately need to stay in an attitude of prayer as we ask Him to help us live for Him. It is a place of surrender, a place where we bring serious concerns to the one who made us. It is a private abode where we pray and petition God, a secluded state of mind where we intercede and stand in the gap for the burdens of our heart. ***"He that dwells in the secret place of the Most High shall abide under the shadow of the Almighty. I will say*** *of the Lord, He is my refuge and my fortress: my God; in Him will I trust" (Psalm 91:1-2).*

Many churches have become too proud to bend their knees and have removed the altars to become more dignified. Some of the modern organizations of today now view Christianity as a bloody and savage gospel and are unfortunately falling away from the foundational truths of redemption. The new age seeker-sensitive philosophies of ministry avoid the altars of sincere meditation in exchange for watching videos about political world events or psychology lectures. Technology can help the church but can also distract the masses from Jesus with entertainment and the feel good stories that compromise truth. It is wonderful to have a positive message that encourages us, but let us also stay focused on Christ and never eliminate the need to constantly examine our hearts and turn away from sin. Yes, it is uncomfortable to deal with our personal issues and take the bold stand to not allow our flesh to lead us but our lives depend on it! Many Christians have become way too relaxed with their daily sins and are deceived to think they can slide by with a lukewarm attitude. *"I beseech you therefore, brethren, by the mercies of God, that ye present your bodies a living sacrifice, holy, acceptable unto God, which is your reasonable service. And be not conformed to this world: but be ye transformed by the renewing of your mind that you may prove* [demonstrate] *what is that good, and acceptable, and perfect, will of God" (Romans 12:1-2).*

Have you ever fallen on the bed on your face or on the floor before God as an act of submission and reverence? An altar represents a place of our humility and weakness - but it is also a beautiful portal to His infinite power. *"And He said unto me, my grace is sufficient for thee: for my strength is made perfect in weakness. Most gladly therefore will I rather glory in my infirmities, that the power of Christ may rest upon me. Therefore I take pleasure in infirmities, in reproaches, in necessities, in persecutions, in distresses for Christ's sake: for when I am weak – then am I strong" (II Corinthians 12: 9-10).* The *Oxford Dictionary* American edition gives the meaning of the word *prostrate* as to; "cast oneself down in humility or adoration, to lay flat on the ground as an act of submission, worship and humility, to be reduced to a helpless condition, a state of coming to an end or exhaustion." In this we see that God wants us to realize we cannot fix ourselves or anyone else in our own strength and reminds us NOT to lean on our own understanding but on His everlasting arms. He wants us to stop trying to be self-sufficient and to allow Him to live HIS life through us. His perfect way is for us to trade our strength and ideas for His strength and ideas. When we lay down our will and obey only <u>HIS</u> voice, we will become the vessel of honor that God can use to offer His clean, pure, living water for all who are thirsty for His presence.

The whole idea of us fighting against our flesh is referring to our old nature, and I can promise that our will does NOT enjoy spending time on God's fire pit. *John 3:30* says that ***"He must increase, but I must decrease"*** and is referring to how the flesh must yield and submit to God's Spirit in order for Him to freely rule and reign within us. Since we have a free-will, we realize that just because we are lying on the coals does not mean our nature stops talking and complaining, for the battle never ceases about who is in control. It is very common to see a *living* sacrifice crawl off the altar and change its mind about sanctification when the heat becomes more than we desire to tolerate. We all go through the same emotional roller coasters in our everyday encounters and have plenty of opportunities to have our private heart to heart talks with God, which means that we all stand on common ground and have the same possibilities to be changed. We also have the same responsibility to make sure our carnality remains constantly in check so that it can remain in its designated place in the graveyard. The refiner's fire can burn away all of the filth and trash of our corrupt, selfish identity, leaving only the clean and pure, sparkling gold identity and character of Christ, but self-discipline is a crucial part of the process.

Everyone agrees the Christian life should NOT be normal or average but should be constantly evolving into a more defined image of Jesus. We start out as a sculptor's block or a potter's raw lump of clay and, very patiently, Jesus the "Master artist" is constantly intervening and tweaking trying to make us what He died for us to be. He has a purpose and vision of what He wants us to accomplish and does as much as He can to encourage us as we ALLOW Him. If we were inanimate objects, it would be so easy to create us and admire our perfection, but what completely changes the concept is that we have a freedom of thought called the WILL that has the ability to choose our thoughts and deeds. If we obtain the revelation of how His divine blueprint is supposed to function, we will understand that surrendering our will is the only way HIS will can be accomplished. But if we are stubborn and determined to live the way we want, our destiny will most likely remain unfinished and the "author and finisher" of our faith will be disappointed. This perception of spiritual advancement includes developing an awareness of the reality of yielding because it is the key to being transformed. The altar is God's workbench where He makes attitude adjustments and timely modifications that are perfectly coordinated with how everyone's personal blueprints can work in perfect harmony with each other.

There are other types of *alterations* like when we remove material or hem a garment in the world of clothing. To alter means to revamp or transform something from the way it was into something different. Think about the word *repent* for a minute. It does not necessarily mean to cry or fall on our face or roll around on the ground. We may do all these things in the process, but the real meaning is to convert who we were into something new. Turning to God implies that we stop going away from God and start moving toward Him which is what the gospel of Christ teaches. Our worship songs and the symbolic sacraments of the faith contain the invitation to examine ourselves from the *inside out*, and that is where the real alteration takes place! Every song, sermon and scripture should encourage us to take care of any spiritual business that is needed and should always point to Jesus as He alone is the only one that can forgive and restore. In *Joel chapter 2, verse 17* we read, **"Let the priests, the ministers of the Lord, weep between the porch and the <u>altar</u>, and let them say, spare thy people O Lord, and give not your heritage to reproach, that the heathen should rule over them: wherefore should they say among the people, where is their God?"** The priests would come from the porch of the temple to go to the altar, and in between this area they were being reminded by the prophet to intercede and weep before the Lord on behalf of the sins of the people. Joel was preaching and compelling the priests to blow trumpets and to call a solemn assembly. He wanted them to sanctify a fast and bring the elders together and for everyone to fall before the Lord and repent and today God is calling His people to rise up and do the same! Humility is an awareness that we are walking, talking, thinking, and abiding on God's *altar* of holiness so that He can *alter* us into His perfect will. *"Lord may our altars not be just pieces of ornate decoration. May my conscience not become calloused but broken with the burdens for souls. Stir me Father; ignite my passion for Your Word and Your ways. Convict me of my sins and my coldness to Your Spirit. Oh God, may the altar of my heart stay wet with my tears of love for You and Your people. Amen."*

Chapter 5

GODLY SORROW

I must admit that even though I have been given the privilege to lead worship over the years, it has not really been a *"zippidy-doo-dah"* continuous flow of joy and contentment. Do not misunderstand me; it is beyond words to be engulfed by His Spirit, and there is no higher place of love and joy than to be saturated with His presence. However, these mountain top experiences many times do not come without struggles and attacks that are determined to hinder our mission. There will be valleys of spiritual resistance along with the battles from our own nature, and most of the time it is a two-headed monster because they both hate to follow Jesus. Spiritual warfare is especially focused on those who lead, and negativity is always ready to bombard us with influences that carry discouragement and accusations. Ministry leaders are faced with the challenges of maintaining enthusiasm as they witness the congregation's day to day struggles to lay down their inhibitions and be at one with God. I believe that very few people in God's family really know what worship and prayer is about or are interested in trying to find out. Our interest in worship is a type of spiritual thermometer that can measure the spiritual maturity levels within the individual's heart. When there is not an awareness of God's presence, there is a limited development of the personal relationship between the individual and the Lord. If there is not a desire to worship or pray, we can be sure there is not a relationship at all. I understand that most of us are intimidated and embarrassed to show our emotions in public, and that comes from our old nature that wants to keep our spiritual life *private,* but I am referring to us building our spiritual life in the seclusion of praising, studying, and praying. I have actually heard people tell me they believe their spiritual life is such a personal matter they will not even discuss their views, but this is just a way of avoiding the subject altogether. Of course this attempt to keep our faith a secret includes sharing the gospel and is just another example of our embarrassment and shame. *Now brother, do not be ridiculous; you cannot tell what is in the conscience of people by the way they act!* Well, we may not be able to see the intent, but we can know that if people are overflowing with the Spirit of God, they will not be acting carnal or ashamed and intimidated to express their allegiance to Jesus! When Judas betrayed Christ, his actions revealed just how committed he was to the Lord, and of course we know the devil would love for all Christians to keep their faith to themselves, so the power of the gospel can remain a mysterious unknown! It is worth considering that if any refuse to be open with their spiritual fervor, and if they are also silent in their prayer life, there is a reason for it, because when anything is filled to the point of running over, we can be assured that it will spill out! May we realize that if we are not accustomed or familiar with His presence in private, we will NOT feel comfortable in giving Him praise and exalting His name in public, and all of our excuses will not be able to hide the truth of how we really feel. We will learn and discover the reasons behind this fact as we continue to grow and see our own lives through the eyes of His will.

I have struggled with trying to understand what God is seeking from us in the world of corporate worship, and to be honest it seems that most of my life I have been chasing a mirage. It is impossible to fathom how stunning the atmosphere will be when we take our first steps through heaven's gates. I am convinced we will absorb the worship within our being and will be mesmerized in a sea of indescribable glory along with the sights and sounds which there could be no human words to illustrate or explain. I believe the translation of words from the book of Revelation that attempt to describe heaven were given so that within our limited imagination we could catch a tiny glimpse, but in that realm the expressions are far higher and more developed because they are truly from another dimension. Praise God, He wants us to reach out and go deeper into His presence now and allow Him to give us a portion of this vision. It is our homeland, it is our world where we came from and where we will return. I have dreamed of feeling the mighty rushing wind of God blowing through the sanctuary and the clouds of God's glory being witnessed by His saints. I have prayed and believed that He desires to speak and demonstrate His power to all who would reach out by faith and experience the wonders of His eminence. I have awakened on Sunday mornings and literally been convinced that the building would shake and that His train would fill the sanctuary as Isaiah experienced. Yes, I am a dreamer, and if I do not encounter this level of His presence in this life, I know I will be engulfed in His breathtaking, awe-inspiring glory in the next life. I know the New Testament saints saw with their very eyes this magnitude of His power, and I have not given up on being in the right place at the perfect time to be a witness of this spiritual reality. One reason why this does not manifest may be the lack of faith and the ho-hum attitude of the saints. If we do not believe, we can be reasonably sure we will not receive. Another thing that could be hindering the move of the Holy Spirit is the lack of reverential fear and Godly sorrow for willful practice of sin. Again, this is why repentance always comes before worship as we cannot go into the holy of holies with a filthy mind and a dark, corrupted heart.

Our flesh man loves to control our attitudes, and because he has called the shots for so long, he thinks he runs our lives (and sadly much of the time he does). However, when Jesus becomes the Lord of our hearts, this old system of thinking that is led by our emotions is not supposed to control us anymore; we are commanded with a higher calling to be led by the Holy Spirit! *But what does this have to do with leading others into worship?* Actually everything! All of our fatigue, worry, apathy, fear, anxiety, depression, sin and strife must be checked at the door, or we can very easily become more of a hindrance than a help. The church does not need any more negativity – it needs purity, dedication to God's truth, and infectious enthusiasm. It does not matter whether we are just sitting in the congregation or preaching the sermon; we must learn to walk in the power of faith, positive confession and the joy and strength of The Holy Ghost. Many have not received the revelation about how to prepare to enter into God's presence and the responsibility of getting into the position to be used. Some are curious to see God move in signs, wonders, and miracles but have never considered themselves as the one God desires to use. Others have never seen God move and really are not interested to know anything about it. It is because they are content to have church just the way they like it in a comfortable and controlled environment. The truth is that most Christians are not spiritually prepared when they get to church, and they do not really want to be used but have settled on observing and judging.

The revelation of what God is waiting for and what He loves to receive from us will come when we finally understand there are no spectators in the realm of worship—or the Christian life for that matter. Everyone that is saved through the blood of Jesus participates in praise and worship because that person has the eternal love and grace of God to be thankful for. Allow me to go further; His blood covenant is a promise to make us heirs to everything He has in exchange for our love and worship. Jesus gave His life to us – the love of His heart, and all He wants in return is the expression and dedication from our hearts. It is a shame that His children do not care enough about Him to devote their "precious" time to studying and praying about God's needs. Many see church as a show to watch but have never thought that they are a part of God's program. It is much easier to let someone else do it because that way they can spend their time and energy judging and criticizing! If everyone was lifting holy hands and magnifying His Name, we would not notice everyone or everything else. It takes commitment in prayer and seeking God's face to be prepared for worship, and to be honest most people are not willing to get that involved. Nevertheless, we cannot make people drink at the rivers of living water; we can only offer to take them there.

I certainly do not want to seem like I have mastered the art of leading worship or have come to a plateau in my walk with Christ; in fact, the more I learn, the more I realize that I know very little. Whenever I feel that I have come to a spiritual understanding of a topic, I usually end up going back to kindergarten and starting all over again. May we NOT feel condemned or embarrassed in our life if there are times when we need to go to the blackboard and erase large portions of our views and start over again. And it is perfectly all right to say "I do not know" in the times when it is true; in fact, it is refreshing and genuine. This takes courage and humility, but God will empower and enlighten those who desire to know His will with all of their hearts. I honestly believe that God does not want us to become so familiar with our *religious rituals* that we lose the meaning of why we are doing them. He desires for all of His leaders to take baby steps according to the directions of His voice because to be over-confident in our human ability is to pave the way for pride and can leave us working exclusively in the emptiness of our flesh. When we lead corporate worship, we must be on guard to detect and avoid distractions that are trying to hinder the Lord's intentions, all the while praying for everyone to become involved and to make the connection with Him. It is no secret that our flesh does not want to worship, because our flesh loves the freedom of walking to the beat of its own drum, and of course the enemy does not want to see us be anointed with God's Spirit in our assignments. Whatever attitudes we bring in with us the people will see them and be affected by them, good or bad. If we allow the little foxes to upset us and make our life miserable, our spirits cannot fully enter into the glory of His presence. To take it a step further, I believe if we are overflowing with negativity and anxiety, we can actually hinder the spiritual atmosphere. The dark-side does not want God's glory to be manifested, and he despises seeing God's house filled with people that are being blessed with miracles as they cry "holy, holy, holy to the Lord God Almighty." Spiritual resistance along with our flesh would much rather see a dead, dry religious church service filled with man's philosophies and everyone bored, sleeping, and daydreaming about what's for lunch. Even when the music is technically good and the people are applauding, it does not necessarily mean the Spirit of God is flooding the atmosphere. It is common for people to release their emotions and appreciate the professionalism of the programs. Many love these comfortable services because there is very little conviction and hardly anything is required of them. They can continue keeping their heads in the sand, and their world views remain protected and secure to do just that. The church is only as spiritual as the people's personal relationship with Jesus! In the church of the *frozen-chosen* the happiest moment of the day is when the last amen is said so they can continue with their life instead of realizing they came to learn how to surrender it. However, where there is a strong anointing and a sincere desire to stay in God's presence, the body will be more concerned with ministering to each other in agape love and spiritual unity.

Do NOT put your faith in a human, but look beyond this natural realm into God's dimension and allow Him to guide you. No pastor, minister, or self-help materials can produce the kind of miracle power that we need. Many can counsel and try to explain what the Lord wants from us, but they are just messengers. Others can sing and preach while stirring us to tears, but that is not our most important resource. Every Christian has been called to plant infectious enthusiasm into the world for the purpose of inspiring and convicting others to know God. Our prayers increase our faith to take what His messengers are saying and use it in accordance with what God has already told us. Each child of the Lord is a minister and representative for the Kingdom of God and has a personal mailbox and has been designed to receive God's truth without a middleman. It is common after a great service for the masses to go home, lie on the couch, and talk about what a great performance that was or how that sermon sure nailed old sister so and so. This is not revival! We have missed the point if all we want is to be emotionally pumped up, soothed, and entertained. It is deception to think that God wants to intervene in other people's lives without realizing that He is trying to do the same with us! The anointing is to be like a contagious virus that inspires us to *pass it on* or INFECT everyone we come in contact with but let us always remember it also applies to our own hearts. Great sermons or awesome times of worship are not to be collected like antique collectable glassware and put on a shelf but are meant to stimulate US to tear down what we have created and begin to allow God to build our lives according to His ideas! Jesus is constantly arranging divine appointments that are so articulated with perfect timing and the highest probability. However, these are not just for the purpose of us relaying something to someone else, because He is also arranging these divine interventions to capture our attention and prick our hearts with conviction with instructions about our need to change. As we spend most of our time trying to untangle the distractions and chaos, it is crucial to maintain our spiritual sensitivity or we will not *catch* the message that God is sending. Many times we are waiting to hear His direction without understanding that God is waiting on us to pray and fast. It seems to be a vicious circle because as we fail to understand the revelation of our destiny, we are also not being able to help others with theirs. We think that ministers are the only ones who plant God's seed, but actually their calling is to pass out sacks of seed to US! The church is where we get the farm supplies and we are the farmers! Worship is incorporated into this process because when we are walking in His Spirit, we love Him for who He is and want to do everything we can to please Him! What more can you say than I love you? And what more can you give Him than your heart? This is a song I wrote on New Year's Day in 1989 called, *"I give my heart to you."*

> *(Verse 1) There've been many, who've called you Lord*
> *And some didn't even know why*
> *Some called on you for all the wrong reasons*
> *And others that didn't even try*

*Then there're the ones who called your name in vain
Like it was your fault everything had gone wrong
But for those who are sincere – their cries you'll always hear
Your love is deeper than any words could say in a song*

*(Chorus) Lord, I finally see
What you've always wanted from me
Of all of the things, that I could say or do
You want me to give my heart to you*

*(Bridge) What gift could I give to lay at your feet?
What kind of treasure could I bring?
Silver or gold, or costly perfume
Or a song of praise proclaiming you as my King?*

*(Chorus) And Lord, I finally see
What you've always wanted from me
Of all of the things that I could say or do
You want me to give my heart to you*

I give my heart. . .to you

Chapter 6

FROM FACES TO FINGERPRINTS

Worship teams are musically coordinated bands of warriors that go before the congregation and lead them into God's holy presence; what happens when we get there is filled with mystery and awesome wonder that is difficult to explain. The main focus of these warriors is to present a sincere, pure offering of worship that invites the tangible presence of God. Worship leaders realize their calling is to be used as vessels as His Spirit is poured through them, which includes the responsibility to sense God's direction so the Holy Spirit can touch the hearts of the listeners exactly where they need His intervention. Seeing the time of worship as a manifestation of God reaching out to those who need His ministry takes the idea of a song service to a complete other realm. Those who feel their job is just to lead a song have missed the point altogether. Many talented people can lead a song, but worship leaders are anointed to usher and escort the listener into God's habitation. I believe that God is going to manifest His glory every time I lead a corporate service, and if it does not happen, I realize it had much more to do with me than Him. All those involved in the Lord's ministry must see the vision that God desires and extend their faith into that revelation because without the anointing of God, our labor is no more than a religious ritual. Worship is not a program or performance. It is pouring out our hearts to God, bowing down before Him, and telling Him how much we love Him.

There are many different styles of music in the world with everyone having a wide variety to choose from. But why are people drawn to a certain kind of music? We are emotional creatures and music has an internal relation with the soul. Far beyond the notes and rhythms there is a spiritual force behind all music whether good or bad. Since God created music, we can know that it has always been a part of His heavenly vision of holiness and honor, but unfortunately the devil is an expert imitator that produces a counterfeit for everything the Lord creates. As much as true worship edifies the spirit of man, the devil's perverted music brings the opposite to the human mind and heart. Demons are assigned to watch us and have been referred to as "familiar spirits" because they are very acquainted with our lifestyles and desires and constantly try to manipulate us with these connections. For example, much of country music has long been associated with the sadness and pains of broken hearts, and disappointments with love relationships. Those who can relate to these experiences become linked to this emotional attachment, and so it becomes like a friend that understands their innermost feelings. Some heavy metal and rap are other examples of how musical movements can produce a camaraderie and promote an attitude that represents a defiance against authority, an *"in your face"* aggressiveness or a shock factor. Young people who are infected with rebellion become connected to this brazen arrogance as a way of relating to and expressing their identity that has been affected by many different kinds of dysfunction. With commitment and loyalty they surrender their souls to the message and many times become calloused enemies of the cross. The music from the dark kingdom carries a spiritual influence of death that knows how to feed the human nature mentality in order to keep the negative character traits stirred up which in turn causes more depression. This merry-go-round of emotional turmoil is the mission of the devil as He is the author of confusion and chaos, and works around the clock trying to prevent the masses from finding true love and peace by generating twisted lies and false hopes of contentment. It is not a secret that many who are involved in the music and entertainment industry have publically made comments about music NOT being about the lyrics but rather the beat. It is common to hear that of all the components that make a song popular or appealing, the lyrics are the least important. I could NOT disagree more. Songs are ALL about the message! The only genuine contentment and freedom is found in Jesus Christ, so it only makes sense that Satan works very hard to distract all people from finding Him! When we sing the Words of God, whatever type of style, we are speaking the positive light of life!

Just because a song is anointed does not mean it will be a popular best seller. There are many psalmists that sing and play music that the masses could care less about. I have come to realize that if people are not walking with God in a personal relationship, they will not feel comfortable with expressions of intimacy to God. Those who keep their distance with Jesus will also keep away from music where they can feel His convicting power. If people are doing everything they can to avoid God's presence, then it only makes sense they will also be aware of anything that is trying to take them there. We choose what we love and have free-will to live the way we want. We can do many things and use excuses to justify our lifestyles, but it is the heart that reveals our identity and true purpose. If we choose to love God, we will follow Him and everything that is connected to knowing and loving Him more. If our hearts enjoy living in carnality, we will preserve and protect our will and our love for the world. God is ready to help deliver us from our frustration and emotional misery but waits patiently for us to surrender our carnal hearts to Him. What will it take for us to have a serious desire for God? Many of us have secret attractions that we love and yet would never admit that we worship them. They may be food, sex, video games, money, or anything that consumes our thoughts and controls our lives. Being entangled with sin may be the reason why certain people cannot stand music that carries the presence of God, and I believe it would be accurate to say the more uncomfortable we are in God's presence, the more we need Him. ***"You shall not make for yourself a carved image of any likeness of anything that is in heaven above, or that is in the earth beneath, or that is in the water under the earth; you shall not bow down to them nor serve them. For I, the LORD your God, am a jealous God, visiting the iniquity of the fathers upon the children to the third and fourth generations of those who hate me"*** *(Exodus 20:3-5).*

I have seen several different styles of music and speaking ministries through the years and have noticed that churches and ministries are like faces in that all are different yet all have similar components. It is true that many are doctrinally off the grid, but usually the differences are "how" the music and sermon are being presented and of course the higher the level of anointing the more powerful it will be! For example, one speaker can bring a word that is theologically accurate but in a *"low key"* mundane delivery, and the congregation just sits there yawning. Another speaker can preach the exact SAME message but inject high energy, charisma, and enthusiasm, and the people will shout, rejoice, and testify how blessed they were to hear such a powerful display of God's power. If both have delivered God's divine truth, what is the difference? It does not matter what arena you would like to consider, presentation measures effectiveness and everyone that has a vision desires to be as effective as possible. So could a powerful presentation generate a strong impression of respect and authority? Absolutely! Could a listener's interest be increased by a speaker's level of passion? Yes! If what you are doing for God is not causing you to be on fire, what makes you think it will cause your listeners to be challenged? Who ever said Jesus was quiet and presented boring lectures?

When you know that what you are saying is the difference between life and death, you will have confidence in your words. Amen. When you have been given the calling to deliver a divine revelation, and are transformed from an orator to a messenger that holds the antidote that can save the world, I promise you are going to have a tank filled with zeal, excitement, and urgency. Jesus knew that what He was saying was not just a strong conviction! He was relaying absolute truth filled with the ultimate authority and power of Almighty God! Each word was dripping with spiritual illumination and had the power to pierce the mind and heart that left the listener dumbfounded! Did Jesus run around and do backflips to prove His charisma? Of course not, but I promise that when He opened His mouth situations changed and they still do! ***"So shall My Word be that goeth forth out of My mouth: it shall not return unto Me void, but it shall accomplish that which I please, and it shall prosper in the thing whereto I sent it"*** *(Isaiah 55:11)*. Everything He did and said had a purpose because He was zeroed in on His Father's business. Should we not be the same? This is an hour when serving milk and cereal is not enough! God wants His ministers to serve the filet mignon Word of the hour! He wants us to live each day like it could be the last day before His return, but this will not happen when we have too many irons in the fire and are overwhelmed with the lust of this world. Many times we are not the victims of being bound with the fetters and chains of bondage but are the ones who willingly asked for it. Only when we make the determined decision to grow up and not allow our toys to distract us will we ever become who we were called to be.

There is nothing wrong with examining what we are doing, how we are doing it, and making sure we are delivering His ministry the way He desires for us to present it. I realize that many will respond and say, *"This is the way I've always been, and I do not need to change anything,"* but this may not be as much about changing style as it is allowing God to breathe life into our work. Being spiritually passionate is NOT a style but rather an overflow from a heart that has been to the mountain and seen God's glory! Standing at the podium as a messenger for Jesus Christ is not the time to serve leftovers or depend on last week's anointing! We need to be filled every hour because we leak, and it is time to seriously consider about re-structuring the way we think about church and our ministry. Jesus is saying to stop trusting in a religious agenda and move away from the bondage of lifeless traditions. If the leaders have lost the zeal and love for what they are doing, then it is time to let someone else provide the leadership until the leader can embrace a vision of God's true reality. The remnant is thirsty for His presence and want to be free in His Spirit and hopefully will search until they find it, but many lukewarm members are satisfied for the leaders to be lukewarm because they enjoy being comfortable. I have heard people say they worship the Lord quietly and are afraid of acting fleshly, but do you actually believe we will contain our emotions in heaven? Anyone that is filled with the true joy of Jesus will explode with an outward display of gratitude. If emotions can be manifested with crying when something happens that hurts us or makes us sad, then why can't people release their deepest feelings of joy and praise to their God? And for those who claim to be quiet natured, do not tell me you are quiet when your favorite team scores or how *low key* you would be if you won a ten million dollar grand prize. Whatever means the most to us in our lives is what we are going to focus all of our energies and emotions into and what we are going to give our highest attention. If we are low on passion with our ministry, it could mean that we simply have too many irons in the fire and are splitting the enthusiasm with something or someone else. Walking in God's presence is our highest priority, and He will not share His glory with anything else including how highly we think of ourselves. For example, trying to pray is very intense spiritual warfare and is no match for the faint hearted. We know we need to seek God's face daily and find that quiet place, but it is not as easy as it sounds. We will say to ourselves, *"after I finish this page I'm typing or after I finish reading this chapter, I will pray,"* or *"I will wait to pray until everyone is asleep."* A common scenario is that many times we end up working late, taking a shower, having a late dinner, becoming very tired, and mumbling something about trying again first thing tomorrow. And then we wonder why our relationship is distant and our anointing is growing weak. God supplies the power, but we are called to supply the discipline. If we cannot control our flesh, then God cannot fulfill His perfect destiny in us. The Christian life is deliberately pursuing God.

You would NOT think that we could become lethargic with our ministry style, but it can happen. We use the illustration of how standing water can become stagnant versus the freshness of a moving stream, and if you have been around the church world for a while, surely you have noticed the difference. There have been many changes in the last few years as technology has advanced along with the package and presentation of styles, and this is wonderful as long as the covenant truth remains the same. Knowing when to adjust and how to revise is important to keeping the people enthused while also making sure the ministries within the church are functioning at the highest levels of quality and integrity. If the church is unorganized, it has the appearance of not caring, and this sends a strong message of laziness, mediocrity, and failure. The first impression of the meeting place needs to be presented to the entire family unit as a clean and safe environment. The assembly should be a praying, loving, compassionate, and giving people that live in God's anointing and in turn the Lord is eager to trust them with increase. If we sing the same lifeless songs and teach the same message every time, it will become mechanical and boring as the atmosphere can eventually turn a place that is designated for celebration and hope into feeling more like a funeral home. People can sense when there is genuine passion and love. If we are not excited about God, how can we expect anyone else to be?

One way we can bring some excitement into our services is to stop thinking that only one or two people are to provide the entire ministry. Pastors need to mentor other ministers and let them exercise their gifts to bring variety into the mix. Have the worship team learn new songs and encourage singers and musicians to minister special music or do special concerts. Be creative with props, prayer lines, dramas, videos, and any type of creativity that can honor Jesus. Invite guest speakers and ministries to stir up enthusiasm that can help the church avoid the rut of doing things the same way. The personality of the church can very easily fall into a traditional, religious parade of going through the motions, and many begin to see the ministry as a comfortable pay check. Pastors that drift away from the fire and ignore that God is trying to get their attention will live in disappointment. It is unfortunate when leaders become closed minded and stubborn and care more about having their way than to see the people suffer. I have heard ministers talk about God "pruning" the people from the church but have never heard them teach about God pruning their own life. Sometimes churches dwindle because those who are thirsty will venture out to find the love, joy, peace, and spiritual nourishment they are craving.

I realize that every Christian is a member of God's church, and we are infused with the Holy Spirit leading us and moving through us. We also see and accept that God does not move in just one specific type of church. There are times when God moves in Baptist and Methodist churches, and there are times when He moves in Holiness and Pentecostal churches even though the styles are different. This can only mean that it is obedience rather than a label that has everything to do with the blessing of God's presence. Every pastor has been given the mantle to lead the sheep, and I believe it is purity and sincerity in the heart of His people that causes Him to want to fellowship with those who are gathered in His name. The ones who choose to allow Him to be the Lord of their hearts and desire to be free in His Spirit prove how much they really want Him to lead the service. We cry out that God is welcome in our midst, and in our prayers we invite Him to come, but it seems to be a contradiction when we refuse to let go of our control. We shout about wanting to have liberty and for Him to take over our lives and church, but with our programs and time limits we seem to be contradicting ourselves. We cannot fill up our services with our own programs while also expecting Him to do what He wants to do.

All preachers, teachers, and worship leaders have natural personalities just like everyone else, and the congregation gets familiar with them just like you would with your boss or a good friend. Leaders that are involved with public speaking on a regular basis learn, grow, and develop their presentation and style of communication over time, and that is normal. Not many people really think about it, but in a church setting there is a fine line between being led of His Spirit and leaning on the abilities of the logical thinking mind. Yes, we live in a flesh body and must use our brains in cooperation with our mouths in order to express our thoughts, but the idea of the anointing is to be used as a channel for God to speak *through*. Saints do not want to hear a human philosophy. They get ready and drive to church because they want to hear what God is saying. People who are serious about their walk with the Lord will not be satisfied with a dry, boring service because God's music and words are to be filled with power and excitement of His presence. The excitement level of the pastor, the leadership, and the congregation controls the thermometer of the personality of a church. The calling to live in this genuine zeal is to everyone that claims to be a follower of Jesus and is generated by living in a close relationship with Him. There is no other way to become fearless and lead the frontline into battle! A dry, survival presentation sets the tone for a dry church but God can use the fire of leadership to ignite an assembly to praise, energy, and love to move in their gifts and labor in the outreach ministries and evangelize the world! I believe we can say the passion for Christ within the pastor can raise the bar and influence the level of enthusiasm of the entire church!

I believe the most important contribution that any of us can make is to PRAY! When we read about the great revivals, we discover the fire was ignited with prayer. The devil is not alarmed with us bragging about how filled with God's Spirit we are and he is not worried in the least just because a new church building is being built. However, he begins to panic when God's people repent and fall on their knees and begin to cry out to the God of Abraham, Isaac, and Jacob. If we know that demons tremble when we enter into our prayer closet, then why don't we spend more time in there? If we believe our prayers can change us and all those around us, then why are we spending so much time watching television? Why don't we open up the church every night for prayer? Because we are too busy and too lazy! Our flesh has obviously laid down the law for us to NOT take this "Jesus thing" to the extreme! Our carnal nature says that an hour on Sunday is more than enough to sustain our religious duty because we have more important things to do. Christ is saying that today is the day to begin rearranging our lives and to give The Lord what He wants. He is waiting for someone to take control of their will and be serious about allowing Him to renew their minds so that HE can re-prioritize their lives. Amen! Or we can continue talking about prayer and worship as very noble ideas but never actually becoming personally engaged. He lives in the Holy of Holies, but you must be willing to go through the tabernacle to know Him and LIVE with Him and this is why many are satisfied to dwell in the outer courts.

Chapter 7

THE WINDOWS OF HEAVEN

Where is this glorious church? It is within us, and its level of manifestation will depend on how serious we are about praying. As most Christians will agree, a person receiving Christ as Lord and Savior is the most important miracle that can happen, and everything we are called to do for God should be a "link" in the chain of proclaiming the gospel that is connected with salvation. Included in this super-natural package of life changing gifts from heaven are being filled with the Holy Ghost, being healed physically and emotionally, and being delivered from the bondages of sin, just to name a few. We know that faith plays an important part of our invitation to experience the abundant life that is included in the atonement at the cross, and this is revealed within the hearing and understanding of God's Word. *What does all this have to do with worship?* Everything! If we believe that worship invites God to come into our hearts and minds as we reach out to Him, and that this exchange prepares our hearts to receive His Holy Word, then we are now ready to discover the revelation of what can increase the anointing and power in this expression of intimate love. The tabernacle of Moses was not only a shadow of spiritual reality but an example of a progressive maturity that becomes more intense the closer one draws near to the Holy Of Holies. *So what is this big mystery?* It is fervent prayer and there are no substitutions. *Oh brother Billy, everyone knows that!* Oh really? Maybe sometimes we forget the basic foundations of our faith, like how prayer is the fuel that generates power to every facet of our being. God has designed the Church to operate within the principles of His Divine order rather than legalism, and prayer has been given to His people as a key that will unlock His glory. Let's start with how the worship team receives prayers to help increase their anointing. Prayer can turn songs into a spiritual, surgical procedure because they contain God's Word. Prayer can raise the level of anointing that will roll out the red carpet for the seed and allow God more freedom to inspire the spontaneous so the messenger can bring the "due season" message with more authority and power. As God's living Word becomes a quickened revelation to the heart and spirit, it in turn generates more faith that releases God's super-natural miracles! Praise God! All assemblies desire to see revival and the Holy Spirit filling the people and the services, but the windows of heaven are locked until the key of prayer opens them. We can complain all day long about how the corporate assembly is dry and dull, but if we truly desire our spiritual life to be better than it has ever been, we are going to have to start doing things we've never done before!

For example, if a lost person is in the sanctuary or someone is in need of a miracle and we have not prayed, this clearly exposes that we are not focused, and we do not have a direction or discernment. Just shaking hands with some of the people does not mean we necessarily love them or even care about them. If we ever become afraid to confront sin and agree to compromise, we have failed our mission. If we are not led by God's Holy Spirit and the Word becomes just another boring history lesson, then we are going to be held accountable for "omitting" our obedience. Servant of God, we ultimately trust God alone but if you are involved with a church, make sure the leadership is walking what they are talking. No one is perfect, but pray for discernment that you might know them by their fruits. ***"Beware of false prophets, which come to you in sheep's clothing, but inwardly they are ravening wolves"*** *(Matthew 7:15)*. Even if you are a pastor, be careful who you allow to speak into your life and take everything to the closet of prayer. Each of us has been given a blueprint and the mind of Christ to understand it along with the strength of God to accomplish it! This does not mean we do not need anyone; we all need each other.

The Lord has NOT called us to organize Him out of His own Church and has never given us the control to do all the planning. Jesus hates a religious ceremony because He knows that a ritual can become a personal idol where we worship our own accomplishments and abilities. This does not glorify His Kingdom or bring true spiritual change to anyone. How can souls be saved without the convicting power of the

Holy Spirit? How can there be changed minds without the anointing that flips the switch in the conscience and enlightens the heart to see truth? How can there be miracles if the infinite God of all creation is not welcome to come into our services to walk among us? Religiosity is the disease that plagues the church world and has lulled to sleep many who claim to be followers of Christ. It is true that lukewarm people are satisfied with a lukewarm church and the windows of heaven will be opened in our churches according to not only our burden to pray, but how much we actually pray.

PART II

THE AWARENESS OF HIS TRUTH

Chapter 8
AN ACCEPTABLE OFFERING

The Bible reveals that God has always been strict with precise instructions about how we are to offer sacrifices involving worship to Him. This should speak to us today and reveal that He still feels the same when it comes to accepting just anything we decide to give Him. And if the situation is serious enough, He becomes very insulted and angry at our disobedience and disrespect. In the past He explained about choosing only the finest animals to be slaughtered and how unblemished everything must be as a type and shadow of the ultimate perfection of Christ as the holy and faultless lamb that was slain for the sins of the world. Whenever anything offered to Him was contaminated or not of the highest quality, there were serious consequences. May I share a passage that reminds us of just how serious He is about this subject and what He expects from our offerings of worship? *"And Nadab and Abihu, the sons of Aaron, took either of them his censer and put fire therein, and put incense thereon, and offered STRANGE fire before the Lord, which He commanded them NOT. And there went out fire from the Lord, and devoured them, and they died before the Lord"* (Leviticus 10: 1-2).

    I do NOT believe God has changed His mind on the issue of respecting His glory, and as children of His Kingdom we must develop the reverential fear of who He is or also face the discipline of His judgment. There are many ways that God can chastise and bring punishment, but whether it is instant judgment or a process, we can agree that it is nothing to take lightly. We must avoid taking Him for granted so that our hearts will not become cold and calloused. The danger of allowing rituals to become routine can sear the tenderness of our conscience. However, we will never become bored or numb with our relationship with Christ because His love is continually refreshing. *"It is of the Lord's mercies that we are not consumed, because His compassions fail not. They are new every morning: great is thy faithfulness" (Lamentations 3:22-23)*. We notice in the tabernacle of Moses how the priests that entered into the Holy of Holies would have a rope fastened around their ankles in case they were found with un-repented sin. For some reason much of the church population does not connect their worship or the condition of their relationship with Jesus for that matter, as being held accountable to the same divine standard. Our spiritual development must include the revelation of having the awareness that the infinite Majesty of the universe requires holiness, humility, and brokenness for anyone that desires to approach Him. The selfishness, foolishness, arrogance, and general carnality that is brought into the sanctuary of the assembly and nurtured within our personal temple is an example of infecting the atmosphere with impurity. Keen discernment must be developed so that we can recognize what is hindering God's presence and distracting other believers from hearing what the Lord is trying to say.

May our worship unto Him be accepted as a holy sacrifice because He will not receive or be pleased with anything else. Worship is not entertainment. It should grieve us when we characterize church services by the performance rather than a sense of divine sacredness. If the spotlight is on anyone other than God, it is not worship. Some may say our new methods are winning more people, but maybe we should ask, winning them to what? To crucify the flesh? To total commitment to Jesus? To self-denial? To true discipleship? To carry their cross? The etymology of the word worship is *"worth-ship"* which declares the worthiness of God to be exalted, and we cannot be afraid to take a radical stand for God's truth. Let us be reminded of Cain and Abel when they both brought their offerings unto the Lord. *"And in the process of time it came to pass, that Cain brought of the fruit of the ground an offering unto the Lord. And Abel, he also brought of the firstlings of his flock and of the fat thereof. And the Lord HAD respect unto Abel and his offering. But unto Cain and to his offering he HAD NOT respect. And Cain was very wroth, and his countenance fell" (Genesis 4:3-5)*. People have always wanted to do things their way, and serving in God's Kingdom is no exception. However, God is not impressed when we try to do His work but choose to follow our own plans. This is because humans hate to surrender their control. I have seen people be incredibly generous but had no intention of submitting their will to God. When offerings are made without the brokenness and purification of repentance through the blood of Christ, these sacrifices are rejected and deemed as a generic substitute that may be intended to fulfill an obligation but are reduced to a gesture of mockery and have no eternal value. It is true that many deeds that are done can be used to be a blessing for others, but the ones that are giving according to their own ideas may discover they did not receive credit for their labors. The entire point of being obedient is to willingly follow His instructions without any alterations or modifications. This is His creation, His salvation, His world, His heaven, and everything within His general and specific blueprint will be accomplished according to His standards of perfection.

> *"Dear heavenly Father, I am humbled in Your presence. I choose to pour out my heart to You until I am empty of myself. Please fill me with Your holiness, Your wisdom, and empower me to WALK as a representative of Your Kingdom. The more I learn about You, the more I realize I know nothing. I repent for my un-cleanness. I am a chief sinner that battles to control my flesh. I have been a terrible example of a Christian as my mouth has spewed negativity, and I have been an enemy to your cross. Create in me a clean heart, and renew a right spirit in me. I realize that I have such a long way to go. I want to know the divine order of how to live and grow in You. I plead with You to build me from the inside out. Wash me with Your blood.*
>
> *I desperately need You to fill me with Your PASSION. Make me hungry for Your presence and help me to develop awareness to Your voice within my heart. If I do not have Your FIRE, I will not come out of my comfort zone. If I do not have Your love working in my conscience, I am nothing. I realize that breaking me and melting is the only way that I can be molded into Your image. Do a strong work in my heart that will literally CHANGE the way I think. I desire to become*

the disciple You have called me to be. I will become the witness You are waiting on so that You can fulfill Your mission through me.

Give me the courage to walk away from the pleasures of this world, and cause me to not be distracted by the attempts of my carnal nature to control me. Help me to overcome the laziness of my body. Help me to forgive others that have trespassed against me. Please help me not to see the church as something to avoid but to see it as a privilege to be a part of Your body. Allow me to see the hearts of those who need Your wisdom and understanding. Help me to share with them the revelations of Your Word. Give me the sensitivity to hear Your voice so that You can use me in your divine appointments. Amen."

When we read the story of how God accepted Abel's sacrifice and rejected Cain's, it needs to sink into our minds and hearts that this was given as a clear illustration that the Lord demands everything that is done for Him to be a certain way. This should be a constant reminder about how solemn we should be in presenting the correct offering with the right attitude in our worship and our labor. This is greatly misunderstood by the masses because of the lack of knowledge, but God is NOT moved to respond to everything He hears and sees. He is so perfect that He cannot go against His laws and principles and cannot be coerced into making deals or compromising His own standards. Since God responds to faith and the condition of the heart, He will not approve of works or gifts that try to manipulate or bribe Him or requests that are tarnished with underhanded motives. *What does all of this have to do worship?* More than we can imagine! Just because God listens to us sing songs and pray or even teach does not mean He will count it as genuine or bless these deeds with His approval. God operates by discerning our faith and judging our obedience, and it will be forever true that He does not let things slide! People all over the world constantly lift up praises with all types of different ideas and reasons (and God hears them all), but if their concepts of Him are not connected with the true God and the correct procedures of His Word, their religion is in vain. The Lord does not accept a generic, flesh based offering just because we went to all of the trouble to present it to Him, because it's not the size of the offering or how much effort we put into it, but rather it must be correct and presented exactly as He requires, or it will not be accepted at all. We can work our fingers to the bone and think we have accomplished much and yet be deceived. Going through the motions of religious rituals with only an emphasis on programs and ceremonies that make us look good is exchanging an eternal reward for a temporary one. Just because some Christians go to church a thousand times does not mean they are guaranteed a front row seat in heaven. The sobering truth is, they may not even get to heaven at all! *Why?* Because we are not earning points with our deeds, we are drawing nearer to Him by loving Him more! If we are not truly born-again through the blood of Jesus, we cannot buy our way in no matter how wonderful we think we are. Another example is that none of us automatically has more favor with God based on the number of times we have read through the Bible. *Why?* Because it is not how much you are into the Word – it is how much of the Word is in you!

As most Christians will agree, when a person receives Christ as Lord and Savior, it is THE most important miracle that can happen. When we become born-again, everything we do should be a link in the chain of proclaiming the gospel so that God can draw and invite others into His family. Spiritual evolution is a major part of God's blueprint for developing our personal relationship with Him and is the heart-beat of the Christian life. *So what does this have to do with worship?* If we believe that our appreciation and adoration for Him prepares our hearts to receive His holy Word, then we are now ready to discover the revelation of His presence! The holy of holies is our secret place, the ultimate destination in the spiritual dimension, and few realize that our relationship with Him is only as strong as our willingness to not only follow Him there but to stay there. *So what is the big mystery about the secret place?* We live in His presence through fervent prayer and intimate worship! *Now Billy, everyone knows that!* Oh really? If we know it and are not doing it then maybe we only have head knowledge and not a revelation.

Have we forgotten that prayer and worship are what keeps the fires of our relationship with God blazing! Developing this intimacy keeps us filled with His Spirit, and this in turn provides the burden and desire to love others enough to pray for them. A perfect example of how we can measure our love is to examine our prayer list. When we are truly walking in agape love, we will release our prayers and intercessions as an act of obedience to His voice and our sincere concern for others. A wonderful addition to any prayer list would be to stand in the gap for the worship team and the pastors so that God can use them more effectively! To be honest, I wonder how many people actually pray for any of the church ministries at all. Do we really believe the anointing releases the presence of God to bring life changing miracles to those who need them? Do we understand that without the fragrance of heaven on any type of ministry it is just another program? We do NOT have time ladies and gentlemen for more lifeless programs! This is the hour that God wants to release His power! Let it begin with US as we take a realistic look at where we are and then pray that He can use us to help Him transform broken lives into new creations! Amen! The chances of these miracles happening are greatly elevated when some care enough about another human being that they will fall on their knees out of sincere love and pray with fervent zeal! Praise God! The anointing establishes the atmosphere and prepares the listener's heart for God's Word while opening the possibilities to inspire the spontaneous. Prayer strikes the match that lights the flame of our faith! The anointing generates God's presence so the messenger can be used as an instrument to bring the *due season* message with conviction, authority, and power! We have NOT been called to build mega churches but have been commissioned to build mega people! It is crucial that we be led by the Holy Spirit in everything that is done in the service (and our everyday life) because God's Word is alive and is the power unto salvation unto all who hear it. Having an expectation for Him to come into our midst should be normal, unless of course we feel that doing our own thing is more effective. Following the Lord's general and specific blueprint should be our highest priority, and we will definitely need His anointing to accomplish it.

Do you believe the average Christian realizes how important their prayers are? Allow me to add to this; do you feel that Christians are aware of what is NOT being accomplished because of the lack of praying? We can easily recognize the sins we have committed and the good deeds we have done, but usually do not want to think about what we should have done but chose to ignore it. One of the pillars of prayer is to hear God's voice and come into an agreement with what He is trying to reveal to us, not to tell Him what we have decided to do. I am reminded of the scripture found in *First Samuel 15:22* where Saul was bragging to Samuel about how much he had accomplished for the Lord. *"And Samuel said, hath the Lord as great delight in burnt offerings and sacrifices, as in obeying the voice of the Lord? Behold, to obey is better than sacrifice, and to hearken than the fat of rams."* I believe many times the Lord is very upset with all of the things that are done for Him in His name, while people never consider asking Him what He wants done. For example, do we realize there are lost souls and those desperately in need of a miracle that NEED us to listen to God's voice about what to say or do? Are things like this the center of our thoughts and conversations or are we too busy laughing about how many chicken wings we ate last night?

All of the things we decide to do cannot be a substitute for what we have been called to do! Oppressive spirits are deceptive which explains how it plagues the religious world and has lulled many to sleep who claim to be followers of Christ. Let us continue reading *verse 23,* *"For rebellion is as the sin of witchcraft, and stubbornness is as iniquity and idolatry. Because thou hast rejected the word of the Lord, He hath also rejected thee from being king."* May the Lord have mercy on us if we become satisfied with playing church and doing just enough to get by. There is more to being an anointed minister than knowing Bible stories and having the ability to scream! It's a deception to think the clergy is an easy profession that allows people to be in charge and a way to enjoy the attention instead of knowing and yielding to the true reason they have been called. Some might say if there is not a noticeable anointing, there will be obvious failure, but just because the presence of God is not evident, it does not mean that some are not cashing in and seemingly having success in the ministry. *How can this be?* For one reason, the masses do NOT know the difference and the second point is that when a person speaks the Word of God, it is the power of God that is being released which always produces results. This does not mean that person is walking in God's perfect will. There are many churches that operate similar to corporations, and I am convinced that God's idea of church and our idea of church many times are not the same. We must face the reality that all assemblies have the opportunity to obey, but all do not have His candlestick burning within them. Jesus gives us the freedom and control to do the planning but only in accordance with His desires.

When musicians and singers meet in the prayer room before service, it is an important time to focus. When I am leading worship, I always ask forgiveness not just for me but for everyone that has a part in the worship who might not have *released* personal sins unto the Lord. Before we begin the service, I will also lead the entire congregation in a simple confession to repent, and this will change the atmosphere within the sanctuary and tear down the walls of darkness and can help bring freedom and peace to everyone in the room. Many times the hindering spirits of heaviness, judgment, and hypocrisy are brought in and need to be confronted. Leaders must have the sensitivity to not only realize what is happening but also the faith and courage to step forward in the authority of Jesus and address the situation. There is nothing wrong with stopping in the middle of the service and rebuking the devil from the premises because that is what God is demanding! Just because our buildings have the name *church* over the door, it does not mean the darkness cannot try to come in and disrupt. The church has been given a sword for offense as well as a shield for defense, and it is time we used both!

Let us take the opportunity to intercede more seriously because a strong, healthy, spirit-filled body of believers does not just fall off a tree but is birthed and continues to mature by seeking His face. The level of spiritual power and purity in a church depends on the people's personal relationship with God that is developed in the prayer closet of spiritual intimacy with Him. Let those who are hungry and thirsty for righteousness remember that the stronger God comes into our lives, the more He expects us to live what we believe. When we sing songs that cry out for His fire and discipline – do we really understand what they are about? Do we even know what an acceptable offering is? For us to have more of Him there must become less of us and that means that somewhere, somehow, we are going to be reduced! *But how?* It is not about losing weight, becoming less popular, or even downsizing what we have accumulated; it is about having less control over our lives. It is simply being willing to throw away our plans and what we want to do and take the key that has the potential to unlock unlimited spiritual success! *What key?* The key of obedience. Christ cannot become evident in people's lives unless they have made a personal intention to allow Him to become their personal master builder. When we are one hundred percent full of ourselves, there is no room for God to say or do anything significant, and this is what us decreasing and Him increasing is all about!

The reason it is difficult for us to say Jesus is all I need is because He is NOT all we want. Many are so blessed with abundance they have never known how life would be without the protection of many different types of security blankets. This is why when we are told to completely trust the Lord it sounds like a foreign language. It's a nice thing to say and do, but our old nature has worked with our carnal mind for so long that it has become a habit to justify leaning on their understanding. Maybe it should be said that we may never realize that Jesus is all we need until He is all we have. Maybe this is why Christ seemed to imply that the more busy people become, the more distance they may find between them and God. When you have everything you need, you don't really need faith, and I believe this has hurt the Christian life. Success can be enjoyed, but it can also be dangerous. We can try to figure out other ways to live and build our own independent way of living, but there are no substitutes for genuine humility. Total dependence on the Father was always the highest priority and intention of Jesus, and He is our perfect example. Many of us have experienced that just because we have a high level of excitement does not always mean everything is going to turn out the way we planned. When our wires become crossed with His instructions, we discover that our emotions may be heading one way while His Spirit is going the opposite direction.

It is healthy to believe that He is going to be there and do all the things He desires, but somewhere in the mix we must not be over-confident in our abilities that lead us to think that it is all about us. Pride comes in a lot of different colors and flavors along with a sneaky version that justifies the situation by boldly proclaiming, *"If it is to be - it is up to me."* This gung-ho approach to ministry may work on special occasions, but as a general rule, the Holy Spirit is a gentleman, and God would rather us walk through His doors instead of us trying to break them down. As in all deceptions, the victims never realize they are guilty while justifying what is happening, and along with a heaping helping of denial, they remain convinced they are sincere and have good intentions. When we are facing times of frustration and our ministry seems to be confusing, we just need to step out of the spotlight for a moment and re-evaluate what is happening. Pray and fast or take a break for a few days and listen to God's voice. More than anyone, He wants us to be in the perfect place at the perfect time, but we must allow Him to deal with our hearts first before He can use us to help others. Only when we suffer through the agony of seeing true reality will we see ourselves the way He sees us, and then we can begin to make alterations.

God wants to flow through us, but the vessel must have a shiny, clean attitude! *"But in a great house there are not only vessels of gold and silver, but also of wood and earth; and some to honor, and some to dishonor. If a man therefore purges himself from these, he shall be a vessel unto honor, sanctified, and meet* [useful] *for the master's use, and prepared unto every good work" (II Timothy 2: 20-21)*. It is true that anointed music is HOLY medicine that can bring healing to every part of us because it is filled with God's Word, but let us remember that He is the surgeon; we are just the operating nurse handing Him the sponge! I believe we can all agree that if we are going to be used mightily of the Lord, we must lead a holy and consecrated life. In today's changing world, there does not seem to be as much emphasis on sanctification because influences and interpretations are distorting our clear understanding of God's intentions. It is difficult to understand how to live in the world but not a part of it, and when the flesh is allowed to dominate our thinking, there is not much of a chance that God can be heard, much less comprehended. When we imagine what could be the most awesome spiritual experience a human could have, many would say, literally seeing God or talking with God. And I must admit that would be the ultimate encounter. But as I stumbled upon an example of this phenomena literally happening, I realized once again that everything is not as it would seem. Just to have a conversation with God does not mean that you are close to Him or would be forever obedient to Him or even love Him for that matter. I believe the Lord tries to speak to us all the time, and we just shrug Him off with a stinking rotten attitude the same as we would a person that we have no respect for. Allow me to continue with the earlier passage found in *Genesis chapter four and verse nine,* where God actually spoke to Cain. But listen to his response! *"And the Lord said unto Cain, where is Abel thy brother? And he said, I know not: Am I my brother's keeper?"* You see, just because we might have a conversation with God does not necessarily mean that we would be automatically thrilled or even polite. There are other examples of conversations that were not filled with lovey-dovey spiritual bliss. We notice that Jonah was told to go to a city called Nineveh and deliver a message, but he ran the other direction because he had prejudice in his heart toward the people and rebelled in anger. We also notice the exchanges that Job and God had between each other, and it is amazing to witness the emotional frustration that was exposed within Job's heart. We would never admit it, but maybe we have acted cold and distant to God's voice on certain occasions when we did not agree with His request, or maybe we just plainly refused to obey. Are these sins a result of being clean on the outside but dirty on the inside or being filled with dead men's bones? Is our bad attitude holding us in misery and preventing us from becoming a perfectly completed jig-saw puzzle?

I know we all get somewhat hungry in-between our delicious meals, but have you ever been starving? I have heard it said that general hunger pains come from signals and electrical impulses that are wired from the stomach and blood system to the brain. This complex network sends communication warnings from all over our bodies to the "main-frame" that sugar and energy levels are dropping and food is needed. We have the choice to respond or ignore these signals, and I can say with confidence that we usually do NOT ignore our fleshly cravings and desires. This causes me to wonder: does our spirit operate in a similar way? We know that when our spirits become transformed through the new birth experience of salvation, we become as little newborn babies. And just like fleshly babies that cry for milk because they need to be satisfied, our new spirits also cry out for spiritual nourishment. Of course the only true spiritual satisfaction is God's Word and His presence. When we choose to commune with Him and feast at His table, we become strengthened and filled with His joy and power just like when we go to an "all you can eat" buffet. But if we ignore the calls and "signals" from our spirit, do they also after a period of time fade away? Mmmmm. . .Drifting away from God's Word and neglecting prayer will cause weakness and spiritual malnutrition because just as there are constant messages traveling within your body to your mind, there are also constant communications being sent to your spirit. They are from God and are in the form of a still small voice that is trying to have your undivided attention. Are you really hungry and thirsty to be closer to Him, or have you neglected His voice and limited your relationship to a small bag of peanuts? ***"Blessed are they which do hunger and thirst after righteousness: for they shall be filled"*** *(Matthew 5:6)*. Staying at His table of balanced spiritual nutrition is not an option, it is our life-source! ***"But He answered and said, it is written, man shall not live by bread alone, but by every word that proceeds out of the mouth of God"*** *(Matthew 4:4)*. The Lord is speaking to us today and saying, "Turn off the distractions this evening and come have a quiet *dinner* with me."

Chapter 9

PLOWING THE FIELDS

"O give thanks unto the Lord, for He is good: for His mercy endureth forever. Let the redeemed of the Lord say so, whom He hath redeemed from the hand of the enemy; and gathered them out of the lands from the east, and from the west, from the north, and from the south" (Psalm 107:1-3).

There should be no difference between corporate worship and private worship because our intention should be the same: telling Him how we feel and what we think about Him. However, there is a good indication that if we do not worship God in the intimacy of our hearts all the time, we are less likely to express our feelings to Him in public. We realize that God wants us to worship Him in our personal day to day activities, but what is He trying to do by having us come together and worship Him corporately? Well, many people have never really quite understood the super-natural phenomena that God desires. Manifest means to be evident, definite, undisguised, unmistakable, noticeable, recognizable, and visible, and His presence is what we should experience every time we come together in His name. We know that our modern idea of church is not perfect, and in fact there are many things that we could say that are negative, but we must admit that God speaks highly of His church as a reflection and representation of who He is. Many have been tempted to throw the baby out with the bath water but there IS a glorious church, and we should do everything we can to help it and be a part of it! Our labor does not mean anything to anyone (from teaching the children all the way to praying at the altar) if it is not Holy Spirit inspired and anointed with the breath of God. The foundation of our spiritual growth is learning, because understanding God's Word is knowing Him personally. His revelation is the heavenly seed and is the crown jewel of our lives (and our corporate services) and is the catalyst of God's power to minister to each spirit, mind, and body, individually, yet all at the same time.

What does all this have to do with worship? Everything! What do you do BEFORE you plant a seed? As natural fields are plowed before the crops are sown, likewise our hearts must also be broken, arranged, and cultivated so the seed of God's Word can be received. Worship softens our natural resistance and prepares the heart to receive God's personal instructions. When we begin to focus on His face and His great deeds of love and grace, we forget about our problems and the fears that come from our spiritual conflicts and focus on who he is. Without the plowing from worship, the seed cannot penetrate a stony or briar-filled heart as Jesus warned us about in the parable of the sower and the seed. It is God's Word that has the power to minister to us, and we should give it our highest priority. When we stop relying on our own strength and futile ideas that we can deliver ourselves or that we can take care of our own circumstances, we can more easily let go of our worries and stress. This deliberate release of our will gives God the opportunity to intervene and remind us that we can always trust Him to help us. As we continue to bow down to our Lord in sincerity and humility, He surrounds us with His presence as the miracle exchange of love takes place between us. As our sensitivity is awakened, we begin to have a stronger expectation and an increased confidence to know that God is transforming us and using us to make a difference in other people's lives.

After we have spent time with Him in the Holy Communion of prayer and worship, our hearts are now broken, arranged, cleansed, and made ready to receive God's Word which is the power unto total salvation. *Why do you refer to this as "total" salvation?* We are being saved spiritually, emotionally, mentally, and physically, or in other words completely! We are being saved daily and even hourly as total salvation is growing and evolving into an understanding of His knowledge to continually learn how to discern His wisdom in order to apply it to every facet of our being. The more we mature in Him, the more we can begin to see our responsibility of being a "garden tool" for God that He can use to help with His miracle ministry of plowing. Of course the enemy has placed a target on us because he does not want us to lead anyone into the abundant life of God's covenant or do anything in God's Kingdom where the power of God can be manifested. The condition of the people's hearts is revealed in *Matthew chapter 13 verse 15*: ***"For this people's heart is waxed gross [calloused] and their ears are dull of hearing, and their eyes they have closed; lest at any time they should see with their eyes, and hear with their ears, and should understand with their HEART, and should be CONVERTED, and I should heal them."*** The devil would rather see a talented but lukewarm musical performance and an intelligent but lifeless speech in church instead of a Holy Ghost inspired demonstration of God's anointing and presence because he knows God's holy, perfect SEED is what brings healing, deliverance, victory, and true spiritual change! Demons realize there are many types of "ground" and if God's people are asleep, the chances are good for the desperately needy to come in and out of church and never receive the Word or a touch from God. The heart must be made ready to receive and to be used, which is why the enemy is willing to engage in a fierce level of spiritual warfare to stop anyone who has the intention to prepare and the revelation to plow.

Chapter 10

IN HIS PRESENCE

D*o you believe that worship has a style?* Well, brother, I think we would need to admit there are many different styles of worship music. I agree in the sense of certain instruments, rhythms, beats, and so on; however what type of style can you imagine is being played in heaven right now? Do you feel that music styles change in heaven through the millenniums like they do on earth? I believe that since music in heaven is in a spiritual dimension, it is less likely to be influenced by style. In fact, with God's perfection and His divine order controlling everything in His realm, I rest assured that whatever is going on, it looks and sounds nothing like we have ever heard. I would go a step further and say that true worship probably does not have a style at all. We see a glimpse of worship in heaven in certain passages within the book of Revelation that describe a person seated on a throne that was the color of jasper and sardine stone and a rainbow over the throne the color of an emerald *(Rev. 4:3)*. There are elders that sit around the throne wearing crowns of gold, and out of the throne were lightning and thunder and voices. There are lamps that burn with fire before the throne and a sea of glass like crystal. And in the midst of the throne there are different kinds of beasts filled with eyes and wings that never rest that cry, **"Holy, holy, holy Lord God Almighty, which was, and is, and is to come"** *(Revelation 4:8)*. As these beasts cry out, the elders fall down before the throne in adoration and worship before Him who sits on the throne, and they cast their crowns before Him crying, **"Thou art worthy, O Lord, to receive glory and honor and power: for thou hast**

created all things, and for thy pleasure they are and were created" (Revelation 4:11). What kind of style would you call that?

Picture this scenario; a group of Christian teenagers are in a church service where traditional hymns are being sung. They roll their eyes and make comments about how boring the songs sound. But across town we find another group of Christian young people shouting, jumping, and weeping as they worship with a Christian rock band that is playing songs with nearly the exact same lyrics but with a different beat. Both styles of music tell how awesome God is; each group plays instruments and sings; both are talented, anointed, and sincere. What is the difference? The power of connection! Just like electricity; when the right wires are connected, the light comes on! And that's okay! Mankind was never intended to be built on an assembly line like a robot. God created us with different tastes because He wanted each person to be a unique, perfect treasure. Our "spiritual circuitry" is what makes our relationship with Him uniquely personal as there has never been anyone like us, and there never will be. All of us being the same yet completely different reminds us of the mystery of the trinity being one God yet three individual persons. He loves all types of worship and praise music because it is not the style but the intentions behind the music that make the difference. It does not even need to be a written song because He loves it when we just tell Him how much we love Him in a spontaneous melody of joy and intimacy.

Most people are convinced their style of worship is correct as they claim to know how God wants to be praised. It is sad but common to see the arrogant look down their noses at the ones they feel are doing it all wrong. Many have never realized that God is seeking for a joyful noise and is worshipped in the sanctuary of the heart. Whether we are walking along the shore or sitting in a forest, He is there and excited that we have come to be with Him and bring Him praise. The place where we enjoy His presence is a state of mind. When our spirits bow before Him in respect and awestruck wonder of His glory, this is the perfect location and the most beautiful demonstration of our adoration as far as He is concerned. Whatever creative ability we have in the realm of producing music for the Lord, it is a blessing to join with the writers of the ages and have in common the same gifts they were inspired and anointed to present to the Lord. Within the songs from heaven we can feel the authors' tears and listen to their souls as they whispered to God how much they admired Him, needed Him and loved Him. The

Bridegroom reaches out to His bride, and she eagerly accepts by telling Him how much she loves Him. The beauty of this communication exchange comes from the heart that longs to know Him in the deepest intimacy and to learn how to love Him completely. Learning to abandon our old nature and yield to Him in obedience because we desire to be one with Him is the true meaning of life. There is no greater privilege than to worship Him, and true spiritual freedom is the opportunity to walk in His presence. It is not an earthly sound that makes a song heavenly – it is when heaven is absorbed in the song. Even the Bible itself would be a boring history book if it were not saturated with God's living Spirit that breathes LIFE into each syllable. Whether we have gifts of art, music, preaching, teaching, writing, giving, building, or any of the many types of serving, we relate and connect with Him in special ways, and these are the unique places where God can create His will within us. He longs for us to grasp the revelation of Him bringing His Kingdom into our earth. ***"Thy Kingdom come; thy will be done - in earth as it is in heaven"*** *(Matthew 6:10).*

Worship leaders have the responsibility to stay in an attitude of prayer and develop the keen sensitivity needed for God to show them which songs He wants to deliver no matter how dated they are or out of touch they seem. As worship participators we need to remember that the songs being presented were not created by God to be only received into our emotions but rather into the inner chambers of our spirits. All who are hungry and thirsty for His presence should be sensitive and excited to know the service is being filled with His instructions and messages as a divine appointment to connect with the listener's heart. We realize that God can take all types of lyrics and styles and transform them into a spiritual language that can minister to each spirit individually. It is not just about the songs we like to play or our personal favorites, it is about being obedient to God's direction and flexible enough to love others and help them to receive God's ministry. It is not the music – it is the words of heaven that have the power! I believe every time we worship Him that He is going to appear in all of His glory and that His compassion will be unleashed on all those who have the faith to reach out to Him. He desires to honor and empower what we are singing. Amen! The question with the worship is the same as it is with the sermon – can you sense what God is saying, and will you "weave" it into your life?

The stage is not a place for us to entertain or be some kind of imaginary rock star, but it is a place of service just like working in a soup kitchen. God provides the ingredients; we labor to coordinate it and serve it, and when the needy choose to receive the food, the Lord does His miracle of providing spiritual nourishment to their souls. This brings me to a very important aspect of the entire worship idea as it relates to the corporate atmosphere. I can use myself as an example because I know who and what I am, and likewise I also realize what I am not. I have always known that I am not an entertainer when it comes to music. I have watched people who entertain and have enjoyed their performances, but spiritual music is from another realm and must be respected as being different from regular music. Spiritual music that has God's Word in it, has the power and presence of God that makes it alive. It is not designed to make my flesh feel good, but rather it is ministry for the soul and this is a huge difference. I have been told that I am not very entertaining when it comes to leading music or when I minister songs the Lord has given to me. I am completely involved with the message of the songs and my own personal worship experience. I hardly ever have eye contact with the listeners, and I mostly concentrate on communicating with the other musicians in the midst of the music. I have witnessed many song leaders in my life where they keep eye contact on everyone and seem to be performing the song as a form of putting on a show. Likewise I have watched the majority of the congregations watch the leader intently and examine the performance with judgment and technical evaluation. Listen carefully; this is NOT worship on either end of the spectrum. A called and anointed worship pastor is not trying to put on a show any more than a senior pastor when he is trying to teach. The worship pastor should be attempting to communicate God's message to the spirit of the listener through the guidance of the Holy Spirit. He should not be worried about eye contact because his eyes should be on God. The congregation should also not be staring and watching the leader because they should be intimately meditating and conveying the way they feel toward the Lord in their personal relationship with Him. In this light, it is easy to detect the spirit of religion and discern the difference between leading and following a song versus everyone worshipping in Spirit and in truth. You see, when we buy a ticket for a concert and go to all the trouble to see our favorite performer, we are glued to that person's every move and every word. *Why?* Because we paid good money to see and hear the performance! When we go to church, we are NOT to be just a spectator of a production. We should be praying and seeking by faith to hear God and fellowship with Him and His people. Consider this the next time you wonder why church sometimes seems no more spiritual than a Broadway musical or a complex organization with time restraints and political overtones. May we learn to be aware of what we are doing and why we are doing it because church is to be a spiritual experience – not a theatrical drama.

Praise and worship is more than just musical emotion *about* God; it is celebrating our personal relationship *with* God. Spiritual worship is exposing our consciences and connecting with our Lord, choosing by faith to walk toward Him – drawing nearer. There is nothing wrong with style because with expanding our variety we increase the potential that can relate and lead different personalities into God and make a bond that maybe nothing else could. I listen to many variations of gospel music and have even witnessed the rap and hip-hop style, and it was awesome! The words were in a different musical rhythm than I am familiar with, but the words are the same and they rhyme the same so what's the difference? Method and technique is just the vehicle that carries the precious contents – the message! ***"So shall my word be that goes forth out of my mouth: It shall not return to me void*** [without fruit], ***but it shall accomplish that which I please, and it shall prosper in the thing whereunto I sent it"*** *(Isaiah 55:11)*. If we take a closer look at the words and themes of praise and worship music from the past, we will discover that the music we are playing today is also very similar. Every generation tries to come up with new expressions but most of the messages are just recycled and released with different instruments to create a different sound. Singers and musicians try to relate to the subject matter in their own style and produce their personal version of what they feel in their souls. Throughout the centuries there have been countless ways to express how much we adore Him, but no matter how many different ideas we come up with to tell God how much we love Him, He thinks they are all equally beautiful. Let us be careful that we do not presume that God favors certain musical styles over others, let us see the big picture and respect how other people connect with God (they love their style as much as you love your style). It is the truth of God's Word that is incorporated within the worship that makes it genuine or false, not how it sounds. You see, worship is far beyond musical trends, popular entertainment, or religious mannerisms – it is where God is known! Can the angels in heaven be categorized as having a particular technique? Did the Psalms have a particular trend? Of all the styles of worship all over the world, is any one style closer to God's heart than any other? That is like trying to say that God's favorite college basketball team is the Kentucky Wildcats. What an awesome miracle that God can touch so many hearts in so many different types of worship services and all of them in a personal way all at the same time! How often we take this for granted and most do not even realize this phenomenon is happening. True worship leaders realize they are a conduit of the Holy Spirit as God uses music to deliver His message. ***"Come unto Me, all ye that labor and are heavy laden, and I will give you rest"*** *(Matthew 11:28).*

Hymns have been a source of spiritual encouragement and strength for many years and are a priceless source of spiritual edification. The stories behind these majestic praises are a tribute to the faith and deep commitment these writers have demonstrated unto God. Christians around the world have enjoyed the blessings of hope, peace, courage, and inspiration from Spirit-filled songs of adoration, and though styles may come and go, the words of these musical love letters will remain strong and sincere. Though this is not a book dedicated to taking sides with hymns or the modern contemporary music, the fact is that both carry the same messages and are just different makes and models that take us to the same place around God's throne. Worship is not even limited to music at all but rather the holy connection between God and man. I have heard for years from the younger generation that hymns are boring and lifeless, but I boldly say that beauty is in the eyes (or ears) of the beholder. Many of the great hymns are filled with the attributes and character of God and His mighty deeds and endless love, so how in the world could people say they would not proclaim those praises and sing those uplifting verses and choruses that tell of God's awesome power? I realize the older music does not have a new sound and what we have chosen to be our own style, but the strange thing is that 50 years from now the next generations will be saying the same thing about the modern music of today. Styles and trends may come and go, but it is the content of the song that speaks to the heart and blesses and nourishes the soul. The Lord is not as concerned with the tempo or how many amplifiers are pushing the speakers, He just wants our songs to be sincere. Worshipping Him in Spirit and truth is to be clean before Him, longing for His presence and humble in our sincerity. Much of what is called worship today is engineered to entertain and please our flesh and is used as a subconscious manipulation to relax and be happy instead of using God's Word as a bright light to carefully examine our hearts. Religion can be so deceiving because it is based on how we look, what we do, and how things seem. Just because it feels good and looks and sounds modern and agrees with our personal views does not necessarily prove that it is anointed for this hour or that it is God's only resource.

"For this cause we also, since the day we heard it, do not cease to pray for <u>YOU</u>, and to desire that <u>YOU</u> be filled with the knowledge of His will in ALL wisdom and spiritual understanding; That <u>YOU</u> might walk worthy of the Lord, unto all pleasing, being fruitful in every good work, and increasing in the knowledge of God; Strengthened with all might, according to His glorious power, unto all patience and longsuffering with joyfulness" (Colossians 1:9-10). Why does Paul mention joy? Because joy enables us to maintain our spiritual strength which keeps us energized in our journey even when our trials become difficult. We will never experience the joy that Jesus intended for us to have if we wait until every circumstance is perfect, because joy is solely based on our relationship with Him! The closer we are to God, the more deeply we can realize what life is about. Joy is not just an emotional feeling but rather it is knowing in our hearts and spirits that God is with us in the calm and in the storm.

The reason we have such a difficult time resisting temptation is because we refuse to let go of its hand. We obviously like what we are being tempted with, or it would not have power to entice us. We want to take a pill and wake up 40 pounds lighter, win the lottery, or depend on some fantasy that will magically give us what we want, but in the end true change will come only when we become determined to abandon our will and live in His. I know a sister that has recently asked the Lord to awaken her at 5:30 each morning so she can pray and confess scriptures before she goes to work. Like a spiritual alarm clock, her eyes now pop open with excitement. *Why?* Because her relationship with her heavenly Father has become a passion and not just a whim! She has received the revelation that becoming saturated with God's Word is being filled with God Himself, and this is the miracle power that empowers us to live as a victorious overcomer! Amen! The Lord is searching for people that literally crave being with Him like the deer that pants for water, people that are infatuated with being intertwined with Him and to place Him at the highest pinnacle of their capacity to love. No doubt He will always do His part, but we must accept the responsibility of self-discipline.

"They shall abundantly UTTER the memory of thy great goodness, and shall SING of thy righteousness. The Lord is gracious, and full of compassion; slow to anger, and of great mercy. The Lord is good to all: and His tender mercies are over all His works. All thy works shall PRAISE thee, O Lord; and thy saints shall BLESS thee. They shall SPEAK of the glory of thy Kingdom, and TALK of thy power" (Psalm 145:7-11).

> *"Father in heaven, I bow down before You this hour and ask that You continue to perform surgery on my heart. Do not allow me to become satisfied with a normal life, but rather continue to stir the flames of my soul that inspire me to want more of You. As I draw nearer to You, I realize this is why Jesus came to die and rise again. It is NOT Your will that I float on an open sea but for me to KNOW where You are sending me and what to do when I get there. Thank You for the covenant that is now established and active for me to embrace. Thank You for all of the blessings You have poured out upon me. Thank You for the Holy Spirit that is a constant source of help and support. Teach me how to worship You and what I must do to continue in my spiritual development, in the glorious name of Jesus. Amen."*

Chapter 11
THE DEFAULT AND THE DIVINE

In this world's system which man is temporarily in charge of, we can all agree there is chaos and the inability to execute perfect justice. Anything that man tries to do without being saturated in the wisdom and anointing of Almighty God may technically function but operates in the curse of the fall. There are two governments; one that is spiritually perfect and ruled with the absolute truth of God and the other that is a flawed, defective system based on darkness and deception. This theological view is not a new revelation, but it must enlighten each individual's understanding, or the Christian life will be no more than just going through the motions of religion. God has always desired for man to abide in His presence, but the conflict of light and darkness within our own conscience is fierce. The natural realm is the only way most people have ever known and have yet to realize it is actually a back-up system. The world is blind and deceived by this imposter world order whose intention is to undermine God's authority and distract mankind from God's perfect will. This is what I will refer to as the *default system* because as we will discover, it is always there to automatically lead us if we fail to reach out by faith and embrace the Kingdom of light. In other words, if we do not cross-over into God's Kingdom, we automatically get the devil by default. This principle has been operating in human civilization since Adam and Eve fell in the garden and will continue with its agenda until King Jesus returns to destroy his enemies and establish His divine monarchy. The default system is ruled by Satan and his army of demons who spend all their time trying to entice, influence, and reinforce the prideful intelligence of man's emotions and opinions. This humanistic, egotistical worldview was birthed in rebellion and is a strategy to convince the natural mind that mankind is the ruler of earth and that all people can successfully fulfill their destiny without God. *"For the time will come when they will NOT endure sound doctrine; but after their own lusts shall they heap to themselves teachers, having itching ears; and they shall turn away their ears from the TRUTH, and shall be turned to FABLES"* (II Timothy 4:3-4).

I will refer to God's domain as the *divine reality* because His perfect Kingdom is a manifestation of His perfect person. He is the Alpha and Omega, the one true God and the Great I am. He designed all things, knows everything, is everywhere at once, and is in total control of everything – period! The devil and the default system are temporal, corrupt, and working on borrowed time, but God's divine order is established on the absolute truth of His honor, His Word, and His Omnipotence forever. *"For unto us a child is born, unto us a son is given: and the government shall be upon His shoulder: and His Name shall be called Wonderful, Counselor, The Mighty God, The Everlasting Father, The Prince of Peace. Of the increase of His government and peace there shall be no end, upon the throne of David, and upon his kingdom, to order it, and to establish it with judgment and with justice from henceforth even forever. The zeal of the Lord of hosts will perform this"* (Isaiah 9:6-7). Abiding in God's divine reality is walking in His Spirit and living in His presence! Transferring our devotion and allegiance from the default system to the divine reality is the revelation of true Christian living. The religious world lives with one foot in the default and the other with head knowledge of Biblical history and legalistic ceremony, while God's remnant disciples desire His Word and more of His person because they are thirsty and hungry for the presence of Jesus! In His presence all fear, worry, and doubt are gone because where God lives there is perfect peace, wisdom, and victory! *"This I say then, walk in the Spirit,* [Divine Reality] *and you shall not fulfill the lust of the flesh* [default system]. *For the flesh lusteth against the Spirit and the Spirit against the flesh and these are contrary* [opposition] *the one to the other: so that you cannot do the things that you would"* (Galatians 5:16-17).

The definition of *default* from the *Webster's New World Dictionary of the American Language* says, "Failure to do or appear as required. Failing to make payment when due. To fail to take part in or finish a contest, to forfeit by such failure." If we can step back for a moment and try to see with the eyes of our spirits, we will attain a very sobering revelation that accepting the default way of living does NOT follow God's divine requirements, thus choosing to forfeit all that God wants to do in us. When mankind disobeyed in the garden, the original agreement was broken and man experienced the consequence of failure. Humans were allowed to continue living in a natural existence and are still being born into the same fallen world that runs its course until they hear the gospel and embrace the sacrifice of Christ that can forgive them and transfer them into His divine reality. Man is given free-will to choose his destiny in this realm, and anyone who does NOT make the decision to accept Jesus as Lord will automatically have the default which includes eternal death. By staying on the course that has been provided and doing nothing, we will experience the consequence of our decision to not be transformed. Those who have won championships in world competition sports did not achieve success by lying around on the couch watching TV and eating bags of potato chips – they became focused, dedicated, and trained hard to become the best they could be. Likewise the prayer closet is the Christians' "gym" or training facility and the place where all strong warriors are developed. ALL humans are automatically born in sin and have the nature of the default system, and if they fail to accept Christ, they will remain in the hopeless destiny of the default because it is the only other option. *"Jesus said unto them, If God were your Father, ye would love me: for I proceeded forth and came from God; neither came I of myself, but He sent me. Why do ye not understand my speech? Even because ye cannot hear my word. Ye are of your father the devil, and the lusts* [desires] *of your father you will do. He was a murderer from the beginning, and abode* [lived] *not in the truth, because there is no truth in him. When he speaketh a lie, he speaks of his own: for he is a liar and the father of it"* (John 8:42-44).

Let us look at a spiritual parallel of a new-born baby taking its first breath and being pushed out of an airplane. At birth our eyes are opened to a prepared environment that is waiting for us to experience all that life has to offer. As humans grow and absorb information, they develop their personal ideas and make their own choices. Each individual life is calculated into measurements that only God knows and has been given a limited amount of time to spend in their visitation on earth. Everyone is offered a chance to be transformed (God's grace) and is a candidate to be spiritually redeemed (Calvary), and all will be accountable for how they respond. From the time we take our first breath, natural forces are pulling us to embrace a system that desires to initiate us with full membership privileges to become a mindless robot, and this will come to fruition if the individual does not awaken and accept divine truth. It is similar with those who are pushed out of an airplane. There is a small thing called gravity, and it is a natural principle very much like the spiritual principle concerning the default system. When something falls in the natural realm, it is headed for disaster unless something prevents it. The same is true when a person relaxes and is content to *free-fall* all the way through life.

This natural realm is designed for us to "go with the flow" of what is socially acceptable and encourages everyone to be satisfied with the status quo. The "pull" of peer pressure is very strong and similar to gravity in the sense that if we just close our eyes and relax, we can spend our entire existence blending-in and agreeing with the system. Thus, it is possible to fall through life without panic or guilt to change anything unless the individual realizes that to continue falling will result in destruction. The independence to trust one's own strength and abilities comes naturally within our human nature and provides a false sense of security that tempts us into believing and agreeing that we do not need to change anything but rather to just enjoy the ride! Everyone is falling, but how many will awaken to the danger before it is too late? All have been given a parachute (the opportunity of grace to reach out to Jesus) and have been instructed about how to use it (the Word of God), and everyone (whosoever will) is given the choice to pull the cord, and if some decide not to, they have charted their own destiny. Each day thousands of individuals choose to continue living in a principle that promises eternal death that is just as real as gravity! Christians have been called to go out into the highways and byways and declare that God has provided His divine reality to rescue the lost from the darkness and destruction of the default system! Our mission is to shout from the housetops that JESUS is the parachute of love and mercy that can save the perishing from falling all the way into the darkness of hell. ***"Be not deceived; God is not mocked: for whatsoever a man soweth, that shall he also reap. For he that soweth to his flesh shall of his flesh reap corruption; but he that soweth to the Spirit shall of the Spirit reap life everlasting"*** *(Galatians 6:7-8).*

When we hear God's call to surrender our wills and absorb the fullness of His life into our lives, then we are spiritually transformed with a brand new opportunity to begin learning how to live in heaven on earth. Those who respond and are yearning to know God more intimately must choose to break free from the old carnal human nature. This is what it means when we sing *"I'm so glad Jesus set me free,"* because when we are delivered from the bondage of sin, we are have the liberty to live in the joy of His presence. Being sold-out to God means we are no longer serving or under the influence of the control of this realm. We have made the choice to embrace God and let go of everything that hinders us from living under the shadow of His wings. Will it be easy to function in one realm and live in another? Of course not. It will take one hundred percent concentration and dedication. Living in this realm is free, but it is not cheap – it will cost us our will. ***"If the world hate you, you know that it hated me before it hated you. If ye were of the world, the world would love his own: but because you are not of the world, but I have chosen you out of this world, therefore the world hateth you"*** *(John 15:18-19).*

It will take a strong determination and a painful sacrifice to cut ties with what we have been used to. Spiritual warfare is more than just a story about David and Goliath; it must become a new creation reality. Some will not really want to go all the way with God because it is much easier to sit in a recliner with a remote and watch the parade. Many have become deceived into thinking they can just play around with religion and that God will just gather us all together and bless everyone as a whole instead of inspecting each person individually. May it be a sobering reminder that all persons will have their chance to explain why they lived the way they did. God's remnant disciples are determined spiritual warriors, not just against principalities and the rulers of darkness and spiritual wickedness, but they are also aggressive with the carnal nature of their own flesh and have learned the revelation of spiritual accountability. ***"And from the days of John the Baptist until now the kingdom of heaven suffers violence, and the violent take it by force"*** *(Matthew 11:12).* We will never overcome the temptations within our own temple or the strong persuasions of our carnal will without the revelation that being a full-time soldier on the front-line is not just a metaphor – but a literal matter of life and death.

In the spirit world there are only two kingdoms, and EVERYONE falls into the category of serving and giving love and loyalty to one or the other. The Lord demands complete devotion, and for those who try to live in both worlds at the same time, they are actually serving the default system already. Many will be surprised in the judgment to discover they were living in a trance of fantasy and presumption. Actions reveal the motives and intentions of the conscience, and whoever is elected to sit on the throne of the heart is the Master of that spirit. Amen! *"Love not the world, neither the things that are in the world. If any man love the world, the love of the Father is not in him. For all that is in the world, the lust of the flesh, and the lust of the eyes, and the pride of life, is not of the Father, but is of the world. And the world passeth away, and the lust thereof: but he that doeth the will of God abideth forever"* (I John 2:15-17).

The less you fight against the default system, the more you will become absorbed in it. God does not want us to be consumed with the control of this world's system but to daily meditate and consume His word. This saturation of His word draws us into the holiness of His presence. Every person will be filled with God or the devil, and the more of one that comes in, the more of the other is squeezed out. Half and half is happily promoted by the default system but will NOT be accepted by God. If the world loves us, then something is very wrong and is a sign that we have fallen into darkness. *"For they that are after the flesh do mind the things of the flesh; but they that are after the Spirit the things of the Spirit. For to be carnally minded is death; but to be spiritually minded is life and peace. Because the carnal mind is enmity against God: for it is not subject to the law of God, neither indeed can be. So then they that are in the flesh <u>cannot</u> please God"* (Romans 8:5-8). The *comfort zone* is when we are choosing to live in the easy path, but let us remember that God has never said that His path will be an easy way. It will be filled with His glory for those who abide in His presence, but it will be an agonizing death for the flesh because we must change everything we have learned and submit to His desires. *"Ye adulterers and adulteresses, know ye not that the friendship with the world is enmity with God? Whosoever therefore will be a friend of the world is the enemy of God"* (James 4:4). Resisting the pull of this world will require being aware of His constant presence and the amount of victory in your life will depend on just how much of God you really want. The only thing stopping us from being filled with God is our flesh! Jesus is with us 24/7 whether we remember He is there or not! Do you believe your life would be transformed if you could see that Jesus is with you, watching you and listening to everything you say every second? Guess what? He is.

The caterpillar is a consumer with a voracious appetite and has been described as a stomach with legs. Through a miraculous process the earthbound insect becomes a heavenly creation of great beauty that rises above the limited nature of the way it used to be. Its appetites are transformed, and its mind is changed, for that which was earthbound adapts to a higher life that now lives in a higher dimension. When the transformation is complete, there is no turning back to the bondage of crawling and scavenging. Yes, we are strongly attached to our carnality, but our Father has a plan to gloriously change all who are willing to become encased or *cocooned* in His presence. The world needs to see how the born-again experience recreates an old life into a representation of God's glory! The instrument of metamorphosis is the cross. It puts to death the old nature that a new creation might be raised up, and from glory to glory we shall be like Him. We must die so that we can live! It is time to arise from the rebellion and spoiled weakness of the flesh so that we can fly with God to the heights of triumph! It is the hour to shut ourselves in with God and not come out until we have touched His face. It is the moment to listen and walk out what we know, for His Kingdom is at hand. Let us shake off the shackles and tear down the prison doors, for behold Jehovah Yahweh has given us the wonder and beauty of His freedom to worship and love Him with all of our mind, heart, and strength! ***"Stand fast therefore in the liberty wherewith Christ hath made us free, and be not entangled again with the yoke of bondage"*** *(Galatians 5:1).*

Chapter 12

A SWEET SMELLING FRAGRANCE

> *"But the hour is coming, and now is when the true worshippers will worship the Father in spirit and truth; for the Father is seeking such to worship Him. God is Spirit, and those who worship Him must worship in spirit and truth"* (John 4:23-24).

Worshipping God is such an honor. I never cease to be astonished and overwhelmed as I try to meditate how awesome He is. As I have spent time alone with Him and serving in the body of Christ, I see myself as just another sojourner that is trying to learn what it means to be a remnant disciple of Jesus. As we focus on developing our personal relationship with Him, it may seem obvious to a few but there are still multitudes that still do not know the difference between just singing songs and actually worshipping Him. Likewise, the same is true with those who believe that going to church is the Christian life. I can understand the confusion because much of worship includes singing, but just singing a song can easily fall into just going through the motions without having God on our minds at all. If all we are doing is singing a song, the most we can expect to receive is an emotional experience. This is not the way it should be. Anointed worship music that is filled with God's Word is not the same as singing about pick-up trucks! Music that tells God how much we love Him is saturated with the sweet smell of heaven. The corporate music presentation in church may display a technically correct program, but many times it can be meaningless in the sight of God because there is not an intimate connection between our spirits and the Spirit of God. Worship is crying out to God, and we should be careful not to turn the battleground – into a playground! Hell comes against us when we worship God even though that is why we were created! Just because we are sitting in church does not remove our free-will to worry about our problems or daydream about what we are going to do tomorrow or about the person sitting three rows ahead of us. Sincerity and humbleness of heart are key ingredients in our worship, and professionalism has nothing to do with it.

If we take a close look at the words and themes of praise and worship music, we will discover they are the same throughout the centuries and are just recycled with new styles. Every generation has its own version of what it may refer to as a contemporary way to say things, but there is no greater expression than, *"I love you Lord"* (whatever the rhythm or style). So it is obvious that praise and worship is more than just music about God; it is our alliance and romance with Him! Spiritual worship is to fall humbly before Him, and this will open our spiritual eyes so that we can enter deeper into the realm where He lives and touch Him and allow Him to touch us. We do not only approach Him with an agenda to figure out what He is doing or why, but we draw near and reach out to Him because we love His person and are hungry and thirsty for His presence. He cannot be contained or controlled by our religious programs or made to fit into OUR ministry schedule. HE IS our ministry schedule and will not bless our homemade blueprints no matter how worthy they are! As soon as we create a system or a formula and think we have it all figured out, we realize He has quietly slipped out the back door. We cannot demand or command Him; we cannot manipulate Him or bargain with Him. How long will it take for us to realize that without our submission to His voice and the empowering of His anointing, our praise service (and our life) will be no more than a "form" of godliness? The focus of our prayers and gifts should always be toward helping others. We reap what we sow and if we sow generously, then God will reward us generously. Opportunities for practicing any gift or talent are truly plentiful, we just need to step out and activate them in faith and cooperate with the Holy Spirit. Jesus is always searching for someone that sincerely wants to serve. Find out where, and be willing to go there. Some allow their gift to become their identity and gauge how involved they become with how welcome they are to contribute. Whether we are invited or not, we must realize we are servants unto God and should not ignore helping just because we do not feel *called* to this area. Yes, there are things we are good at but let us be careful that we do NOT develop an attitude that tries to manage and control our abilities by only being available to minister within our comfortable *field of expertise*. The Lord loves to teach humility because it prevents us from following our own voice. If God needs a toilet cleaned, then He can make us a toilet cleaner. If He needs the grass mowed, He can make us a maintenance person. In God's eyes there are no insignificant labors for Him. Also, let us not be envious to do the work that others are doing but sincerely ask Him to reveal and open doors for us to do what needs to be done. There is never a crowd doing the work that is not being done, as there will always be room for everyone that is willing to serve. It is arrogant and selfish to allow the perception of our gifts to determine our service because we should realize that God can equip us for any service. His grace is sufficient for any task; we just need to lay our pride aside and trust Him. This positive attitude of doing the work that needs to be done will result in dependency upon God and not ourselves and will work toward establishing the revelation of humility while providing an opportunity for the manifestation of additional gifting's from within us.

God is not just searching for ability alone – He is seeking availability! He already knows who he has given His gifts and abilities to, as this is a part of His foreknowledge, but our free-will responsibility is to offer these talents back to Him as a sacrificial offering of thanksgiving and adoration with a broken and contrite heart. This is why worship should not be a burden but rather a joy and privilege to express the way we really feel about Him and what He has given to us. When it comes to our ministry and the church, there seems to be differences of opinion as to "who does what" and this can cause feelings of rejection. Many times the attitude of the leadership is not really caring about the calling God has given to an individual but rather what area they can guide that person that will help their overall cause. For example, if you are a Psalmist, and no one in your local church is interested in your gift, but instead they are trying to recruit you to be a greeter - be careful. It is true that serving the Lord is a privilege in any capacity, but let us always take these situations to the Lord because God has given the specific anointing and gift to YOU! Maybe the Lord is telling you to be patient and that He will make a way for your ministry. It is also possible that the church music ministry is being controlled by politics and maybe this is not where Jesus wants you to be. If the pastor is not responsive to your gift, this is a red flag. God has a definite place for you to share your contribution and wants you to be respected and appreciated as a vessel of honor. We all have a chair at God's table, and no one is slighted, ignored, or not considered good enough. Yes there is a price to pay for knowing Him, but the sacrifice cannot be compared to the honor of serving Him. God appreciates the heavenly fragrance of an elderly saint worshipping Him in her garden the same as a church choir with a complete orchestra. This is a song that was given to me in 1992 called *"What is the ministry."*

> *(Verse 1) It's not the beauty of the building - or the size of the crowd.*
> *It's not how well you dress – if you're quiet or loud*
> *Success is not measured - by what is in the offering plate*
> *But it's knowing we're walking in God's will every step of the way*
>
> *(Chorus) It's all about brokenness, and humility*
> *Compassion for others, instead of only love for me.*
> *Father help me to know, what is my true priority*
> *Teach me – what is the ministry*
>
> *(Verse 2) Praying in secret – for those who are in need*
> *Not to be religious, but when we feel the Spirit plead*
> *Recognizing our Father's voice – with the desire to obey*
> *No matter how inconvenient, or out of the way*
>
> *(Bridge) We are all time ministers, to be the salt and the light*
> *Witnesses embracing truth – about what is wrong and right*
> *Living testimonies – of all that God can do*
>
> *Vessels of honor, for Him to pour His love through*
> *(Chorus) (We need more) brokenness and humility*
> *Compassion for others, instead of only love for me*
> *Father help me to know what is the true priority*
> *Teach me, help me to see, show me – what is the ministry*

A very special story is found in the gospels and is a powerful illustration concerning giving our lives as an offering of worship to God. In *Mark the fourteenth chapter* we read where Jesus is visiting with some friends and eating dinner, when a woman approaches Him with an alabaster box of very expensive perfume. She breaks the box and deliberately pours it on His head as one would anoint for a very special occasion. Let us read the story; *"And being in Bethany in the house of Simon the leper, as He* [Jesus] *sat at meat, there came a woman having an alabaster box of ointment of spikenard very precious; and she broke the box, and poured it on His head. And there were some that had indignation* [anger] *within themselves, and said, why was this waste of the ointment made? For it might have been sold for more than three hundred pence, and have been given to the poor. And they murmured* [complained] *against her" (Mark 14:4-5)* Notice that as the religious crowd criticized this lady, our logical thinking will step in every time we think about being radical for Jesus. We are blind as to what is really valuable in this earthly realm until we receive the revelation of who He is! If He told us to give all of our money away, would we refuse? Just how important are the things of this world compared to pleasing Him? In order to do *extraordinary* things for God, we will always be confronted with resistance from our carnal nature and the devil. However, the heart that is completely sold-out for Christ will not care or worry about what other people say or what our selfish mind thinks about it. Our love for Jesus must be stronger than our intimidation from anything else! Let us continue: *"And Jesus said, Let her alone; why trouble ye her? She hath wrought a good work* [beautiful thing] *on Me" (verse 6).* Her box of perfume represents everything we are and all that we have, and when we empty our heart of love onto Him, He can begin the process of filling us with His glory.

When we choose to go to the next level with Jesus, the revelation of our destiny becomes clearer as we realize that the fragrance of our love is released when the box becomes *broken*. How long are we going to rub a little drop of our love here and there? It is time that we allow the Lord of heaven and earth to break our hearts of stone so that we can pour every drop of our lives onto Him and others. We will never live in the awareness of His presence until we love Him enough to be emptied. Abiding in Him is staying in the attitude of humility, and through our brokenness the world will sense His awesome love. When we submit our wills and give Him all that we have, we can enter into the bridal chambers and advance into the deepest levels of intimate adoration. This woman's offering was a type of priestly ministry as she poured out her highest devotion upon the majestic and perfect Son of God. These perfume boxes were historically given by Jewish parents to their daughters for a dowry. On a bride's wedding night this costly fragrance was to be emptied out upon her husband's feet and across the bed at the marriage consummation similar to the act of submission performed by Ruth at the instruction of Naomi to Boaz at the threshing floor. As we see this humble servant surrendering her entire dowry (her hopes and dreams for the future) for Jesus, we are witnessing a declaration and confession of complete and undivided love, trust, respect, faithfulness, desire, and expectation. Is this the type of *lifestyle* you are searching for?

Chapter 13

EVERY KNEE SHALL BOW

"O give thanks unto the Lord; call upon His name: make known His deeds among the people. Sing unto Him, sing psalms unto Him: talk ye of all His wondrous works. Glory ye in His holy name: let the heart of them rejoice that seek the Lord. Seek the Lord, and His strength: seek His face evermore [continually]" (Psalm 105:1-4).

Julius Caesar was one of the most famous mortals that ever lived. Many have said that his intelligence was head and shoulders beyond the dispensation in which he lived. But let me ask today, did angels announce his birth, and did the earth shake or the sun refuse to shine at his death? Did he have any part in helping God create the universe and everything in it? There is only one true God, and it is He alone that spoke all things into existence. Did Caesar have the power to lay down his life, and then take it up again? And has anyone except God ever had the power and authority to transform a soul, or raise the dead? Caesar and all the earthly kings and kingdoms are just historical figures of the past, and were it not for God giving them the air to breathe they would have been forgotten long ago. All of the kings and rulers of the earth are like ants in God's sight and pass away quickly like an early morning fog as the sun rises. Every idol and treasure will rot and decay; every false god and every earthly kingdom will pass away because they are not divine. There is only one God that is worthy of all praise, and He will be exalted for all eternity. *"And all the angels stood round about the throne, and about the elders and the four beasts, and fell before the throne on their faces, bowed down and worshipped God saying, Amen: Blessing, and glory, and wisdom, and thanksgiving, and honor and power, and might, be unto our God for ever and ever. Amen"* (Revelation 7:11-12).

Why are we being reminded about God's Omniscience? Because He is the only one in the universe that is worthy to receive all glory and exaltation. Omniscient means that He is ALL knowing and no other being has this ability. Is there another deity that is Omnipotent or Omnipresent? Of course not! The Father created all things including Lucifer and is deserving of all love and adoration from us not just because of what He has done but because of who HE IS! There is only ONE TRUE GOD that can forgive sin and only one price that can pay for mankind's iniquities and that is through the perfect blood sacrifice of Jesus Christ. There are many spiritual roads and religious philosophies, but Jesus is the only bridge to heaven. All the words that have ever been written by mortal man are just ink and paper, but God's words are alive and filled with life changing spiritual power. The Father, Son, and Holy Spirit make up the trinity Godhead and are the one and only true God of the past, present, and future. He is God Almighty, the invincible warrior, the King of all kings and the Holy One of Israel! *"And being found in fashion as a man, He humbled Himself, and became obedient unto death, even the death of the cross. Wherefore God also has highly exalted Him, and given Him a name which is ABOVE EVERY name: That at the name of Jesus EVERY knee should bow, of things in heaven, and things in earth, and things under the earth; and that EVERY tongue should confess that Jesus Christ is Lord, to the glory of God the Father"* (Philippians 2:8-11).

Chapter 14
SEEKING AFTER A SIGN

Being involved with the church environment is challenging because it requires working with people. It is a place that can be beautiful when everyone is in one accord with Jesus and it can test our spiritual character when emotions become involved. With His mercy and patience, He has allowed me to take baby steps of maturity toward the freedom that comes from learning His truth and how to love. A portion of my seeking has included asking the Lord to enlighten me about His church and it has taken me a long time to acquire the wisdom that people may be complicated individuals and at times difficult to deal with, but God loves them very much. I've also learned a deceiving part about this discovery is that we often forget to look in the mirror and realize that we are also a part of the problem. He has revealed to my heart that I have been guilty of having pride, and of course I thought it was everyone else. Generally speaking, most of the time we think we are somehow exempt from arrogance and are easily convinced that our self-discipline, knowledge, and strict awareness of our conscience keeps these types of dark attitudes from *sneaking* into our lives. But, as we have said many times, deception is a silent killer that can secretly hold us captive within our minds and hearts like an *invisible man* without us even recognizing it.

The mystery is that it is invisible only to the one who cannot see it and is usually very noticeable to everyone except the ones that are thankful they do not have it. Like all fruits of iniquity, this one is especially common in those who think they know a lot about their favorite subject and have spent much time learning about it and of course, religion is not exempt. The general idea is that some people believe they know more than anyone and commonly have a difficult time listening to someone else that might have a new or worthy insight. Many times even though we are highly persuaded in our conclusions, things are not always the way they seem. I believe we can agree that all of us are like this to a certain degree, and the difference between those who continue learning and growing in God's wisdom and those who are hindered by their denial comes down to being cautiously open minded—Not in the idea that we accept everything, but to be sensitive to the Holy Spirit where we can recognize that pride has become an unwanted resident within our hearts and is preventing us from moving forward. May we remember, *"A wise man will hear, and will INCREASE learning; and a man of understanding shall attain unto wise counsels" (Proverbs 1:5).*

In our state of ignorance and blindness, pride can also cause us to have a calloused conscience where we spend more time criticizing the way people live instead of having compassion and praying for them and demonstrating how Jesus wants us to live. I did not mean to spend this much time about the dangers of arrogance, but I certainly needed it for my own soul. My intention is to continue learning how to be a remnant disciple, and as we will see, the reason for mentioning pride is directly connected to my views about worship and the church. If we are to be effective servants for His Kingdom, we must be willing to undergo extensive surgery to remove this heart *blockage* that holds us in bondage and prevents God's nature and character from being evident in our lives. It is true, the Bible says that we have the mind of Christ, but this does not mean we know as much as He does. It just confirms that if we can know what He is thinking, we can carry out His will. *"For who hath known the mind of the Lord, that he may instruct him? But we have the mind of Christ" (I Corinthians 2:16).*

Without being able to discern His mind we have no clue as to what He is saying or how to please Him. Many of you have experienced wounds and disappointments in the church and realize that some were the faults of others and some were your own. I have also had times of rejection and disagreement and must confess that it has been my perception of how I thought things should be that has frustrated me. It is common for the average church to be filled with armchair quarterbacks, but there is no excuse for our lack of meekness, forgiveness, and understanding because without these attitudes we are only making it worse! Yes, there are times when wise counsel and correction is needed but only in the spirit of love and longsuffering. I have finally realized that it is not how much we can do but rather how much we let go of, and the more we try to make the corporate assembly into what we think it should be, the more it begins to be molded into our own personal version of church. The church is a highly complex organism that is socially accessible, politically vulnerable, and spiritually empowered, and will only become what God wants it to be when we invest our energy and enthusiasm into serious prayer.

While it is true that many do not comprehend truth, there are some that do, and if we build walls around our reasoning, our opinions can sometimes betray us. When we refer to a specific topic, it is important to remember not to include everyone because there are usually exceptions. For example, to say the church has failed, we are saying there is not a single person that can be found faithful. If our discussion about the church is to remain intelligent, we need to remember that devotion for our Lord was never expected or foreseen to be huge but actually rather small. When *Ephesians chapter five* talks about the glorious church, it did not say that it would be massive because *Matthew 7:14* says, **"Because straight is the gate and narrow is the way which leadeth unto life, and FEW there be that find it."** He was emphasizing a holy, spotless bride which consists of the remnant disciples that are few and far between. Within many assemblies there could possibly be only a handful of true disciples, and as it may be true that the church as a whole has not followed God's voice, it does not mean that everyone that attends is only a religious spectator. God invites all who hear HIS Word to respond and will save all that are His, which gives us the assurance there will be a band of overcomers, a victorious bride, and a holy remnant that He is excited about and that He has lovingly prepared a place in eternity for them!

I know the Bible teaches about groups of people that have gathered together to worship God since the beginning. There have been praise and music leaders that teach and relay what God is saying to the people, and giving tithes and offerings that were used to support the ministries and outreaches of these groups. We observe everything from the Old Testament where we see Moses and the tabernacle, the congregation of Israel, and the law of God's Word all the way to the Pharisees, the temples, and the observance of religious ceremonies and sacrifices in the day of Jesus. Then after Christ we see the New

Testament Christian church developing in the callings, offices, and gifts of the Holy Spirit, having meetings in the upper room and the revival at Pentecost. Continuing, we read about the condition of the seven churches in the book of Revelation, and all of this gives us a small insight about these assemblies of believers that were organized and that observed the commands and commission of God's plans. But I must admit that I am still confused because I have been thinking that the church would arise and become a visible representation of God's glory on earth. Instead of the restoration of the tabernacle of David, mostly what I have witnessed in my life has only been a gathering of believers that follow a routine of three songs and a sermon. However, the reason why I began with mentioning about my pride is because evidently my views have been distorted by my lack of understanding. It all has to do with comprehending the mystery that the church is NOT the building down on the corner that serves as a practical *meeting place* for God's followers.

The literal church is a sold-out individual that is a member of a collective remnant of disciples all over the earth that make up the body of Christ. Within this reality is recognizing that every assembly may have a few of these true saints but also contains a number of people that are not true Christians and others who are living in carnality. Seeing this revelation, it is understandable why the mighty rushing wind does NOT blow through the buildings or angels are not seen flying throughout the sanctuary. The disappointment of not witnessing the manifestation of God's glory is now put in the perspective that a major part of the general church population is NOT living a holy life in the Spirit and does not have any intention to do so. Could it be this lukewarm attitude that explains why the building does not shake and the service is not as miraculous as God desires for it to be? I believe so. In order for God's presence to be revealed, His glory must be alive and active within the life of the believer which reveals the corporate church is a direct reflection of the heart of the people. Yes, the Lord desires to move mightily when His children meet together, but He cannot manifest the literal glory of His throne in the brick building across the street when the majority of the members do not believe it and do not want it! Since His children are the temple of the Holy Ghost, I believe this mystery is only being revealed to those that have become determined to seek Him with all of their hearts and are willing to take control of their old natures. In other words, He does not give His revelations to those who do not care one way or another. *"Ask, and it shall be given you; seek and ye shall find; knock and it shall be opened unto you" (Matthew 7:7)*. These are the ones that will be engulfed in miracles and be used to represent the Kingdom of God. The beauty of holiness and the perfection of His holy love will be the demonstration of His presence and will be accompanied with the power and glory of His person. God longs to reveal His wonders to those who passionately desire to live where He lives.

I have poured out my heart to simply say that I have been expecting something that will not come the way I thought it would. This is not to say that God will not manifest Himself in our meetings, but He is going to release His power through individuals that have become refined and willing to be used as His holy instruments. These remnant overcomers will conquer their flesh, and as they surrender the control of their wills, He can fill them with the power of His Spirit to do His miracles. It is faith that releases God's authority that will generate these miraculous deeds for His honor and purposes. These holy expressions of love and obedience will NOT be treated as pearls before swine or a carnival side show of unexplained magic tricks but will be done according to God's perfect will and always an extension of His unmeasured mercy. I have envisioned the glory cloud would fill the church sanctuary and the foundations would shake like Isaiah talked about in chapter six. I have heard people testify that during a worship service they saw gold dust falling from the ceiling, colorful auras or angels that manifested above the congregation. I want to be clear in what I am saying; God is NOT against manifesting His glory, but the problem with us weak humans is that if we are not careful the phenomena can capture our attention and bring an imbalance. For example, I noticed with the gold dust testimony that nothing was mentioned about God's Word, healings, salvations, or how the Holy Spirit had convicted anyone to repent or given a revelation that changed someone's life. All that was talked about was the sign.

Maybe people like me spend so much time trying to witness the super-natural that we forget to love and intercede for the people like Jesus does. Instead of spending more time in my prayer closet learning how to live a holy life and allowing God's anointing to be a blessing to everyone, I became frustrated and critical with everyone's failure to live up to a certain standard. Yes, much of the modern church style is providing more sensationalism and entertainment to hold people's attention, but a good suggestion would be to not spend as much time worrying about why other people have not yielded their wills and just do what Jesus is telling us to do. May God help me to learn that I CANNOT change anyone! To even think that we could transform a congregation and set them on fire for God is arrogant. The best chance for people to be touched through our lives is for them to see Jesus in us, and if they cannot see Him in our lives then why in heavens name would we think we have a ministry? We are getting the cart before the horse if we are worrying more about the glory cloud than about the people to be discipled. When we are living in the awareness of His presence and have allowed Him to become our Lord, people will sense the anointing and be convicted to search for His truth. Again, a heavenly phenomenon is wonderful, and God wants to do them and can perform them anywhere He wants, but I was looking in the wrong location! Instead of coming to the service and waiting for the glory cloud to fill the house, we must realize that He desires to manifest His power and love in our hearts and souls ALL the time! If His presence is going to be revealed when we are in church, then someone who is anointed by God will release it, and everyone will recognize it! If the people are NOT prepared and NOT expecting God's glory within the church and have no desire to experience it in their life – then it will not happen! We wonder why the services are dry and are without demonstrations of His power and we must realize these are some of the reasons. He will not force His presence, and I believe that many times He feels that He is NOT welcome. The level that He can move among us and in us comes down to how determined we are to surrender our lives to Him. It is time to pull out the song "I surrender all" and read the words very carefully to see what they mean! A church assembly that is filled with sin and apathy is nothing more than a room of religious spectators and in the Bible these are the ones who never received from the Lord. ***"What? Know ye not that your body IS THE TEMPLE of the Holy Ghost which is in you, which ye have of God, and ye are not your own?"*** *(1 Corinthians 6:19).*

I am not suggesting that He cannot or will not manifest His presence in a sleepy church, but I am proclaiming it is time to wake up and allow Him to send a great revival to our souls! I do not intend to be someone that only seeks after a sign, but I just want everyone to SEE His majesty and be filled with His love. I am learning the revelation that this must happen through the way I LIVE and not to just keep waiting for it to happen in a church service. *"A wicked and adulterous generation seeketh after a sign; and there shall no sign be given unto it, but the sign of the prophet Jonah. And He left them, and departed" (Matthew 16:4)*. Everything the Lord is trying to do in the earth He desires to do through His disciples. What we call church has been infected by the same religious spirit that contaminated the Pharisees and Jesus feels just as angry about it today as He did then. Our programs and rituals cannot take the place of allowing God to *possess* us! Only when we surrender our independence can we be considered a wise virgin whose lamp is filled with the oil of complete dependence on God.

I have been in many services where much of the time was spent trying to *pump* everyone up into an emotional state of excitement. As a worship leader, I learned over the years how to do this myself, and in some churches where this is normal, if the worship leader and pastor do not perspire through their shirts, and a few saints don't run around the sanctuary a couple of times, they have not had a good service! Without offending either side of the fence, emotion is not necessarily bad, but it is not the anointing. Amen. I believe there is a time for emotion to be released when the anointing of God is thick, but if it is NOT there, we should stop attempting to make it happen or force the issue! Our discernment should give us the sensitivity to know if the anointing is there or not, and if it is NOT, it is a clear indication that prayer is lacking. I look forward to seeing the gifts of the Spirit activated and believe that purity and praying in faith has unlimited power with releasing the manifestations of God. I pray to see miracles of healing along with outpourings of God's presence that bring salvation and deliverance, and to tell you the truth I am disappointed when it does not happen. However, I now realize that even though it is wonderful to have heavenly expectations, the amount of spiritual demonstration depends on the levels of personal sacrifice and obedience. *What do you mean?* If the people are not walking in His anointing and do not desire to see heaven come down, the Lord will not *interrupt* the meeting with His presence! Obedience is better than sacrifice and emotion cannot take the place of the anointing because God does not provide generic substitutes! It is time we understand that it is God's presence radiating from within our hearts that allows Him to use us for HIS glory. If you and I really want to see Jesus manifest His presence, let's fast and pray for a week while we ask Him to open the eyes of our understanding. Let's make a prayer list and intercede every day for the lost in our network so they might be saved. And let's pray an hour before the service and cry out for His Spirit to be poured out on our assembly. Mmmmm. . .it seems we all want the fishes and the loaves but start huffing and puffing when it comes to fighting on the front line of spiritual warfare. It is true that God has done many awesome miracles through the ages, and He has many more that He is waiting to release, but who will become a vessel of honor and be willing to be a *conduit* of His power! God has plenty of lightning, but is having a difficult time trying to find a living lightning rod.

> *"I am sorry Lord for all of the times I was looking for Your miracles instead of looking for You. I wanted to see Your power without desiring to see my need to be transformed and filled with Your Spirit. Forgive me for looking for You all around me – and not within me! Your truth was there all the time, and I could not see it. It was like I could not see the forest for the trees. Thank You for speaking to my heart and revealing truth about emotions and the anointing. It is so easy to become confused, and I pray for all Christians who are living in denial and the lack of understanding. Stir the hearts of your pastors and all of Your warriors. Convict us to fall on our faces and learn Your holy revelations. We do NOT know it all, and when we think we do, we are already caught in a prideful snare trap of delusion. Help us O God; we are desperately needy for You. We love You. Amen."*

PART III
THE AWARENESS OF HIS LOVE

Chapter 15

CONSTANT AWARENESS

"He heals the broken in heart, and binds up their wounds. He tells the number of the stars; he calls them all by their names. Great is our Lord, and of great power; His understanding is infinite" (Psalm 147:3-5).

Do you appreciate the fact that God is with you when you are mowing the lawn or doing the laundry? Do we realize that when we do something wrong, even if no one else will find out about it, that He is there? It is not like He is down the street or even down the hall. He has a front row seat to everything we think and say because He lives within us. It is a revelation to discover that God is much more aware of us than we are of Him, and if I could condense the purpose of this book in one sentence it would be to encourage us to STRIVE *(make great efforts to achieve)* to become just as attentive to God's constant presence as He is with us. I am reminded that within the discipline of Theophostic counseling, an empty chair is always brought into the therapy session as a representation that God is not only being welcomed to sit in with the conversation but is actually present. This is for the counselor and the counselee to have a visual reminder that even though we cannot literally see God, we can have a conscious recognition that He is listening and is being given the liberty and consideration to intervene however and whenever He so desires. This is a small illustration of how we can develop an awareness of God's presence as a lifestyle.

We have talked about worship as an organized meeting in the corporate setting of the assembly, but there is another view of our personal relationship that is the highest form of love, obedience, and devotion, and that is the being consciously acquainted with God as our most trusted friend. There are many levels of spiritual maturity and graduating into a closer walk with Christ will be determined by the proportion of our determination to know Him. Since we have concluded that going to church does not prove that someone is a Christian, then can we also agree that even participating in a praise service is not necessarily worshipping God. It is true that singing unto the Lord can (and should) be a part of expressing our love and gratitude, but *John 4:24* says, **"God is a Spirit: and they that worship Him must worship Him in spirit and in truth."** *So, how do we know if we are worshipping Him in spirit and truth?* Within the context of this passage, Jesus is having a conversation with a woman and is revealing to her several things about her personal life that was making her uncomfortable. She attempts to divert His attention away from her problems, but He refuses to be distracted about the subject of true worship. His point was that worship is not confined to an external ceremony but is a matter of the heart that is directed and influenced by God's truth. Unless there is sincere passion for God, there is no spiritual worship, and unless we have a personal knowledge of the God we worship, we cannot worship in truth. The more we know about God, the more we appreciate Him, and the deeper we come to know Him, the more intimate our worship will become. It does not say they shall just *sing songs* in perfect harmony with an expensive sound system and this will make them worshippers. Whether in deed or thought, one must have the intentions of divine love or our offerings and expressions will be tainted with the smell of ulterior motives. Many of our religious traditions have failed to teach God's Word clearly, and many have become confused by the subtle deceptions of what a follower of Jesus should be.

The masses are proud of their church attendance and how they participate in a worship *service* every week, but as we have said before, this is NOT necessarily a confirmation of our spiritual devotion or obedience. It does not take a lot of convincing from our un-renewed mind to deceive us into thinking that going to church is connected with going to heaven. Many are resting in the comfort and security of church attendance like something contained in a safe little box that we visit and leave. This *museum* attitude can tolerate going to church but does not worry about the homework. If we went to a seminar that promoted a guaranteed way to become a millionaire in 4 weeks, we would buy a ticket, bring our notebook, sit on the front row, and take notes! (You know where I am heading with this). Many have never wanted to understand that church is a place where we load our guns and fill our canteens, which makes perfect sense because most have no intention of enlisting as a soldier. *Why?* Because there is nothing in it for them! This is why things like love and prayer are not crucially important to the average person. Churches have taught that Christians go to heaven, so with eternity secure they are thinking it does not matter. The real question is whether they have ever really accepted Christ at all. The tiny amount of time that we do meet together in church was really created to be like a *time-out* in a game where the players go to the sidelines to join together in the safety of unity, catch their breaths, get a drink, wipe off the sweat and blood, listen to instructions from their coach, and be reminded of their purpose and destiny, then go back into battle! Whatever your personal metaphor of church, an important rule to remember is that we are NOT at war with each other! We have been called to enjoy the precious attribute of UNITY that is the result of our humility when we come together in love. It's not how much the church is into Jesus; it's how much of Jesus is into the church. And when we have conflict, it is usually advertised from the pulpit as a warning against the devil, but the truth is that our most intense warfare is trying to cast down our carnality.

    The Christian has been called to walk and abide in the Spirit of God, and this can only be accomplished when we allow the Lord to fill our minds and hearts with His thoughts. For many years I was guilty of seeing the church as the only place of worship and that we should try to spend as much time in service as possible working for Him. I was often frustrated because there were many other parts of the service that seemed to hinder and harness the presence of God. What I eventually have come to realize is that instead of the church service being my entire personal worship experience for the week, it should be considered as a training session where I learn how to worship Him as a lifestyle. The same way a sermon is not the only instruction we should receive all week but rather should be an inspiration and enhancement to our personal Bible studies, the same with prayer, giving, and so on. When college students go to class, listening to the professor's lecture is not the only requirement for the course, but rather is only a fraction of the reading and writing that is necessary! Our corporate meetings should be like practice sessions that help us become more experienced and better prepared as we go out into our network and serve in God's ministry.

When our spiritual experience is based on feelings and the legalities of tradition, it can be compared to an adrenalin rush that is a fast and furious burst of emotions but has very little to do with God. True worship is a level-headed continuous steady stream of positive thoughts and appreciation for what He is doing in our lives that does not go up and down like a roller coaster. *How can we live like this?* We become determined to train our mind to work with our spirit instead of allowing our mind to take orders from our will. I will amen that myself! Worship is not just going through the motions of a religious program so that we can appear holy; it is demonstrating our convictions every moment! What we do and the way we act in church is easy. The real challenge is how we act when we are in a fox hole, and the bullets are flying over our heads, or when someone opens a car door and bumps our car. Years ago, the Lord spoke to me through a prophetic word that God would give me a gift to write songs, but there was a tiny condition - I would have to walk them out! This has been difficult, but I am finally beginning to realize that just because some people can produce truth and help others connect with God, it does not mean they have the revelation of the message themselves. I realize the perfect scenario would be for us to receive the revelation and then feel qualified to teach others, but many times I believe that since all of us have only such small amounts of understanding, He can still use us for His purposes while "hoping" that the truth we are sowing will continue to grow within us. The same is true with worship as it has nothing to do with the quality of our vocals, our style, ability, or how long we have been playing; it is all about how much of our heart we have given to Him. For example, if the pastor is NOT living by his own preaching and the worship leader is focused only on the sound of the music, then church has become a job and not a ministry! Just because our hair stands up on the back of our necks or goose bumps run down our arms means nothing to God if our walk does not match our talk. I have personally known individuals that have spent many years claiming to have built a strong spiritual life, but in the end they discovered that their vessels had holes in the bottom. For some reason, the Word was on their lips but never became activated within their minds and hearts to create the transformation that could change who they were. As strange as it may sound, we can trudge through what we think is a Christian life without a true comprehension of what it means, and disturbingly it is easy to do.

The first part of *Proverbs 23:7* says, **"For as he thinks in his heart, so is he."** This is a wonderful spiritual principle that exposes the contents of our hearts and what we say and do as evidence that can be used against us. We cannot be limited to only living a religious performance in the church environment because our words and deeds will eventually reveal our true identity. Only when loving God becomes a personal passion will we begin to worship Him everywhere we go and in everything we do. Let us learn how to worship Him while we work, when we take hikes into the mountains or when we are with our families. Let us praise Him when we are walking on the beach, on vacation, at the grocery store, pumping gas, or in the waiting room. Praise and worship is a state of mind within the one who truly loves God with a whole heart! He is calling us to come away with Him; can you hear Him? He is beckoning for us to get alone with Him in a private, secret place of refuge. It is not a geographic location but a quiet and holy habitation where we can concentrate and talk with Him. It is a spiritual mighty tower of solace and security where we can empty our consciences of all stresses, fears, worries, and concerns. Within the intimacy of His presence is an environment where we can sing and cry at the same time and where we can become saturated with His joy and be overwhelmed by His endless love. **"Thou wilt keep him in perfect peace, whose mind is STAYED on Thee: because he trusteth in Thee"** *(Isaiah 26:3)*. The Lord gave me this song in 1985 called *"Get alone with me."* It was written in first person as a tender plea from His heart that reminds us of how much He desires to be close to us.

> *(Verse 1) The sound of many voices, saying come here go there*
> *Everyday life distractions from everywhere*
> *I know there never seems to be enough time*
> *But remember my word says that if you seek me you will find*
> *He that hath an ear let him hear*
> *What my Spirit has to say*
> *If you'll draw near to me, I'll draw near to you*
> *Staying close to me is the only way (I'm waiting)*

(Chorus) Come get alone with me, come get alone with me
Meditating on my word, living in my presence
Find the time – to get alone with me

(Verse 2) I desire the secret place in fellowship with you
For I have many things to share
But for you to hear my voice
You must make the choice to spend time with me
My child you will find that the battle's in your mind
Don't allow the enemy to steal our time
I will make you stronger don't put it off any longer
You are the branch and I am the vine

Chapter 16

MORE THAN MUSIC

"And take heed to yourselves, lest at any time your hearts be overcharged with surfeiting [overeating], and drunkenness, and cares of this life, and so that day come upon you unawares [unexpectedly]. For as a snare shall it come upon all them that dwell upon the face of the whole earth. WATCH ye therefore, and PRAY always, that you may be accounted worthy to escape all these things that shall come to pass, and to stand before the Son of man" (Luke 21:34-35).

We all have the potential to become like Christ. When we are born again, we are given a deposit of living gospel seeds that come from the fruit of the Spirit and have the potential to grow and produce the character of God. As caretakers of the gardens and orchards of our hearts, it is up to us how much we allow His nature to develop and be demonstrated in us. When it comes to worship, our love for Him becomes more than a just a picture of flowers; it becomes a literal flower garden, and since we are the gardeners, we have the responsibility to eliminate the weeds and keep everything watered with obedience. As always, the flesh hates to be disciplined or become involved with commitment, but like anything else, the more we learn and practice, the better we will be. In this natural realm, whenever discipline is being enforced, it is for the purpose of training to win a competition, to receive an award, or to excel and become successful and victorious, and the general idea remains the same in the context of the spiritual life. Being an overcomer for Jesus Christ has never been advertised as an option. Our salvation has a unique mission and destiny, and losing is not God's idea of an abundant triumphant life. When we fail to construct our lives according to God's blueprint, it is usually a failure on our part to follow directions. Every Christian has been called to utilize all that the Father has provided along with the accountability to fulfill His will. The victorious perception is as much about conquering our flesh as it is about pulling down strongholds and will require total devotion to His instructions. Walking holy is not just a religious thought or phrase but a demand from God that works hand in hand with our determination to follow Him. He is the shepherd, but many sheep are still arguing about details within the contract agreement they have signed. The Christian life is no longer rolling the dice, but now it's all about learning how He has prepared a specific destiny for us and what it's going to take to accomplish it! If faith is the substance of things hoped for and the evidence of things not seen, then we could say that love is the substance of our passion and the evidence of how determined we are to prove it.

Within the beauty of holy intimacy between God and man there is a seldom mentioned mystery called the covenant vow. It is the highest form of relationship and is comparable to the husband and wife bond of matrimony. This holy *exchange* of complete commitment and devotion simply means that all we have is His, and everything that God has is ours; however, it is based on obedience and the condition of our heart that measures how serious we are about it. If we are surface Christians, we will be interested only in the basic blessings and eternal security that a Savior can provide. If we choose to be disciples, we are committed to following Him into the depths of His presence as the LORD of our heart no matter where He may lead. This vow involves the tears of the servant mixed with the Master's delight. *"Weeping may endure for a night – but joy comes in the morning" (Psalm 30:5)*. Our weeping represents the breaking of the heart in humility and sorrow as His presence pulls us closer and opens the eyes of our conscience that we might see His infinite compassion and mercy. Is there anything on earth worth more than these precious times of worship with the creator, redeemer, and lover of our souls?

Sin has a subtle way of slowly creating a *film* of dirt which is a result of carnal compromise. In our hurried life, we have the free-will to ignore the calling of the Holy Spirit to come into the secret chambers and spend time with God. If we do not develop a strict lifestyle of self-discipline, we can slowly allow our emotions and flesh to lead us and influence our thoughts with negativity and sin. However, this deception does not go unnoticed in the Spirit realm, and, in fact, it has definite consequences concerning our personal relationship with Jesus. Each hour that we ignore our need to repent and restore our fellowship, the further away we drift into lower levels of lukewarmness. Our passion and the awareness of His presence fade away while our flesh continues to enjoy the freedom to indulge in fleshly temptations. Our spirits cry abba Father, but cannot overrule our free-will because we have been given the freedom from our creator to choose what we do and whom we will serve. This condition progresses until one day our heavenly Father intervenes by revealing how we have hurt and disappointed Him. Praise His holy Name for the grace and mercy of His conviction as He comes to rescue us from ourselves as a shepherd would leave the ninety-nine to seek the one. In the deepest part of our conscience, (the inner voice of our moral or ethical self that tells us the difference between right and wrong) we become broken through conviction and shame and respond with intense sorrow from within the core of our being. After we have asked Him to forgive us and cleanse us, we are refreshed and renewed in the beauty of His mercy, grace, longsuffering, patience, and love. This is where the inner chambers of our soul become flooded with joy unspeakable as our security, peace and fellowship with Him is restored. When is the last time you have wept because you have been overwhelmed with His love and humbly allowed Him to break your heart and cleanse you? ***"The sacrifices of God are a broken spirit: a broken and a contrite heart, O God, thou wilt not despise" (Psalm 51:17).*** The word *"contrite"* means completely penitent and thoroughly remorseful as a result of guilt and shame. Humility and meekness put others before themselves and becomes the perfect environment for His agape love, while pride is the exact opposite as it protects and justifies the heart to remain selfish and calloused. If it is our desire to be a student of worship, we must become acquainted with the lifestyle of humility because we cannot walk in His Spirit without it.

There are many levels of maturity in the body of Christ. The religious masses love to hear about all the blessings God has for them along with a steady flow of motivational lectures, but the problem with *nursing the bottle* along with a steady consumption of chocolate cake is that we can become malnourished and unbalanced in our spiritual perception. I am NOT against being encouraged because we do need it;

however we must also see the big picture of not only the reality of the way God sees everything and everyone, but more personally how He sees us. This is where many immature believers usually need to leave because their mamma is calling! If your church announced a weekly Bible study that was going to be about sanctification, I would guess that you would probably not need to put out very many chairs. This is not being negative – it is being truthful about ALL of us! I am guilty and do not spend nearly enough time deeply examining my heart, and this is because we all have the same common problem—and that is our flesh wants to rule our lives. I can do a general assessment and say a quick prayer and keep running along the path of spiritual routines, but this does NOT necessarily increase my spiritual maturity!

If we stay in the battle long enough, there will come a cross-road moment where we will come face to face with truth about ourselves, and we will CHOOSE whether to follow Him or walk away. The amount that we progress and develop into His image will depend directly on how convinced we are of our need to change. If we do not believe we need to be adjusted or modified, we will NOT pursue the image of Christ and His glory or complete His blueprint! Conviction brings revelation, and until we allow His Word to do His perfect work in our hearts, we will remain the same! Many have tried to live their spiritual lives exactly as they have lived their physical lives, but that is not God's way. We look in the mirror and see ourselves and decide what we will do to change the outside while God's command is for us to search from within and see ourselves the way HE sees us on the inside. The truth is that until we abandon our will we cannot not live for Him at all. The concept of being made holy in the image of God can become a meaningless religious slogan if we do not have the revelation of sanctification. If we depend on our *title* of Christian or a cross we wear around our neck to take the place of His refiner's fire, we are living in a fantasy land. For those who presume that just because they go to church they are automatically fulfilling God's specific will, I pray the conviction of God's Word will awaken them and reveal His divine reality. We cannot live the way we want and expect His approval! ***"And what agreement has the temple of God with idols? For you are the temple of the living God. As God has said: I will dwell in them and walk among them. I will be their God and they shall be my people. Therefore, come out from among them and be separate, says the Lord. Do not touch what is unclean, and I will receive you. And you shall be my sons and daughters, says*** *the Lord Almighty. Therefore, having these promises beloved, let us cleanse ourselves from all filthiness of the flesh and spirit, perfecting holiness in the fear of God"* (II Corinthians 6:16-17 and 7:1).

Many believers are an embarrassment to God and a disappointment to the world because they have never allowed themselves to be transformed by the renewing of their minds. Ouch! The world does not need to see another hypocrite but does need to see unwavering loyalty to God's truth! It is true that we have been called to be *set-apart,* but from what? We are to be separated from the default system to keep from being contaminated or infected with sin, and be constantly purified by His blood to be a holy witness of God's love. This type of preaching can be tolerated until someone reveals how much being purified is going to cost, and this is when many will back away. It is easy to just live a religious formality, but it is difficult to hand over your old blueprints to God and watch Him throw them away. You worked hard on your future and all the plans and ideas you have been looking forward to doing. You had your life ALL planned out and now you are being required to lay them down? I watched a movie one time about a man that spent his life looking forward to retirement when he would live the rest of his life sailing around the world on his boat. He was consumed with making sure every detail was perfect, and when he finally set sail, he was told that his wife was expecting a baby. The plan was to have no children, and now to say the least his life had become a twisted agony of bitter-sweet emotions. He was now faced with letting go of one lifelong dream in order to embrace another one. Yes, our independence means our life and is the reason why there is a large crowd on the broad way and a small crowd on the narrow way. Our carnality must be crushed and crucified just as the body of Jesus was nailed to the cross! In order for us to live the resurrected life of victory over sin, our old natures must die an agonizing death. Many will say that there is no suffering for the Christian because Jesus paid for everything. It is true that Christ paid for our sins with His blood, but to eliminate our suffering as we deny our flesh to keep it from dominating us is just bad theology. We do not learn how to live for God lying on the beds of ease; we learn in the times of difficulty when there is *nothing* to depend on but Him! The agony from sacrificing our carnality is crucial for our spiritual development and will flow directly in context with how much we really love God. If we have NOT allowed Jesus to have control, we will NOT be pleasing to Him as faithful servants. When God pushes you to the edge, trust Him completely because only two things can happen; He will either catch you when you fall or will teach you how to fly!

So what makes the difference between those who desire to walk in sanctification and those who live carnally? It is either the lack of spiritual instruction, or severe heart disease, or both. It is all Christians' personal responsibility to study and pray and listen to what God is telling them, but in many cases it seems that people just avoid thinking about what God cares about. I am not trying to appear to have arrived at walking in His Spirit because, to confess openly, I am guilty of doing this. I realize that most of the time we are NOT concentrating on the mission at hand, and I believe this comes as a result of our minds not being renewed. We may have a great time of intimacy today, but we spring a leak, and tomorrow we are empty again. The vision and goal should be for us to be consistent, but that will come only with determination and discipline. **"Brethren, I count NOT myself to have apprehended: but this one thing I do, forgetting those things which are behind, and reaching forth unto those things which are before, I press toward the mark for the prize of the high calling of God in Christ Jesus"** *(Philippians 3:13-14)*. It is God's intention for us to develop a sensitive awareness to sin which can lead us into being holy; however this will manifest only when we decide to adopt an attitude of Godly sorrow about sin as a trait of our character. There is a huge difference between recognizing sin and resisting it.

A personal friend made a comment about my ministry the other day and said that within my songwriting and my article writing that God is saying the same thing over and over in hundreds of different ways, and it is about the condition and intention of our hearts. I thought about this statement, and I must agree that in the last thirty years, God in His graciousness and patience has been trying to tell me how much He wants all of my life not just parts of it. It is true, the contents of the conscience expose who we are, and reveal everything about us, and I know that He wants to be the Lord of everyone's life. We all invest much time and energy into our service for God, but what if all the personal communications He has spoken to you are just for you and Him to enjoy together, would that satisfy you? The first thing we want to do is share what we have learned in secret, but what if it was just for our personal spiritual growth? Maybe sometimes we run out and try to teach others what He is trying to reveal to us before we have even applied it. Mmmmm. . .It is more likely that He desires for us to incorporate it and demonstrate it as a part of our life first, and then in due season we can relay it with confidence because we have lived it.

I know we wiggle and squirm because it is uncomfortable to think about sacrificing our pet sins and the things we do that are not right. I mentioned Godly sorrow a moment ago, and I wonder if we even know what it is. As a Christian, have you ever done something or said something that, after it was over, you felt ashamed? Have you ever felt heaviness in your soul over a sin, and you tried to shake it off, but the nagging misery just would not go away? This is a glimpse of the sorrow of sin. Godly sorrow is a blessing in disguise as it allows us to feel the guilt of doing wrong and the sadness that God feels from our failure. If we could realize how much it hurts Him when we disobey, it would definitely help us to do better. If we are willing to discern truth and stop sugarcoating our *rose-colored* image, we may discover that our consciences contain things we need to deal with. Can we really worship Him in the fullness of joy if we are hiding things and do not want to let go of them? The main thing that hinders us from worshipping Him is that our sin has caused distance, and this guilt is why people do not want to go to church. Our most joyful times of being in His presence will always be when our hearts are clean and completely surrendered to Him. Good news! Father is doing a work in His people right now! He is preparing His children not just for a one way ticket to paradise but is filling them so they might be able to abide in His Spirit now! There are spots and wrinkles in our bridal garments, and He is saying to come away from the world and let go of all those things that are trying to steal our affections. Rebellion and idolatry will cause our hearts to grow cold and numb, and worship will be the first to fall to the bottom of the priority list. We must stay in an attitude of repentance so that He can continually restore and maintain our connection with Him. To think that worship is based only on music would be to miss the beauty of living in the quiet contentment of His presence. Our sacrifice of praise is the demonstration of our obedience and is directly connected to the depth of devotion we have for Him. *"But the fruit of the Spirit is love, joy, peace, longsuffering, gentleness, goodness, faith, meekness, temperance: against such there is no law. And they that are Christ's have crucified the flesh with the affections and lusts. If we LIVE in the Spirit, let us also WALK in the Spirit"* (Galatians 5:22-25).

Chapter 17

THE LEADER OF SONGS

"And David and all Israel played before God with all their might, and with singing, and with harps, and with psalteries, and with timbrels, and with cymbals, and with trumpets" (I Chronicles 13:8).

Most people do not understand the daily balancing act that church leaders go through trying to manage people without causing a religious mutiny. Managers in the secular world can relate to the headaches and pressures of trying to organize individuals with diverse personalities, but the ministry is even more complex with the addition of spiritual considerations. People always want to share their ideas, opinions, and expectations, and the Christian realm is no exception as each man or woman has a personal interpretation of how church should be. What most people fail to realize is that all the other parts of the body also have their own unique revelations about what to change along with the same intensity and fervent passion as others do. In simple terms - we want control.

Leaders that are sensitive to the Holy Spirit will listen to suggestions and advice and consider them with prayer and meditation because they know how important it is to have an open mind and a clear conscience. Much prayer and wisdom is needed in the leader's life to avoid categorizing people with prejudice and opinions because this hinders the ability to perceive and comprehend a possible confirmation of what God is saying or may really want to do. Judging critiques the outside appearance, but discernment recognizes the spiritual connection with God. Church leaders are constantly dealing with everyone's ideas about how worship services can be made more effective which can easily lead them to become overwhelmed and distracted. As a subconscious escape, the leaders may become less open to listening and lock the gates of their tolerance and enthusiasm to consider the thoughts of others. This attitude can hinder and cause a dysfunction in their personal lifves and ministry and over a period of time may cause the leader to develop a habit of wearing a *mask* of friendliness and being seemingly interested in suggestions but inwardly can be completely ignoring everyone. Isolation has its place and is sometimes much needed, but it is not where we develop a false security that gives way to a negative mentality to only listen and trust our own ideas. There is a fine line between retreating into isolation to listen to God's voice versus independently leaning on the way we believe things are. We must never forget the Lord can use the most unlikely person to speak into our lives, which is why the leader must have his receiver on God's frequency and his spiritual antennas up at all times.

Every Christian is called to be A leader but not everyone is called to be THE leader. The Lord loves all of His children equally but gives different levels of authority and responsibility as He sees fit. Those who are chosen to be directors and managers in God's Kingdom are like connectors (reminds me of the plastic caps that twist electrical wires together) that can lead people into Jesus and show them how to grow and augment their personal relationship with Him. A strong leader is actually more of a facilitator that can generate confidence and encouragement in others by getting them to understand and follow God's vision to work together with others within the body of Christ. Whatever your philosophy of leadership, we can say that learning how to follow teaches us a great deal about how to lead. The higher the role of facilitators, the more humble and willing to serve they need to be. Those in authority must develop spiritual discernment so they can make sure that everything is being done in the will of God and not the arm of the flesh (including their own). In the Bible, we have studied David and know that he was a person after God's own heart, and if we look closer we will see how an attitude of repentance was a key to his intimate relationship with the Lord. The concept of being willing to decrease so that God can increase has become somewhat of a theme within this work but can happen only when we choose to spend time with Him. True Christian leaders will not compromise the truth but will do the right thing, not just for the curtain call of vain glory but simply because they genuinely love Jesus and His people.

Everyone agrees that a worship pastor needs to have the gift and anointing to lead others into the presence of God, but this is not the only qualification. There must also be a personality that is sincerely concerned and driven by a strong agape love for everyone. Ministry leaders need to be able to counsel, mediate, teach, and lead by example as a person of integrity, fairness, patience, and spiritual perception. There may be several people in the worship team that can sing solos and can lead songs, but the worship pastor is the one who needs the anointing to manage everyone into a working unit that can flow in not only the music but in their relationships with each other. It is crucial to have the ability to learn the art of maintaining unity and a balanced harmony within the many variations of temperaments and diverse dispositions. Leaders cannot be so strict that they smother the liberty and joy from the activity, while on the other hand it is also important to not be so laid-back or intimidated with fear that they fail to address problems and establish order. If we want to be respected in the field we are gifted in, then we must remember that meekness is not weakness but strength under control. Let us operate with knowing that all people deserve to be treated with dignity and that loving others as we love ourselves is giving God the honor for who they are and what He wants to do in them.

The worship pastor is always trying to challenge and stretch the ones who are gifted and becomes excited to step back so others can lead. Spiritual sensitivity allows the leader to take a special interest in encouraging young people for the sake of seeing them grow and advance into their gifts and callings. Youth that are trying to find their ministries in the field of music especially need to SEE the Holy Spirit move through the worship, and a true leader will help demonstrate how the gifts function so the church of tomorrow can learn how to become strong leaders and walk in their anointing. Mature leaders are patient and care about the person more than the talent as our calling is to build people not a legacy. Those that have been selected to be the head of a ministry have the responsibility to allow others to broaden and emerge as they become a resource for encouragement and edification to the body. The calling of a worship pastor is not to be a vehicle or platform to advertise a personal ministry or push a professional career agenda but is to be more like a chef that can take many wonderful ingredients and with the careful measuring, mixing, and concentration, they help prepare and serve a wonderful banquet of God's love to everyone. Every ministry is a privilege to serve and represent the Lord of glory and should not be taken for granted or used as a way to draw attention to ourselves.

People love to share their ideas, opinions, and expectations just like in everyday life, and all members should feel that their opinions are appreciated, but for ministry leaders it takes a keen discernment to sort out the fleshly thoughts from the anointed perceptions. It is true that most humans are convinced they know what is best, but what they fail to remember is that other people of the body also have their own unique revelations about what to change along with the same intensity and fervent passion as they have. Experienced leaders will always need to take suggestions and advice to the place of prayer and meditation because they know how essential it is to have an open mind as they listen to the Holy Spirit. Mature facilitators realize that first and foremost they are humble servants, and this realization will allow them to see the practical reality that the ultimate mission is for everything to be done in the power of God – NOT human ability, intelligence, or strength. Leaders for Christ must invest time alone with Him in prayer and personal worship as they learn that their life is the result of a vow to represent God and be accountable to a cause that comes from another dimension yet is manifested for all to know and appreciate. The position of a worship pastor is NOT reserved for a haughty spirit of pride that loves to have authority over others or who gets a charge out of being in *charge!* It is an opportunity to be a helper and supporter that can guide and assist others to grow and find their place among the challenging yet satisfying world of musical evangelism as we communicate the gospel of Christ to the entire world. *I Peter 2:5* talks about each member being a ***"lively stone,"*** and *Ephesians 2:21* mentions that we are a ***"building fitly framed together,"*** so with this train of thought we are becoming mature and learning how to be not just a worship team but a committed member of the body of Christ. We practice living for Him and serving Him throughout the week because the more skilled an individual becomes, the stronger the entire group becomes. Every team member must see the big picture of this unified *sound* of love and collaboration without becoming jealous or envious of those who are more advanced or might be experiencing a season of rich anointing. Let us rejoice and be happy for one another when God chooses to bless other individuals. Rejoice with those whom God is using today, and in His timing (and our attitude) He may be able to use us tomorrow! It is very important for the entire team to concentrate on God with the eyes of their hearts and be reminded their efforts are an offering for His glory. Our purpose is to honor God - our calling is to edify His people, and our destination is His throne. Just like the spies who brought the report from the land of Canaan, people are listening and depending on our attitudes and visions. If we project a negative way of thinking, the people will be discouraged, but if we are positive, we can plant many seeds of victorious thinking. Let us realize the way we present ourselves has a direct influence on our network as those around us are watching and listening to every word we say. It is a personal revelation to resist the snare trap of carnal communication and consider that the words we speak reveal what we believe and who we are.

Those who dedicate themselves to a worship team or any type of ministry understand that sacrifice and humility are more important than talent because attitude is the thermometer of our effectiveness. Whether you are a leader or operate in a support role, everyone is held accountable to the same standards and considered by the Lord to be equally valuable in the Kingdom. Amen! It is ALL about a unified effort that is pressing toward the goal of seeing the super-natural manifestation of God. It is NOT about who is more professional because the gifts and talents are mixed together to produce one spiritual sound. *What is this sound?* It is the sound of our enemies falling at our feet! Amen! It is the sound of thundering hooves from the horses of God's army that is protecting us and constantly fighting all around us so that we can fulfill God's will! It is the sound of triumph in the Name of Jesus! It is the sound of the Lion of the Tribe of Judah that is coming for us! Amen! Worthy is the Lamb that was slain!

Our heavenly Father is sharpening, teaching, and developing each of His children all over the world at the same time. Everyone is at a different level in his own personal relationship with the Lord, and we must be aware of this beautiful, constant snapshot of progressive maturity. Leaders need not only observe and discern others but also consistently search within themselves for the motives and intentions of their own thoughts and actions. Laying down our agendas and submitting our talents in order that we might see God's Kingdom flourish is the purpose of becoming a musical bridge builder. Laying down our wills in order to know God intimately is the reason we live. This attitude and state of consciousness is nothing new because the daily Christian life always involves sacrifice, sensitivity, and surrender; *it is the nature of Jesus*. Being a leader is not creating our own visions and concepts of God's power and glory but simply listening to His voice and confidently following the perfect destiny of His purpose. It is basically inviting Him to come into our midst and worshipping Him for who He is.

The relationship between the lead pastor and the worship pastor plays a vital role in the spiritual anointing of the corporate church service. In order to have a smooth transfer from music to teaching there must be a bond of trust and a unified connection of thought between these two individuals. As the worship leader begins the journey and leads the people into the presence of God, it is the senior pastor that has the overall vision, discernment, and Holy Spirit *"inspiration"* for the entire service. Somehow in the realm of space and time, the service is usually transferred from the one that has been leading and then passed to the one who will take it. I call this "passing the baton," and in this holy crossroad we continue moving smoothly toward our specific destination which is to allow God complete liberty to move among us. It is like the Lord is in the control tower, and the pilot and co-pilot are flying the plane. The co-pilot can fly awhile, but he hands it over to the pilot who knows *how, when, and where* to land safely. Each minister is trying to listen to every word that is coming from the flight coordinator as the service hinges on the willingness to follow and obey. There is not a lot of discussion about this subject, probably because most have not really thought much about it, and many rarely even notice this occurrence. When I am leading worship, I do at times become lost in God's presence, but when we are coming to the point of intimacy and soaking, I can feel myself becoming aware of the lead pastor and will try to find eye contact with him when I sense the time to transfer the service is coming closer. I've noticed that many times the lead pastor also *awakens* from his time of personal adoration with Father and becomes sensitive to the right moment to step in and take over. I love for the transfer to happen while the Holy Spirit is thick and the music is still playing gently and God's presence is still moving on the hearts of the congregation. It makes for a seamless hand-off when God's glory is intense, and this time of wonder and joy gives the pastor the option to continue with spiritual gifts or a specific direction of praying, or if he does not feel persuaded to linger, he can gently bring it to an end and continue moving forward with the service.

While we are on this conversation about the relationship between the worship pastor and the senior pastor, I want to include the topic of authority. It is generally agreed that the lead pastor has been trusted by the congregation to be able to hear God's voice. I am not saying he is perfect but only speaking in a general sense. There is a submission of all church related ministries, similar to how we all follow orders where we are employed. If you are a new worship leader, and are being guided by the senior pastor about song selection or anything connected with the worship service, do not be offended. This is a part of your maturity process that God is doing in you. The Lord is trying to teach all of us about humility and yielding our control to others that are in authority over us. This is very difficult to do especially if we are convinced that we can do perfectly well on our own. This is NOT the point! Even when those who are leading us miss the Lord's instructions, this is still valuable wisdom that can be used by everyone in our continuing education. On the other side of the fence, those who have matured and grown more experienced as worship pastors and ministry leaders need to be recognized by senior pastors as also being able to *listen* and *obey* how God is leading. A senior pastor must be careful to NOT fall into the habit of micro-managing every ministry in the church. There comes a time when leaders must develop TRUST in their fellow ministers and respect them in their spiritual labors. God is to be the one in control, and all of His servants are just trying to hear His voice - together. Sometimes pastors want everything to enhance and confirm their message, and that is fine if that is what God wants. However, if there are several different messages being presented through word and song, this does not automatically mean confusion. It may just reveal that several people were dealing with several different problems, and God in His endless compassion was trying to touch each one individually. Or it could confirm that the pastor was not in tune with the Holy Spirit, and others that had been praying were. Let us be quick to repent and acknowledge if we miss it because this transparency unveils our sincerity. It is God's church, His sermon, and His songs; let Him minister to every person the way He desires! Christ calls and assigns senior pastors as leaders of His assemblies and they are surrounded by fellow co-laborers in the ministry. The spirit of unity is at the heart of what makes the corporate assemblies function, and His love provides the power for the anointing. There is a divine order within the body that brings strength and glory to God's church, and it is an honor to witness this blessing.

Chapter 18

LEARNING TO LET GO

In part II, we glanced at a true account about Mary and Martha, but as many of you know there are different versions of this event, and some say there may have been two separate occasions that involved similar expressions. Whatever the occurrence may be, I want us to glean more from the perspective of how desperate we should be to abandon the natural so that we might embrace the divine. *"Now it came to pass, as they went, that he entered into a certain village: and a certain woman named Martha received him into her house. And she had a sister called Mary, which also sat at Jesus feet, and heard his word. But Martha was cumbered about much serving, and came to him, and said, Lord, do you not care that my sister has left me to serve alone? Bid her therefore that she help me. And Jesus answered and said unto her, Martha, Martha, you are careful and troubled about many things: But one thing is needful: and Mary has chosen that good part, which will not be taken away from her"* (Luke 10:38-42). It is true, we all have busy lives, but it is good to learn how to develop an awareness of our priorities. God never promised we would have an easy way, but He intended for us to have joy in the journey with Him.

How awesome to be able to see into the life of Jesus with stories about real people that Christ interacted with. Here are two sisters that were friends of Jesus, and they had such different personalities. Martha the choleric was the busy organizer, the *worker bee* that was always thinking, going, doing, and unfortunately complaining because everyone else was not taking part in the bombardment of labor. Mary seemed to be more of a melancholy type that was less stressful, but serious, and sensitive, who took the time to enjoy the beauty of a meaningful personal relationship. It is easy for any of us to drift into being a Martha because our flesh feels right at home living in the pressure cooker of a demanding emotional world. All you have to do is let your spiritual priorities go for a moment, and you will find that you have drifted far away from the peaceful shore. However, no one ever drifts into being a Mary. This is a thoughtful, conscientious life that has lived in both worlds and knows the difference. These individuals have developed the discipline to stay focused on what is really important to them by spending time alone with God, and in their calmness they have made the choice to listen to the Holy Spirit. They are constantly aware of how both heaven and earth beckon us to come and spend our energy, attention, and concentration, and have made the decision to follow the way the truth and the life. Every day we make crucially important decisions to either allow ourselves to become entangled with the cares of this life or to break free by choosing what is good and holy. We do have a certain amount of responsibility that we need to take care of, but we also must make time to sit at the feet of Jesus and bask in the wonders and majesty of God. Notice the last part of the verse: ***"Mary has chosen that good part, which will not be taken away."*** What does this mean? I'm glad you asked!

The world can bring much persecution against us and can make our lives very difficult, but no one can take away our love for Jesus! The relationship that we are building with God in this life will stand forever. Our external choices may be removed, but we will always have the internal choice to worship Him. True worship is work! It is more than just reading about it or thinking about it – it is doing it! And just like prayer, it is not as easy as it seems, as many times it is a full battle gear war against our flesh where we need to get serious and use self-discipline against our flesh while also trying to rebuke the devil in Jesus' Name. Those who are involved with worship spend time through the week listening to songs, praying, and trying to feel a spiritual connection with God about the songs, practicing at home, typing, chording, transposing etc. . . . Then we make an extra effort to practice during the week and also come to church early to practice before each service. This *busy work* can push our buttons and irritate our emotions if we allow it. Do we always feel like doing all this? Of course not, but we push through it and realize that in the sacrifice of praise there is the blessing of being obedient and enjoying His presence.

Let us remove our thoughts away from the *microscope* of self and look through the *telescope* of the world and see that it is not only the worship team that battles the flesh and the devil, but all members of the congregation are also fighting in their own individual skirmishes as they try to stay focused on the prize of the high calling in Christ Jesus.

    An interesting story was told by a minister, and I would like to share it with you. As an evangelist, he had stayed in the homes of Christians from time to time throughout his forty years of ministry. He said that on one occasion, he was a guest in the home of a woman who had seven children, and though she had a large home to care for and attended to her husband's family business in her spare time, he never saw her aggravated or frustrated. There was always the fragrance of Christ about her life, and he marveled at it. While staying in their home during a conference, one morning around five o'clock he noticed light filtering in past the door; so he opened it very quietly and saw this woman kneeling by her piano. He quietly closed the door. The next morning the same thing and every morning after that. So he finally asked her. *"What time do you rise to seek the Lord?"* She replied, Oh that is not my decision. I made a choice long ago that when He wanted to have fellowship with me I was available. There are times when He calls me at five; there are times when He calls me at six. And on occasion, He will call about two o'clock, I think, just to test me. Always she would get up, go to her piano stool, and worship her Lord. He asked, *"How long do you stay?"* Oh that is up to Him. When He tells me to go back to bed, I go back. If He doesn't want me to sleep, I simply stay up. Do you not sense the heartfelt devotion as she made a deliberate decision to go beyond the worries and cares, beyond the inconvenience, the schedules and demands of the daily routine, all the while developing an awareness of His presence. Have we not been called to do the same thing? Throughout our lives we must learn that being busy does not necessarily mean we do not have time for God, because there are individuals who have nothing to do and yet still do not attempt to spend time with Him. In fact many times it is the busy ones that realize how much they need Him to accomplish all they have to do. We are the ones that decide in our free-will how we appropriate our time. No matter how demanding your *natural* life becomes, your *spiritual* life can still flourish if Christ is the most important person in your life.

Chapter 19
HOLY GROUND

We notice that one of the most well-known passages about holy ground is found in *Exodus 3:5*: ***"And He** [God] **said, draw not nigh hither: put off thy shoes from off thy feet, for the place whereon thou standest is holy ground."*** *What is the Lord saying?* Holiness is the highest attribute of God, and He does NOT overlook sin. In fact, every practicing sin that is not under the blood of Jesus must be dealt with. Holiness is NOT of man. Living in God's holiness is the foundation of His general and specific will for us and is the result of the combination of God's sovereignty and man's responsibility. In the above passage, we must be careful to realize that the ground is not holy, but rather holiness is being in the presence of an Almighty God. This is not just something the Lord was trying to teach the people in the Old Testament, but is an illustration of how ALL beings must approach Him. It was a warning that our heart is being analyzed and that sin is very offensive to Him and also how easy we can disrespect Him with our attitude. Do we ever think about this when we come into the church setting? Christians, especially in our modern culture have become too relaxed and have neglected to become aware of the reverential fear of His holiness. May we rekindle the desire to be awakened and realize who we are worshipping. The point of this book is to ask the question why the same seriousness and level of sensitivity we experience when we take holy communion cannot become the state of mind we live in every moment.

When He designed for us to walk with Him, He knew how difficult it would be for us. Since He is holy and we are not, He knew that He would need to INFUSE His holiness within us in order for us to have an intimate relationship with Him. He has always wanted for us to realize that He is listening to our thoughts and observing our deeds every moment, but the process of grasping this revelation takes a while and much longer for some than others. When He uses the term *abide* with Him, He means to live and dwell in His Spirit, and this is exactly what He is waiting for His people to embrace. Without a vision of His divine identity, our subconscious produces a lower, earthly way of thinking that sees Him as just another king trying to rule us. It is true that we can relate to the earthly Jesus; however let us not forget the reality that He was always God the majestic creator of the universe. When men and their new styles and ideas of seeker-sensitive church try to present Jesus as just a man with a ministry, it is much easier to manage and deal with Him, and we become more comfortable with His teachings. The liberal crowd tries to portray Him as a regular guy with regular problems in order to make Him more approachable. The truth is that no one can approach Him unless miraculously drawn by His super-natural power of grace, and no one with a right mind would be rude or for heaven's sake challenge His authority! The idea of humans evaluating and speculating about Him is an insult and is advertising His holiness like an option on a new car or a brand name of clothing. This is a lack of knowledge and a carnal attitude that has mitigated the understanding of absolute truth to the church and the world. The lack of respect for God is one of the most dangerous seeds that has ever been planted, and it is very noticeable how secular humanism has helped people grow into a distorted concept of who God really is. When His perfect supremacy and absolute truth becomes disregarded, it does not take long for His identity to become misinterpreted and mingled with false interpretations, which opens the floodgates to heresy. Lukewarm Christians are not needed to add to the confusion - the blind are already deceived.

    God is so holy and mysterious; He can be fathomed only through tiny glimpses in the spiritual realm. We must leave Him high and lifted up above all things because that is who He is and where He is! We sing that we long to touch Him, but as we try to take Him into our imaginations, we discover He is too much for us to fully comprehend. Why do the angels in *Isaiah chapter 6* cover their eyes and feet and why do the twenty-four elders in *Revelation chapter 4* fall down before Him and cast their crowns? Because His glory and Majesty are so overwhelming and spectacular, we are reduced to a state of being dumbfounded as we lie on our faces before Him. He holds billions of galaxies in His hand, and each galaxy contains billions of stars; He knows every thought in every mind, every tear that has ever fallen, and is keenly aware when a sparrow falls to the ground - all at the same time! Praise Him forever! He is so magnificent and omnipotent that darkness tries to run and hide as the brilliance of His glory illuminates as far as the East is from the West. Infinity, eternity, and perfection are His attributes. As He passes by, our eyes ache from the reflection of His eminence, and through the cleft of the rock we become breathless with His splendor. Those who have seen and been in the presence of His angels fall on their faces as dead men because it is too overwhelming to the mortal senses. So how could we as mere mortals possibly fathom that we could stand before the Almighty God and survive? We talk about His presence all the time but never realize that He has lowered the intensity level of His glory down to a tolerable *voltage* just so that we humans can sense a portion of His power without being evaporated. When will we realize there is no difference when we step on stage and experience the holy power of God's presence than when Moses was told to remove his shoes? When will we desire to proceed through the outer courts of praise into the paralyzing glory of His presence like the Tabernacle priest that carried the blood into the Holy of Holies? He is the same yesterday, today, and forever, and His demand for holiness has not changed. **"Follow peace with all men, and holiness, without which no man shall see the Lord"** *(Hebrews 12:14).*

I believe the reason why many do not respect Him is because they do NOT believe Him! The church is filled with doubters and those who seldom exercise faith, which explains why many do not sense the danger of disrespecting Him. If we do not live in His Spirit all through the week and respect His presence in our everyday lives, our holiness meter will reveal our carnal lukewarmness when we go to the assembly. We try to figure out why our church services are dry and powerless, but it can be easily traced to the lack of our spiritual awareness. Is it going to take God telling us to take off our shoes in order for us to obtain the revelation of His holiness? When we are having corporate service, we should have the mind set to act like we would if we were in heaven standing before His throne, but instead we behave as if we are in the hardware store buying a package of nails. When we disrespect Him, it reveals our lack of maturity and wisdom to know the realities of His person, and when we do not take Him seriously, as we mentioned earlier, it is similar to taking the communion without self-examination. It is a very serious and dangerous act of mockery to stand before God without a humble and repentant state of mind and spirit. We must have confidence in believing He is who He says He is, because without this revelation of His holiness, we could very easily begin to lower the standards of our own morality if we have not already. Our concept of God affects how we act, and this in turn can have an influence on others, either good or bad. People are watching how we respect God and are building their views from what they observe in us, which divulges that we are not taking God seriously and concluding it means nothing to us. It is important to remember that no one can live perfectly, but this does not imply we are to become inattentive. We will never be able to truly worship Him unless we know that we can depend on Him completely, and maybe this is why many are not involved. The Christian life is a progressive order; when we believe He is perfect, we can worship Him in truth. To personally know Christ is to love Him, and those who love Him will worship Him in the beauty of holiness. In the realm of worship there must be a sense of awe and reverential fear accompanying our divine wisdom. As our relationship grows stronger, we learn to trust Him as the perfect authority of all things and know that He is worthy of all adoration. Crystal cathedrals, stained glass windows, silk robes, or lofty speeches have nothing to do with holiness! Only when a humble heart has been in His presence will it begin to understand the path of purity. ***"But as He which hath called you is holy, so be ye holy in all manner of conversation; because it is written, be ye holy; for I am holy" (I Peter 1:15-16).***

Chapter 20

THE BRIDAL PROCESSION

It would be incomplete to present a collection of thoughts about worship without including the precious revelations of truth from the Tabernacle of Moses. The beautiful symbolisms of salvation and the types and shadows pertaining to the Christian journey are life changing to say the least. When we research and discover the intricate details of God's plan for mankind and the depths of His divine love, we become overwhelmed with His determination to save us. He is so perfect and holy that we need to keep these treasures of wisdom close to our hearts to remind us of our spiritual requirements and His perfect order when it comes to recognizing His holiness. When we realize that true salvation is woven within the covenant of Jesus' blood and our commitment to follow Him, it becomes clear that lukewarm religion will not be accepted in the beloved. The question that each of us must ask our own hearts is just how far do I choose to go into this procession? At which stage or level will I dare not venture any further? Am I prepared to let go of my life and take hold of His? Am I prepared to not stop until I am at His mercy seat?

Through the years I have come to realize that God has a certain way of doing things, and that most of His principles are set in stone or can be referred to as absolute truth that cannot be compromised or substituted. This divine order is seen in everything from the glimpses of heaven, the universe, His structure of authority, His blueprints for salvation, and the earth's creation just to name a few. In all things He has a certain way of doing things because His ways are perfect. He has never failed and does not need any back-up plan; neither will He ever go back on

His Word. He has given the world mercy, grace, and forgiveness, but there are also certain guidelines that even He cannot betray, or it would be a failure within His nature and character. For example, in order to be born-again a person must come to God under the conviction of the Holy Spirit, and that takes place by hearing the gospel. As individuals stand in the crossroads of decision, they must by their own free-will choose to accept Christ by faith as their Lord. They must trust with all of their hearts that His blood has forgiven their sins and transformed their spirits from death to life.

When these steps are followed, The Lord miraculously transforms their old spirits into a brand new creation, and they become born-again into the family of God. This is a process that was designed by God, and there are no short-cuts, alterations, tolerances, compromises, or modifications. It does not matter how many different religious creeds or ideas there are in the world that promise eternal life, if this divine blueprint is not followed through — the sacrifice of Jesus Christ on the cross of Calvary – there is no salvation. Of course we have always seen religious interpretations of how to get to heaven, with all kinds of different rules and regulations and promises that God will give people credit for their deeds – but the truth of the gospel stands unmovable! The result of dying and not being born-again is eternal death, and there are no other options. This is just one example of absolute truth that carries the reputation of His divine perfection and cannot be substituted with a generic replacement.

These absolutes can also be seen when it comes to worship, though I have no intention of becoming legalistic about how we approach the Lord. However, I believe His instructions were meant to be followed, and that it matters greatly to Him as we learn and obey His will. There are layers or levels of truth which is why God placed emphasis on the importance of our studies and seeking His truth as a progression of becoming wiser. Most people are satisfied with surface knowledge and have no desire to go deeper. One reason is because our natures recognize that more understanding includes more responsibility. So, in order to keep life simple and pleasurable, the masses follow their own custom-designed world view that includes homemade answers for life's most difficult spiritual questions. The concept of incorporating the Tabernacle of Moses into our worship falls under this category and includes the realization that we have grown from children into more advanced stages of maturity. Of course we must include the fact that the more we advance in our understanding, the more is also required of us. *"When I was a child, I spoke as a child, I understood as a child, I thought as a child: but when I became a man, I put away childish things"* (I Corinthians 13:11).

This is not to say we have arrived at a "holier than thou" spiritual plateau, but rather the more we learn, the more responsible we are to live what we know. A wise man realizes the more he knows the more clearly he can see how little he really does know. God understands where we are in our spiritual development and has longsuffering and patience with us, but I believe He desires that we eventually grow up from being in kindergarten to advancing and progressing into the higher levels of learning. The idea and ultimate purpose behind spiritual education is accepting the process of becoming stronger and more mature in His Spirit which are both vital change factors within our quest to fulfill God's specific will. Transformation is a crucial aspect of the prize we are pressing toward because the extent that we are changed is based on how attentive we are to His instructions! *"But we all, with open face beholding as in a glass the glory of the Lord, are CHANGED into the same image from GLORY to GLORY, even as by the Spirit of the Lord"* (II Corinthians 3:18).

Let us now begin the journey of not only our eternal salvation but also our daily salvation. *What do you mean?* If we meditate on this illustration of spiritual order, we will see two things happening at once. We will begin to understand the divine plan that leads to everlasting life and the path to His presence while we are in this corruptible body. This was given by God to allow us to see a glimpse into the reality of our redemption and to reveal how we are to live in the reverential fear of His holiness. Many have accepted only the invitation to have eternal life without considering the conditions of His blood covenant. It is challenging to ponder how we can be rewarded with eternal salvation when we have neglected His requirements to press toward the mark of the high calling in Christ Jesus which is the crucial aspect of His TOTAL salvation. We must perceive that His general will and His specific will are designed to work together in order for us to accomplish the destiny of His perfect will.

We notice that within this designated earthly habitation for God's presence are different colors of curtains and fabrics and different types of materials that symbolize how Christ is intertwined within the life of the believer. The pure gold represents His deity, and the silver symbolizes the redemption He has provided while bronze stands for judgment. While we are trying to visualize how the structure was enclosed, allow us to pause for a moment and see the colorful materials that were used and what they represent to our faith. There were 4 symbolical colors of linen used in the tabernacle along with a tremendous amount of detail in the rods that held the fabric so the tabernacle could be completely enclosed: BLUE - God came from heaven; PURPLE – the highest royalty in the universe, as Christ is the King of kings; RED - the blood sacrifice of the Messiah the Lamb of God; and WHITE – the perfect, sinless purity of Jesus the Lord of all. These are but a few of the many intricate details and illustrations that are intended to awaken and enlighten us to the intricate designs God has provided for our salvation. As we advance in His Spirit, we are curious about these realities as a vital part of our higher education and should be eager to learn what they mean to us personally. May we receive confidence and joy to know that when He was on the cross, we were on His mind, and may this concept create within us a deeper appreciation and admiration for what He has provided. These are examples of patterns, representations, and hidden mysteries that are waiting to be discovered and the reason why we study to show ourselves approved unto God. What is more interesting or satisfying than to spend time learning what great lengths He has gone to just to show how much He loves us. Why would we not want to know as much as we can about the love of our lives?

THE ENTRANCE

"Enter into His gates with thanksgiving and into His courts with praise" *(Psalm 100:4).*

As we begin our journey, let us recognize there is only ONE entrance which is a divine spiritual truth revealing that there are no back-doors, no other secret openings, no climbing over the top or tunneling from underneath for those who have their own ideas about how to reach eternal life. There is only one true God, and there is only one way to approach Him, obey Him, love Him, and worship Him. **"I am the door; by me if any man enter in, he shall be saved. . ."** *(John 10:9).* It is the way of His gospel that exposes how lost, blind, and hopeless we are, and through this humble realization we reach out by faith and accept His wonderful offer to exchange our filthy rags for His righteousness. *"I am the way, the truth, and the life: No man cometh unto the Father, but by Me" (John 14:6)*. The religious world is confused with so many variations of interpretations and philosophies, but this tabernacle clearly reveals there is only one divine order of truth pertaining to the Christian life. This is an Old Testament prophetic illustration that revealed the coming Savior of the world who was and is the reality of the full gospel truth of total salvation. *"There is one body, and one Spirit, even as you are called in one hope of your calling; one Lord, one faith, one baptism, one God and Father of all, who is above all, and through all, and in you all" (Ephesians 4:4-6)*.

The gate was 30 feet wide and was located directly in the center of the outer court on the East end and was covered by curtains made of finely woven linen. There are so many intricate details pertaining to the articles and furnishings, and it is fascinating to read about them in the Exodus and Leviticus. It is such a blessing to study and see the revelations of their spiritual significance. Everything that was implemented has a meaning and is a reflection of the eternal vision of God's covenant promises to man. The praises of thanksgiving signify that a soul has entered into the kingdom of God and is overwhelmed with joy in knowing that he has been redeemed. This entrance into the salvation of the Lord begins with accepting the blood sacrifice that is found just inside the gate, which is a violent and disturbing image but yet a beautiful illustration of how we must come into God through the blood of Christ. This cleansing from the forgiveness of our sins allows us to enter into His courts with a fresh new spiritual existence. This creates a depth of appreciation and a vivid awareness of what has been given so that we might be redeemed. The brazen altar is in the outer court and represents Christ being our sacrifice and us reaching out to Him by faith. It is wonderful that some have agreed to accept His offer of eternal life, but sadly many never proceed any further into the depths of His glory. The spectators refuse to comprehend that His total salvation blueprint includes our *continual* development that enables us to advance into knowing God's mind and becoming an image of Christ. For those who are satisfied to live in the outer court, I must say that I am perplexed and can only intercede for these individuals that they would not allow their carnal wills to prevent them from living in the bridal chamber.

From a praise and worship perspective, the gate and the outer court are where we celebrate all that He has done. Praise and thanksgiving are joyous and exciting expressions of how grateful we are for His mighty deeds and His power, love, and victorious demonstrations. This attitude of gratefulness is connected with our awareness of His presence. When we have Him on our minds, we are naturally always thankful for who He is and what He has done. When I lead worship, I usually begin with songs that are bold and upbeat with the content of how God is mighty to save and how much He wants us to have victory over the enemy. It is a time to let go of our problems and the worries that are trying to keep us distracted from the encouraging truth that He is in control! I am a believer in positive confessions and will many times start with proclaiming and declaring that we are overcomers, to remind us that God is for us. I speak God's Word that is filled with positive energy, and this generates faith into the hearts of the listeners so they can forget about their mountains for a while and shout praises to their Lord and King. This rise of faith and expectation changes the atmosphere and chases away the dark spirits that are trying to hinder and prevent the manifestation of God's presence. Again I am not trying to establish a legalistic agenda but only explaining my concept of the divine order concerning the progression to our ultimate objective which is the holy of holies. We can see many times that just singing a song or two and moving on with the program does not go any further than the outer court. True spiritual worship is a journey that involves many different stations and levels of participation and may we spend the time we need to make sure we arrive at our destination.

THE BRAZEN ALTAR

***"I am the good shepherd: The good shepherd gives His life for the sheep"** (John 10:11).*

As we enter the courtyard, we become awestruck with the Brazen Altar. This is where the priest would sacrifice animals as a covering for sin, which is a type and shadow of Christ as the Lamb of God being sacrificed as the only price that can forgive our sin. This symbol explains the great redemption and becomes a foundational pillar of our praise and personal expressions of love for Christ who has saved and forgiven us from eternal death. The brazen altar or bronze altar was situated right inside the outer court but the lost are not permitted entrance into the courtyard because they have not received His Spirit. This altar was lit by God's holy fire and is a gruesome bloody illustration that is not meant to be beautiful to the natural eye but rather a reminder of the depth of God's mercy, forgiveness, and love. The Hebrew root word for *altar* means to *slay* or *slaughter* while the Latin word *Alta* means *high* as this instrument of destruction was built on a raised mound of earth, and we are reminded that it is also a symbol of the hill of Golgotha where Jesus was crucified. His cross, which was lifted up, became the altar of blood sacrifice that satisfied the debt for our sins that nothing else could repay. The altar was an illustration to show the Israelites that the first act toward a holy God was to be cleansed by the blood of an innocent creature and the cross carries the same concept that humans cannot have a relationship with God unless they are made presentable through the perfect blood of Jesus, the Lamb that was slain.

It was made from the wood of the acacia tree and overlaid with bronze which is symbolic of judgment against sin. The altar measured 7.5 feet on all four sides and 4.5 feet deep with four horns projecting from the top. The horns represent power and strength, and as blood was smeared on the horns of the altar, it symbolized the power of the blood to atone for sins. Likewise, the power in the blood of Christ has become the *horn* of our redemption that not only covers but forgives and washes away our sins completely. We still sin on a regular basis, but now the price that Jesus paid has the authority to forgive and cleanse when we approach Him with brokenness and sorrow. ***"The Lord is my rock, and my fortress, and my deliverer; my God, my strength, in whom I will trust; my buckler, and the HORN of my salvation, and my high tower"*** *(Psalm 18:2)*. The concept behind the word *atonement* is to be made just, holy, and righteous; it is to provide satisfaction for God's requirements. It means to make amends for, to compensate and make restitution for. Jehovah's law demanded death as the penalty for sin, and through these sacrifices the atonement or payment was provided. The priest would slaughter the animal, sprinkle its blood in front of the veil of the holy place, burn the carcass, and pour the remaining blood on the altar. This was a portrayal of Jesus' blood that was sprinkled on the mercy seat of heaven and not only covered but erased our sins as the ransom for our souls. ***"God made Him who had no sin to be sin for us, so that in Him we might become the righteousness of God"*** *(II Corinthians 5:21)*.

As we lift up our sacrifices of praise, our songs are saturated with the theme of the gospel – and they should be! Why is it called a sacrifice of praise? Because our flesh hates to do it! Our carnal nature has no desire to be involved with anything spiritually positive. We must force our minds and wills to step aside, and with this bold determination we can release our feelings and communicate to God how we feel. Our spirits love to praise, worship, pray, and do all things that are related to obeying God and being in His presence. ***"By Him let us offer the sacrifice of praise to God CONTINUALLY, that is, the fruit of our lips giving thanks to His name" (Hebrews 13:15).*** The songs that proclaim about God's great love and the awesome price Jesus paid in order to set us free can be celebrated in fast songs at the beginning, in the slower meditation of intimate worship, or anywhere in between.

LAVER

"That He might sanctify and cleanse it with the washing of water by the Word" (Ephesians 5:26).

Next we find the Laver, which was a basin of polished brass that was filled with pure, clean water giving the effect of a mirror when we look down into it. Since we are born-again and have celebrated the sacrifice of Jesus and exalted the Lord with thanksgiving and praise, we are now going deeper into discovering what is being required for us to be His child and abide in His Spirit. This conviction and sensitivity is a reminder from the Holy Spirit of our need to live honestly and transparently as we conduct regular self-examinations within our hearts. This mirror also is a type of the Word of God which, if we look with our spiritual eyes, we continually see our need to change. The water in the laver is a type of God's Word that has the power to transform our thoughts and cleanse us from the inside out. This washing and cleansing is NOT an option like we would decide whether or not to take a shower. Being pure is a determined state of existence and a responsibility for us to maintain with constant prayer and fellowship. Water is a type of the Holy Spirit that instructs us and guides us into purity and holiness. Once again, Christ is symbolized in the water, for He is the Word *(John 1:1)* and the One with the Holy Spirit. *I Corinthians 10:4* reveals Jesus as the water that came forth from the rock that was smitten. Water and blood came out when Christ was pierced on the cross. As we live in an attitude of humility and brokenness from what Christ has done, we sincerely repent of our sin and allow our consciences to be cleansed and set free. We are also completely immersed in water as a picture of the burial and resurrection with Christ within the command and ordinance of baptism. To satisfy God's requirements of repentance at the brazen altar and cleansing at the laver we must decide if we are going any further into the tabernacle. God has established order into the miracle of salvation and has woven divine order into His holiness but does not force anyone to love Him. His blueprints are specific details of His will, but He leaves it up to our own free-will to continue or turn away. He will not accept a compromised offering, and we will not experience the joy and peace with Him if we allow un-repented sin to live in our hearts. Many souls are living in agony because they refuse to spend time at the laver, and since we can go no further into His presence without forgiveness, this clearly explains why many in the local assembly have very little enthusiasm when it comes to praise and worship. They have drawn the line and are bound by their own rebellion and experience the distance from God because of their impurity. We are at a crossroads to either stop here and live in the outer court and just be a *surface* Christian that only wants a certain amount or to let go of all we have in order to be all that He desires.

We are now leaving the outer court and going into the Holy Place. The outer court measures 300 cubits around, and 5 cubits high. This calculation represents 1500 years from Moses to Jesus, the law age.

TABLE OF SHEWBREAD

"And Jesus said to them, "I am the bread of life. He who comes to me shall never hunger, and he who believes in me shall never thirst" *(John 6:35).*

As we enter into the Holy Place, we notice the table of shewbread and slowly but confidently realize that we have made a serious commitment to continue moving forward in our fellowship with Jesus. We were like babies that desire the sincere milk of His truth but have grown stronger and are learning and growing more mature in our intimacy with Him. As we draw closer to Him, we notice that the songs we sing are taken more seriously and filled with personal meaning and expression. We are becoming more sensitive and beginning to think more deeply about what we are saying and are experiencing a stronger burden of love for others than we have had before. This table of bread symbolizes Jesus Christ as the bread of life - the Jehovah Jireh of everything we need and all that we are. We are to *digest* Christ and His Word as they become our very source of life as we allow His power to transform our minds and change our hearts until we become one with Him. As He is absorbed into our souls and saturated in our conscience, we receive His character into every fiber of our beings. As we embrace His Word, we put our trust into His blood covenant that promises the abundant life of spiritual benefits and blessings that come with being a royal priesthood and child of the King. In Holy Communion, Christ is symbolized as the satisfier of our hunger and in the partaking of His broken body we are reminded of Him becoming the ransom that could only be satisfied with His body and blood. In our reverence of His sovereignty our hopeless spiritual condition becomes revealed and we are awakened to our need to live broken before Him. As we remember His blood, we become filled with humility and gratitude for His grace and the great price He paid to rescue us. He was beaten and crushed as He became the only offering that could satisfy the payment for our redemption. The ingredients that are in the bread are all blended into one loaf which is Christ our all in all, the same as we are individually a part of the ONE body of Christ – the people of His heart.

THE GOLDEN LAMPSTAND

"Then Jesus spoke to them again saying, I am the light of the world. He who follows me shall not walk in darkness, but have the light of life" (John 8:12).

"In Him was life; and the life was the light of men. And the light shineth in darkness; and the darkness comprehended it not" (John 1:4-5).

We are still progressing into the beautiful life of servants of the most high. We are remnant disciples that are learning that worship and prayer are the foundations of living in the awareness of His presence. We are actually praying for others and notice that our hearts and attitudes are becoming more meek and humble. We are finally making the heart-wrenching decision to abandon our old plans and dreams as we grow stronger in our intimate relationship with Him. We are learning to pull away from the chaos and spend quiet time with Him in the inner chambers of our conscience. We have pulled away from the religious system and the meaningless programs of man's pride and control and are seeing Christ as the illumination of our lives and how important it is for us to allow His light to shine through us. This lampstand is actually called in the Jewish world a menorah. It was made from one solid piece of gold, beaten into the shape of 7 stems *(7 spirits of God yet unified as one)*. This lamp was filled with oil, which also represents the Holy Spirit. There were 3 different kinds of ornaments on the stems. There were 3 knobs *(the bread of life, the light of eternity, and the incense of everlasting joy)*, 3 flowers *(the way of salvation, the truth of His Word, and the life of sacrifice)*, and 3 almond bowls *(the Father, Son, and Holy Spirit)*. There were 3 sets of 3 ornaments on each of the 6 stems, and 4 sets of 3 ornaments on the middle shaft. This adds up to 54 ornaments on the stems and 12 on the shaft, totaling 66 ornaments, representing the 66 books of the Bible. *"Your Word is a lamp to my feet and a light to my path" (Psalm 119:105)*. This is a divine confirmation concerning the amount of scripture we have considered as the only true inspired written Words of God. We as the church are to be light-holders, having God Himself living inside of us. The story about the wise and foolish virgins is an example of how we must be filled with the oil of the Holy Spirit, lit with His power; then as He burns within us, the world can see the only light that can reveal who Christ is and our desperate need for Him. We are reminded in this story that we are to be prepared for His coming and be filled with His Holy Spirit in order to be received by Him. *"Afterward came also the other virgins, saying, Lord, Lord, open to us. But He answered and said, verily I say unto you, I know you not* [do not recognize you]*" (Matthew 25:11-12)*. We have made the conscious decision to focus our eyes on His face and not become entangled with the distractions of life. We are beginning to realize that the more of us there is to see, the less of Him there will be, thus we are determined to allow Him to shine within us - whatever it takes. *"Ye are the light of the world. A city that is set on a hill cannot be hid. Neither do men light a candle and put it under a bushel, but on a candlestick; and it giveth light unto all that are in the house. Let your light so shine before men, that they may see your good works, and glorify your Father which is in heaven" (Matthew 5:14-16)*.

THE GOLDEN ALTAR

"These things I have spoken to you, that in me you might have peace. In the world you will have tribulation: but be of good cheer; I have overcome the world" (John 16:33).

We are now taking a step where only the front-line warriors and remnant disciples have dared to follow. The spiritual life with God has many levels, and these are directly related to how far we are willing to go with Him, or in other words, how much of Him do we really want! Our understanding of worship is becoming more clear because we are not just singing songs anymore, we are literally telling Him how we feel. The religious masses have no problem with receiving from God and enjoying all that He has given and all that He will do. However, the crowds begin to thin out when we begin to explain that the Lord is seeking someone that is willing to become a *living* sacrifice. Our spirit wants to be a vessel of *honor* but our flesh does not desire to become a soft piece of clay in the hands of the potter. The golden altar represents holiness and sanctification and is a crucial step in the process of KNOWING God and learning how to sincerely live for Him. *Romans 12:1* says, **"I beseech you therefore, brethren, by the mercies of God, that you present your bodies a living sacrifice, holy, acceptable unto God, which is your reasonable service."** This is where we are faced with the decision to crucify our wills, get control of our minds, and dedicate ourselves completely to God. This might sound like a simple and reasonable act, but it is the most difficult thing we will ever do. It is surrendering our control to Jesus so that He can begin to control us. When we talk about yielding our wills, we are declaring that we are no longer the captain of our own ship but have turned over complete control to our new master. This means that living with God has advanced far beyond meeting with Him once or twice per week, but is developing a *lifestyle* of constant communication and obedience. It is within this awareness we are changed into His image! We are learning what it means to invite Jesus to sit on the throne of our hearts and be the LORD of our lives. We are learning that our lives are not our own, and we have been bought with a price, so our highest mission in life is to listen to His voice and obey Him. This is far beyond the normal way of living and will result in the world rejecting us and moving away from us. Do not be discouraged or sad because the way you have chosen is becoming more narrow - it is also filled with more joy. This realm of His Spirit is far beyond our natural understanding, and holding hands with the creator of heaven and earth is the more glorious than words can say.

We are now leaving the Holy Place and entering behind the veil, into the Holy of Holies. The Holy Place measured 20 cubits long X 10 cubits wide X 10 cubits high, which represents the 2000 year church age.

Chapter 21
SPIRITUAL INTIMACY

A thick curtain separated the Holy Place from the Holy of Holies. This curtain, known as the veil, was made of fine linen and blue, purple, and scarlet yarn. There were images of angels embroidered into it. The word "veil" in Hebrew means a divider or separator that hides, but what was being hidden? It was actually shielding the holiness of a perfect God from the nature of sinful man. The curse of the fall had closed the door to man and God having a close relationship like Adam and Eve had with Him. This was God's way of reaching out to man in love and trying to explain that soon a Messiah would come as a precious Lamb that would re-open the door of intimacy and become the bridge that could re-unite them once again. God's presence required such reverential fear that anyone who entered into this place, except the high priest, would die. Even though the curtain has now been removed, we are still reminded in our walk with God, that He is still the same person that demands honor and respect for who He is.

THE ARK OF THE COVENANT

> *"Let us be glad and rejoice, and give honor to Him: for the marriage of the Lamb is come, and His wife hath made herself ready" (Revelation 19:7).*

Now that we have enrolled into the advanced discipleship course and are allowing our lives to be turned inside out, we are ready to proceed to the Ark of the Covenant and become students to what God has *for* us and what He requires *from* us. This is the ultimate destination of our worship and is the highest honor, for there is no greater joy than for Him to be the Lord and King of our hearts. We are beginning to see that we can actually live in the earth but be citizens of heaven at the same time, but it will take many modifications to our minds. When we are "engaged" with Jesus, we long to be with Him as His future bride, and as the soon coming bridegroom He will bring an end to this world and usher in our eternal marriage together. Now is the time to be wise virgins and make sure that our lamps (our hearts) are filled with oil (His Spirit). Only those that have cast down their wills and allowed Christ to become their Master can enjoy the fullness of being saturated in His glory now and forever. Amen.

The furniture in this room has no light except the Shekinah glory of God himself. The ark was a box made of acacia wood *(strong, long lasting wood which symbolizes Christ as incorruptible)* overlaid with gold inside and out *(representing deity)*. It had 4 rings *(eternity – never ending kingdom)* made on the sides of the box *(representing 4 corners of the earth, perfect balance, and the 4 gospels)* where long poles could slide through, and the box could be carried without directly touching. The presence of God was so holy that if humans touched it they would be instantly killed. The ark is a type of Christ, which represents deliverance, protection, and preservation just as Noah's ark was a type of savior, grace, ransom, and deliverance. When Christ died on the cross, the veil in the temple was supernaturally torn completely apart symbolizing that a new reconciliation had been established between the divine and mortal – Jesus Christ the Son of God—and that now nothing was separating man from God. The mediator and high priest of all eternity came to bring restoration for the severed relationship that man had lost and provided the opportunity for the world to accept Jesus. This invitation for salvation was also offered to every saint that died in faith and was abiding in paradise since the beginning of the world.

As we are now clothed in His righteousness, we have been made worthy through the blood of Jesus to approach Him face to face, be joined with Him in the new covenant, worship Him in the Spirit, live in His presence, and be with Him in heaven forever. The Ark was the habitation of God on the earth, and now we are the habitation of God on this earth. Praise His Name! Now we are the temples of the Holy Ghost, not made with hands, and sin no longer is the veil that separates and prevents us from being with Him. The Father made a way to redeem us with the blood of his only Son because He loved us and missed us more than anything. Three articles are found in the ark. First, the rod of Aaron, which budded, representing the 100 fold return, the fullness of power, judgment, fruit of the spirit, authority, and the resurrection. This rod was made of wood, which was once alive, then when cut became dead, then supernaturally came to life again, representing Christ coming to earth, dying, and resurrecting. Second, the golden pot of manna symbolizing the never-ending provision of Jesus as the bread of life and the giver and sustainer of life. And third, the Ten Commandments or the law of Moses which is a type of the eternal, literal Word of God, which contains all of His promises, prophecies, and judgments. All of these truths are given to us to help explain who He is and who we are IN HIM. When we worship Him in Spirit and Truth, we are singing and expressing our love for Him and acknowledging all of His attributes and character traits. It is as an encouragement to our spirits when we confess what He has done for us, and this becomes the word of our testimony when we declare all that He is IN US! *"To whom God would make known what is the riches of His glory of this mystery among the Gentiles; which is Christ in you, the hope of glory"* *(Colossians 1:27).*

THE MERCY SEAT

"And while they went to buy, the bridegroom came; and they that were ready went in with Him to the marriage; and the door was shut" *(Matthew 25:10).*

Have you ever thought about being married to God? How would you respond to Him? Would you be faithful? Many have never realized the holy vow of receiving Christ as their Lord, but in all reality that is exactly what salvation is. Do you realize you have been pronounced husband and wife? When we speak of spiritual intimacy, we are relating to the passage in *Ephesians chapter 5* that reveals the symbolism of a man and wife representing the relationship between God and His people: *"This is a great mystery: but I speak concerning Christ and the church"* *(v.32).* In this light, our closeness to Him in this realm may only scratch the surface to the eternal bliss of literally loving Him and being with Him forever. Are we really infatuated with Him as we should be? Are we that much in love with Him that we want to constantly spend time with Him in the secret chambers of our consciences and continually tell Him how much we love and adore Him? There is a world of difference between the outer courts of religious activity and the spiritual affection we enjoy when we are with Him. You see, unless He is the Lord of all – He is not Lord at all.

The mercy seat is the lid of the ark and is overshadowed by the wings of two golden cherubim, one on each side. The high priest would once a year sprinkle the sacrificial blood of animals on this mercy seat to be accepted by God for the covering of the sins of the people. This was a shadow to how the Father one day would sprinkle the blood of His Son Jesus to completely forgive the sins of whosoever would believe on Him. These sins in the tabernacle before Jesus were temporarily covered, but when Jesus shed His blood, our sins were permanently washed away and forgotten. His blood has now set us free from the law of sin and death. We are sons and daughters of God because the born-again experience is a blood experience; it is a family bond, which intertwines us with God as heirs to all of His promises. This is our resurrection from being eternally dead to becoming raised to life eternal. We actually become His children by being born from Him - to Him and are not just servants but a chosen generation and a holy nation as members of His royal family. When Moses would go in, he could audibly hear the voice of God speak *(Numbers 7:89)*. God loves us more than anything in the universe, and we shall be with Him forever. With the pure, sinless blood of Jesus being accepted by the Father, we can be assured that He accepts us and that our sins are completely forgiven. Oh the wondrous cross! Praise Him forever! It is the miraculous symbol of death and life. ***"Verily, verily, I say unto you, except a corn of wheat fall into the ground and die, it abideth alone: but if it DIE, it bringeth forth much fruit"*** *(John 12:24).* We have the confidence in knowing that every promise that was ever made by God is true and will never fail and have been guaranteed access to enter into His throne boldly as fully entitled blood covenant partners. His last will and testament is written; His blood is His signature, and His resurrection is His seal. All glory to His name forever!

THE HOLY OF HOLIES

"For on that day shall the priest make atonement for you, to cleanse you, that ye may be clean from all your sins before the Lord." "And he shall make an

atonement for the holy sanctuary, and he shall make an atonement for the tabernacle of the congregation, and for the altar, and he shall make an atonement for the priests, and for all the people of the congregation. And this shall be an everlasting statute unto you, to make atonement for the children of Israel for all their sins once a year. And he did as the Lord commanded Moses" (Leviticus 16:30, 33-34).

Let everything that hath breath praise the Lord! We are now in His presence and bow down to His Majesty! We are worshipping Him in Spirit and in truth. *"Having, therefore, brethren, boldness to enter into the holiest by the blood of Jesus, by a new and living way, which He hath consecrated for us, through the VEIL, that is to say, His flesh"* (Hebrews 10:19-20). This is what spiritual restoration is all about. This is the big picture of Christ and the outline of His salvation! When Adam and Eve sinned and were cast out of the garden, they lost the priceless treasure of the universe: God's presence. The chasm that was separating our personal relationship was a distance that no man could cross until the Father sent His only Son to become the reconciliation between Himself and His creation. Salvation is His gift of compassion on a fallen world, and His grace is our opportunity to accept Jesus Christ by faith. This in turn transforms us from a state of hopelessness into a righteous position where God's presence can inhabit. In the tabernacle the priest would enter under the most pure conditions and offer the blood of animals for the temporary forgiveness or *covering* of the sins of the people. This type and shadow was a symbol of Christ becoming our high priest whose blood was sprinkled on the mercy seat in heaven for the permanent forgiveness for the sins of those who would believe in faith. *"For Christ is not entered into the holy places made with hands, which are the FIGURES OF THE TRUE; but into heaven itself now to appear in the presence of God for us"* (Hebrews 9:24). This is not a place where the lost can rejoice because they are still blind and undone. Those who are NOT saved by His blood do not understand His Word or the concept of worship because they are still held captive within the default system and their lost spiritual condition. Our spirits must be transformed for God to live inside of our hearts so that we can experience His presence now and in the next life. These divine silhouettes are similar to the parables that Jesus told for the purpose of unveiling deep spiritual truths so we might comprehend how much love and sacrifice He gave so that we could be together. *"And this is eternal life, that they might know you the only true God, and Jesus Christ whom you have sent" (John 17:3)*. We pray for understanding so that Yahweh might be unveiled to our minds and hearts. To know Him is our destination and the purpose of our journey; to love Him is the meaning of life, and His presence is our greatest reward. We are not just pressing toward Him in our worship; we are dwelling with Him in the secret chambers of His holy of holies every moment! Living in the awareness of His presence has now become a lifestyle of worship.

There is no greater gift or miracle in the infinity of time than what was done on the cross. We cannot work to earn this gift because it is a price we could never pay. The cost of our ransom was paid in full to deliver the elect from eternal separation from Him. His children of light will forever sing worthy is the Lamb that was slain to receive all glory, power, and honor.

This dispensation is coming to a close and the final chapters, including judgment, are drawing near. The Holy of Holies measures 10x10x10 cubits, adding up to 1000, which represents the 1000 year millennial reign of Christ upon the earth. This 1000 year period will be a time when God will rule the earth as a Monarch with complete authority and His people will be working and enjoying this wonderful "prelude" to the future when heaven's gates will be opened. This event will not happen until after the tribulation, the rapture, the anti-Christ, and Armageddon. Be encouraged and filled with anticipation to worship Him in the glorious freedom of joy today, and begin to celebrate the inexplicable wonders of His glories!

> *"Heavenly Father, You are so perfect and so infinite. We cannot fathom what You have done for us or what You are planning for our future. We are so grateful for all of these details and hidden truths of Your last will and testament that confirm how much You love us. Lord, help us not to have fear or anxiety about surrendering our wills. Give us peace and confidence to know this is the only way to Your throne. Help us to have a greater understanding of what You expect from us. Help us to see that with more revelation, the more You are requiring*

from us. Enlarge our vision of You. If this does not cause us to walk holy before You – what will? We fall down before You in awe of who You are. Please continue to have mercy and patience with us. Many do not mind entering into Your gates and the outer courts but have made the decision not to go any further. Help them, encourage them, and pour out Your hope and peace to them. Help us, strengthen us to become bold and determined to LIVE at Your mercy seat and to have the burden to help others find their way to where You are. In Jesus Holy Name I pray. Amen."

PART IV
THE AWARENESS OF HIS MAJESTY

Chapter 22
THE ANOINTING

I have heard and read about the anointing of the Holy Spirit most of my life, but it is difficult to understand the mysteries related to His work. The Holy Spirit is the third person of the trinity and is just as much God as Jesus and the Father because the three are united as ONE which is another mystery all in itself. The Spirit world is difficult to understand because it is a realm that is on a much higher level than our natural senses and reason to press deeper into our petitions for discernment, perception, and extra measures of faith. Nonetheless, is the specific job of the Holy Spirit to anoint and empower individuals for God's purposes? or is the anointing simply being filled with God's presence? or a combination of both? It is much like the questions about whether the singer or the song is stirring our heart, and is it the ability of the speaker or the content of the message? Whatever the case, I am sure we can agree that communications become alive when channeled through the spirit and emotions of the heart whether on the giving or receiving end. The word *Messiah* means THE anointed one along with *Chosen One*, and of course we realize that Christ was and is THE Word and is equipped, and empowered, as the fullness of Godhead bodily to establish His Kingdom. ***"How God anointed Jesus of Nazareth with the Holy Ghost and with power: who went about doing good, and healing all who were oppressed of the devil: for God was with Him"*** *(Acts 10:38)*. As Jesus was returning back to heaven, He sent the Holy Spirit also known as the comforter to become personally involved with everything we do. He is not a vague, ethereal shadow, nor an impersonal force, He is a real person to help and strengthen us in our everyday labors as we are directed by God's voice. We do not hear it being taught, but since the Holy Spirit is God, it is perfectly fine to worship Him and pray to Him. Amen. However the anointing process operates, we can know that we are *chosen* in Christ before the foundation of the world and are now *anointed* to fulfill God's general and specific will. ***"Now He which establishes us with you in Christ, and hath anointed us, is God; who hath also sealed us, and given the earnest of the Spirit in our hearts"*** *(II Corinthians 1:21-22).*

"So how does this relate to me and what does all this have to do with worship?" When followers of Jesus desire to do God's will in any form of ministry, they must allow Christ to be Lord and be anointed with miraculous power and wisdom from the Holy Spirit, or their effectiveness will be limited to the strength and abilities of the flesh. ***"The Spirit of the Lord God is upon me; because the Lord hath anointed me to preach good tidings unto the meek; he hath sent me to bind up the brokenhearted, to proclaim liberty to the captives, and the opening of the prison to them that are bound"*** *(Isaiah 61:1).*

Every child of God has special gifts and callings and is anointed in these areas. It is a shame to think that some people have not sensed or recognized what they have been called to do as a part of the body of Christ. May the Lord continue to reveal to all of us the precise details of our destiny as we become enlightened and encouraged to accomplish our mission. We can do an extensive research of the definition of anointing and follow each scripture reference in our Strong's concordance, but that still might not explain how the Holy Spirit works. There are references to the Greek word *CHRISMA* that relate to the act of smearing and rubbing an oil or fragrance all over someone which helps us to visualize that if we are truly saturated with God's anointing, there is no way we could not smell like heaven to everyone we meet. Mmmmm. . . This is the level of Holy Spirit enablement that can turn an uneducated fisherman into a skilled orator who can be used to pierce the hearts of a multitude and leave their mouths gaping in astonishment. We find references to sacred anointing oil made of olive oil, myrrh, cinnamon, cane, cassia and various spices which were used in the Old Testament to anoint certain individuals and within the tabernacle which included the ceremony of consecration for the priests as they were being set apart for spiritual service *(Lev. 8:10-30; Lev. 21:10-12; Num.4:16).* The anointing also refers to the official dedications of kings *(I Sam.10:1).* We notice the Spirit of God blessing Saul with authority after he was anointed as king over Israel and then empowering David when he was anointed as king *(I Samuel 16:13)*. So how does the anointing of the Holy Spirit work? First, we must recognize that it is not the power of the oil itself but rather the oil becomes a symbol that is used as a point of contact when the Lord is directing and blessing with His power and authority. We are the vessels and His presence becomes the contents! Or we can think of is as His Spirit becoming the garment that surrounds us as it radiates His character. It is a way that God can help guide and manage us into His perfect will without forcing us.

When we read about oil that is applied in any type of spiritual dedication or prayer, we see is as a substance at the point of contact for divine commission that, even though it has spiritual connotations, is similar to the gel that is smeared on the paddles of a defibrillator to help re-start the heart. It is a conductive material that is *between* the receiver and the power that is being delivered but is not the power itself. We can see that oil was used in the New Testament when Jesus sent out the twelve disciples and gave them authority over evil spirits, and they anointed the sick, and they were healed. **"And they cast out MANY devils, and anointed with OIL many that were sick, and healed them"** *(Mark 6:13)*. The anointing is heavenly power that enables earthly people to do God's spiritual work on the earth! *Unction* is another term used for anointing and refers to being rubbed down, covered, and insulated, all of which renders the individual holy, protecting and separating us to God. There are several different verbs in the Greek that describe the word *anointing*. One is *ALEIPHO* which is a general term used to describe an application of refreshing oil to the head and feet after washing, or to apply ointment to the sick, or to apply spices to the dead. The Greek noun *CHRIO* is confined to sacred holy oil that is used with a symbolical meaning of spiritual application as a synonym of the person of the Holy Spirit. This gift of the Holy Spirit is the all-efficient means of enabling believers to possess the truth of God's wisdom through illumination, revelation, and demonstration. Today it is very common to anoint those who are called into God's service with oil as they are commissioned and ordained with the laying on of hands by the elders. We anoint babies as a dedication to the Lord and also use oil when we praying for demonic deliverance, and protection against evil spirits.

One of the most common uses of anointing oil is for healing, **"Is any sick among you? Let him call for the elders of the church;**

and let them pray over him, anointing him with oil in the name of the Lord: and the prayer of faith shall save the sick, and the Lord shall raise him up; and if he have committed any sins, they shall be forgiven him" (James 5:14-15). We can see that God's Word has many examples of saints that were involved with the practice of being anointed or anointing others for service, such as Daniel, Elijah, Elisha, Joshua, Moses, Aaron, Isaiah, Samson, Abraham, Isaac, Ezekiel, Jeremiah, Peter, Stephen, Paul, John and all the way through the Bible! These were all average people who became divinely empowered to accomplish God's visions such as Martin Luther, John Calvin, and all the martyrs who were given the anointing to die in faith, such as Hugh Latimer, Nicholas Ridley, John Bradford, John Wesley, George Whitefield, Jonathan Edwards, the list goes on and on. And of course the great preachers like Spurgeon, Tozer, Finney, Moody, Graham, and the list goes on. God is waiting to anoint all who will take up their cross and sacrifice their lives to do His will!

As you already know, trying to work for God's Kingdom has times of triumph and joy along with many disappointments and frustrations. In our ministry journey we learn through trial and error that there is an obvious difference between the glorious *unction* of the Holy Spirit and the noble (yet dry) efforts of the flesh. We can tell when the anointing is on us, and we can also sense when He is moving through others, but since we are filled with the Spirit, why is He not surging through us and allowing us to glow red-hot with His power all the time? Maybe we are not always in a *position* to be endued with power from on high. *What do you mean?* Since God has His finger on our spiritual pulse, it makes sense that He releases as much spiritual current as He can according to our awareness and the condition of our hearts. He has the sovereign decision to empower us in His way and His time but is conditional according to our dedication. Since much of our effectiveness depends on us getting into the position to be empowered, then we can blame it on our disobedience. If God still chooses to use us, then it is purely unmerited favor and a blessing of His marvelous grace. For the sake of theological consideration, let us agree that it is our responsibility to stay filled with God so that we can be ready to be used in season and out. Concerning preaching, teaching, music, witnessing, or whatever the task, the anointing definitely makes the difference between just plain words and a spiritual energy that penetrates the soul and blesses the heart. I have been in services where the anointing was so strong that people flooded the altars after a simple sermon because God's Word is not from this dimension as it contains the power of conviction to penetrate the soul. *"Now when they saw the boldness of Peter and John, and perceived that they were unlearned and ignorant men, they marveled; and they took knowledge, that they had been with Jesus."* (Acts 4:13)

We notice an example of David's musical anointing in *I Samuel chapter 16 and verse 23: "And it came to pass, when the evil spirit from God was upon Saul, that David took a harp, and played with his hand: so Saul was refreshed and was well, and the evil spirit departed from him."* The anointing changed the atmosphere, drove away the oppression of evil, brought deliverance, and ministered healing to the vexation of the mind. When the anointing comes, it is not just a talented performance connected to an emotional feeling but rather God's ability being demonstrated through a chosen vessel. We are given heavenly blessings from God's throne of love and mercy, such as Jesus' blood providing our salvation and the eternal security of His promises. Along with these foundations of our faith we must include the anointing of the Holy Spirit because it is the fuel that runs the engine of our spiritual lives, and without Him we are nothing more than a *vehicle* broken down on the side of the road. Our anointing is like the key ingredient of a fabulous recipe which stimulates the world's appetite for Jesus, but without Him even the dogs will turn their noses up at what we attempt to serve. The anointing is being used in our change process and is the only power that can draw others to repentance. All Christians have the anointing of God in them, but there is a *general* anointing and a *specific* anointing. For example, every Christian has a general anointing to evangelize and pray, while specific anointing's are for gifts like singing, teaching, or administration, mechanical talents, and so on. For those who are trying to find their specific anointing or desiring a stronger anointing, we can agree that fasting and praying enhances spiritual clarity. Spending more time with Jesus will replace our thoughts of this natural realm with revelations of the heavenlies. Fasting and praying can create a stronger sensitivity to God's voice in making decisions, increase boldness to proclaim His truth, give us more compassion for souls and a greater understanding of His Word, and the determination to lay down our wills and become transformed into the image of Christ. The anointing transforms our ministries from being emotionally driven to Spirit empowered!

Many do not realize that God's anointing is allowing them to excel at what they do, and in this light we can say they are taking this enablement for granted. It is true that we invest long hours in the things we love, but leading worship is not exactly like this. When we attempt to do things for God, it is usually the opposite of this world's way of thinking because we are not producing it on our own (which explains why at times it is so frustrating). Yes, we can practice and prepare our music and our teachings, but this in itself is NOT what is making it more spiritual. It is all about God *touching* what we are doing! I believe in working hard, and practicing with the instruments and vocals, and making sure the service is a certain way, but that is only sharpening the tools so that God can use them to do HIS labor. I realize that higher quality music is more pleasant to the senses, but professionalism does not guarantee a higher level of anointing because our hearts must be in tune as well as our instruments. It is difficult to find the line of balance between raising the bar of the music while not becoming an obsessed tyrant and ignoring the sensitivity of the Holy Spirit. Sure, people might enjoy the worship, but many just listen to it as a performance and leave without realizing what was said. I am convinced that being a part of a worship team seems to be one of the least appreciated labors in the Kingdom, but do not be discouraged, because you are learning the realities of a true servant. Look around and notice the lack of appreciation for Jesus. Did I mention the worship team needs lots of prayer? By the way, who is going to pray? True worship leaders have pastors' hearts because they care about each person and take a personal interest in their lives and spiritual development. I have learned over the years how crucial it is to pray for each member of the team each week. This is not boot camp; this is real war, and we who lead the army into battle are actually on the front line, and the ammo is live! EVERY facet of the church needs all the prayer covering the people can give.

I want the music to be as good as it can be. I listen to different bands each week, and I focus on certain worship songs and enjoy the way they encourage my spirit. I can sense God's presence in a song, and I try to hear God speaking His message of the hour just like I would absorb a sermon into my spirit. As someone that is responsible to select the songs we will sing, each week I feel like a pharmacist that fills the prescription from the Doctor. The worship pastor becomes a messenger just like the lead pastor, as they communicate what God wants to say (and many times these will complement each other). Worship and preaching are not always to be presented as warm and fuzzy feelings because soldiers need to be stimulated and provoked when we meet corporately so they can learn how to soberly view the Christian life. Yes, worship music is focused on our love and appreciation for God, but it also contains a spectrum of topics pertaining to our daily experiences that can be used as weapons of positive confession. There are times we need to be stirred and made aware to tear down the gates of hell, and there are times we need to learn how to love, stand in faith, and forgive. Whatever the mission, we cannot afford to be lulled to sleep with soft, powerless, chocolate candy sermons and sleepy pillow songs. True praise and worship will include sensitivity, energy, and enthusiasm that will bring encouragement as the storms of life are raging, to dance and shout the victory, to be filled with confidence and hope.

God desires to rise up big in our hearts and minister His words in the right places at the right times. Leading worship requires humility as we become reduced so that Jesus can be lifted high and His tangible presence can be manifested and encountered among His people. Many have never felt His presence and believe this is just a part of the religious jargon of popular catch words and phrases, but God's presence is a literal, tangible reality that can be and should be felt and enjoyed. It is exciting that in heaven we will be submerged in the depths of His being. Here is a definition of *tangible* from the American Edition of The Oxford Dictionary: *"Perceptible by touch; definite; clearly intelligible, material or substantial, real or actual, rather than imaginary or visionary, solid, manifest, actual, evident, discernible, definite; not vague or elusive; without doubt."* The presence of the Lord is not symbolic but is real because God is real! Just because we cannot see Him does not mean He is not there. He has promised to be in our midst whether we are alone or in the assembly, because He is an active and willing Father that listens to our prayers and intervenes in our lives. He is with us, in us, and all around us. ***"Fear thou not; for I AM WITH THEE: be not dismayed; for I am thy God: I will strengthen thee; yea, I will help thee; yea, I will uphold thee with the right hand of My righteousness"*** *(Isaiah 41:10).*

We are not cranking up the volume so that our talents can be admired but so the gospel and glory of God can be noticed as a lighthouse of hope from the darkness and fear of a lost world. We shout unto the Lord with our praise and thanksgiving for what He has done as a testimony of His power as we boldly proclaim His works and His love to all who have an ear to hear. Our vision is to minister to people's needs – not to build organizations! Total salvation is the message of deliverance and hope, and Jesus is worthy to be praised for the generosity of His mercy and grace, but when we operate in the flesh while trying to accomplish this great commission, it is like climbing a cliff. Some have described the anointing as a time and place where our gift functions smoothly and with ease. Others say that when they are experiencing the anointing it seems natural, and they do not need to work it up. If it seems nothing is happening in our ministry, we just need to remember that either we are preventing it from being released or the Holy Spirit is not ready for us to proceed. *"I will go before thee, and make the crooked places straight: I will break in pieces the gates of brass, and cut in sunder the bars of iron. And I will give thee the treasures of darkness, and hidden riches of secret places, that thou mayest know that I the Lord, which call thee by name, am the God of Israel"* (Isaiah 45:2-3). We want and need the anointing in our ministry, and we will learn that sometimes we can sense it and other times we cannot. We can have it one night and not the next but even in the times when we are struggling, we walk in faith and simply do God's will. If we have to work it up, we have probably gone outside our anointing into our own *bag of tricks,* and this is a type of manipulation that no one needs. Some have walked through dry seasons and have become so discouraged they have even questioned their calling. These trials of our faith are won with being steadfast in fervent prayer, for it is in His presence that a clean heart and a right spirit is nurtured. Within our sense of desperation we come to know that in our weakness He is made strong. In *Matthew chapter 4* we notice that Jesus fasted 40 days and nights, and we can agree that much of this was to subdue His flesh so that He could focus and concentrate on the task at hand. Walking and trusting the Holy Spirit's anointing makes the difference between us being at peace in our ministries or us suffering under the weight of weariness and disillusion. Let us also remember that we do not engage in today's spiritual activity with yesterday's *leftover* anointing! May we develop a continual expectation for a *fresh* revelation of His presence! *"The Lord is my strength and my shield; my heart trusted in Him, and I am HELPED: therefore my heart greatly rejoices; and with MY SONG will I praise Him. The Lord is their strength, and He is the saving strength of His ANOINTED"* (Psalm 28:7-8).

I am sure that all of God's people would say they want the anointing, but not all are willing to allow it to be developed in their lives. There are some of His children that are doing many great things, but they are working outside of where God wants them to be. For example, some individuals are called to be teachers but are trying to be pastors because it provides a salary. This is trying to *make it work* for their needs instead of following His plans. And then there are others who have been given the anointing to be used mightily in the Kingdom of God, but they have used it to promote their own fame, glory, and financial gain. For example, I personally believe there are many in the music industry and the business world that have been given a specific blueprint to devote their lives to building God's Kingdom but have intentionally said no thank you. In our spiritual journeys we need to think seriously about our divine destiny and sincerely ask Jesus if we are working in the exact field that He has designated for us. Each of us that is serious about our specific blueprint should examine our lives and ask for help to discover where we are, what we are doing, and why. In *I John the second chapter,* the writer states that we have an ability to know our calling. ***"But you have an unction from the Holy One, and you know all things. I have not written to you because you do not know the truth, but because you know it, and that no lie is of the truth"*** *(verse 20-21).* If you are willing to do what God calls you to do, He will not only create in you the desire to do His will, but He will also furnish the anointing to complete it. ***"And I will pray the Father, and He will give you another comforter, that he may abide with you forever; even the Spirit of truth; whom the world cannot receive, because it sees him not, neither knows him: but you know him; for he dwells with you, and will be in you"*** *(John 14:16-17).*

As we have said before, everyone is not called to be a pastor, teacher, prophet, apostle, or whatever the mantle may be, but everyone is called and anointed to a personal, specific spiritual responsibility. Whatever the Lord has drawn on our specific blueprint, He has anointed us to accomplish it! Amen! The worship team is a perfect example where the gifts, talents, and abilities for music are evident to prove the calling for this particular ministry. It is true that talent is not needed for a person to worship God because all of His children can lie on their faces all day in intimate worship to Him and can put on the garment of praise and dance before Him until they collapse with exhaustion without any true musical gifts. However, this is NOT the same as being called and anointed to lead others into worship or to have a specific ministry. It is heartbreaking to witness individuals trying to force their desire to labor in a field they are not anointed to work in. We purchase CD's and books and listen to our favorite singers, preachers, and worship bands, not just because they have good intentions but because they are highly skilled and anointed and minister to our spirits. The mantle of spiritual music is like every other gift and calling in that it is not just something that anyone can do; it is like a divine puzzle that fits together perfectly only when each piece finds its designated place. Learn to know the anointing within your spirit, and you will not be deceived, confused, or intimidated by what the world may think about you. Begin to train your mind to lean on the Holy Spirit by confessing daily that you have the wisdom of God and that you know the difference between what is of Him and what is from your imagination. Pray that you can become more aware of the Holy Spirit every minute so that He can guide you even in the small things. This is how we develop sensitivity to our anointing as a *perception* for direction.

In the times when you must make crucial decisions, just stop and ask yourself, what is it that I really feel in the deepest part of my being? *James 1:5 says, "If any one of you lacks wisdom, let him ask . . ."* Jesus said in *John 16:24 ". . .ask and you will receive. . ."* and in *John 2:27, ". . .the same anointing teaches you of all things. . ."* If you are determined to trust the anointing, you will discover this is the wisdom of God that is being used to renew and transform your thinking through the Holy Spirit for your benefit! We can also miss the beauty and blessings of God's provision when we believe the anointing is available only in times of formal or official ministry. Divine appointments are a perfect example of developing spiritual awareness through the anointing—in everything from talking to bringing someone a cold drink on a hot day to mowing an elderly person's yard. *"A man's heart devises his way: but the Lord directs his steps" (Proverbs16:9).* Jesus said in *John 14: 26, "But the comforter, which is the Holy Ghost, whom the Father will send in my name, he will teach you ALL things, and bring ALL things to your remembrance, whatsoever I have said to you."*

For further reading and study you can turn to a wonderful passage of scripture found in *I Corinthians 12:14-25* that reveals how God anoints people for unique purposes and different ministries. Many have become entangled with frustration because they have drifted from their callings to do things they were not called to do, or have tried to be like someone else. Some may listen to teachers and singers and try to imitate them only to discover that the attempt does not have the same power or effectiveness. *Why?* Because God has anointed that person's blueprint that only works with them, the same that He has given you a unique anointing that will only work with you. Our wells are dry without God's anointing, and He will NOT automatically bless everything we do because the truth is, it is not really our lives, our ministries, or our destinies! The Lord never promised to bless our plans, but rather the idea is for us to seek His face and find His will, then to work hard to obey so that He can fulfill <u>HIS</u> vision in us! It is true that just because a ministry is being blessed financially that it is not necessarily a confirmation that it is anointed; however many do believe that money follows ministry. In *Psalm 37:4*, David said ***"Delight yourself also in the Lord; and He will give you the desires of your heart."*** The Lord is saying that if we will place HIS WILL as the highest priority in our lives, His Word will CREATE the desires of our hearts, and our love and energy will be directed by the Holy Spirit to help us be successful.

The anointing is crucial when it comes to timing as many step out into their ministries before the Lord tells them to. They may have sensed the call in their lives, and others may have given words of encouragement, but let us remember there is a time table with the Lord's perspective of maturity and divine appointments. Let us remember that Jesus knew His ministry and calling but only stepped out into His ministry when the time was right. I heard a story one time about a young man that came to church and was filled with excitement. He said that he had been praying about being a missionary for a while, and he had finally heard the Lord say "go." After a year in the mission field, he came back very discouraged as he was exhausted, had been sick, and was financially wiped-out. He admitted that after fasting and praying and desperately seeking God about what had happened that he had only heard the first word of God's original answer. In his excitement he had not stopped long enough to hear the entire message which was, "Go - and sit down and wait for my perfect timing. You have much to learn before I send you." Our anointing is very closely associated with our spiritual sensitivity, and it's fine to be excited, but we are NOT to get ahead of God or think more highly of our abilities than we should. If we know our designated areas and operate in God's Spirit, others will be aware of it, and we will not need to advertise or push our way into opportunities (that is a tough one). If we feel the urgency to prove our ministry, this could be a sign there are critical components that are missing and are preventing us from having the balance needed to be effective. It is much better to have people invite you and desire for you to minister than to have them trying to avoid you. When it comes to ministry, our anointing can say more in two words than we can try to prove in ten concerts or lectures with our natural abilities. If we abuse our anointing, we have received our reward, and if we are laboring without the anointing, it will be obvious to everyone who has spiritual discernment. *"Now we have received, NOT the spirit of the world, but the Spirit which is of God; that we might know the things that are freely given to us of God." "But he that is spiritual judges all things, yet he himself is judged of no man. For who has known the mind of the Lord, that he may instruct Him? But WE have the mind of Christ" (1 Corinthians 2:12, 15-16).* This is a very powerful verse and should be used as a part of our daily confessions. When we are talking about abiding in God's Spirit under the anointing of His presence, is there anything more important than to have the mind of Christ?

Chapter 23
REVERENTIAL FEAR

"The fear of the Lord is the beginning of wisdom: a good understanding have all they that do His commandments: His praise endures forever" (Psalm 111:10).

As we move on with this fascinating subject, I want to say that God is filled with patience toward us who are trying to learn how to live for Him. He knows who is really sincere and the motives of every heart. He knows who is genuinely hungry and thirsty for the entire buffet of His Word, and He rejoices with those who love Him and want Him to be their Lord and Master. If we are blessed and judged by the words of our mouths, then it would only be wisdom to pray for the discipline to be careful what we say. The power of words is for our benefit so that we can speak our visions in faith and believe that God can and will create the fruit of our lips. He is cheering for us and has a strong desire for His children to *seek* Him so we can *find* His will and have the courage to live it out. There is a terrifying and paralyzing type of fear that does not produce good results and this is not the fear we are referring to. The reverential fear of God is all about respect and is the only appropriate response to approaching our creator and redeemer. If we can learn how to develop an awareness of His presence as a lifestyle, there will truly be a miraculous difference in our conduct. *"O fear the Lord, ye His saints: for there is no want to them that fear Him" (Psalm 34:9).* Our spirit is birthed within an atmosphere of true worship and longs to dwell in a state of brokenness, admiration, appreciation, and reverence. This will become a reality only when we become determined to NOT allow our wills to control us.

I have been in many different church services throughout my life that seemed to operate in a business-as-usual attitude, which left me to wonder why and how does this happen. I have spoken to members of these congregations, and it appears they are interested in having the Lord in their midst and are actually perplexed as to why things are the way they are. I have asked what they believe could make it livelier, and they agree that a special person could probably ignite a Holy Ghost fire, and this would *rev-up* the church to a higher level of spirituality. My response is if Jesus cannot stir your heart, why would you presume that anyone else can? Mmmmm. . . Humans can stimulate our emotions, and a charismatic personality can momentarily make us excited and enthused, but without a personal revelation of Christ, we generally exist as defeated, miserable, unhappy, and discouraged souls that are incarcerated within a mediocre religious existence. If any Christian does not pray, worship, praise, and jump for joy continually throughout the week, they are most likely not going to do it when we come together! And if they do come to church and put on a show, it usually has no real substance. If the congregation lies around with a lethargic attitude during the week and does not think about God until they return to church Sunday morning, the service will be a reflection of how the people have lived all week! Many churches are filled with sleepy religious people because their carnal wills are being allowed to hold them hostage. ***"Wherefore my brethren, as ye have always obeyed, not as in my presence only, but now much more in my absence, work out your own salvation with fear and trembling"*** *(Philippians 2:12)*.

An example of understanding a glimpse of reverential fear is found in the book of *Job*. The conversations between Job and the Almighty are so amazing that we should visit these sobering responses from time to time just to maintain a perspective about who we are and who God is. When the Lord is asking such questions as, *"Where were you when I was measuring the universe,"* it causes us to humbly fall on our faces before Him. I was talking to an older saint recently about this subject, and he mentioned that it seems nothing stirs him or moves him anymore. Over many years, he has heard thousands of sermons and sung worship songs over and over until now even hearing about Jesus being crucified does not break his heart anymore. It is like his conscience has become calloused and numb to the messages, and his faith has become a tired ritual. I believe this is happening all around us and is directly related to why the churches are lifeless! *But what causes this apathy?* Well, we can blame it on the devil, but that is NOT the problem. It is falling away from our first love and losing our reverential fear of God. When water sits still and is not allowed to flow, it becomes stagnant. It does NOT matter how many years a person has attended corporate assemblies; the true concern is how close that person is living to God. Familiarity can become an enemy as we remember that those who watched Jesus grow up did NOT respect Him when He became God's voice! The danger of backsliding is very real, and I know it sounds ironic, but it is actually possible to wear our tires out going to church while slowly drifting away from the One we are so faithfully trying to serve.

It goes back again to the concept that we are to be developing our relationships in our prayer closets and not relying on church to satisfy all of our spiritual needs. Satan has no problem with God's people attending church as long as they leave their own *wills* ruling on the throne of their hearts. He knows that if anyone's love for God becomes reduced to a religious ceremony, that the world will be less salty and not only will that individual be held in bondage, but will not have the anointing or desire to set anyone else free! However, the devil becomes worried when he sees someone praying and studying God's Word because when God's people begin to understand revelation knowledge, they can see His will, and when we can know His will, we can follow it and accomplish the great and mighty things that God wants us to do! Our brains function in the natural realm, but God's wisdom comes from the super-natural dimension! The Christian life is like going back to being a baby and starting all over again with learning how to function, operate, communicate, act, learn, think, and speak. Allowing God to re-wire our minds in order to process our emotions through a new spiritual filter is very difficult and uncomfortable, which is exactly why most people would rather remain the same. Learning how to allow Christ to sit on the throne of our hearts instead of making our own decisions is so painful, no wonder only a few choose to do it! Only when we snap out of our trances and recognize who God really is, will we walk in the awareness and reverential fear of His holiness! I can say with all confidence that if we do not have a reverential fear for Him now, we will soon. ***"For we know Him that hath said, vengeance belongeth unto Me, I will recompense, saith the Lord. And again, the***

Lord shall judge His people. It is a fearful thing to fall into the hands of the living God"(Hebrews 10:30-31).

Much of the church world has become lackadaisical about Jesus, and until we let go of *our* wills, we will never live in *His!* You see there is this often unnoticed danger that arises once the honeymoon of being born again starts to wear off. The conscience begins to identify that this stranger (Jesus) has not only been visiting as a guest, but has moved in permanently AND desires to implement a whole new system of thinking and living. The brain along with our old nature draws up a survival or self-preservation strategy and begins to send out warning messages, like "Houston we have a problem," to the body and the emotions. It does not take long for our wills to figure out there is now a huge conflict between the way we have always lived and the way Jesus wants us to live. Our carnality rises up in defiance and declares war (if we allow it), and we are faced with a crucial decision. If we want to be the overcomer in this life that God requires, we must bind and gag our old nature. Our former self is supposed to be crucified with Christ, but with some Christians it is more like a vampire that operates in the dark and avoids the light. One day we are happy and filled with peace because we have spent time with God, and the next day we give in to temptations as Satan joins forces with our old nature and pushes all the buttons where we are weak and vulnerable. Many times this surprise ambush is so tempting that we fail before we even realize what has happened, which shakes us to our foundation and commonly happens right after a wonderful victory. We just do not want to submit, nor do we want to do things that we hate to do. It is the same reason that Jonah ran away from the Lord when God gave him direct orders to go to Nineveh and preach repentance. His will wanted them to suffer while God's will knew that love covers a multitude of sins.

We respond to truth in a positive or negative manner. The human will is fashioned with the capability to accept or reject information, and within this reality, every time there is an opportunity to learn, the heart will always make a decision to apply truth or walk away from it. This explains why many have no enthusiasm for Bible study and are not interested in spiritual growth. Recently, I offered to fill in for a Bible study class that was being held on a Saturday evening. No one showed up. The following day was the Super bowl and 40 people came to church that afternoon to watch the game. *So, why do people choose to remain in a lukewarm attitude?* Let me say this gently – we do not want to change! Change can be an exciting word filled with anticipation and expectation, but it can also be a threatening word to those who love everything the way it is. People have all of God they want! If we really wanted more, we would turn off the TV, and pray and worship every night. Now that may seem fanatical, but it is not rude or condemning. It is just a factual statement and a very uncomfortable one I might add. God is available every second, but most call on Him only when they need something. For example, we had a radio at work a while back that sat on top of our filing cabinets. People would come in every now and then and turn the dial to a station that played popular songs and crank it up. With going in and out of the office all day long, I would listen to the songs, and many of them would bring back memories of my past which most of the time would be associated with things that I was not proud of. The point is that I found these songs stayed with me, and I began to hear these tunes in my head all the time even when I came home. They began to replace my praise songs and were distracting my focus of spiritual topics that I write about every day. You see, listening to the radio seems like an innocent thing, but the enemy found a crack in my armor and was now dragging my spirit down while attacking my mind and stirring my emotions in a carnal way. *What should I have done?* I finally came to my senses and removed the radio completely! *Hello?* We cannot afford to be distracted by the corruptible junk of this world that has every intention to hinder us from walking in the clarity and beauty of His holiness. ***"The fear of the Lord is a strong confidence: and His children shall have a place of refuge. The fear of the Lord is a fountain of life, to depart from the snares of death" (Proverbs 14:26-27).***

Be careful what you think about and what you watch. You are the one who decides what you drink into your senses. It is your responsibility to stay in an attitude of reverential fear for who He is. It is easy to fall into the dangerous deception of trying to make concessions by measuring and calculating how much carnality we can include along with our relationship with God in order to have the best of both worlds – it will not work! There is NO room for sin in the life of a believer! Keep yourself pure, for you are a servant of the Most High! If we want to be a minister of fire and have church services filled with the glory of God and to be used in constant divine appointments, we are going to need to become vehement in our praying. Those who are filled with His Spirit can hear His voice because they have made the investment into His divine reality. If we are cold, indifferent, and confused as to why everything seems dry and dead, maybe it is because we are backslidden. God does NOT let things slide and is no respecter of persons. He will convict us when something is wrong, and it is our responsibility to repent instantly. Removing the logs in our own eyes begins with self-examination as purity is the result of obedience.

Chapter 24

CRYING IN THE WILDERNESS

"As it is written in the prophets, behold, I send my messenger before thy face, which shall prepare thy way before thee. The voice of one crying in the wilderness, prepare ye the way of the Lord, make His paths straight" (Mark 1:2-3).

There are certain idioms and phrases that are connected with events that parallel and symbolize meanings. In the verse above we understand that it is about John and how he was the one who went before the Lord to help prepare for His entrance to earth. This particular phrase of *"crying in the wilderness"* is commonly used as someone who expresses an idea or opinion that is not necessarily popular with the masses. For example, "she was a lone voice crying in the wilderness about the need to save the whales." Within our topic of worship, we sometimes feel that no one is listening to our concerns about drawing nearer to God. I have seen worship leaders after the service have a troubled look on their faces and seem almost sad with disappointment from the lack of response. I have noticed many times how they will pack up their gear and leave quietly without hardly talking and move through the crowds with very little encouragement for their labor. I am aware and can relate to them because many times I have felt the same way. It is important to remember that we worship God, NOT man's approval. We are the friends and servants of Christ, and if our hearts are clean - He loves it! The masses may quickly forget about our ministry, but let us rejoice in knowing that God considers what we do as a mission accomplished, and He will never forget it! Look beyond the way things seem, and keep working, weeping, praying, and preparing the way for Jesus because we are also a forerunner for Him in the network He has placed us in.

It is perfectly normal for us to desire to be more knowledgeable and prepared for ministry. We might be considering going to Bible College or thinking that being musically trained will sharpen our craft or make us more equipped and charismatic to lead others. And we may even be convinced that if we dedicate more hours for practice each week and remember to pray every day for God's anointing that we can do a better job. No doubt it is wonderful to examine our hearts and focus on issues such as attitude, sin, apathy, fatigue, as we may discover that we are not spending enough time with the Lord and realize we have become stagnant and are just going through the motions. All of these things are great ideas and will definitely help, but may we remember that we cannot actually make our ministry successful; we are just instruments for His purpose. It is His church, His music, His anointing, and His miracle power. When the song service seems flat, we can blame the song selection, the style, the musicians, and the people for not being focused, but what about the times when you can rule out these possibilities and do everything you know to do, and it still feels like you are on a different planet? This is a perfect opportunity to see what happened and do everything we can to get on the right page with Him – then all we can do is rest in faith and enjoy His perfect peace. We continue going forward and trust in what we cannot understand because we KNOW we have heard from God! ***"Now faith is the substance of things hoped for, the evidence of things not seen"*** *(Hebrews 11:1)*. Did you sincerely pray that God would lead the service? Did you actually call each musician and singer by name and ask the Lord to anoint and use these people to do His will?

When God's Word is spoken through the music, there is definitely spiritual power going forth whether we think it is or not! When prayers are being offered to Him, He is listening and moving to answer them! Our songs are positive confessions that shall NOT return void! So even though it may seem that nothing is happening, we must learn to trust Him with the eyes of our hearts and know that something did! Amen! If we confess failure, we are agreeing with the darkness that is trying to defeat us, and we are confirming it with our own doubt! This is putting more faith into our *defeat* than our *victory,* as our negative confession is establishing what we believe! Listen carefully! If we have sincerely prepared under the guidance of the Holy Spirit and presented our labors in obedience to God's voice, we must let go of our presumptions and truly believe that what was released was used to perform God's perfect plan in spite of our uncertainty and speculations! Anxiety is one of the emotions we experience in the difficult gap between the vision and our manifestation. In these crossroads we can choose the easy, comfortable direction and throw in the towel, or we can stay the course, become filled with His determination, and continue standing in the heat of battle. I know this is much easier said than done, but this is where patience must be allowed to have its perfect work. The flesh will cry, and our internal agony can push us and test us to our limits, but God is an ever present help in time of trouble. He is there to help us through these difficult situations with His encouragement and compassion. Yes, there will be times when it seems you are walking in a barren environment and there is no relief as far as you can see. This is not a negative confession; it is just a part of the fallen world and the classroom of life. The Lord gave me a song one time that said, *"When I was crossing over bridges that eyes could not see – I knew that someone was praying for me."* Your ministry is going to cost you in more ways than just financially, but when He says to give whatever it is, remember He is trying to teach us when to hold on and when to let go. We have all these ideas and visions about the ministry, and we can be as prepared as we know how to be, but after all is said and done, our success will reveal just how serious we are about doing it His way.

Remember, many times the peep hole we are looking through does not reveal the entire view. If we become distracted with thinking about the time we are investing and the sacrifices we are making, we may lose our focus about why we are living like this! An important part of having the mind of Christ means that we understand there are many things going on in our circumstances that He is doing *behind* the scenes. Sometimes it is not what we see but what we do not see that brings surrendering our lives for Him into a clearer perspective. *What does all this have to do with worship?* For those who are called to lead others into the presence of God, it is a word of wisdom and encouragement that reminds us that all we have belongs to Him. Of course this involves giving up our control and abandoning our wills, and many Christians may ask, what is so good about being weak and helpless? Because it is the beauty of truth! Accepting the revelation of submission and obedience allows us to realize that in our weakness He can finally take total control. As a counselor, I have been in situations where all

I knew to do was fall at His feet. Those involved with ministry understand what it feels like not be able to come up with a dazzling answer, and in these times of helplessness all I knew to do was to hold tightly to God's hand and depend on His mercy. I have had a father ask me why his son and daughter in-law and their four children died in a house fire, and trust me these are not questions that anyone would look forward to facing. I am known to rarely be at a loss for words, but there are times when I am speechless and dumbfounded, and all I know to do is bow before Him in humble reverence. In my times of weariness and uncertainty I have witnessed the power and strength of God that accomplished more than I could have ever dreamed of - I just needed to get out of His way.

Yes, there are many reasons for our disappointments, and much of it can be traced back to our attitudes, but Praise God He is always with us and has the solution to satisfy every problem. Have you ever wondered why there are days when it seems that everything goes wrong? In the times when songs and sermons feel dry and boring and life seems to be a disappointment, is it our lack of interest and spiritual investment, or are we having a flood of hormones and disruptive emotions? And then on other occasions we find ourselves riveted to our seats, pierced in our hearts, and moved to tears all at the same time because we feel as if the glory of God has engulfed us like a surfer that falls into a twenty foot wave, but is it because we were more prepared and receptive that day? This causes me to wonder about the times we blame others for not being able to represent God more effectively, but I would say that most of the time it is more about us failing to have our dial on the right channel. When will we begin to acknowledge that the problems are not always someone else? The one who delivers has the responsibility to give within the anointing, and the listener has the responsibility to receive within the anointing. When there is a problem on either side, we lose a vital part of the connection. Since God's amazing grace looks beyond everyone's faults, we can say that the closer we are to Him, the more we will see everyone the way God sees. Within the spectrum of wading through our feelings, we realize there is always room for more of Him in our lives, which was the theme of this song, *"More of You."*

*(Verse 1) There was a time in my life, when all I
thought about was me
Never considering the price I would pay, for living so
selfishly
But it's hard to know what's true, when all you can
see is you
I'm glad your specialty takes old hearts, and
makes them new*

*(Chorus) I know there needs to be much less of me –
and more of you
Because the more of me there is to see the less that
you can do
Help me to step out of the way, so the world can see
what is true
When there is less of me, there can be – more of you*

*(Verse 2) Had it not been for you allowing me to see
my desperate need
I would have still been on that dark and lonely road,
continuing to be deceived
But you're the potter of compassion, who loves to take
a heart of clay
And with the patience to mold it, a little each day*

*(Chorus) I know there needs to be much less of me –
and more of you
Because the more of me there is to see the less that
you can do
Help me to step out of the way, so the world can see
what is true
When there is less of me, there can be – more of you*

Chapter 25

THE LEVITES: PIONEERS OF PRAISE

The ancient world of praise and worship is fascinating and worthy of research for those who desire to learn more about how mankind has expressed his adoration to God throughout the centuries. Since creation, man has offered sacrifices as a way to show his affection, devotion, and love. Musical worship has been from the beginning and even included Lucifer as a leader of angelic choirs and heavenly musicians that produced the most beautiful sounds of praise and worship to the glorious majesty of the Almighty. Through the centuries man has developed his abilities and has made instruments to play along with his shouts of joy and thanksgiving and this reverential fear and desire to proclaim God's awesome power has produced libraries of written songs and organized musical presentations. Our spiritual relationship with God is definitely enhanced with music, and we use these gifts to help us express our feelings toward Him.

If we look at *I Chronicles chapters 15 and 16* we notice several things that are difficult to understand completely but are still very interesting. There are words through translation that have become like missing pieces of the ancient world of music such as *second section, porters, alamoth, and shemineth*. They could possibly pertain to musical scales, harmony, octaves, modulation, pitch, rhythm, beats, notes, chords, keys, and other related musical structure. Whatever the case, we can be sure that certain individuals were chosen to lead in specific areas of wind and string instruments similar to our orchestras, and those who directed these sections would be what we would call a maestro or conductor. Vocals were separated into sections, and the entire musical symphony was developed by many leaders in their own fields of expertise including trumpet and cornet teachers, cymbal instructors, psaltery and harp teachers, choir and vocal directors, music arrangers, in conjunction with the psalmist and prophetic song writers.

We have actually been given a record of some of those who participated in the historic account when David brought the Ark of the Covenant to Jerusalem. He chose the children of Aaron (the Levites) to literally carry the ark and be in charge of watching over it and required them to be anointed, sanctified, and ready to minister in worship for the occasion. We see *He'-man* and *A'-saph* were appointed to sound the cymbals and *A'-zi-el* on the psaltery. *Az-a-zi'-ah* on harp, *Je-du'-thun* and *Be-nai'-ah* on the trumpet, and *Chen-a-ni'-ah*, who is referred to in *I Chronicles chapter 15 verse 22 and 27* as the master of the song, was evidently very talented with instrument and vocal arrangements. We can see the Chenaniah ministry today in those who organize and facilitate choirs and worship teams as God anoints their abilities and uses their keen perception of music to relay God's messages to the people and bring glory to His name. These mantles are very rare and are specific callings within the body of Christ. The Chenaniah is a leader of leaders, able to not only manage talented individuals but have the ear to hear the sound of heaven and the ability to coordinate and manifest that sound to God and His people. We also notice in *chapters 25 and 26* that musicians and singers were appointed to minister songs in the house of the Lord which was referring to the temples made with hands and in our dispensation also includes the heart that is sanctified within the temple of the Holy Spirit. In modern day comparisons we can see how worship pastors, choir leaders, organists, pianists, soloists, conductors, the chair order of an orchestra, the engineers, sound and graphic technicians, and the performing arts are all parallels of these ancient patterns. The expressions of worship were taken very seriously with much practice in order to present the perfection that God is so worthy of. Likewise, it is appropriate to maintain strict and precise requirements and a desire for quality in our worship as long as it does not turn into a prideful performance or an attitude of legalism.

It is awesome to realize that what we are doing each week comes from a ministry of music that represents the organization and coordination of a worship band 1000 years before Jesus! We have the writers, arrangers, teachers, musicians, singers, and leaders that have been appointed by God to adore Him in His house today just as they did. We see how powerful and anointed these services were, and the sound must have been impressive, but it is interesting to note that in the Old Testament they were praising and dancing around a box that represented God's presence. We are so much more blessed in that now WE ARE the box that is filled with the Holy Spirit and the presence of God within us. We are not limited to worshiping the Lord in a certain location or only in the corporate assembly, but we can dance, sing, shout, wave flags, or bow before Him and become soaked in the calmness and radiance of His presence anywhere we want.

Those who dedicate themselves to a worship team realize that sacrifice and humility are more important than talent because attitude is the thermometer of our effectiveness. Whether you are a leader or a supporter, everyone is held accountable to the same standards. In a worship team, each person is contributing and representing a vital part of a unified vision and has willingly become a servant to God's service as well as to each other. We are all responsible to develop and share our gifts, and our musical mission is all about submitting our feelings so that Christ can minister through us. It is challenging to assemble a group of talented people and humbly work together, and it is NOT the place to permit carnality to hinder the overall vision of what we are trying to do. Just like the ancient music world, everyone that is musically talented does not necessarily have the mantle to lead worship, or write songs, but each musically inclined person has been given specific gifts and abilities and is just as equally anointed. When it comes to length of worship time, if it is anointed, it does not matter how long it goes because who wants to walk away from the presence of God? In His glory we are energized and will not grow weary. But when the music is struggling to get on track, choppy, confused, wrong chords, without timing, having technical problems, or even a bad mix, it hinders the flow and is not as enjoyable. Chaos is misery, and it would be better to cut it short than to allow it to continue in agony. This is where the leader must decide how to react. It is not the end of the world, and we just put it behind us and regroup. The key is to stay focused on humility because we are all in this together and everyone is highly valued and appreciated. Like the parts of a smoothly running engine, the spark plug is just as important as the fan belt. The armor bearers, weapon makers, medics, uniform makers, and cooks are just as crucially important to a military battle as the ones who fight on the front lines. Respect is a product of maturity. No matter what part you play – you are needed. It is a team effort, and in the rank and file of divine order with the gifts and callings of God, we always have peace and admiration for each other's ministry in the spirit of love.

Chapter 26
THE AGONY OF DISRESPECT

I have some questions for you today. Do you have certain goals for your ministry that have not come to pass yet in your life? Do you often wonder when or if these visions will ever be manifested? Do you sometimes speculate that maybe you have done something to prevent your ministry from being much larger and more effective? Have you ever felt that no one respects you or what you are doing? To some Christians, these questions do not bother them at all because they have never really felt the call or any desire to lead a ministry or become publicly involved with serving as a frontrunner in God's Kingdom. However, there are others that have sensed the drawing power and conviction from the Lord to do some type of work that has eternal value, and for these individuals it can be said that finding clear answers and open doors can many times be a challenge to say the least. What we have done either before we were saved, or even after for that matter, can never prevent us from becoming as close to God as we desire. NOTHING can stop us from having as much of God as we want! You see, there is a HUGE difference between something that tries to *distract* you – and something that has the power to *stop* you! We know the devil is trying to distract us and our flesh hates anything to do with Jesus, but neither one of these forces can prevent us from becoming all that God desires for us to be. Since our un-renewed mind wants to make all of our decisions, maybe it is more like asking just how much of Jesus do we want? And that, my friend, will depend on how serious we are about taking control of our wills.

If we have made mistakes and feel that we are not worthy to represent Him, we are being condemned by the dark side in hopes that we will forget the idea altogether. We can have all of God that we want and walk as close to Him as we desire. One of the most powerful character traits within the character of Christ is forgiveness, and He will stand against anyone in our defense. Actually, this revelation is much of the reason why we are forever grateful to Him. He forgave us because He loved us so much, and He wants us to understand that unless we function with this same mindset toward others, our ministry will be no more than sounding brass and a tinkling cymbal. If we want others to respect us, we need to treat others the way we are longing to be treated, and that includes sincerely encouraging them in the things they are involved in. How else can we expect to grow if we are not open to being spiritually stretched? If we refuse to expand and become a bigger person for God, then we will remain watching from the sidelines as an envious, bitter, pouting, frustrated, jealous, and resentful spectator. These religious pity parties are simply the result of not having love, and this attitude will NOT improve until we allow Jesus to change our thinking! Asking Him to give us His love will clean the windows of our souls so that we can see more clearly and realize that it is not about the world respecting us – it is about seeing everything like Jesus sees it.

Great news! God is trying to get in touch with you! Sometimes it seems that we are like ships that pass in the night, but make no mistake - it is NOT God that has taken His attention away from you. Most of the time we say we are waiting for Him, not realizing that He is waiting for us! Amen. In these wilderness occasions it is important to spend time with Him in order to become more aware of how He is trying to intervene. You do NOT need the respect of man to PROVE your ministry! The only thing you need to establish your gift as valid is to be confident that God has called you, endorsed you, equipped you, anointed you, and is commissioning you! When you are confident of this, your level of effectiveness will depend on how serious you are about being obedient. If you truly desire to be a remnant disciple, but are constantly running into brick walls, there are solid realities you can rest in and know that God has NOT forgotten His plans HE has put within you! Actually, if you study the leaders of the faith (especially Christ) you will see their lives were led by God, yet they did not always have an easy path. Even in the world of secular endeavors, those that have eventually become successful and popular may have had a long history of disappointment, but they also had a key quality called *perseverance*. God uses the ones that have failed and fallen because when they heal and learn from their mistakes and finally get it right, they are stronger than ever and ready to reap a good harvest. Experience and hard work does not always make one wiser, but it is what we *learn*, and this unlocks unlimited potential for what He can do through us! Just because you are having a season of stumbling blocks does not mean that you are destined for defeat; it just reveals you are being given the opportunity to see them as stepping stones within the fine-tuning stages of His perfecting process. Those who overcome seemingly impossible obstacles realize the dynamics of determination (nothing is impossible with God) and place ALL of their trust in knowing that Christ IS their victory no matter how violent and dark the storm! ***"Being confident of this very thing, that He which hath begun a good work in you will perform it until the day of Jesus Christ"*** *(Philippians 1:6).*

Number one: EVERYONE has a gift from God! The ones who say they have nothing to contribute are usually just trying to wiggle out of the commitment and responsibility to serve. Since this life is a training ground for the next life, it would be a good idea to recognize your gift today and begin to find places where you can use it! You may not want to get involved with other people or all the headaches that go along with being a part of a team, but allow me to remind you that you will be working in heaven in unison with the entire assembly of heaven. The more we give of ourselves now, the more God will bless us with later because we have earned His trust by following His commands. In the parable of the talents, we see that Jesus Himself is teaching and was very serious about this issue. He is trying to focus and drive home the point that what we do with what we have been given will be seen as a measuring tool of our thoughts, desires, and love for Him. If we respect His Word and the glory of His being, we will be intense about obeying His voice because we know we will face Him one day and give an account of our deeds and our attitudes. Those who pray for wisdom and divine appointments and develop spiritual sensitivity will be watching and waiting for opportunities to do His will. A divine principle is being revealed in this story that promises we will be given authority to rule and reign with Him according to our diligence to follow His instructions. ***"His lord said unto him, well done, good***

and faithful servant; thou hast been faithful over a few things, I will make thee ruler over many things: enter thou into the joy of thy lord" (Matthew 25:23).

The reason I mentioned the fervency that Christ was emphasizing here is that we notice at the end of this story, He does not compromise or fail to deal with the consequences of laziness and rebellion. I am not sure the church has taught the importance of being actively involved with our callings, along with how much God is expecting from what He has given to us. It seems an underlying political attitude within religious church government that the church does not really want the people to become overly involved with demonstrating their callings because it would reveal the lack of need for paid ministry. Many churches want to use people's energy to help them build their ministry so that they can have all the recognition. Let us continue reading in *verses 28 and 29: "Take therefore the talent from him, and give it unto him which hath ten talents. For unto every one that hath shall be given, and he shall have abundance: but from him that hath not shall be taken away even that which he hath."* We notice an interesting point here that if Christians refuse to develop their spiritual gifts, most likely they will lose the ability to use those gifts. However, for those who give their lives into serving God and obeying Him no matter the level of resistance, they may end up accomplishing even more than they ever imagined. The organized church through the years has taken much of its management style from the traditions of the natural business world and is partly to blame for the idea that compensated clergy is to do the work of the Lord instead of Christians examining their own hearts to discover their own callings. The concept of a few leaders being in control and for the people to finance God's work has falsely reassured the masses that spiritual authority within the Kingdom is only for paid clergy. The truth is that every follower of Christ is a minister and will be held accountable for not following a personal, specific blueprint! The spiritual life is a gradual progression of training and development for all saints to become experienced warriors that serve faithfully on the frontline for the sake of all that is precious in God's sight. The pastor has a specific office, but every disciple of Jesus has been commissioned to be a minister of the gospel.

Number two: Many say they want to do God's will but are really just placing all of their confidence in the hope that He will bless their own plans. This is a statement that requires a complete examination of our conscience with the eyes of our heart. If we truly seek to follow every tiny detail of our building process, God will reveal truth and expose our deceptions. You see, people can do many things in God's name, and lots of Christians are very busy with religious activity, but the question remains; are they paying attention to the specs and codes of the plan? Of course it is much easier to add details and modify here and there, but our contract does not have a *tweaking* clause that allows us to rearrange the structure just because we want to make it more comfortable. How often are we faced with the decision to obey Him and then try to think of everything we can to avoid His instructions? I believe that God is not nearly as impressed with what we do as much as He is with our willingness to obey. I'm sure there are many that have been called to the mission field but refused to go. And what about the ones that were called to the ministry yet never yielded their hearts to God's service because they were afraid of what it might cost them. The most popular excuse for NOT following God's compass is that people are not willing to abandon the things they hold dear. I keep going back to the rich young ruler, but until yielding our wills becomes a life changing reality within the very depths of our souls, this will remain just another Bible story. Evidently, the young man had done well and was no doubt a respected man of the community, but when he presumed that he had attained the plateau of the Christian life – he was mistaken. The powerful illustration that Jesus was trying to explain was that this man had articulated the Christian life around all the things he loved so that everything fit perfectly into his carefully drawn out designs for a comfortable life. Even though he had done notable works, he had never really surrendered his will and after reading the fine print was depressed to discover this was the heart of the issue. We also must come to terms with this revelation and become enlightened to this same truth or our lives will not have the opportunity to spiritually advance any further that he did. We are not to be proud of our deeds; we are to be thankful for His mercy that allows us the privilege to surrender our lives to Him. This is the highest level of spiritual living unto the Father. *"And He* [Jesus] **was withdrawn from them about a stone's cast, and kneeled down, and prayed, saying, Father, if thou be willing, remove this cup from me: nevertheless not my will, but thine be done"** *(Luke 22:41-42)*.

Number three: Be ready to be rejected. If you think that laboring in God's Kingdom or spreading the gospel is like passing out twenty dollar bills, you have never tried it! I would say one of the most discouraging aspects of the ministry is the seemingly endless lethargic attitudes from those who know you are a Christian and for what you have been called to do. And it is shocking, but many times you will find that those whom you thought were close brothers and sisters in the faith are the ones rolling their eyes as an obvious way of NOT wanting to be associated with you. Listen carefully; everyone has their own interests they are focused on, so it is wise to realize that others are not really that concerned with what you are doing. Yes, this can be discouraging from time to time, but realize the Lord is giving and directing you, and just stay focused on your mission until He tells you to do something else. The world did not particularly care for what Jesus was doing either but that did NOT stop Him. Be encouraged! Follow God above all things.

Rejection is very hard on the ego (and that may be a good thing), but as long as Jesus is guiding and anointing us, we can be content, happy, and grateful. Remember when Christ was arrested, a young girl accused Peter of being one of His disciples like he was contaminated with some type of plague. As the crowd became focused on this accusation, Peter fell apart and lost his courage to stand boldly with the Lord. In the fear and anxiety of the moment, he angrily cursed and denied that He was a follower of Jesus in order to save his own skin. Of course he later regretted what he had done and wept bitterly because he knew he had failed, but the point is that we must be prepared to handle rejection and lack of enthusiasm toward us and Christ. It is good to be aware that we are following the Lord and working for Him because we love HIM and we are a minister of the gospel to everyone because we love THEM! If we are doing it for any other reason, we have lost the scope of our purpose and will become vulnerable to resentment.

Speaking of resentment, please listen to me carefully. Rejection is associated with many different types of negative emotions and is the cause of countless Christians turning against the organized church along with destroying relationships among God's people. Being offended gives way to the idea of being caught in a snare trap. Envision a person walking along and stepping their foot into a loop which activates a mechanism that tightens the loop and "catches" the victim by lifting them above the ground and suspending them upside down. This illustration allows us to see that when someone does not recognize the danger of dwelling in their emotions, they are constantly riding a roller coaster of frustration over and over. Our flesh interprets rejection as disrespect and if we allow ourselves to live in this vicious cycle, we are vulnerable to constantly being hurt and entangled with our feelings because this is the only world we know. We all suffer from what we do not know which is why the Lord desires to teach us a brand new way of thinking and living! You see, when we choose to harbor unforgiveness, this opens the door to the consequences of being ineffective in our ministry, family, friendships and more importantly becoming disabled in our spiritual relationship with God. We will NOT be able to function in peace and love within the Holy Spirit if we hold on to resentment and bitterness! To even imagine that God does not hold us accountable would be like believing we can handle rattlesnakes while expecting the people we are upset with to be bitten! However, there is good news! We have been given the key that can unlock our bondage from being controlled by our feelings; we can learn incorporate God's divine truth and begin training our mind and conscience how to step over into God's joy filled dimension and stay there. You are the only one that can make the decision to stop living as an easy prey for the devil. Rejection, resentment and being offended is a "button" the devil will push every day until we figure out that we do NOT have to live this way. If we are rejected – so what? Jesus was rejected and disrespected but He KNEW the truth and walked in compassion for the unlearned! If you will sign up for God's transformation boot-camp and be willing to step out of your old way of thinking, He will deliver you from this agonizing trap and show you how to live in His cycle of freedom that is a *lifestyle* of love and joy.

In most cases across the board, the way people react toward you and your calling is nothing personal - it is spiritual. Remember the old saying, *"birds of a feather flock together?"* All of us are individuals and have different desires, specific interests, and hobbies that we make time for because we are captivated by what we enjoy. It is even common for Christians to have their priorities out of order and cherish different kinds of idols that take preference over being obedient to the Lord. For example, you would think those who follow Jesus would enjoy reading Christian books and articles about their faith or listening to Christian music that edifies and encourages their spirits but that is NOT always the case. Many who call themselves Christians do not even read or study their Bibles or worship God at all. So if you write, sing, teach, or create any type of spiritual contribution to the body of Christ and expect fellow Christians around you to be jumping up and down about your talents, you will probably be disappointed. *Why does that bother us?* Well, we say we want people to interact with God but many times it is because we want respect, and we desire someone to pat us on the back and appreciate what we are doing. I know we are human and this is somewhat normal, but if we can get over ourselves for just a moment, we might learn how to be content in knowing that Jesus respects us whether anyone else even remembers us! People are not flippant toward us because they do not like us or believe our ministry is not a quality and worthy cause; they are just simply NOT interested in it! You and I cannot afford to be offended at them because resentment is sin! Just stand back and see the big picture and realize that people are about as enthused about what you are doing as they are about praying or anything else that takes them deeper than they want to go! Life is filled with so many distractions that it is not difficult to find something to steal away their attention. By the time they finish reading the newspaper and magazines, surfing the net, texting, e-mailing, face-booking, and watching TV in the evenings – there is no time left. The masses are allowing the enemy to *bind the strong man* and they are not realizing why their life is being ransacked! We need to get this straight; we are not praying for them to listen to us, and we cannot change their hearts or make them rearrange their desires. We are simply praying they will return to their first love.

Most Christians have been raised in a church environment and naturally associate praise and worship in the context of a corporate setting. To some, it has never occurred to worship God beyond the four walls, and this is a perfect example of the limitations (some might say deception) of religion. When God does not capture the imagination, it is easy to see how people can just go through the motions and become numb to what is being said and done within the church and in their everyday lives for that matter. This way of thinking can develop into a bad habit of only turning to God when we need a favor. Spiritually this may seem elementary, but I honestly believe that though many Christians have heard about having a personal relationship with Christ, they have never really had one. I have been in many services throughout the years, and it is not unusual to notice people (no doubt daydreaming) just standing there yawning as if they were bored to tears, yet these are the same people who the night before were screaming, jumping, and crying for their favorite sports team. How could that be? How could a Christian be so enthusiastic and aggressive with something that has very little meaning, and not be interested in the opportunity to proclaim Jesus as the Almighty, Eternal King that will reign forever? There are several reasons, but one is that in the natural realm humans can actually SEE and know what is happening, and in turn we emotionally respond to it. Whether it is waxing a vintage automobile, or displaying a cabinet of trophies, or lusting after the opposite sex, it is the VISUAL that tempts our egos, drives our lusts, and captivates our attentions. In most cases it is not even our possessions or accomplishments that bring us great satisfaction but rather the journey.

Nonetheless, in church, we usually do not see the manifestations and demonstrations of the super-natural (when is the last time you talked to someone that has literally *seen* God), so without anything to visualize, it is tempting to just follow the normal church routine of singing some songs, listening to a prayer and a sermon, and going home. And there is nothing necessarily wrong with this, but if we are convinced that Sunday morning church is the same as taking up our cross, this is where we have a problem. The dilemma with an immature mentality is not having a developed spiritual vision of what God desires in our personal relationships with Him. Christians that are serious about their intimacy with God will NOT be satisfied with a religious facade but will be drawn to learn and know the specific details of their missions on earth. Focused disciples have a passionate desire to hear with their spiritual ears and to observe with their spiritual eyes in order to become a participator not only in the church community but within the covenant of Christian living!

Worship needs no songs, instruments, music, or beautiful stained glass buildings. Worship does not even need a voice because if the voice is unable to speak, God can still recognize and know the intentions from within the heart. Worship is simple, and all that we add to help demonstrate our affections are only *enhancements* to our spiritual experience. The show business attitudes have diminished the spiritual anointing of many who began their callings and ministries with right motives, but they learned to love and crave the attention and started to believe the applause was for them. The enemy of our souls is always ready to encourage us to praise ourselves! Worshipping our heavenly Father in Spirit and truth is very simple, like prayer, but is commonly faced with very strong resistance. Spiritual warfare is real and will challenge just how serious we are and what a value we have placed on living in His joy. Until our desire to worship our Lord becomes greater than our temptation to ignore Him, we will never do it! True worship is not complex as there is beauty in simplicity. Do you remember the story of the little drummer boy that played a simple beat on his drum as the only gift he had for baby Jesus? What could he give to the creator of the universe? What can any of us give? Our hearts are ALL that we have to offer and yet the most difficult to let go of because they contain the freedom to do what we want. Our songs, books, poems, artwork, sermons, and labors for His Kingdom are just millions of individually unique ways to simply say I am devoted to you forever.

It is such peace and a feeling of awe to recognize the power of His person and the love and beauty of His presence. However, within the thoughts and dreams of heavenly bliss and the glorious mysteries of the spiritual realm are stipulations. Of course God is love and desires that everyone reach out with childlike faith and embrace Him, but His principles and character cannot compromise His perfection, and included in His infinite truth is His holiness. The more pure and holy we are the closer we can be to Him. The more filled with carnality we choose to be, the more distant we find ourselves from Him. So I would not be revealing the entire truth if I did not mention that the life of freedom and joy in His presence is conditional upon our sanctification. It is sin that keeps our spiritual eyes blinded and our hearts distant, darkened, restless, and heavy. Until we abandon our wills and let go of our independence and humanistic fantasies, our intentional rebellion will continue to be exposed to God. If we are so heavily drugged and deceived by the control of our flesh, it will not be possible to enjoy the blessings that come with walking in His Spirit. When we allow our hearts to become hard and dry with worldly lusts, we lose the sensitivity that is needed to hear His voice and discern His wisdom. But if we make the choice to absorb His love, His mercy and grace will empower, persuade, and convict us to repent, and in turn He will forgive and restore so that we can be made presentable to Him.

Have you ever been in the presence of God? *Well, brother I think so; I'm not sure; how would I know?* If you have been born again, your new spirit is from God and directly connected to Him. Whenever a person receives Christ, there is a definite bond between the spirit of the child and the Spirit of the Father, but the potential of how close the two become depends on how much the child responds. When we pray, meditate, and confess His Word and worship Him as our Lord, we can sense the presence of His person because we are identified through the blood of His Son. It is awesome to know that since He lives in our hearts, we can walk through the forest or along the beach, and feel His presence because He is there! It is easy for Him to speak to us and influence our minds from the inside, but unfortunately this is where free-will comes into play, and most of the time our old natures are so strong they will not permit our minds to listen to His voice. If it were up to our flesh to decide when to worship God – we never would! It is only the determination of the transformed and renewed mind that receives the message from the new born spirit that says it wants to be with God and is ready to obey whatever He is saying. Until people receive the revelation of learning how to walk and abide in God's Spirit, they will step right past Jesus and never recognize Him. Many have NOT been motivated to read, study, intercede, worship, develop faith, do His works, or speak positive confessions, in order to get on the same page with God's will. Most have not been taught or *"challenged"* to pray before we go to church so we can receive God's Word and be anointed in a divine appointment with someone who may need our help. How many pray for the pastor, the worship leader, the musicians, or the teachers before they enter the church door? For that matter how many Christians pray each morning that God will guide them in the sensitivity of His voice throughout the day? The same is true with how many Christians have never trained their mind to live in a state of discernment. How many live with an expectation that God is going to perform daily miracles and believe that God will use them to help save a soul? And how many pray that faith will arise within the congregation so that a Holy Ghost fire of repentance, renewal, zeal, and dedication will burst forth? How many know God's will when it comes to praying for the sick and those who need deliverance? If we live without a bold confidence and positive expectation that God is going to reveal to us how He wants to move, we are getting exactly what we are anticipating – nothing!

If Jesus Himself miraculously appeared and stood at the podium on a Sunday morning, how would you react? Would you just sit there? Would you applaud Him? Would you go up and shake His hand? Just to stretch our imaginations, what is going to be your response when this life is over and you meet Him face to face? Will you embrace Him? Will you fall at His feet and tell Him how wonderful he is and how worthy He is to receive all worship, love, and glory? Number one: Actually, HE IS surrounding us all the time, but evidently we are not aware of Him. Number two: If we are not really interested in bowing before Him now, what makes us presume we are going to desire to do it then? Do we really think there will be complaining in heaven because it will be tiring to stand up so long or that the music will be too loud or that we will need to leave early so we can get a good seat at a restaurant? Allow me to say again, some of our lethargic attitude is because we are just not interested or thinking about Him very much. *Why?* Because our free-wills are constantly absorbed in planning and enjoying what we want to do. Maybe this could be a sobering indication that we really do not want to have that strong of a relationship with Him and are NOT as much in love with Him as we thought.

Chapter 27

THE MANTLE OF LEADERSHIP

No, this is not about vocal scales, running around the block before service, doing jumping jacks, or going through instrument warm-ups. This is about a much more difficult type of training – it's the pain *(and gain)* that comes from being flexible in our thinking and in how we respond to others. Our lives are filled with character development opportunities but that does not mean we are making the right choices. *What is missing?* Well, we could begin with desire, love, and awareness for our fellow man because leadership is all about trying to help others be all they can be. You see, it is better to lead from behind and put others before you especially when victory is being celebrated. *Why?* Because true leaders are more concerned with watching over everyone else and are ready and willing to move to the front line only when there is danger. When your heart develops this type of attitude, people will respect and admire your leadership because they will know it is genuine.

In ministry or leadership positions, we must learn to bend without compromising. We ascertain much by trial and error, and when we adapt and incorporate God's wisdom, we can know that He will help us become a trusted leader. Respect does not come over night but is earned over time. Let us remember that true leadership is the capacity to convert vision into reality and takes very serious dedication and determination. If we cannot convince others to see the light – at least let them feel the heat! Allowing God to melt and mold us is good for us because it expands our potential. Being versatile makes us more effective because everything we do is closely associated with getting along with people. In psychology, the five-factor model points out five dimensions used to describe human personality; these are openness to experience, conscientiousness, extraversion, agreeableness, and neuroticism. Those in public ministry would especially do well do incorporate these ideas into their lives and be able to recognize them in order to be all things to all people. If we could just perform our ministry and go home, it would be easy, but since our faith is a lifestyle, God wants to teach us the beauty of genuine relationships (and that, as many of you know, is the challenging part). I want us to look at two areas that will test our attitudes as we function in our gifts within the body of Christ.

First let's notice the view from the singer/musician/sound person or any position associated with worship. All participants have their own ideas about what role they are to play in the music. They may see themselves as a potential leader, a qualified soloist, lead instrumentalist, or always ready to suggest new music for the team. There is nothing wrong with these visions and contributions in themselves (these are blessings) as long as it is understood that timing is the key for them to be fulfilled. A tree brings forth its fruit in its season, and the leader is listening to God's plans and instructions. Patience is a tool that helps us to grow and expand our character and in the setting of a worship team, we need to keep our emotions and attitudes in check or the seeds of frustration can quickly grow into a crop of strife. For example, let's say someone brings a song to music practice and really wants the band to learn it. The leader is then faced with an awkward situation and must have the wisdom and strength to handle the decision as an anointed facilitator. If the worship leader has prayed all week about song selection, practiced, and believes he has exactly what God wants to minister, he or she needs to lovingly respond that, *"we will listen to the song and learn it in the near future."* On the other hand if the worship leader has been seeking a new song that will speak to the congregation in a special way, then it can be accepted as a divine appointment and received joyfully as God's song of the hour. It is very important to notice how the person that brought the song reacts, because it can make a huge difference in the atmosphere and likewise can affect the entire band. If the person accepts the decision to learn it later with sincerity and a good attitude, the band remains healthy and strong. If the person feels rejected and becomes offended, the band could possibly become vulnerable to an infection of heaviness and discord. Thus, the beauty of flexibility has its chance to shine (or fall prey to rebellion). The team is only as strong as its weakest link which reaffirms the need for each member to stay in an attitude of humility and prayer.

Another illustration would be those who desire to sing specials or wish to be added to the worship roster to sing or play. Some may need more practice to develop a higher skill level; others may not yet be in the position to be used but are still developing and have great potential for the future. Or it may be a situation where the individuals have not yet found their true callings and really need to seek God's face for their unique paths that He has ordained for them to follow. It may sound strange, but many people are not aware of their inability to sing or play music. This will eventually lead to confrontations that will allow truth (in love) to bring revelation and reality to those who really want to know God's perfect plan for their lives. Remember – true leadership radiates encouragement. I have seen people with great amounts of determination and discipline as they prepared, prayed, cried, begged, practiced, pushed, and done everything to make themselves available for music ministry but were just laboring in an area they were not called to do. Just because a person enjoys music and wants to participate does not necessarily mean that person has been chosen and anointed by God to labor in that particular field. We also forget many times there may be something in the person's spiritual life that needs to be dealt with, and maybe the Lord is sitting them out until the issue is resolved. This is another example of how discernment is necessary in leadership and how a leaders involvement with individuals must be done in the spirit of patience and personal concern. Church is about much more than a music program or a religious service – it is about knowing and caring for others.

Though it is true that being prepared is very necessary, we must be ultimately led by the Holy Spirit. If we set our agendas in stone and lock our programs in without even considering the moment by moment whisper of the Lord, we will reap the disappointment of a religious presentation. It is true that God gives directions ahead of time, but who can say He will not test our sensitivity and obedience to be led by His Spirit spontaneously? Leaders must walk in the Spirit and be ready to *change gears* when the Lord wants to do something special in the service. They must have the confidence to change the direction of the service when the songs have been selected and the bulletins have already been printed. Many churches that are lifeless have disregarded the anticipation and excitement of God's leading and have fallen into the comfort and security of their own ceremonies and would not allow someone to interrupt their precious programs that have been chiseled in stone. I have never understood where we adopted the idea of having only a certain way of doing things and a limited amount of time for the service. What would it matter if we worshipped first, preached last, or stayed all day and night in the presence of God? I am reminded of when Jesus asked the disciples, can you not pray with me for an hour? May we never become afraid to be spontaneous. ***"Preach the word; be instant in season, out of season; reprove, rebuke, exhort with all longsuffering and doctrine" (II Timothy 4:2)***. If the way you live is inspiring others to learn more and become more – you are a leader.

People are always suggesting new ideas because every person has a personal creativity. The leader must realize the fine line of releasing these talents which bring life to the body and the sense of accomplishment and spiritual growth to the one ministering. The other side of the coin involves the danger of harnessing the collection of gifts that God has allowed these leaders to oversee with selfishness, pride, and issues of manipulation. Leaders are placed in the church by the Lord Himself to help encourage people according to the character of Christ. Leaders are to have an aura of humility and are NOT to act like they own the church! Here's a good one; let's say the lead pastor wants to do something out of the ordinary like spontaneously dropping a song or replacing a song. If the worship leaders are to function in the peace of God, they must not allow their emotions to get them upset (if they disagree). The enemy may whisper to the worship leader that outside forces are trying to ruin the worship set and that others who are seemingly not listening to the Holy Spirit are intervening and ruining God's plans. Music ministers may feel they already have the direction, and others are not considering how hard they have worked and planned the service. This is a crossroads moment that can go to a place of blessing or a place of resentment. Leaders are able to react quickly with spiritual maturity as they choose to *go with the flow* of the spiritual current. This attitude can make or break this transition and definitely affect the entire service. Again, it is about reaction and the decision to yield that is crucial. If those in authority make decisions to change direction, it is on them - not you. There are times to take control and times to submit to control, but in all things have love, joy, and contentment that you are being a humble servant with a pure heart.

Yielding our will in order to know God intimately is the reason we live. This attitude and state of consciousness is nothing new because the daily Christian life has always involved sacrifice, sensitivity, and surrender - it is the nature of Jesus. Being a leader is not creating our own visions and concepts of God's power and glory but rather listening to His voice and confidently following Him. It is not about supervising the house of God according to our micro-management guidelines, it is about making sure we are sanctified before God, then reaching out to others in agape love. Every service is a challenge to be spiritually sensitive to whatever *procedure* the Great Physician may want to do and is usually outside of our tiny box of familiarity. As each individual person in the body is a work in progress, we should want to see God's people connect with Him and receive His blessings every time we come together. With the same love and compassion that has been shown to us, may we invest our time into others that we might help equip them in their spiritual journey. This might sound like a simple noble deed, but I assure you it will require advancing into a more serious spiritual maturity of caring.

It is no secret; we all like to do things a certain way and we all have our own ideas about how and what to do about everything (especially church). There will be times when we must deal with those who want to dominate what we are involved in. We will be faced with confronting them boldly or avoiding the situation entirely. Each choice might be the answer in specific situations but our focus should always be love and forgiveness. A true leader takes a little more than their share of the blame and a little less than their share of the credit. Those who are involved with ministry leadership discover the role of facilitator comes *pre-loaded* with many types of challenges. The moment we enter into the arena of authority and responsibility, we automatically become a magnet for resentment, jealousy, politics, challenges, competition, complaints, strife, and criticism just like a manager at a place of employment. As many of you have learned, enjoying success while being led by God's wisdom is accomplished only through constant prayer. A leader knows the way and shows the way as there is a special anointing needed when trying to counsel, finding a balance in mediation, or needing to make difficult decisions, and discerning God's will in these places is NOT an option. Praying for the Lord's patience and having a true concern for others is the foundation that builds relationships, and if we keep a good attitude, the Lord will give us the grace to minister in areas that we would normally avoid. Imagine how understanding and forgiving the Lord is every moment - and we are praying to be a reflection of HIS image.

Chapter 28

A LITTLE LEAVEN

When we hear the words "contemporary" and "modern" within the realm of today's church, we may think of discarding or re-structuring the older traditions and streamlining with a new, fresh approach to presenting and serving God. In some assemblies this has been the case, but there are still a number of churches that do not desire to change their styles of music ministry and will have a *traditional service* notice included on their signs to publicly identify their views so that everyone can know what to expect if they are thinking about visiting. Whether we stay with the older formats or transition into the new look and sound, neither style will necessarily make a ministry more anointed. Yes, technology has changed the face of how things used to be with supposedly improving the presentation of the gospel, but we must be careful that we keep Christ at the center of what we are trying to do and not become more excited with how we are doing it than why. I have often wondered what if we did not have the big sound systems, cushioned chairs, and air conditioning; would His Word still be enough for His people to gather together? Some ideas can be God-inspired and are fine as long as we stay in a spirit of humility and the reverential fear of God. Without the Holy Spirit and the anointing of God in our music and teaching, we are no more than a high-tech motivational seminar. We must emphasize that worship can very easily be converted into something it was never intended to be. Deception does NOT have a conscience, and nothing is off limits to its power of influence. When we see worship as something that makes us feel good in our flesh more than inspiring us to be willing to do what the song is saying, then we have distorted the intention of our purpose. When worship becomes a lifestyle of being aware of God's presence, we will easily recognize the difference between a sincere intimacy of appreciation and a professional performance of talent and charisma. Children need to see and experience the glory of God and how the Lord has called the church to worship Him. It is good to bring the children into the service so they can hear God's Word and witness the demonstration of His power. It is very important to take the time and explain the realities of what goes on within the church because we learn from what we see, hear, and experience. Becoming actively involved and becoming a genuine example allows them to know first-hand about the Christian life, and training the next generation is one of our highest responsibilities.

Many in the church just go through the motions and do not recognize the difference between what is anointed and what is not. For the true disciples that really know Him, the closer they are to God the more sensitive they are about the spiritual realm. When God's people truly see a glimpse of Him, they are left with awestruck wonder and begin to comprehend just how holy and how glorious He is. ***"And all the angels stood round about the throne, and about the elders and the four beasts, and fell before the throne ON THEIR FACES, and worshipped God" (Revelation 7:11).*** This is not a terror or a dread that we would feel threatened or in danger but rather an awareness that every being in heaven falls to the ground because of His holiness. God does not present Himself or His Kingdom as weak or compromising and does not suggest that He can be approached with anything less than an attitude of purity, humility, and seriousness. Likewise, He listens to our every word and demands that we be uplifting and encouraging to the body of Christ. It has never been an option to abide under His wings or to live in His presence without examining our hearts for anything that would offend His perfect holiness. It is crucial to develop this mindset when we come to Him in prayer, worship, and meditation in the corporate assembly or in our prayer closet because He will not be mocked. If we have anything negative to say, let us run it past Jesus first privately, and most likely He will tell us to keep it to ourselves! We pray and plead for Him to come into our midst, and we say we desire to come into His Holy of Holies, but do we really want His holy fire to purge our minds and reveal our secret sins?

It is very interesting to notice in the Strong's concordance at the many references to the word *holy*. Since God associates His church with being pure and spotless, it might be wise for us all to become more sensitive to how He wants us to live. The word *holy* is mentioned 611 times and *holiness* is referred to another 43 times, which gives us a clear indication that God is very serious about us being on the same page with Him. Our lack of respect for authority in the world has unfortunately bled over into our lack of reverential respect for God. This rebellious state of mind and resentment is a dangerous example to the youth and can bring a corruptible influence along with calloused emotions into the church. Many believe they can watch what they want, say what they want, and expose their hearts to all kinds of evil without being affected, but this belief is a deception. The lukewarmness of an individual has a drastic impact on the rest of the body, and if several in the congregation open the door to the world and drink of its filth, the church can suffer and develop a suspicious, cold, religious personality. We have heard about lifeless services and actually felt an atmosphere of depression and apathy and wondered where in the world this could come from. It comes from the reality that sin is in the camp which means some have brought their dirty laundry in with them. The building is just brick and drywall and cannot be blamed for the environment, but when attitudes are brought in and mixed together, the building becomes a mixed spiritual container within one body. We are reminded of this in the story of Jonah, where we see a man that is being disobedient and rebellious toward God. When we are living in willful sin, it is not only affecting us but all who are around us. When Jonah boarded the ship to Tarshish, his sin nearly destroyed every life, and the remedy came only when he was removed.

The church can be filled with God's glory like the temple in *Isaiah chapter 6*, or it can feel like a sad funeral; it all depends on the condition of the people's hearts. We can realize the meaning of the leaven in *Matthew chapter thirteen* as how powerful an influence can be. The text says, in *verse 33,* that a woman hid some small pieces of leaven in three measures of meal and the whole seven and a half gallons became leavened. This story gives several different powerful insights. The positive reflections are seen in the practical example of how yeast is microscopic yet has a dramatic effect on huge amounts of dough. This is a parallel and type of how the Kingdom of God started with Jesus and 12 disciples yet steadily grew to cover and change the world. Leaven changes from within, the same as God's Spirit also changes the heart and then eventually begins the process of changing the mind and behavior. The negative analogy reveals how contagious a tiny sin can be to our conscience and those who are watching and listening to us. Microscopic amounts of negativity, criticism, complacency, and bad attitudes can slowly but surely contaminate an assembly and hinder the worship and overall spiritual health of the body along with a dismissive influence to our friends and family. If we continue to use the illustration of how susceptible we are to influence, we can also see the possibilities of how powerful an optimistic and positive way of thinking can be in influencing those who communicate with us. We certainly have the opportunity to be a bright light of encouragement, hope, and love if we can grasp the power of this revelation. Becoming aware of our power to influence could actually become our most effective ministry! If we would allow our minds to be renewed, we could walk in the image of Christ every moment and this is the heart of the message of this book.

I cannot over-emphasize how important it is for everyone to pray and worship during the week before we come together instead of just showing up at church to see what everyone else is doing! It takes only one person that is being oppressed with a spirit of gossip to bring a negative, disgruntled attitude among the entire church. A spirit of slumber comes from the dark side and is sneaky as it calmly persuades us that everything is all right, while at the same time wanting to leave an opinion of all that feels wrong. Lethargy is a morbid drowsiness that gently invites us to lay down our weapons while we are on watch and lean back for a little nap. This may sound innocent, but it has a strong impact on how effective we are for God. ***"O generation of vipers, how can ye being evil, speak good things? For out of the abundance of the heart the mouth speaketh"*** *(Matthew 12:34)*. For example, as Christians we are NOT to be going along with the crowd at work or at school just because we want to *let our hair down* and play both sides of the fence. The same is true about not coming into the sanctuary to laugh and joke about what we watched on TV last night, when people all around us are hurting and lost. I am not implying that anything that is said which is not directly related to the service is necessarily evil or has corrupt intentions, but we are just observing that whatever is at the center of our thoughts will usually come to the surface. In this light, we can easily discern what people have on their minds by listening to their conversation. The place where we approach His presence is where we should be concentrating on what we have been praying about. Amen! If we have not been praying or even concerned with what will happen, it is easy to understand why we are not excited or filled with anticipation. It is good to evaluate how many souls we are affecting with our words and deeds. Our lives need to have *substance* and that comes from demonstrating the *evidence* that Jesus has truly changed us! Work hard to become the person you want people to remember you as being. I will also include a suggestion, that we be careful in what we bring into the service to use as an enhancement to help minister to the people. Let us make sure that whatever we intend to do or say is from the Lord. We are not desperate to find something to say or perform; we are desperate for His presence and trusting that He can lead HIS service (and our life) the way HE desires. For example, moving in prophecy is wonderful as long as it is being led by the Spirit. We do not want to speak into people's lives unless we are sure it is from heaven. ***"For God is not the author of confusion, but of peace, as in all churches of the saints. Let all things be done decently and in order"*** *(I Corinthians 14:33, 40)*. We are reminded that the concept of church may be much different in the eyes of God than what man has imagined, and this is not the hour to take His instructions lightly or presume that Christ will tolerate a lukewarm church or a compromising lifestyle. It is much easier to construct our own concept of the way we want God to be, in order to live the way we want to live. God is the way He is no matter how we think He is. ***"Remember therefore from whence thou art fallen, and repent and do the first works; or else I will come unto thee quickly, and will remove thy candlestick out of this place, except thou repent"*** *(Revelation 2:5)*.

PART V
THE AWARENESS OF HIS INTENT

Chapter 29
REFINER'S FIRE

"For our God is a consuming fire" (Hebrews 12:29).

"And I will bring the third part through the fire, and I will REFINE them as silver is refined, and will try them as gold is tried: they shall call on my name, and I will hear them: I will say, it is my people: and they shall say, the Lord is my God" (Zechariah 13: 9).

God is the Master Designer and yes, He has a very specific design for our life. He has standards and expectations along with intentions and hope that we will somehow discover what He is thinking and allow Him to implement His design within us. He has a beautiful purpose for us and a definite reason for everything He does except there is only one problem; We rarely pay any attention. He tries to speak to us in order to bring awareness to our spiritual life because He desires to reveal a very important message. He wants to be our personal Lord and purify our conscience so that we can be transformed into a holy representation of His glory. *So, what is God's refining fire and what does it have to do with worship?* His fire brings purification similar to the process that melting gold requires extreme heat to eliminate the dross. This beautiful symbolism illustrates that our level of purging has a direct effect on how close we can be to Him and how *filled* we can be with Him. When we pray for God's fire to fall within us, we are crying out to Him that we finally see how our sin is preventing us from being close to Him AND that we are willing to let Him do whatever it takes to continue His holiness process. The more holy and pure we can become, the more presentable we are to approach His presence. If our desire is to be filled with His Spirit and walk hand in hand with Him in this life, this can only be fulfilled when we allow Him to melt us and re-create us into a vessel of honor. ***"But who may abide the day of His coming? And who shall stand when He appeareth? For He is like a REFINER'S FIRE, and like fullers' soap: And He shall sit as a refiner and purifier of silver: and He shall purify the sons of Levi, and purge them as gold and silver, that they may offer unto the Lord an offering in righteousness"*** *(Malachi 3:2-3).*

> *"Father, Bring Your refining fire into my heart and burn out all the sin and carnality. Make me white and pure and so aware of Your presence that I cannot sin without the agony of Your conviction. Give me the revelation of the awareness of Your presence. Give me the desire and courage to crawl on Your altar and allow myself to burn until there is nothing left but You. May I lose my identification and embrace being a light holder for Your glory.*
>
> *Please help me to resist the temptation to over-indulge in everything my flesh wants. Reveal to me what true maturity is and how to dwell in the awareness of Your presence. Haunt me with Your conviction until I surrender my will. Change my heart, and transform my thinking. Teach me how to know Your will and see others like You see them. Give me will-power over my flesh to walk away from temptations and not to put my trust in the securities of this world. Help me to have the heart of a servant that I might finish my course in blazing zeal and diligence. Give me a courage and determination to stand in the times of persecution so that my life might become the word of testimony of Your faithfulness. Give me boldness to speak Your holy wisdom. Give me Your anointing that breaks the yoke of bondage that can open the eyes that are blind and in all of these petitions, may I passionately and intimately love You and return to You the only thing You have ever wanted from me. . .my heart. In the Holy Name of Jesus Christ. Amen."*

Isaiah chapter 29, verse 13 talks about people that claim to love God but in reality are speaking only words. *Matthew chapter 15 and verses 8 and 9* repeat this message: ***"This people draweth near to me with their mouth, and honoreth me with their lips; but their heart is far from Me. But IN VAIN they do worship me, teaching for doctrines the commandments of men."*** Remember Christ in *Matthew chapter 23* absolutely blasted the religious world and proclaimed that on the outside everything looked fine and decent but their hearts and spirits needed to be changed into the divine nature of Christ. The Pharisees were constantly reading the scriptures and conducting a strict lifestyle of legalism, but Jesus rebuked them because their ideas about serving God were based on pride and human intelligence. They were comfortable *doing* works in the name of God but had no intention of allowing Him to burn away their carnality. Christ becomes our LORD through a process of purification, and this in turn helps lessen the strong influence of our wills. Along with the renewal and transformation of our minds, we develop a conviction to apply the discipline and awareness to resist sin which is a significant pillar of our Christian foundation. Unfortunately, this spiritual undertaking is commonly neglected.

"For thou, O God, hast proved [tested] ***us: thou hast tried us, as silver is tried" (Psalm 66:10). What does that mean for today?*** I believe it simply means what it always has; the Lord knows the hearts of every soul, and all will go through the same process. Religious organizations have always attempted to develop philosophies, mysterious doctrines, and legalistic regulations as we realize the counterfeit *spirit of the age* loves the pomp and ceremonies that are based on political agendas. People are always looking for shortcuts and easy formulas that can bypass the true spiritual principles of God's holy divine order, but God has a certain way of doing things, and no one escapes the refiner. For example, relativism and tolerance are slowly creeping into every facet of life and are especially targeting the church. This worldview is very dangerous as it proclaims that any type of view or religious interpretation is received gladly by God, when in reality this concept is a deadly deception. There is a huge difference between worshipping in Spirit and Truth and just going through the motions of human opinions. There cannot be many different interpretations of truth because there is only one Jesus! There are not ten thousand prophets, kings, idols, or religions that can offer eternal salvation – Jesus Christ is the only bridge that provides the salvation connection between God and mankind. This new way of thinking wants to do away with the idea of being refined because it is much easier to live the way we want and believe what we choose, instead of submitting unto the God of heaven and Him alone. The God of the Bible is truth and will not accept one molecule of error. Let us look at another example of rejected offerings: *"Not everyone who saith unto me, Lord, Lord, shall enter into the kingdom of heaven; but he that doeth the will of my Father who is in heaven. Many will say to me on that day, Lord, Lord, have we not prophesied in thy name and in thy name have cast out devils? And in thy name done many wonderful works? And then will I profess unto them, I never knew you: depart from me, ye that work iniquity"* (Matthew 7:21-23). God does NOT compromise, and there are no secret or special deals. His Word is His general will and is given to each person on the fair equal basis that He will judge perfectly without favoritism. There will NOT be 100 billion interpretations that will be considered - there will be only one.

Of course we realize that offerings to false gods have no heavenly significance, but many forget that even Christians are not guaranteed that everything they give is accepted. Just because people say the name of Jesus or speak the religious lingo does not mean that God automatically responds to it because the spirit world also has fool's gold. People can sing songs in church while daydreaming about what they need to do when they get home, and even though the songs may sound good, it is not true worship. The same is true with repetitious prayers that cry and put on a show so that everyone can see how spiritual someone is, or even fasting that is done to prove how humble and holy the person is. Our motives behind our obedience will determine the fate of our rewards and crowns because our works and deeds will be judged. This must become a personal revelation and incorporated into the renewed mind as a divine word of wisdom directly from God. There will be some whose contributions may seem small in the eyes of the world but will be significant in God's Kingdom. The same can be said of those who accumulate impressive religious accomplishments only to find their works were burned. *"For other foundation can no man lay than that is laid, which is Jesus Christ. Now if any man build upon this foundation gold, silver, precious stones, wood, hay, stubble; Every man's work shall be made manifest: for the day shall declare it, because it shall be revealed by fire; and the fire shall try every man's work of what sort it is. If any man's work abide which he hath built thereupon, he shall receive a*

reward. If any man's work shall be burned, he shall suffer loss: but he himself shall be saved; yet so as by fire" *(I Corinthians 3:11-15).*

The Lord is available every moment of every day and waits patiently for His children to acknowledge Him. In this view, we can agree that holiness is not only a choice but a responsibility for the ones that claim to be His disciples. With all of this talk about the fires of cleansing, it is easy to see why everyone wants His blessings but not His refining operations and procedures. *Refining* means to improve and perfect and this is a beautiful illustration of our spiritual evolution. His purpose of keeping a fire constantly burning within us is to eventually consume all of the garbage of our old natures so that we can have clean hearts which enables us to maintain a mental awareness of His presence. You see, our spirit is already aware of God and is constantly crying, *"Abba Father"* which means the challenge is to take the initiative to bring the mind, flesh, and will into subjection to the Holy Spirit so that together with our spirit we can enjoy God's abundant life. Listen carefully; if Jesus is not constantly on our minds there is no way we will ever take Him seriously! The same attitude and focus on Christ when we worship Him in church is the same frame of mind we are to have when we worship Him as we change the oil in our cars. I am reminded of how reverent we are to be at the communion table and how serious we consider this time we spend in deep meditation with God. We examine our consciences and repent of our iniquities because we do not want sin in our hearts before we go behind the veil with Him. We humble ourselves in holy fear before Him and focus on the great price that He paid with His blood and body so we could be made righteous. I realize this is easier said than done, but we are to live in this type of awareness every moment! The same mindset that the priests had when they went into the Holy of Holies is the same attitude we should have as a *lifestyle!*

When it comes to our worship, we talk about examining our hearts and asking God to forgive us and cleanse us of our sins before we enter into worship, but if we are living in a constant state of sensitivity, we will maintain this same high level of holiness at all times. We can say with all confidence—if we are NOT ready to surrender our wills, then we are not going to consider being consumed! And without being consumed we can never become the pure vessel God has called us to be! Those who have the revelation of awareness are learning how to listen and are interested in knowing (and completing) the intricate details of His specific will. May we continue to pray each morning that He will lead us into His perfect will throughout the day, and before we go to sleep let us commune with Him as we reflect and examine what we have done until all is well with our souls. Repentance is asking Him to purge us and make us clean, and in turn this will release our joy and freedom in His presence. Many come into the service bound with the stress of sin, and these heart conditions hinder the atmosphere with the spirit of heaviness. We cannot make ourselves clean, but we can ask Him to forgive us, and then accept His righteousness through His ministry of reconciliation. It is true that He paid for our sins when He went to the cross, but we still have the responsibility to live holy lives and abide as a living sacrifice. How could the condition of our hearts not have a direct effect on our anointing and the presence of God in our thoughts and conversation? How could our attitudes and motives not influence our prayers and worship? May we bow before Him with broken and contrite consciences in the spirit of gratitude and present to Him an offering of adoration that will be accepted as a gift of our love. *"The refining pot is for silver, and the furnace for gold: but the Lord trieth the hearts"* *(Proverbs 17:3).*

Each day our lives are filled with choices about yielding our plans because it is God's desire that we become walking, breathing, spiritual offerings. But what many fail to remember is that each and every sacrifice will either be accepted or rejected depending on three major areas. NUMBER 1. We must know God personally and have a relationship with Him. Deeds from those who are not born again are blessings to others but are not honored by God for eternal rewards. NUMBER 2. Obedience is the key to success. When God speaks, it is a part of His specific will and requires that we respond *exactly* as He says, and He will honor those deeds. Ideas that we come up with that try to bring attention to ourselves, and busy work and labor that we construct in our own thoughts and plans are not a part of His perfect plan, and He is not obligated to bless them. NUMBER 3. The intentions and motives within our hearts reveal why we do what we do, and God will use this to decide how we are rewarded. Does this mean that some religious work and deeds are in vain and not accepted? I am afraid so. Trying to impress our way to heaven and earn His favor with our own strength is not the same as trusting in God's righteousness to guide us and wanting to please Him. This gives us a glimpse of why it is so important to live in the awareness of His presence. *"But He knoweth the way that I take: when He hath tried me, I shall come forth as gold"* *(Job 23:10).*

Chapter 30

GUARDING OUR JOY

I was thinking about how we try to live in the natural realm and the spiritual realm at the same time and how this *balancing act* makes it difficult to live in victory. The natural realm is always coaxing us to be happy while the spiritual realm is trying to teach us the meaning of joy, and learning how to tell the difference will take more than just a passing thought. I am reminded of the story in the original animated holiday classic, *"When the Grinch stole Christmas,"* and I admit that I had never seen the spiritual symbolism until it dawned on me that the community of Whoville represents God's saints, which are peculiar to say the least but nevertheless enjoy the simple pleasures of spiritual peace and happiness. The Grinch represents Satan, who on the other hand is filled with envy and hatred and is determined to *steal* their spirit of hope and cheerfulness. The Grinch believes that if he can take away their material possessions, he can crush the essence of their joy, and of course we all know the joy of the Lord is our spiritual strength. He does manage to steal all of their earthly goods and even the last bite of food, and just when he is ready to enjoy listening to all of their cries, he is stunned to discover they do not really care about their loss. The Who's are not affected at all; in fact they begin to hold hands and sing and laugh and love each other just the same. Yes, it is a simple cartoon but a powerful skit that reminds us how we must NOT allow the pleasures of this world to dictate or identify who we are! The Grinch thought the Who's were led by their emotions and that he could easily destroy their hope, but he finally realized they were actually victorious over him because they had a more mature view of the meaning of life. I wonder if the *Who's* might be short for *WHOsoever* will? Nonetheless, it was proven once again that nothing can stop true love!

What does this have to do with worship? Well, how can we worship without joy and love? If our lives are based on emotions rather than on the spiritual, we will not only be unstable in our thinking, but we will worship only when we feel happy. Living in the awareness of God's presence is all about loving Him and adoring Him NO MATTER what is happening or how things seem! For example, if we are discouraged, the first thing we fall into is feeling sorry for ourselves. But being filled with God's Spirit is constantly recognizing and being aware of what is going on all around us and making the choice to walk in His truth and life even when situations are not going right. It is easy to be happy when things are going good, but the way we respond and what we say while being under pressure is the word of our testimony! Knowing who He is and who we are in Him will give us the revelation of what He wants us to do and say when all hell comes against us. (Pause). The Who's did not put their happiness and security in fine clothes, beautiful new cars, crystal cathedrals, delicious foods, or a bank full of money, and neither will we! *Why?* Because our province is not on this earth – our true habitation is in heaven! Satan knows that if he can influence us to build our lives on the pleasures and securities of this world that we will put more faith in materialism than in God's Word. When people take the bait and become comfortable in this foolish way of living, then the devil attacks with attempts to steal our possessions and destroy our health which will ultimately leave us defeated and destroyed. He works night and day trying to set people up so that he can tear them down, hoping that we might give up and throw in the towel. But hallelujah! God has a people that CANNOT be defeated by attacking their flesh or their stuff! God's remnant warriors are learning that a lifestyle of worship is not about how we feel but about who He is! Amen! No matter how wealthy we become, the key is NOT to trust in riches. It is fine to have wealth, but be careful that wealth does not have you.

God's word says in *Nehemiah 8:10*, *"...for the joy of the Lord is your strength."* And as we study the true meaning of joy, our spiritual eyes are opened to how it is the heartbeat of our spiritual lives. Joy is the *revelation* of who God is and who we are in Him, and this is the gateway to including worship into our relationship. We know the understanding of knowledge may keep us from perishing and combined with a Godly attitude could be our most powerful weapons in spiritual warfare. Realizing that we are under constant surveillance from the enemy with the intention to attack us is crucial to understanding why Christianity emphasizes the importance of knowing how to study, worship, and pray. So it only makes sense that learning how to handle situations and circumstances while keeping our human nature under control is the vital lesson we must exercise if we want to maintain a steady flow of victory. When we walk in joy, it is impossible to derail us or shake us, and this is what causes the enemy to become so frustrated that he moves on. Growing strong in the Lord is learning to realize that material things are just passing through our hands, but our thoughts, motives, and actions are eternal.

The more we venture out of our caves and look around in this great big world, the more we will run into people that are hurting and have had very dysfunctional histories. I know there are many who are blessed and have led sheltered lives, but if we take the time to listen, we will notice that many have not had it so easy. It is much more comfortable to mind our own business, live in isolation, and just focus on our own needs and desires, as the idea of *out of sight – out of mind* is used as an excuse to keep us from thinking and worrying about other people's problems. But it does NOT excuse us! It is amazing how the less we know about suffering, whether intentionally or not, the less we are concerned to pray. This leaves us more time to concentrate on our desires and converts our intercessory prayers into a *bless me* confession and consequently reduces the needs of others to just a passing thought. Ouch! I was thinking the other day about people like Mother Teresa that abandoned her life so that she could help others. She evidently started out with a burden and a compassionate heart, and the more she became involved, the more it became apparent that she had found her calling. To her, helping and giving became a revelation within her soul, and I believe this should be the attitude of a true disciple of Christ. When we think of giving, we always think of money, but there is so much more to consider like what we are giving, how much we can give, and why we are giving. In *Mark 12:43-44,* we are reminded of the poor widow that gave two cents into the treasury while many of the wealthy were donating large amounts of money. **"And He** [Jesus] **called unto Him His disciples, and saith unto them, verily I say unto you, that this poor widow hath cast more in, than all they which have cast into the treasury: for all they did cast in of their abundance; but she of her want did cast in ALL that she had, even all her living."** When we think of a person's gift or calling, we usually have ideas like a profession or something someone can be good at, and for many this may very well be the case, but it seems only a few actually discover that our lives were given to us as a gift, and in turn we are to give our lives back to God and the world as a gift. In this light, we see giving on a grander scale as not giving something we have, but rather giving who we are. According to the flesh, the *normal* way of thinking is to give God His *portion* but the absolute truth in relation to God's specific will is for us to drop our nets and return our lives back to Him.

Have you ever been at work and watched how people act and listen to what they say with the intention of trying to imagine where they are and how they got there? I have been in crowds of people that seemed downcast and were outspoken about how much they hate what they are doing and where they are in general. They act as if they are entangled in a miserable existence like prisoners that cannot find a way out of their seemingly hopeless circumstances. This helpless feeling of failure infects their consciences and their minds with emotional negativity that haunts their souls with dark clouds of depression. When we are not where we need to be with God, it seems we are in a deep hole, and as we look up, we can see the sky but cannot figure out how to climb out. I can say today; there is no hole so deep that God cannot reach you! There is no island so remote that He cannot hear your cries! There is no place so dark that God's light cannot find you and rescue you! The God of all creation wants you to be filled with His joy, but it all depends on your perception of reality. The three Hebrew children were in the fiery furnace, BUT SO WAS GOD! Remember, it is never WHERE you are that establishes your victory – it is who you are WITH! You and God make a majority, and nothing can stop you from His love but you!

I have been to the valley of despair; it is the most miserable place anyone could ever be. I do not enjoy anything about it, and though I have never seen or felt a literal hell, I would cast my vote that depression is earth's version of it. Have you ever noticed how discouragement paralyzes and encouragement motivates? I know what it is like to suffer emotionally and to be consumed with the torture that comes from being offended, hurt, neglected, backstabbed, deceived, not appreciated, and disappointed. I realize that many have had it much worse than I, and my problems have been small compared to others that have suffered a great deal; nonetheless, this life is filled with troubles, and most of them are more than we can handle on our own. In these times of nagging worries that try to drag us through the valley of anguish, the last thing we desire to tell God is how much we appreciate Him, but praising Him is EXACTLY what we need to do!

At times we all wrestle with different weaknesses and trials that cause torment within our minds and souls as they are either targeting us as victims or taunting us with our own mistakes. And while we are walking over these hot coals of pity, it usually does not make us feel any better to hear the old saying: *it is not the crisis - but our reaction*. However, beyond the blinding pain there is a divine truth in that statement which actually holds the key that can unlock the door to our healing. Jesus stands on the other side of this door, and if we can stop crying long enough and let Him in, then hopefully we can listen and take baby steps of faith and allow Him to fix what is broken. *But Billy, it seems you are taking my misery lightly and implying that the pain is not real.* I am not saying the pain is imaginary or just in your head because I realize it is very real, but I would be wrong not to mention how much of it can be defeated by your faith and determination and can be replaced with joy. *It is easy for you to say but how can just words heal a human being?* The greatest mystery has been unveiled and given to whosoever can receive the revelation of the power of words. Listen my friend—He IS THE WORD that saves the lost, and His authoritative truth goes far beyond a printing press! When we agree in faith with what He has promised – His Word does NOT fail! When we ingest His Word into our lives and stand upon this truth with all of our hearts, His power is released within us to create whatever miracle we need! The good news is that when we make the conscious effort to look beyond our misery just for a moment, we will recognize within our spirits the hand of a merciful God reaching out to us in compassion. As recipients of His patience and longsuffering, we can focus on the one who created us, and humbly reach out and trust Him and embrace the Savior of our souls. It is not what happens in this realm but rather knowing that we followed His directions while it was happening. When He holds us in His arms of grace, we are overwhelmed in His perfect peace and strengthened with His merciful counsel. **"Unto the upright there arises light in the darkness: He is gracious, and full of compassion, and righteous"** *(Psalm 112: 4).*

I realize there are chemical imbalances and psychological disorders in these fragile temples and times when we are genuinely attacked and wounded, but strong soldiers must NOT curl up in fetal positions in the foxhole and pull the blankets over their heads. Times of resentment and bitterness are where the weak in faith and the fearful tie handkerchiefs to their machine guns and begin to wave them to the world as a message of surrender. Saints, how can battles be won when we give up on our trust and confidence in God? There is so much work for us to do in these last hours, so many souls that are watching us, so many young ones that need Jesus, and so much of God's Word that needs to be spoken. I once knew a Christian that was very involved in the things of the Lord for many years and was even considered a fanatic most of the time. Even his own family did not want to come around because they could not endure the sermons. Sadly, this person battled a serious character flaw his entire life and as he could never get it under control, at times it would rise and show its ugliness. One day it would be all about living in Jesus, and the next day there would be a melt-down cursing screaming fit. This individual was unfortunately struck down with a debilitating illness in the later years, and instead of using all of the knowledge and insight from a life of listening and speaking God's Word, he continued to allow the flesh to control the mind and responses. The lesson we can learn from this is that it's not the amount we are exposed to God's Word but the amount that actually becomes planted within our hearts.

It is revelation that *renews* the mind and *transforms* us from death unto life. And it is always our responsibility to activate self-discipline as a crucial part of our spiritual character because a major pillar of our salvation experience is being delivered from our old way of living. The only surrender we should ever be a part of is the yielding of our old nature to Jesus so that we can be a faithful witness and representative of His Kingdom. People are depending on us; they need our prayers, our time, our help, and our encouragement, and most importantly they need to know that having a relationship with God is REAL! Yes, there will be hard times when we are punched right in the mouth, and there will be seasons when we have done everything we know to do and still feel like we have failed. But in these times of frustration, we must learn how to control and discipline our flesh so that God can display His nature within us. What good would it be to tell everyone how wonderful it is to walk with Jesus and yet they never saw us live it? The Christian life is not supposed to be like searching for Big-Foot! Be prepared. There will be times when we blow-it and fail in front of the ones that are depending on us, but after a season of mourning and grieving and feeling sorry for ourselves, there must also be a time to arise, wash our faces, put our armor back on, and return to the battlefield in the confidence that God is developing us and teaching us how to learn and grow stronger through experience! Yes, the novice is still learning, but the veteran warrior is to eventually learn how to be a true Christian.

Who will discover the revelation of seeing themselves in the *telescope* of the big picture instead of focusing in the *microscope* of self? People that believe everything revolves around them, who are self-centered, and are always concerned only about their own feelings, usually have a pocket full of tickets to ride the roller coaster of disappointment and depression. At times I have been one of these people, and it is amazing how I could not see how self-absorbed I was. Serving the god of self is a sin of idolatry. We all need not just a revelation of Jesus Christ but a revelation of our own hearts because how can we know God if we do not know who we are? We must desire to see the reality within our consciences and then be willing to deal with it, and third we must be willing to pay the price of transformation. It is unpopular to acknowledge, but many times our frustrations are the result of NOT cooperating with God's intervention. One of the best ways to snap out of depression is to get up and go somewhere with the intent of helping someone. Pull yourself away from the mirror long enough to see how others are living, and your problems will begin to fade. Walk through a children's cancer ward at a hospital or read *Fox's Book of Martyrs*, and all of a sudden you may think your life is not really as bad as you thought it was. Go out and buy some cards and send them, with no hidden motives, to those you know. Donate to a proven charity or buy a needy child a toy and give it in the name of the Lord or maybe give a donation to the Bible league so that people around the world can know Jesus. Take the time to visit a person in a nursing home and take a good look around while you are there. I have a wonderful suggestion that will encourage you and bless you beyond words. Simply take a pen and paper and write down as many of your blessings as you can think of, and within no time at all you will see the world AND yourself with a *more appreciative* perspective!

If we do not learn from our trials, then our distress has been a waste. Crisis situations are opportunities to put our faith and patience to work! How can we be defeated when God is for us and working constantly on our behalf? He was even involved in the middle of Job's trial. Maybe the reason we struggle is because we are fighting Him for the steering wheel. If we let Him drive, I believe we would be more likely to enjoy the ride, don't you? Is there such a thing as counting it all joy when the blacksmith is holding us to the fire and shaping us with His hammer? I'm not saying it is easy, but actually, yes. If we KNOW that God is making us into what He has called us to be – we can count it all joy! We may suffer trauma, turmoil, or even persecution, and no doubt it is all uncomfortable, but we must eventually get back up and dust ourselves off in order to get back into the race. Remember, when the blacksmith is finished with his piece, he does not throw it in the corner and forget about it. He has worked diligently to produce his vision because he intends to use it for his specific purpose.

God knew you and planned you before the foundation of the world and has been taking care of all the fine details to bring you to this place and has every intention to use you NOW more than ever before! He is trying day and night to polish you and challenge you to be a strong and effective instrument to accomplish His purposes. Sure, the world is falling apart because of sin, but that is exactly why we cannot afford to throw in the towel. Do not allow unforgiveness, bitterness, or being offended to render you powerless. ***"No man can enter into a strong man's house, and spoil his goods, except he will first bind the strong man; and then he will spoil his house"*** *(Mark 3:27)*. You are the strong man, and whenever you become discouraged, your pity binds you and holds you captive to the enemy that desires to control your life. True healing is all about forgiveness, letting go, turning the page, and continuing to move forward. To remain wounded and bitter is to be plagued with the ongoing torture of emotional and spiritual infection. It is time to advance to the next level of maturity and let the wounds turn to scars (from the inside out) that remind us how God is our *Jehovah Rapha,* the Lord that HEALS us! The deeper the pain the more valuable the lesson, and as you learn from the trials, allow them to build your character and wisdom so you can teach from your experiences. Step back and see that our lives are all about becoming what Jesus died for us to be and how effectively we can be used to help others do the same. To God you are a masterpiece! Pray for awareness and understanding. Watch carefully for His unseen hand, and listen intently for His still small whisper. ***"My son, despise not the chastening of the Lord; neither be weary of His correction"*** *(Proverbs 3:11)*.

The normal advancement and progression of spiritual growth is to be developed like a child to an adult, but unfortunately the majority of the masses experience only *physical aging,* not spiritual maturity. There is nothing more disappointing to God than seeing an older person in the flesh still nursing the bottle in the Spirit. He cannot use undeveloped babies to fight wars because if their stability is based on their attraction for the default system, they will never be able to stand. If there is anything that can stop them, it will, because the most sensitive button they have will be pushed constantly until they learn how to not let it bother them! Learning the mystery about how to hold on to joy in the midst of our trials could be the deciding factor between success and failure in our missions, including consequences now and in the final judgment. We must guard our joy day and night and keep it secure because our strength is at stake! The Bible speaks of being an overcomer in this life and how it is accomplished through the blood of Jesus and the word of our testimony. This is a double attack strategy that uses the blood of Jesus as a defense and protection while the positive confession of His Word establishes the divine reality of His will. As we speak God's truth in faith, we are tearing down the strongholds of darkness, and His sword becomes our offensive weapon to *engage* in the battle and drive the enemy back to where he came from. How serious are you about protecting your precious JOY?

Chapter 31

BURNED OUT OR BACK SLIDDEN?

Ministry on any level has its share of special moments of gratitude and blessings along with wounds and disappointments. This statement is not being negative, but rather it is facing the truth concerning all leaders and how they must prepare for the headaches of a complex and critical world that is filled with strong-willed individuals. Praise God, each person is a blessing in some individual, personal way and unique from everyone else, and leaders must learn to read personalities while developing a keen sense of knowing how to connect and mediate in order to be successful. We all experience stress at work along with every other facet of life, and the church is no different.

In today's world of medical breakthroughs we do not need to be doctors to realize that stress is very hard on the body. Our adversary has known for a long time just how powerful a weapon stress is and how it can be used against us to break us down. It is true the weapons of our warfare are not carnal, but it is nearly impossible not to feel the emotions that come from situations. We also cannot deny that our spirits operate out of a temple of flesh, and yet somehow we must learn how to deal with issues in a way that will keep us from collapsing. God wants us to be happy and healthy because He knows we need this vehicle to minister out of. What good are we as teachers, counselors, and warriors if we are sick and in bed with exhaustion and discouragement? Just as it is important to take care of our temples and not abuse them with our eating or sleeping habits, we also must learn how to manage the relentless pressure of worry and stress.

Many doctors now agree that reducing mental stress is more beneficial than physical exercise, and it is now realized that the feeling of hopelessness is as harmful as smoking a pack of cigarettes a day. New studies published in separate journals of the American Heart Association have come up with the numbers that prove what we all knew deep in our consciences all along: Emotional and psychological stressors, especially depression and anxiety, have a negative impact on our glands, organs, nervous systems, and brains. When leaders end up in a *"burned out"* state of mind, we know that somewhere, somehow, they have probably been trying to carry too much of the load. Many times we do not realize how heavy the load, or how far or how long we have carried it. Unfortunately, the advancement in stress-relieving drugs has not necessarily been a *cure all* for these problems. Medications may give temporary relief, but questions arise as to side effects and dependency. Pharmaceutical companies promote drugs and supply doctors, who in turn give the drugs to patients, and while it is true that many problems are chemical imbalances, there arise spiritual questions about why leaders cannot find the healing and peace they are constantly trying to promote. Yes, ministers are human and face physical and neurological difficulties, but many seem to think they know more or have an inside edge when it comes to healing.

The truth is, ministers have the responsibility to seek God's Word and have an open door to God's throne just like everyone else. Of course, leaders are also not exempt from the constant warfare of demonic torment, influences, and temptations that are very real. For example, I personally believe that a root of bitterness along with resentment, hatred, jealousy, unforgiveness, and rebellion can cause physical sickness, and in severe cases produce fatal diseases. Psychological stressors, especially depression, hopelessness, and anxiety, can stimulate hormones that bombard the heart, forcing it to beat as if in a constant state of *fight or flight*. Ingesting God's Word can increase faith, but we must remember that it is not a one-time event but more of a maintenance program. Praise and worship can also bring calmness as a healing side effect to the body, because within the pathway of His presence we are drawing closer to His person, and His touch can cause what we think is impossible to melt away into the miracle we have been seeking. I do not believe it is scriptural that Christians can be possessed with demons, but I can see clearly they can be oppressed with every type of possible attack. The enemy can detect our weakness and focus on influencing our old nature, and this confrontation with familiar spirits is serious spiritual warfare that is fought in the combat zone of the mind. We must implement a strategy to resist negative persuasions that desire to be absorbed into our thoughts and NOT allow them to be accepted within our conscience. This becomes sin and can saturate our system with corruption and deadly consequences of pessimism. *"Cast your burden upon the Lord, and He shall sustain thee: He shall never suffer the righteous to be moved" (Psalm 55:22).* These problems are NOT figments of the imagination but are very real and damaging. However, I also believe that God is THE Great Physician and desires to heal us completely IF we sincerely cry out to Him! Praying, meditating, worshipping, reading, and studying God's Word are all powerful connectors to the never failing healing balm in Gilead – Jesus Christ! NOTHING is too difficult for Him, and He has never failed!

It is no secret that all of God's warriors that are shaking the gates of hell have a *bull's-eye* on them. It is not a negative confession to admit that we are in a raging battle with the devil – it is spiritual reality! You notice that I described those who wear the target as God's warriors because just owning a Bible does not strike fear in the enemy and does not automatically give anyone spiritual respect from the devil, or from God for that matter. There is a huge difference between people who play religious games and those who choose to abandon their wills so that God can keep them on the narrow path of His will. I believe that in the realm of the Spirit, both Kingdoms are well aware of those who are giants for God, and it would only seem logical that the intensity of battle would be directly related to the level of the warrior's obedience and anointing. Today we are seeing a stronger pull from the world to compromise God's Word, and many in the church are slowly becoming desensitized to sin. The enemy does NOT worry about those who have a Laodicean attitude, but rather he is very concerned toward those who take sanctification seriously and are not afraid to go before God's throne boldly.

What does all this have to do with worship? Satan hates worship! And everyone that loves to worship God! The devil wants to stomp out all true praise to the Lord because it drives him crazy, and he will shoot every arrow he can think of to disrupt and hinder the flow of the Holy Spirit. Our adversary doesn't mind a dead religious ceremony (in fact he creates and promotes them), which means he definitely recognizes the difference between a Holy Spirit infused service and a manmade program. He can see in the spirit dimension and is fully aware of the glory of God's presence in the hearts of His people. Satan might laugh in the aisles of some dry churches, but when God's children invite the King of Kings to come in, and they cry out in holiness and humility, the devil packs his bags and heads out the back door! God does NOT live in empty buildings – the church must BRING GOD in with them! Amen! Church was never intended to be so comfortable that we yawn through our traditions and become like mesmerized zombies. Many assemblies have become fat and satisfied on the steady diet of prosperity teachings and material blessings of this world but have ignored the call to live holy lives. These are the members that worry about what they have invested in the natural realm while never considering that investing in the spiritual realm is the true reality of God's specific blueprint for their lives. Yes, it is true; these are the same individuals that are always negative, gossiping, and murmuring about the church because deception prevents them from seeing that their selfish heart is actually being exposed as a result of having nothing spiritually invested! The true church, however, comprehends that corporate meetings are a time to be refreshed and become participators in ministry to the body. Our meetings are a time to learn more about Jesus, but many Christians have never understood that meetings are also a time to demonstrate what they already know! For example, intercessors choose to invest their time and energy into God's Kingdom because they not only believe in the cause but have been given a burden to pray. They are the ones who will not be critical of the church because they do not want to tear down what they are helping to build! These saints avoid being judgmental because they have asked God to teach the people and open their eyes about how to live in His nature. They cry out to see a vision of God's glory, and they know what it means to suffer and agonize in intercession as living sacrifices for Him.

When those who proclaim to be Christians have never learned about the realities of spiritual warfare and have not received the revelation about being aware of God at all times, they are still like babies on bottles. The Lord is disappointed in saints that choose to remain immature, as we must have a constant flow of spiritual nutrition and be willing to act on what we learn. Satan smiles in delight when he looks at an army of spiritually undeveloped *toddlers*. It is time for all of us to *grow up* and *stand up* in the name of Jesus, and I'm not talking about learning how to be a blacksmith that forges his own sword; I am talking about obeying and living by the two-edged sword of God's Word and fighting on our knees in prayer. Yes, we will have opposition, severe trials, and waves of discouragements that will inflict wounds to our hearts (if we do not compromise), but Praise God, we have reinforcements! We are surrounded by the Lord and His heavenly host of ministering angels that are waging war all around us on our behalf. Let us be filled with His victory as we shout unto God with the voice of triumph! When we stand with God we are invincible no matter who or what comes against us! Amen!

Chapter 32

THE RELIGIOUS SPECTATOR

Those who know how to value God's gracious presence will be more fervent in their prayers and more serious in their walks. These are the faithful ones that have received a glimpse of understanding and know the difference between *"making"* a sacrifice and *"being"* one. Our intentions are supposed to be established on His will, and His blessings are directly connected with our obedience. It is His Kingdom and His spiritual principles. ***"I beseech you therefore, brethren, by the mercies of God, that you present your bodies a living sacrifice, holy and acceptable unto God, which is your reasonable service. And be not conformed to this world: but be ye transformed by the renewing of your mind, that you may PROVE what is that good, and acceptable, and perfect will of God"*** *(Romans 12:1-2).*

We must constantly be aware of the difference between our talents and abilities and God's direct commands. Just because we call what we do a ministry does not automatically mean it is God's anointed mission. Working night and day to impress Him (or others) has no influence or spiritual power unless we are directly connected to His specific will. The smells of burning flesh and incense of the ancient world were part of the works of man's sacrificial obedience according to God's perfect details. They were all honored when done in the right way with the correct attitude but rejected when offered without purity or with the wrong intentions. Today our sacrifices are also based on faith and the motives of our hearts. Without following His direct instructions we can do nothing but make a lot of noise - but when we follow His voice, there is unlimited power to change the world. The Church is a designated place to bring the sacrifice of praise – not the place to bring criticism, darkness, or negativity. The *spectators* have a tendency to pick everything apart instead of working toward unity. The *participators* will discover their places of ministry and pray fervently for the revelation of what they are to be AND intercede for others so that God can help them also. True disciples will enter into God's sanctuary filled with His anointing and are READY to release their love and excitement into the body. We should be prepared to minister with our gifts and pour out our adoration to the Lord, because the level of power, signs, and wonders is determined by the amount of pureness and faith that is in our hearts. I know a brother that comes into church fully charged and ready to release every time he comes in! He does not need to be primed because he prayed before he came and has one foot in heaven before he steps into the sanctuary!

Stop for a moment and consider what we sing about. Every week we cry out for His refining fire and purification process. We say we want His fire to fall down and burn up our carnality. We confess that we desire to lay down our wills and be completely sold out to Him. We proclaim how we want to be sacrificed on His brazen altar and how we want to go into the Holy of Holies, but just because people can sing the songs and shout amen, does not mean they really want it! The participator is really serious about being changed – *the spectator just hears a song*. The participator is hungry and thirsty for God's truth and His presence – *the spectator is sleepy and hopes for a short sermon*. We sing about the blood of Jesus, being filled with the Holy Spirit, resisting sin, living in the secret place of His presence, being victorious, doing miracles in the Name of Jesus, touching the face of God, seeing His glory, and on and on, but does everyone really understand these concepts? It is true that many do not know what all of this means, but what about the ones that have understood it - but refuse to submit? People will always have a passion about the things they are serious about! Spiritual awakenings are personal! We will have a life-changing moment only when we see ourselves included in God's plan. The problem with many leaders and veteran saints is that they have fallen into the deception that the Word of God is speaking to everyone but them. Amen! When someone becomes consumed with a desire, nothing can stop him! But what flips the switch that brings this spiritual illumination? Until we have a personal encounter with God about each aspect of the Christian life, we will continue to go through the motions in that area. Without revelation there is hesitation, and the spectator will never know the difference between a religious deed and a lifestyle of love.

How much of God do you want? What an odd question! Everyone knows God cannot be measured. Oh really? Maybe it depends on which path your brain chooses to consider. And hold on a minute before you start thinking about miles and light years. I am not talking about trying to find out what size He is, but rather how much of Him you are willing to *add* to your life. *Some may ask, what does this have to do worship?* Well let's see . . . how about everything! Here's a revelation; the more of God we have in us - the more we will love to worship Him. We advance in our levels of knowing God, and this is directly related to how determined we are to make more room for Him. When people deny their flesh and spend more time with God, they develop a craving for His presence. They love His Word and think about Him all the time. They stay in an *attitude* of worship and are passionate about praying and serving. No one needs to pump them up – they are already excited and ready! They know the way to the Holy of Holies because they go there all the time. They do not want to sit around in the outer court; they want to embrace Him. Do you enjoy being intimately close to the one you love all the time?

You see, it may sound strange, but most people already have as much of God as they want! They have allowed their *glass* to contain only as much of the living water as they are comfortable with. Yes, there are many that will live their entire lives without having a desire to add more of Jesus to their lives, and when a group of people have developed this way of thinking, you will find a stagnant church that is numb and lifeless. Think about it for a moment; we could be the image of Christ if we became determined to be (by the way, we are supposed to be). Amen! Is there anything that could stop us from being everything He died for us to be IF we really wanted to? The problem is that when we incorporate more of Him into our lives, some of our control must be thrown out. So in order to have the best of both worlds, we try to squeeze our wills and His will together, which gives us a perfect example of a frustrated and discouraged religious life. God will never compromise the way He has designed the Christian life to be. He wants to completely fill us (now there's a concept). Are you satisfied to get your toes wet, or are you willing to get your hair wet? Will you choose to sacrifice, or to live the safe, comfortable normal life? Will you make an investment in God's church and be a radical disciple for Christ, or are you satisfied with being a critical spectator? God wants ALL of us, and He desires that we would want ALL of Him. Will you throw away the teaspoon and allow Him to be poured in? or do you already have all of Jesus you need?

Chapter 33

GOD'S TANGIBLE PRESENCE

"And the Lord, he it is that does go before thee; he will be with thee, he will not fail thee, neither forsake thee: fear not neither be dismayed." (Deuteronomy 31:8)

God's presence is one of the most popular concepts in our Christian vocabulary and yet filled with mystery. How is it we say we can really discern and sense Him being near at certain times, yet it is common knowledge that He lives inside of us all the time? Maybe the reason this enigma is so difficult to explain is because we are thinking about it backwards. Maybe it is not that He comes around only every so often, but rather we sense Him when we become aware that He is there. Mmmmm. . . . The first part of *James chapter 4 verse 8* says ***"Draw nigh to God, and He will draw nigh to you. . ."*** which reveals how God has developed a pattern of His laws and principles pertaining to our intimate spiritual relationship with Him. Can I really feel Him? Yes! And I am so thankful that I can always know He is there! Some saints read how Abraham and Moses had encounters with God, and they think that now it would be impossible to have a spiritual experience like that. *Why?* They do not acknowledge God in their everyday lives as a living Person that is standing right next to them, listening to them, and trying to communicate with them. Just because history has recorded the ancient stories of glory, clouds of fire, and His voice thundering from the heavens, does not mean He has stopped communicating or intervening. ***"Jesus Christ the same yesterday, and today, and forever"***

(Hebrews 13:8). Developing our spiritual hearing might mean more to us than we think, especially if we do not want to miss when the last trumpet shall sound.

God is more than a leather bound book; He is a present, tangible reality! His *presence* has always been and will always be, which is why He is called the Alpha and Omega. As the supreme ruler of heaven, earth, the universe, and all things, He is Omnipresent, which means He is everywhere at once. The underground church in China experiences God's *presence* at the same time He is with a person in Chicago in a prayer closet. He is Omniscient in that He sees and hears everything and knows all deeds, all thoughts, and all knowledge. He is Omnipotent which means He is the eternal, Almighty, divine deity of all other gods and infinite in His power and authority as Lord and King of all. God's *presence* is the mercy of heaven that falls like drops of eternal love on the world. He is perfect, and the essence of His holiness demands reverent fear and respect from anyone who would even consider approaching Him. Jesus was God manifested in the flesh so that all people could see the demonstration of His Word. *What does that mean for us today?* We can now see the character and image of His person through His remnant disciples who allow Jesus to become a reflection within them! We are to be like trees whose branches are hanging loaded with whatever ministry is needed, who give protection from the wind and rain, and who provide shade for the weak that suffer from the scorching heat of trials and discouragements. However, in order to be a strong healthy tree that can be all things to all people, we need to have deep roots and receive regular nourishment! The rain and sun from heaven is absorbed within us and we flourish with His character in order to present Christ to the world. Our legacy is not about carving our names on the trunk with our accomplishments, but it is about making an impression on the hearts of those we came in contact with. It is the way we live that will be remembered more than what we said.

I was raised in a traditional Baptist church, and as I try to remember about God's presence, I can recall hearing loud inspirational messages and people saying amen, and the songs were led by a person that used hand gestures for timing. Hymns were accompanied by a pianist, and we used hymnals as our source for congregational worship songs. Sometimes a choir or an individual would sing a special song. There would be long altar calls that pleaded with people to come forward, and we would sing several verses of songs such as *"I surrender all"* at the end of each service. I can relate to these traditions because when I was fourteen years old I went down one Sunday as the altar call was being given and surrendered my life to Jesus, and I thank Him for those mercy and love filled salvation messages. I'm sure my parents made comments about the power of the Holy Spirit, the anointing and how strong God's presence was, but I cannot really remember them mentioning anything about it. I also do not remember hearing that much about miracles, but I'm sure some people were healed and delivered. God's anointing comes when someone cares enough to pray in faith, and this expectation increases our sensitivity and expands our vision for what God wants to do. For many years now I have been involved with God's presence as an active listener, and I cannot imagine stepping onto a stage without the confidence of knowing He is with me. Without encountering Jesus our programs are just a lot of hot air, but with God's presence the atmosphere becomes charged with the power and authority of heaven.

There is great joy in walking with God as a clay cup of honor that holds the priceless treasure of His living water that will never run dry. We live in-between a natural realm and a spiritual dimension both of which are constantly compelling us with the instructions to either press forward or to pull back. Each day we are challenged to discern the voices from this earthly realm that fight against us and try to hinder our advancement toward our destiny, and it is no wonder why we have difficulty hearing the one voice that really matters. We fight to deny our flesh the control and domination because we know our feelings and temptations can become enmity against God's Holy will for us if we do not allow our minds to be transformed. We want to fulfill our spiritual missions, yet we are often too weak to accomplish them, and, to be painfully honest, most of our failures can be traced to our inability to implement self-discipline. The Almighty God holds the keys that can unlock all of our obstacles, but He can intervene only as much as we let Him. Our relationship with Him is conditional upon how much of our wills we surrender. We know that we must lay down our agendas and pre-conceived plans and ideas so that He can fulfill His vision in us – but when will we do it? For this to happen there must first be a true desire to change and a sincere conviction that admits we desperately need Him ALL the time. We must pray and ask Him to give us a genuine spiritual thirst and hunger for His presence, or we will never surrender our hearts. Look around; you see people all day long that never even give Jesus a consideration in their decisions. They are so occupied with living their lives that He never crosses their minds. We can understand how the unsaved are not flowing in the Holy Spirit because they have not even connected with God yet, but what about people in the church? How can Christians assume they have everything under control and live a satisfied lifestyle of not calling on Him until they have a crisis? How sad that many who profess to be saved will gladly accept the golden ticket to heaven but do not want Jesus to interfere in their lives. This is NOT what God had in mind for us but is a twisted deception of being a victorious overcomer!

True love and unity comes when people empty themselves out and then sincerely cry out for God to fill them with His glory. When we just want God for who He is, we are willing to accept His truth no matter what it requires or how painful it will be. Spiritual maturity and passion will grow stronger as the *will* is being crushed. A room filled with lukewarm Christians who believe they can manipulate Jesus might be content with a relaxed agenda but will continue as a lethargic, ceremonial gathering and nothing more. True worship awakens, provokes, stimulates, motivates, and challenges the heart to accept God's instructions to live in radical faith, obedience, strength, and peace. For many Christians, including pastors and ministry leaders, it can be said with tears; they have settled for less because they do not want any more. How many who claim to be saved actually avoid God's presence because they know what He is demanding? Could it be possible that some who would willingly trade a personal relationship with Jesus for an empty religious lifestyle have knowingly walked away from worshipping Him forever?

Chapter 34

A STILL SMALL VOICE

Awareness is a very important part of our Christian faith and one of the most difficult to develop. We have no problem being aware of ourselves because much of the time that IS the *only* person we are considering. We might consider stretching out a little because we are curious or if it might help us somehow, but it cannot be said enough that what we all need to be aware of more than anything is the presence of Jesus. *And what does all of this have to do with worship?* I thought you would never ask. When we think about the Holy Spirit in the corporate assembly, the first thing that comes to mind is the responsibility of the senior pastor to teach the Word of God and for the worship pastor to be *led* by God to minister the carefully selected songs or possibly someone who steps forward to be used in the demonstration of one of the gifts of the Spirit. However, the still small voice of God can be heard by ANY of God's children, and all of us have the responsibility to act upon what we hear. The general congregation must realize that everyone kneels at the foot of the cross and is equally important as a working member that represents God's Kingdom and is jointly fitted together and called to minister life to each other and the world. Each member (not just the leadership) has a responsibility to speak and demonstrate what the Lord is saying for the purpose of edifying the entire body.

It is true that most of us are NOT aware that we are being watched constantly and being held accountable for our words and deeds. The more we progress in our Christian development, the more we are held to a higher standard. *Luke chapter 12* provides us a clear picture about this topic in the context of *verses 43-48* and is concluded with the statement that *"For whomsoever much is given, of him shall be much required."* Our words are a very simple but powerful act we do that REVEALS so much about us. Let's just focus on our time in church with one another and look at something very common yet extremely important. It is just as devastating to say the wrong thing - than to not say the right thing. For example, if we have an opportunity to give encouragement to someone but decide to just shrug it off, then that person can go out the door without the much needed word of hope and strength that may be so desperately needed. Maybe that person was going through a marital crisis or had been to the doctor and is waiting for test results. God could have arranged a divine appointment for us, and we denied the manifestation of the blessing because we did not want to get involved. Could we be sitting next to someone that has been considering suicide because of being unable to deal with the pain and disappointment of life? Could this service be the last hour of hope for someone? Has this possibility ever crossed our mind?

Here's another example. What if a woman was not sensitive to the clothes she wore to church and was willing to *reveal* more than her good personality? This may sound silly to some, but it is another perfect illustration of the importance of being aware that what we do and say has a direct effect on others. It is common knowledge that men are sexually stimulated with what they see, where women tend to lean toward the emotional realm, and of course we know that all humans are weak when it comes to temptations. We realize the church is a place that should be off limits to this type of scenario, but we also know there is a considerable amount of carnality in those that are still learning how to live in Christ. What if a lost man comes to church and is a candidate to hear the gospel, yet while he is there becomes distracted by people talking about what happened in the big game OR a particular female gets his attention because she decided to wear a sexy outfit that particular day? The worst case scenario would be if he entertained perverted thoughts during that church service and became so absorbed in his carnality that he walked away from the altar call and had a horrible car accident and died. What if our being critical or rude caused some to turn away from the church because they were offended? What if God told us to give someone a financial blessing, and we chose not to because we thought it did not matter, and that person went to bed hungry that night? What if we spend more time watching television than we do thinking about how we can help be a blessing to others? What if the church failed to grow and become excited because we failed to fast and pray for revival? *James 4:17* says, **"Therefore to him that knows to do good, and does not do it, to him it is sin."** Isn't that the sin of omission? How many souls are depending on people like us to be obedient to God? How much of our specific blueprint are we NOT following? Who will care enough to consider what is at stake?

I want to tell a true story that happened just a few weeks ago. A friend of mine is the pastor of a small church in a nearby town and is blessed to have a lady that is faithful in attendance. Her husband would come every now and then but seemed to keep his distance. My friend had visited the man, and he confessed that he had drifted far away from God in his life, and the cares of life had caused him to become selfish and calloused over the years. He was now 74-years-old, set in his own ways and was just floating along in his own world. On this particular Sunday morning, he and his wife came in together as they had done several times before, and nothing seemed unusual. The congregation was nice to them and everything seemed perfectly normal. My friend had been interceding for this man as the Lord had put a burden on his heart about him. The music team went through their praise and worship, and then my friend preached the message. He gave an altar call, and all of a sudden the man walked down the aisle and fell on his knees and began to cry out. People were amazed but very happy and relieved to see someone like this surrender his life before God. They all prayed with him and spent some time with him after the service. My friend said he seemed to glow with excitement, and there was a sparkle in his eyes. The very next day he had a severe stroke while driving to a café for breakfast and wrecked his vehicle. His brain was so damaged by the stroke it could not support his organ function, and as they removed the life support, he quietly passed away. It allows us to stop and think for a moment just how important it is for everything we do in the church not to be taken lightly because eternity is only a breath away.

Many different thoughts come to mind when I think of this story. Was it something that someone said? Maybe some other people told him with tears in their eyes that they had been praying for him. Maybe he felt the convicting power of agape love, and it stirred his heart. Was it a certain song that the Holy Ghost used to pierce his soul, or was it the life-changing power of God's Word that exposed his desperate need for a Lord and Savior? Whatever it was, someone was used by the Lord, and we all can agree there is no greater miracle. God is trying to prepare us as His instruments because He has so much He would love to do. He sees the future and knows each minute what is going to happen, which makes how we walk in His spirit have so many possibilities. Imagine how much more God could do in OUR lives if we were *turned on* 24 hours a day and *tuned in* to His frequency instead of all the other things we watch, listen, and give our time to. Jesus was always concerned with what His Father wanted, and likewise we need to walk and think about our Father's business and as always this includes discernment and being sensitive to the needs of others. Some may say that God will accomplish everything He wants to do whether we participate or not, but that may not be the case. If we are NOT interested in God enough to become sensitive to His voice, then how can we be used? If we do not *believe* that it is our responsibility to be a ***doer of His Word,*** how will anything be accomplished? Are we just presuming and taking for granted that He will always use someone else to do what we have been called to do? In *Matthew chapter 13* we have a disturbing true story of how much work God wants to do and how the lack of faith and obedience can prevent change. When Jesus officially began His ministry, He came into his hometown trying to teach, but the people somehow allowed their familiarity to become an offence and thus prevented them from receiving His message. *Verse 58* says, **"And he** [Jesus] **did NOT many mighty works there because of their unbelief."** The concept of victorious Christianity is to make a difference in people's lives every day, but allow me to ask a couple of questions: are we having a positive or negative effect on those in our network? Are we being aware of our accountability? Are we thinking or even concerned with what people we know might be privately facing? The degree that we will be used in the future to help rescue the perishing depends on the amount of time we spend in the place of prayer developing our spiritual sensitivity and agape love. And we will only go through all of that if we love God.

Chapter 35

THE PSALMIST

"And it came to pass, when the evil spirit from God was upon Saul, that David took a harp, and played with his hand: so Saul was REFRESHED, and was well, and the evil spirit departed from him" (I Samuel 16:23).

In the eighties, I was given several prophecies about me being a psalmist within the body of Christ. I had not written a song before this time, but one night during a revival in 1984, an evangelist in the middle of his message stopped, pointed to me, and prophesied that I would begin to write the *new song* of the Lord. My wife Cheryl and I went home that night and wondered how this was going to come about. A few weeks later, I was at work, and some words came to my spirit, and I scribbled them down on a piece of paper. When I came home, I pulled out the tattered paper, picked up my guitar, and sang the complete song as if I had known it for years. My wife reminded me about the word of prophecy, and both of us just stared at each other in amazement. This was the beginning of an interesting journey of writing and singing messages that would just come out of the blue without any effort on my part. Soon after this, an older couple in our church gave me *$1500.00* to record my first album, which was the first of many. The next year, I received a confirmation from two different prophets while I was attending a worship Symposium in Freemont, Ohio, that I was NOT just a lyricist but would be required to WALK OUT every word that was given to me. This has also proved true, as it has been some *hard walking* through, experiencing the discipline, demands, and penetrating truths of the rigid standards that Jesus is calling all of us to live by. I have received several other miracle financial blessings throughout my ministry for recording projects and one even included a brand new Martin D-35 guitar, but the most sobering part of this testimony is that included with these miracles there has been an anointing on the music that is difficult to understand but can be sensed with the perceptive heart. My wife has said that late at night when the house is quiet and I am singing these songs back to the Lord, there is a tangible peace and presence of God that fills the house. The fragrance of heaven is given from Him as He gives His gifts and then cycled back to Him as we give Him worship and glory to His Name forever.

There are many different ideas and interpretations of musical gifts of prophecy, song writing, and spiritual mantles of leading worship. In our modern world of organized church assemblies there are levels of understanding that are directly connected with a pastor's theology concerning the manifestation of musical gifts. This in turn has a serious impact on the extent God is able to become involved with "His" ministry in the corporate service and how the people learn to respond to the Holy Spirit. There have been many times that I have written songs before the service, and they have perfectly corresponded with the sermon as a spiritual confirmation of God's thoughts and desires. One of the most widely known and respected Psalmists of all time was King David. Many studies have been done on his life, and all clearly reveal that he was a child of destiny. He had a strong anointing on him as a young lad and was as fearless as he was gifted. He was a man after God's own heart, and God loved him and walked with him in his greatest victories and through his failures. Along with several Old Testament books that reveal much of David's life as a warrior and King, the book of Psalms highlights him as a gifted musician and Spirit-led song writer of at least 74 of the 150 Psalms. The book of Psalms also reveals several other highly skilled musicians, singers, and anointed psalmists such as Asaph, Jeduthun, Neginoth, Muthlabben, the sons of Korah, Solomon, and Ethan.

The different musical styles of churches fall anywhere between not having instruments at all or only singing hymns, to complete orchestras and full contemporary prophetic worship bands. Some traditional churches may have only an organ or piano, but hopefully all respect music as not only a vehicle to receiving the promises and commands *from* God but also for all saints to release praise and thanksgiving back *to* God. Assemblies that do not recognize the prophetic ministries are missing a very important aspect of the spiritual communication between God and His people as a vital link to how the Lord desires to touch and minister in the hearts of His children. A Psalmist is usually defined as a person who writes sacred songs. This particular gift moves in the prophetic music realm and is practiced by a sensitive and anointed person that has keen discernment and creative talent to receive and relay revelation from God to the listener. These people most often play an instrument and are given songs from the Lord that flow with their instrument and vocals in a unique way. They are not practicing, training, or trying to learn how to be a psalmist – they are selected by the Father to function in this capacity. A Psalmist is just like any other person that has been given a spiritual gift, and we are reminded that individuals cannot choose their gift, but every calling is a part of each person's specific mission. Every child of God has been chosen and given the anointing to be used as a unique prophetic *channel* for God to flow through just as all the other gifts and offices within the body of Christ.

Separating songwriting into categories is difficult because most people never think much about it, but one thing everyone can agree on; music moves the soul. Lyrics are like poems that are set to musical melodies, and spiritual music can bring identification to certain belief systems. Christian music is dominantly about Christ, His Word, and the Christian life, but sometimes can be more specific with doctrinal subjects and personal interpretations. Most Christians refer to songs that are not about God or His Kingdom as secular, worldly, carnal, fleshly, sensual, heathen, humanistic, or corrupt, but it can be dogmatic to believe that all music outside of the church environment is bad. Some songs are light and innocent and can actually cause the emotions to be uplifted with happiness, encouragement, and a sense of well-being. Other songs can be serious and intense as they passionately tell true stories like a seamstress at her spinning wheel or a ship that went down, yet without necessarily being evil. Of course we all know that Satan has influenced millions of people around the world with negative brands of his dark musical poison that he has intentionally perverted into a destructive weapon. He also realizes the power of music that has close ties with the soul and loves to entertain the masses with mirages that sparkle and promise satisfaction only to be revealed in the end as illusions of death and ruin. The bottom line is that music is a vehicle that contains a dynamic that can stir the emotions to violence and self-destruction or spiritually calm the savage beast. When God is in the music, He can minister His rest and bring healing to the hearts that are hurting, and this is the type of music we need much more of.

The Psalmists were (and are) writers of musical messages that contain spiritual illumination. These communications are a direct link from the Holy Spirit that challenges and provokes the hearer to listen deeply with the spiritual ear of the heart because hidden within the music are the mysteries that reveal the mind and character of God. The Bible says in *Revelation 3:22*, **"He that hath an ear** [is sensitive and in tune with the Holy Spirit] **let him hear what the SPIRIT has to say to the churches."** The key to listening has a great deal to do with *desiring* to hear, *disciplining* our flesh, and *delighting* ourselves with His holy instructions. It is common for the Psalmist to minister songs that are written in first person because many times they will relay the message just as the psalmists heard the Lord say it to them. Many of the songs I have written are about commitment, holiness, purity, sacrifice, and surrendering our wills, and we should not be afraid or intimidated to deliver these messages but pray for strength and faith that we may obey what we have been told. I have ministered in many churches and small groups over the years and thought that people would enjoy these spiritual communications, only to realize that God's Word is razor sharp and was piercing the comfort zones and secret places that people did not want to deal with. For a long time I was confused and felt rejected, but now I can see more clearly how the conviction of God's Word brings frustration, silence, rebellion, guilt, anger, sorrow, and a mixture of emotions that causes all of us to examine and ponder what we will do with what we have heard. Here is one of those first-person songs that have always been a soothing personal message of comfort that reminds me that God cares and loves us so much. The Lord gave this message to me on December 23rd, 1985, and it is called, *"Healer of the broken heart."*

> *(Verse 1) My child, your heart is broken*
> *You think that nobody knows, how you feel inside*
> *But my child, have you forgotten*
> *That no matter how far you run, there's no place to hide*

(Chorus) I am the healer of the broken heart
I'll bind up all your wounds, I'll never leave, I will always be there
Let me break the chains that hold you captive
So that you can have a brand new start
Come unto me, I am a healer of the broken heart

(Verse 2) I bore your griefs and your sorrows; I feel your hurt and pain
You've carried those burdens far too long
I'll more than heal your body; I will heal you through and through
Cause being free is where you belong – and I want you to know that

(Chorus) I am the healer of the broken heart
I'll bind up all your wounds, I'll never leave, I will always be there
Let me break the chains that hold you captive
So that you can have a brand new start
Come unto me, I am a healer of the broken heart

Psalmists are sensitive individuals and can keenly pick up on ideas and thoughts and learn to write down their musical messages and relay them back to God in the secret place of meditation. It is very common for psalmists to play and sing in tears as they serenade their love to an audience of one. It is not uncommon for these *thinking* emotional personalities to feel isolated and conclude that only a few can understand or relate to their interpretations of spiritual views, dreams, and visions. This mantle is more than a natural talent of skill and cleverness because their ability to minister in the anointing is originating from the dimension of the Spirit. Psalmists feel protective of what they have received, as they believe they have been given something that is very serious and consider it holy. They hesitate to play their music just anywhere but rather desire to share it with those who sincerely want to hear spiritual mysteries and connect with the mind and presence of God. They feel that only a few can interpret the meaning and do not feel the need to perform or the entertainment aspect. Non- Christians and carnal saints who live in the outer courts will avoid the ministry of the psalmist (run the other way) because they sense God trying to intervene and knock on the door of their consciences, and of course none of us really like the idea of a burning altar and God calling us to lie down on it. In this light, the psalmist is like a musical prophet that declares the specific message from the Lord without trying to soften or compromise the meaning. If you have this calling and are not being welcomed by the masses – do not be discouraged. Stay in the spirit of prayer, protect your messages, and trust that God will use you to relay His engrafted Word to touch the hearts of those He has prepared.

The spontaneous Song of the Lord is a beautiful, special gift of musical prophecy that should be a precious asset in our corporate meetings but unfortunately has nearly become extinct. We hear an occasional tongue and interpretation and maybe (every now and then) a word of knowledge or a word of wisdom, but many have never heard the spontaneous song of the Lord manifested. It is delivered in the same manner as the other vocal utterances in a "thus sayeth the Lord" type of message, except it has a musical melody. It is more likely that you will see this spiritual phenomenon within the environment of the Charismatics, Full-Gospel and Pentecostals, because they highly regard praise and worship in their services and are more free and open to the voice gifts and all forms of musical expression. Let us not forget that it is a beautiful although rare expression of musical prophecy when sermons are sung instead of being spoken. The anointing within these special times of communicating can be charged with Holy Ghost power. Generally speaking, the traditional churches intentionally do NOT make room for the unorthodox in their services for these messengers of the divine. Man-made creeds and doctrines establish rules that limit how the style and personality of the church should be when it comes to the congregation speaking to God and allowing Him the opportunity to speak and minister back to the people through His Spirit.

This musical gift is different from *singing in the spirit* which is also instinctive but is simply expressing our feelings to the Lord and worshipping Him in our own words without preparing ahead. Singing in the Spirit is an outward, holy, connection between our spirits and God's Spirit and is a beautiful accompaniment to our written worship songs, but again must be given the time and space to evolve and come forth. The worship team must prepare the way with times of instrumental interludes that create the environment for the freedom of spontaneous worship. If no room is given, it is insulting to the Holy Spirit and quenches the intensity of God's intervention. The same is true when we are learning to pause and wait on the Lord for the manifestation of what He wants to do. Worship that is technically *cut and dried* leaves no window for adding or extending the songs that can drift into more spiritual liberty and opportunity. The only thing needed to open the door to this heavenly sound is for the musicians to softly repeat a few chords and for the people to clear their minds of this world's distractions and focus on the Lord Himself.

When worship has brought us to the entrance to the Holy of Holies, and God's presence is heavy in the atmosphere, it is crucial to proceed with extreme sensitivity. There must be an awareness to pause that gives the Lord an opportunity to speak. If the service is cut off because of man's need to continue with his agenda, God will step back and not intrude. The Lord is always knocking but will not force Himself where He is not welcome. This gift ventures into the prophetic realm of messages to God's people that includes warnings, corrections, edifications, promises, exposing secrets, giving directions, confirmations, encouragement, hope, comfort, and declaring visions of spiritual symbolism. This *new song* will usually arise from the stillness and tranquility in worship but can manifest wherever saints are meditating in God's presence and thirsty to hear from the Lord. It does not need music to manifest and can effectively be released acappella into the atmosphere when the divine appointment appears. God knows the perfect place and time for all of His gifts to be released, and it is up to all of us to walk close to Him so that we might be ready when He calls. The manifestation of prophecy, with music or without, is a sign and wonder that builds confidence through obedience in the one that releases it and encouragement through faith in those who have an ear to hear it.

Worship is a journey that begins at the gates of thanksgiving and proceeds through a series of life-changing levels and experiences. Each section of the tabernacle of Moses and each piece of furniture is filled with powerful symbolism that reveals how much God loves us and what He has done for us. Our entire Christian journey is seen through this holy blueprint that exposes the levels of our commitment, dedication, and love for Him, along with His requirements and expectations from us. Our spiritual understanding is beautifully laid out in this type and shadow as it continues all the way to the mercy seat where we stand face to face in the glory of His presence. When worship has brought us to the entrance of the Holy of Holies and God's aura has flooded the atmosphere, it is crucial to proceed with extreme sensitivity. Let us prepare our hearts to release God's revelations and prophecies. May we dream to step out into His anointing and go beyond the written lyrics, notes, and arrangements with joy and excitement! Venture out in "free-worship" and sing in the Spirit! Learn how to tell Him in your own words the way you feel about Him with songs that have never been sung before, expressions from the deep inner chambers of your soul, and let us experience the freedom and joy of true worship.

I believe it is very possible that Mary sang the Magnificat as a spontaneous song unto the Lord. Individuals that have the *blessing* of being used in any type of prophetic vocal or musical gift, operate under the anointing of the Holy Spirit. Just as the words of wisdom and knowledge, and of tongues and interpretations, are used to communicate God's instructions to the body, the musical prophet is included in the *family* of vocal prophecy gifts. The heavenly melodies and the arrangement of words and rhythms are used by the Spirit to pierce the conscience and bring healing, edification, correction, and deliverance to the souls of those who have an ear to hear. This is far beyond the natural senses of emotion but rather comes from the omniscience of an all-knowing, all-seeing, divine deity that understands individuals' hearts and what they need to hear at that moment. It is a *Rhema* word that is used as a confirmation of the spoken word and a supernatural manifestation that will build faith and strength. Spiritual music connects God with His creation and builds the bridge of a deeper more intimate fellowship. Musical prophecy is a vital gift that is for the edification and encouragement of all.

The devil knows all about *spiritual* music because as Lucifer he led worship in heaven and is evidently quite gifted and experienced. Since he is an expert musician and singer, he has learned much about human nature and how to manipulate music style to fit the desires of the generations. He understands how arrogance and pride can ruin a person's heart. He comprehends how music is connected with our lusts and desires for power, and how subtle music can be in influencing the soul. We have heard of familiar spirits, and this is one way Satan can manipulate and control human emotion. The dark side of music can bring depression and establish defeat by compelling the listener to confess negativity and dwell on emptiness. Our words create our destiny, and the devil uses deception to get people to *sing along* to songs that are filled with the declaration of death and destruction. Amen! Much of the world's music is naturally filled with lies, lust, and hopelessness because it is coming from a doomed kingdom whose agenda is to kill, steal, and destroy. When we allow our senses to drink in the subtle messages of humanism and carnality, these seeds begin to grow, and we begin to evolve into what we are thinking and saying. We must guard our ears and eyes to prevent us being transformed by the relentless pollution of our minds and realize that fleshly music is not just harmless entertainment but a spiritual danger. Be careful with the little catchy tunes that get stuck in your head that tempt you to keep confessing them over and over. Poison can be made to taste sweet if enough sugar is poured into it.

Many times the spontaneous song of the Lord will arise from the stillness and tranquility of worship. It does not need music to manifest and can be released into the atmosphere when the divine appointment appears. God knows the perfect place and time for all gifts, and it is up to all of us to walk close to Him so that we might be ready when He calls. The manifestation of prophecy with or without music is a sign and wonder that builds obedience in the giver and faith in the hearer. Years ago I remember going to a worship symposium, and I witnessed the flow of the prophetic songs of the Holy Spirit as they were being birthed within the worship. In this scenario the worship team must prepare the way with times of instrumental interludes that create the environment for the spontaneous. If no room is given, there will be no room for the gift. If there is no desire for the gift or a decision to not allow the gift, naturally there is little hope for the manifestation. The same is true when learning to pause and wait on the Lord for the manifestation of the other vocal gifts. Worship is a journey that begins at the gates of thanksgiving and proceeds through the tabernacle, the furniture, and should continue all the way to the mercy seat. When worship has come to the Holy of Holies and God's presence is heavy in the atmosphere, it is crucial to proceed with extreme sensitivity. How can the Lord step forward when we do not allow Him the window of freedom? If the service becomes a generic *"machine"* because of man's need to continue with his agenda, God will step back and NOT interrupt where He is not welcome. How many churches have enjoyed the beautiful buildings, the strict organization, the intellectual agendas and professional programs while leaving God to sit on the front porch to wait until they are finished?

There is a huge difference between a song leader and those who are worship leaders, because the song leader is thinking only about the song while the worship leader is listening and waiting for prophecy. Just because someone has the natural ability to lead songs does not mean he is a called worship leader. The same is true with someone who enjoys singing and someone that is called to sing. The worship leaders will usually have the anointing to weave God's word within the music. They can exhort the people with whatever God gives them to say in the form of spoken words or spontaneous song. The beauty of free worship is also used very effectively when the words are allowed to come and be incorporated into a series of chord patterns. Sometimes a song can continue with just the chords being played which opens the door for new words. Worship should be a joyful conversation with God, and as free and sincere whether we are walking along the Ocean, chopping wood, or in the secret place of our prayer closet. Of course the type of church and the theological views will dictate the liberty of worship, but the Lord will help lead all of His people to find their perfect place in His Kingdom.

Pastors that are open to the gifts of the Holy Spirit and are hungry for the supernatural signs, wonders, and miracles of God's power will provide a more welcoming atmosphere for the Lord to manifest His glory. This invitation will provide a safe haven and favorable environment for those that love God's presence and flow in the gifts of the Spirit. All laborers who work in the Kingdom need encouragement and a freedom to develop and mature in what God has given to them. ***"Now there are diversities of gifts, but the same Spirit. And there are differences of administrations, but the same Lord. And there are diversities of operations, but it is the same God which worketh all in all. But the manifestation of the Spirit is given to every man to profit withal"*** *(I Corinthians 12:4-7)*. Just like every other gift, the purpose of musical prophecy is to simply edify and build up the body and to bring glory and honor to the name of Jesus Christ. It is important to remember that we are not to rush or put time restraints on God's service. It is HIS service! When we sincerely desire for Him to take over our time together, then we must wait and respect how He wants to move. The churches would never admit it but planning everything around the flesh is actually telling God that we do not need Him. He recognizes this as us saying that we can control this on our own and for Him to go away and come back when we are finished, and by the way Lord, please bless what we are doing.

PART VI

THE AWARENESS OF HIS MERCY

Chapter 36

INTENTIONS OF THE HEART

Life seems to be judged not by what we do but the spirit in which it is done. The same goes for those who try to appear religious by doing good deeds, like being generous, or who think speaking loudly means that someone is being sincere or directed by God. I believe we can say that many times religious acts are done with the purpose of trying to ease the conscience or just wanting to be seen. For example, just because people can sing or play instruments, does not mean they are always spiritually connected with what they are singing or even thinking about God at all. It might just be an opportunity to perform so that everyone can see how talented they are or because they are making a salary. Others might make it a point to brag about how much money they give in the offering because they want the power, popularity, recognition, favor, and glory that goes along with authority and control. Let's keep in mind that just because individuals are gifted in a certain area or have an impressive resume, it does not prove they are automatically the best choice to be used in a specific church ministry. There could be several factors to consider such as timing, attitude, sensitivity, maturity, and availability, just to name a few. It is the motives and intentions of the heart that will reveal why they want to be involved and if they are ready to not only step into the position but have the anointing and humility to be effective.

What about those who strive to be a board member, elder, or deacon, not because they want to serve God's people but because they love to be in control? Here is a another one; the Bible mentions some individuals who love to pray long prayers in public because they are just putting on a religious *show* to demonstrate how wise and knowledgeable they are. May we listen to these words from Christ about how motives are the foundations of our deeds: *"Take heed that you do not your alms before men, to be seen of them: otherwise you have no reward of your Father which is in heaven. Therefore when thou doest thine alms do not sound a trumpet before thee, as the hypocrites do in the synagogues and in the streets, that they may have glory of men. Verily I say unto you, they have their reward. But when you give, let not your left hand know what your right hand is doing: That your alms may be in secret: and your Father which sees in secret himself shall reward you openly. And when you pray, thou shalt not be as the hypocrites are: for they love to pray standing in the synagogues and in the corners of the streets, that they may be seen of men. Verily I say unto you, they have their reward"* (Matthew 6:1-5). And let us not forget *verse 7, "But when you pray, use not vain repetitions, as the heathen do: for they think that they will be heard for their much speaking."* As a standard rule to consider, it is not who, what, or how much – but why.

Unfortunately many church members limit their personal worship experience to singing a few songs in a corporate assembly each week and are content to *visit* God in His house. This concept has been an enemy to the Christian faith since the beginning. *Why?* It seems that many have not comprehended that going somewhere to be with Him cannot be compared with having Him live within us. These outer court participants consider themselves faithful by setting aside a couple of hours each week to associate themselves with others within a social organization and attend a religious program that in their own mind has earned them another ribbon of righteousness. I am not against the idea of going to church; however, if this is the extent of some individuals' personal spiritual development, it becomes a concern that they have missed the point of what church and the Christian life is all about. The assembly is not our life, but rather helps us understand the awareness of God's presence and how to incorporate Christ into every part of our life. The objective is to obtain a revelation of Jesus as the LORD of our hearts and not just a historical account of Him as another Bible character. We are not to completely plan our daily agendas and then try to *squeeze* Him into our schedule, but rather we place Him at the center of everything, and learn to filter everything through Him. This is the lifestyle of a remnant disciple, and since God knows the thoughts of every person, our intentions that are associated with our actions will be the evidence of our current and future judgment. *"And that, knowing the time, that now it is high time to awake out of sleep: for now is our salvation nearer than when we believed. The night is far spent, the day is at hand: let us therefore cast off the works of darkness, and let us put on the armor of light"* (Romans 13:11-12).

I believe many people wear a mask in church (and life in general) because it is a defense mechanism to protect what they are trying to hide. We learn at a very early stage in life that it is easy to appear to be something we are not because no other human really knows what we are thinking. We learn how to adapt and say the right things as a form of deceptive manipulation while being able to conceal our true attitudes and feelings. For example, why do seemingly innocent children choose to lie? Because when they learn that negative activity results in serious consequences, their consciences develop a built in escape hatch that causes the human brain to create quick thinking along with many clever disguises to avoid punishment. *What does this have to do with worship?* When we have the honor to be in the presence of God, we discover it is a place of honesty and purity and not the time to think that maybe we can get away from something. We are not as clever as we think and certainly are not fooling God. The Lord can see our hearts as clear as crystal, and if we continue to convince ourselves that halfway clean is good enough or partial sincerity will be sufficient, we will be confined to remain in the outer courts of His presence or worse. When individuals see life as a game, they fail to realize how the deception they use on everyone else is also the very same spirit of lies and manipulation that is being used against them and influencing their consciences to live a distorted, generic existence. The devil has come to steal, kill, and destroy everything he can and hopes to betray us right in front of our noses without us even noticing it. Deception believes we are a certain way while NOT realizing we are actually something else.

Going through the motions of religion has never impressed God. *"Because you say, I am rich and increased with goods and have need of nothing; but you do not see that you are actually wretched, and miserable, and poor, and blind, and naked: I counsel you to buy of me gold tried in the fire so you may be rich; and white raiment that you might be clothed and that the shame of your nakedness will not appear; and anoint your eyes with eye medicine, that you may see"* (Revelation 3:17-18). The need for genuine transparency is crucial in our spiritual understanding of who we are and who God is. What kind of relationship can we have (with anyone) if we are not honest? If we cannot perceive the truth about the way we are, then how can we see God the way He is and worship Him in Spirit and *TRUTH?* If we cannot understand the reality about our spiritual condition and are NOT walking in the awareness of His presence, then we are not on the same page with God at all, and our worship is in vain. Understanding the Lord is all about recognizing His requirements to be holy, and those who are His followers will not just pretend to be consecrated, they will practice what they preach!

What is happening to sanctification? Somehow the idea that it does not matter what the condition of our hearts is when we worship the Lord, has leaked into our religious world views and philosophies. The enemy has quietly crept into the field at night and sown tares of false doctrines into our spiritual thinking because he knows the more we flood our senses with the voices and images of the spirit of this age, the more we can argue and justify carnality within our consciences. Minds and hearts that are filled with lust, anger, lying, perversion, resentment, envy, hate, and witchcraft cannot find virtue and the peace of God, which is the foundation of spiritual worship. The new-age, seeker-sensitive church culture is turning more to entertainment and the feel-good experience that artificially soothes the troubled conscience while resisting and avoiding the power of God's Word that produces true holiness. The chaos and confusion of a heart influenced by demonic suggestion and the carnal desires of undisciplined emotions cannot worship God in Spirit and Truth. Repentance is becoming an archaic word that is considered irrelevant to the science of modern religious thought and is being abandoned because it opposes the humanistic theories of social freedom. Jesus confirms the importance of repentance from the Old Testament and strongly emphasizes the continual process of asking for forgiveness and being cleansed from sin in the New Testament. The church must not tolerate blatant rebellion if it is to preserve its integrity, or be intimidated to keep from confronting the powers of darkness. It is our responsibility to develop our spiritual discernment and have the courage to deal with whatever tries to disrupt or discredit the body! If we become afraid to address situations that could damage the cause of Christ, then we have become guilty by association! Jesus is enough to satisfy our thirst for fulfillment, contentment, and peace, and we are NOT to compromise our purity and sanctification in order to appear more lenient or lower our standards just so the world can feel more at ease. Many have rejected Him as their source and have turned their attentions for a different *flavor* of water, instead of allowing His Word to encourage and empower their spirits. Some are trading the message of abandoning the will for constructing a comfortable belief system with *strange fire* and the carnal attractions of the world. MAN SAYS - if we do a certain number of deeds that God will accept them no matter what our motives are. GOD SAYS - He will reward only those things that are done in the right way with the right reason!

Those who have willingly adopted a double-minded attitude about the Lord's will have become infected with a lethargic and relaxed way of living which opens the door for the lust of the flesh to make decisions by controlling the thoughts. *Are churches automatically exempt?* No. This hypocritical way of living has put much of the church into an induced coma, but all hope is NOT lost! Anyone who is serious about dropping the nets and following Jesus can turn around and become a new person today! In His power, any of us can become true, honest, holy, and pure if we make the decision to give Christ complete control and allow Him to refine us into pure gold! Those who are serious about allowing God to change them, know they must begin with God's living Word which is His general will, and then progress into discovering their personal destiny which is God's specific will. Spending time with Him each day and absorbing His spiritual anti-biotic within our minds will cure our infection of rebellion and transform our hearts, heal our minds, and fill our spirits with His nature and character. ***"For the Word of God is quick, and powerful, and sharper than any two edged sword, piercing even to the dividing asunder of soul and spirit, and of the joints and marrow, and is a discerner of the thoughts and INTENTS of the heart"*** *(Hebrews 4:12)*. God's Word transforms our minds and consciences along with our attitudes and motives with a physical, mental, emotional, and spiritual Holy Ghost revival! What percent of our lives do we want to dedicate to Him? Fifty percent? He wants ALL of us and is waiting for us to want ALL of Him. Be careful about following the crowds; if no one else wants to go, do not let that stop you from following Jesus. It simply comes down to what we decide is most important. When this song came to me, it was as if the Lord was having a conversation with me, so I wrote it like I heard it. On July 18, 1984, I sat down at the kitchen table with a pencil and paper and scribbled it down in just a few minutes. I picked up my guitar and played it like I had known it for years: *"Intentions of the heart."*

> *(Verse 1) There is nothing you can do; there is no where you can go*
> *There's nowhere that I cannot see, my eyes run to and fro*
> *You can pull your shades and lock your doors*
> *You can think the thoughts that no one else will know*
> *You may deceive the world, and even yourself*
> *But I'm the only one who really knows*
>
> *(Chorus) It's the intentions of the heart, I know the price*
> *It's not how much you're offering, but it's the sacrifice*
> *I know you better than you know yourself,*
> *But you let your games keep us apart*
> *I know the reasons why you do the things you do*
> *I know the intentions of your heart*
>
> *(Verse 2) Someday your heart will be opened, and laid out before my throne*
> *Your works good and bad will all be judged*
> *The hay and stubble from the gold and precious stones*
> *But Lord, look at all I've done for you*
> *You know I've given more than all the rest*
> *My son my words will forever be true*
> *More is not always the best*
>
> *(Chorus) It's the intentions of the heart, I know the price*
> *It's not how much you're offering, but it's the sacrifice*
> *I know you better than you know yourself,*
> *But you let your games keep us apart*
> *I know the reasons why you do the things you do*
> *I know the intentions of your heart*
>
> *I know the reasons why you do the things you do*
> *I know the intentions of your heart*

Chapter 37

THE SECRET PLACE

"He that dwelleth in the SECRET PLACE of the most high shall abide under the shadow of the Almighty" (Psalm 91:1).

What *is the secret place?* It is not a geographic location but rather a place from another dimension. The inner-most chambers of the heart and soul is a place where God and man fellowship and is the most precious sanctuary in this realm. God has come to dwell within the conscience of His creation and enjoys living in the constant communion of love and relationship. This *secret place* is where we learn the lifestyle of worship and how to live in the awareness of His presence. What we learn in the private when we are alone with Him molds us into what we are when we are walking in our daily lives. For those of us who desire to go deeper with God, we will realize the most important aspect of our thoughts and deeds must be based on the Holy Spirit leading us and moving through us, and this is learned in the secret place. *"But whoso hearkeneth unto Me shall dwell safely, and shall be quiet from fear of evil" (Proverbs 1:33).*

We know that God does NOT move in just one specific type of denomination as there are times when God moves in Baptist and Methodist churches, and there are times when He moves in Holiness and Pentecostal churches even though they might be a little different. These groups have wonderful intentions, but His focus is to be evident in the lives of those who follow Him! Personal obedience has everything to do with the level of God's presence, not what we call ourselves or a name over the door as some believe. If we stop and think about it, God favors obedience, but the confusion is about who knows His will. If all of God's people would spend more time in the secret place, the chasm of disagreement would become smaller.

In our spiritual relationship with God we are led by the Holy Spirit and listen as He guides us into truth. Likewise, in the corporate assembly the pastor has been given the mantle of leadership to help guide the service under the direction of the Lord along with the contributions from the body. I believe it is purity and sincerity that God recognizes in the hearts of His children that causes Him to want to fellowship and bless those who desire His presence. The ones who cry out in the secret place to be filled with His glory are the same ones that will be more serious about Him in the corporate assembly and in their everyday lives. The ones who choose to INVITE Him to lead their services and that desire to be obedient to His Spirit reveal how much they really want Him there by the way they live. We can say many things with our lips like, *God is welcome in our midst,* but the words are a contradiction when we refuse to let go of our control. We can shout about freedom and how we are yielding to His Spirit, but if our agenda (in the church and our daily affairs) becomes more important than what He is saying, then our failure to relinquish has limited and hindered Him from doing what He wanted to do. You see, He is the only one that should have an agenda and our desire should be to follow it! Amen! It is fine for us to have an organized program as long as it goes along with His plans because then we are working with Him instead of wanting Him to work with us. This is confirmed when there is a strong anointing along with the manifestation of His power and glory.

Whatever we pursue with the energy and devotion of our strength will be found as the object of our emotional and spiritual praise. If Christ is found seated on the throne of our hearts as Lord and Master of our lives, then He alone will be the focus and adoration of our deepest intimacy. When this genuine love for God is found in the spirit of humility, there is nothing that will hinder the external release of thanksgiving and exaltation unto Him. We will boldly stand with courage and joy as we proclaim that He is the only one that has ever or will ever be Praised! The remnant disciple that lives in a conscious state of seriousness about the Lord discovers through time that maturing in Christ is a process. The phases and levels of learning to know God along with the complexity of human behavior can hardly be grasped by the young novice. Our spiritual journey can be seen as a unique road map that is intended to lead and guide everyone to a specific destination, and this entire process is all about growing deeper in our faith, hope, and love relationship with Him. Allow me to give a warning while traveling down this interstate—that blessings and refreshments can be found in the occasional *rest areas,* but we must avoid the temptation to build our homes and live there. It's all right to take a breather, but this personalized guide has a step-by-step route that leads to a designated objective, and we need to keep moving forward! We also might be directed every so often to take side roads and exits that are uncomfortable and will lead us to visit strange places, but as we have said before, our mission is a customized calling and every journey will require spending much time in the place of prayer and listening carefully for divine appointments, which should be the highlight of our journey.

As God uses the expression of being filled with His Spirit, He is trying to explain that our hearts are like containers where there is no limit to how much we can absorb of Him, and this encouragement to continue *being filled* also allows us to notice that possibly we can LEAK and lose some of His presence or drift away if we do not *maintain* this ongoing process. In this light we can see how crucial it is not only to press toward the mark of becoming filled with Him – but also to STAY filled. **"And be not drunk with wine, wherein is excess; but be FILLED with the Spirit; Speaking to yourselves in psalms and hymns and spiritual songs, singing and making melody in your heart to the Lord; Giving thanks always for all things unto God and the Father in the name of our Lord Jesus Christ; Submitting yourselves one to another in the fear of God"** *(Ephesians 5: 18-21).* This passage begins with comparing alcohol consumption and feelings of intoxication with the overwhelming spiritual joy that comes from being saturated in God's presence. Paul, the author, goes on to reveal the secrets of how we can encourage ourselves by confessing God's Word out loud as a form of worshipping Him in Spirit and truth. We notice that he is trying to explain that we do not need to wait on someone else to sing or preach – we must take the initiative to approach God on our own. *Why?* Because our relationship is not based on a corporate meeting or actually anyone else, it is developed within the intimacy of personal adoration and determined obedience. Without this direct accountability with Him we will not be fully engaged with Him, and without His anointing and power, He is NOT able to use us to accomplish His will! Paul concludes with the importance of being grateful to Christ which is directly *attached* to a humble appreciation and meek attitude that allows us to be submissive not only to the Father but also to one another in the reverential fear of God. All of this (which is the heart of Christian living) can happen only when we desire to see there is more to life than ourselves. We do not have to get dressed or go anywhere, spend money or announce it in the newspaper, to spend time quietly alone with Jesus – we just need to decide if we really want to be there.

There is nothing wrong with examining what we are doing, how we are doing it, and making sure we are delivering His ministry the way He desires for us to present it. I realize that many will respond and say, *"This is the way I've always been, and I do not need to change anything."* But this may not be as much about changing style as it is about allowing God to breathe LIFE into our work. When we can function only within a certain style, there may be more of a connection to the style than to God Himself. Is being spiritually passionate really a tradition or style? or is it an overflow from a heart that has been to the mountain and spent time with God? We are living in the last hours before Jesus returns, and now is NOT the time to serve leftovers or just go through the motions! God's remnant disciples are thirsty for His presence and want to be free in His Spirit and will search until they find it! I have heard people say that worship is personal and we do not need to practice it where everyone can see, but do you think in heaven we will all go into our mansions and worship privately? Anyone that has true joy is always ready to *explode* with an outward display of gratitude because they cannot CONTAIN their love for God! Amen! If emotions can be manifested with crying when something makes us sad in the world or laughing when we are happy, then why can't people release joy and praise to the Lord? And for those who claim to have a quiet-natured personality, please do not tell me you are quiet when your favorite team scores or how low-key you would be if you found a buried treasure. Whatever means the most to us is where we give our highest attention and express our strongest emotions. We must include with this topic of dedication the idea that when we are NOT sold-out to something, we can easily be talked out of it, which leads us to wonder why there were only a handful of followers at Golgotha. Jesus healed, fed, and preached to thousands during His ministry. Were they embarrassed? Did they think more of their integrity than of openly supporting their Lord? If we are lukewarm in our interest for the things of God and are not burdened for souls, it could mean that we are sharing our enthusiasm with something or someone else. Maybe we are afraid that others will think we have lost our ability to reason. Walking in God's presence is our highest treasure, and He will not share His glory with anything else - including how highly we think of ourselves.

You would NOT think that front-line warriors could become infected with a spirit of slumber in the ministry, but it can and does happen. We have heard the illustration of how standing water can become stagnant, versus the freshness of a moving stream, and if you have been around the church world for a while, you can look around and see how easily the congregation can become relaxed and satisfied. We can package the church in many different containers, but it is the content of covenant truth that must remain the same. Knowing when to do things differently is important to effectively meet the needs of the people and help them stay enthused for new spiritual growth. If we sing the same songs and teach the same message every time, it will become boring, and result in a dry, packaged, sleepy atmosphere. It is true that many churches need spiritual CPR to *revive* them; however, a PERSONAL revival is the only thing that will make a difference! The most important part of our calling is not only telling others how much God loves them, but also proving how much we love them! People must know that a true Christian will sincerely walk across town to help them, and this level of concern and sincerity allows them to see the love of Jesus in us. If we are so busy with our lives that we project the vibes that we do not really care about them, it is time to start over or let someone else be the leader. It is very discouraging when we realize that a facilitator of God's Kingdom is more concerned with developing the success of a personal ministry than loving the people. A true servant is focused on the Great Shepherd and His sheep!

A wonderful approach to understanding church authority and governmental leadership is to stop thinking that only one or two people are to provide the entire ministry. Pastors need to mentor other ministers and let them exercise their gifts to bring variety and balance into the mix. It is vitally important to develop more leaders that can expand our innovations and inspirations to spread the gospel. Let us encourage singers and musicians to minister special music or do special concerts. We can encourage individuals and help them become teachers, counselors, evangelists, pastors, love teams, youth leaders, and children's directors. It is especially the pastor's responsibility to create an atmosphere of *vision* along with accountability and responsibility that can develop maturity and enthusiasm. Each of us has a special gift, and as a brick is laid into a wall, our contribution is equally important and needed within the local church. We can have guest speakers and invite effective ministries to generate excitement so the congregation might be stimulated and inspired to discard their comfortable rut of doing things the same old way. We can fall into a habit of leaning on our traditional, religious routine of going through the motions and become satisfied with mediocrity if we do not take the initiative to occasionally back away and receive a fresh perspective. Pastors that ignore when the Holy Spirit is trying to get their attention and continue being stubborn, doing things their own way, will live in the disappointment of deadness. There are times when God may call the ones who are serious about the Spirit filled life to pray and fast for the church and intercede for the people to repent and allow God to re-light His candlestick within the assembly. If the leadership continues to ignore the Lord's beckoning for change and has decided it will NOT allow Him to have His way, then those who are NOT being spiritually satisfied may be released to find the nourishment they need.

When we read about the great revivals, we discover the anointing was IGNITED with intercession and fasting, which is done in the secret place of spiritual intimacy. The devil is not alarmed with us bragging about how filled with God's Spirit we are. Satan does not care how large the offerings are or is not worried in the least just because a new church building is built or even if it is filled to standing room only. Our carnal natures say that an hour on Sunday is plenty because we have more important things to do! Do you see your relationship with Jesus like punching a time clock? Will you take control over your will and allow Christ to renew your mind so that your life can be re-prioritized? Or will you continue talking about prayer and worship in the secret place as a very noble idea but never actually become personally engaged with it? Learning how to love God comes from wanting to live with Him. This is the sacrificial path that demands total surrender and also contains the splendor and glory of a love that cannot be measured. Spending time with God is calling us but it seems there is a *force-field* around it that does NOT want us to enter in, and this resistance is called spiritual warfare. When Paul preaches to be *filled* with the Spirit, he is referring to the Holy Spirit and in accordance to God's Word, and before we begin to think of how we can wiggle around it, this is NOT an option! The Bible will never be compromised or be reduced to a book of suggestions but rather is a detailed instruction manual about how to become what Christ died for us to be. The reason most people live in a state of lukewarm spiritual mediocrity is because they simply refuse to obey God's commands. The idea is simple: the more closely we follow – the brighter our light becomes.

None of us can take God seriously while also being absorbed with our own lives. Our mind has convinced us over the years that we can have both – but it is not true. This time it is not Paul speaking but Jesus Himself: ***"No man can serve two masters: either he will hate the one, and love the other; or else he will hold to the one, and despise the other. Ye cannot serve God and mammon"*** *(Matthew 6:24)*. There is good and evil in this life and the human free-will chooses which one it will serve every breath we take. The idea of worship is not automatically limited to God because worship is a reaction to something, and that includes desires associated with the devil. It is our will that decides who our Lord will be. This verse is specifically referring to money and materialism but is definitely NOT being *limited* as the only other master. Most people do not realize that what they love has anything to do with serving something or someone, and this is because they fail to remember that the external temptations and idols of this life do NOT cause us to become servants. These are only influences that tempt us and can only lead us when our WILLS unanimously *vote* them into power. Until we allow Christ to govern *every* part of our beings, it is our wills that remain the chief executive officers of our lives and captains of our ship! The desires that attempt to capture our imaginations are only entertaining our rebellious natures – NOT controlling us. For example, alcohol never controlled anyone until the *will* made the decision, and then the mind told the body to pick up the bottle and take a drink. Pornography has never chased anyone down and forced that person to look at it and lust, it was the *will* that entertained the imagination of sin and was given control and intentionally tracked it down and devoured it! Many do not take the spiritual life very seriously and have not realized that it is a constant campaign from *candidates* who strongly desire to win the elections within our hearts and that our personal vote from our will determines what level of Christian we are.

I want us to go deeper into this thought of Christ becoming personal, and I would like for us to turn to *John chapter 19*. In this section we read about the exchanges between Jesus and Pilate, the crucifixion of Christ, and eventually his death. In *verse 25*, we notice that His mother Mary did not run away but is seen bravely standing by the cross in the emotional trauma of agony while watching her innocent child be tortured. ***"Now there stood by the cross of Jesus His mother, and His mother's sister, Mary the wife of Cleophas, and Mary Magdalene."*** I want us to think for a minute about just how personal this event was for the mother of Jesus. Everything she had experienced and seen in the past 33 years was beyond human understanding as she had been so blessed to have been chosen to give birth to the Savior of the world. She was completely convinced in her mind, heart, and spirit that Jesus was the Son of God, and there were so many miracles that proved who He was, she could hardly remember them all. Her life was NEVER THE SAME after she conceived and began to carry Jesus as He became and remained the *center* of her being. Do you see where I am going with this? Only when He begins to grow within us and becomes the focus of our existence can we give birth to Him, but He cannot be expressed or released from within us until we are *overflowing* with Him! He did not grow inside of Mary to remain hidden within her – His destiny was to be launched into the world to do His Father's will. Likewise, our salvation is not about being pregnant with an idea or opinion about Jesus, but to *deliver* Christ to the world so that everyone can see Him and know Him! I am not saying it will be a painless delivery, but in a unique way of thinking we see that the Father's desire is for us to born-again in Christ, and in turn for us to allow Him to be delivered through us.

After Jesus died, was buried, and rose again, I want us to continue thinking about His mother and His disciples. We notice in today's world when something tragic happens to a child that sometimes the mothers will turn to the legal system or even Congress to try and pass a law that will promote awareness or might prevent a crisis from happening with another child. This is because the mother (parents) has taken the event so *personally* that it is ALL they can think about. Those who are directly affected by tragedy do not take what happened lightly; neither does the impact of the reality fade away quietly. When Mary went back to the routine of everyday life after Jesus eventually went back to heaven, do you believe she just stopped talking about God's plan of saving mankind? Do you think she spent her days talking about how Jesus was just a good kid that was passionate about religion? Definitely not! She was CONSUMED with God's plan of salvation and was POSSESSED with His divine truth that she knew was real! She birthed the gospel and the ransom to redeem mankind from eternal death! Yes, of course she was a fanatic, and I'm sure she could hardly think of anything else, but why are we not the same way? For one reason, we do not think about what happened to Jesus in the same personal way she did. *Why not?* He was not our child but was someone else's. In the same way we do not feel the deep sorrow when we see those mothers on TV pleading their case before the world. It is because these are not our children, and these problems do not *directly* affect us. We are not dealing with these specific difficulties so we are not as concerned or interested as they are. However, if our teenager was killed by a drunk driver, I guarantee we would want to speak with the president of the United States to see if he could do something about how to prevent this from happening again as an honor to OUR innocent one who tragically lost so young a life.

With the same attitude, it seems that Christianity has become a sleepy addition to our already hectic lifestyle, and instead of us being fervently passionate about Jesus and the burden for souls, we are intimidated and embarrassed to be an aggressive messenger of His gospel. It appears that if God actually lived inside of us (He does), and we had the opportunity to release Him to the world (we do), this would be (should be) the most ultimate PERSONAL mission anyone could have! Amen! There is no doubt our wills are so strong and dominating that they have threatened us and intimidated us to keep this extremist business under strict control! And obviously we have allowed ourselves to take our precious Lord for granted! Will we ever become so determined to be a radical Christian that we forcefully discipline our wills into submission? Do we really desire to be led by His Holy Spirit? or is this just a religious thing to say that makes us seem spiritual.

Chapter 38

MAKING THE INVESTMENT

It never grows old to realize that Jesus is our friend and is doing everything He can to help us live in victory! He is not a religious concept that we can manipulate, and His power is not something we can use to become famous; He is a merciful God that just wants us to stop and listen to what He has to say. When we make the conscious decision to become serious about what life is all about, we are granted the privilege of knowing the spiritual reality of His person.

I am convinced when we come before God with humility, brokenness, and desperately needy for him, we will find him. Maybe we should rephrase that and say it this way - in His compassion and mercy, He finds us. However we connect, the question remains; do I really desire to sit at His feet, drink from His cup, and lay my head on His chest? It is a common response to want all that we can receive, but many have never understood that even though salvation is based on God's grace, it also includes our responsibility to surrender our lives to Him. Receiving Jesus into our heart is accepting the holy vow of being in covenant with our creator, and this is much more serious than is taught. It is true that God's love is unconditional, but our personal relationship is based on the agreement of *mutual* commitment. He ransoms us and redeems us with the understanding that He is to be our Lord and Master, and as we develop in the comprehension of our pledge to Him, the promises of His truth become manifested through our lifestyle of obedience. This simply means that His covenant is conditional upon our determination to fulfill His will. Our potential levels of spiritual sensitivity are designed to advance into an awareness of His presence and eventually into a lifestyle of walking and living with Him.

No matter what we are involved with in life, a right attitude is always one of the most important attributes we can have. There are inspiring stories about those who were left alone to scrub the pots and pans or that sat on the bench during games and never had any playing time but did NOT allow hardships and difficulties to steal their joy. They discovered a very important principle that very few possess. They learned how to look beyond temporal circumstances and not become absorbed in feeling sorry for themselves while keeping their eyes on the vision of future success. In church, there have been times when I did not have a good attitude, and what I failed to realize was that the person who was already in the position I wanted was being honored by God because of that person's faithfulness and favorable spiritual temperament. Being competitive would be like a runner in a track meet that tries to crowd out the one next to him by stepping over into the other's lane. May we be reminded that the rules of disqualification sometimes also apply to the spirit realm because the Lord is NOT happy with these carnal motives, whether we are more talented or not! There will be times when others that are not the most gifted are chosen to be the leader! *Why?* Because their hearts are clean and can be used as a pure vessel of honor to pour out God's Spirit which is what servant-hood is all about. The reason we find ourselves sitting and observing is because God is trying to renew a right spirit within us and teach us the revelation of humility. Our responsibility is to present our gifts back to him as a sacrificial offering of thanksgiving and adoration because there is much more to leadership than winning a popularity contest. When serving Christ becomes a burden or a pressure to perform, something has infiltrated our soul and clouded our vision. For example, if a worship leader position became available and two people were trying out for it, one may technically be a better singer but not necessarily the better overall leader. Being a person of integrity and a good steward includes many different character traits, and when it comes to qualities such as being trustworthy, faithful, humble, generous, self-controlled, disciplined, mature, well respected, and able to teach, we can see that it is important to acknowledge the big picture instead of zeroing in on one thing. Do not allow the stress of dealing with others and the aggravation from ministry cause you to become upset and leave. Be careful to avoid the distractions and frustrations that want to pull you away from the tenderness of His touch. Misunderstandings and twisted thinking can build walls that gradually become a prison cell that can hold us captive to our own distorted imaginations. Genuine spiritual growth causes us to contemplate more thoroughly, and as we trust His wisdom, we will realize that we cannot force doors to open in our ministry. God is perfectly capable of opening them for us when He knows we are ready. The simplicity to His unspeakable joy is to focus on Him alone, and this is where His Word moves from our head - into our heart.

Brother Billy, how often do I need to confess my faith and speak it with my mouth? Well, it all comes down to just how much victory you want. We can go down the list of those who made the investment, but it always ends up with the same answer; we get what we pay for. Many are asking how long do I need to fast, intercede, and pray, and how long do I need to believe and wait and hold on to my petitions? Others want to know how much of God's Word do I need to learn, and how much more serving do I need to do? How much forgiveness and love do I need to demonstrate, and how much longer do I need to sacrifice and give? Well, do you want to be a sold-out Christian or all talk and no walk? We must establish that the Christian life is a lifestyle and NOT a part-time job. We also need to clarify that we not a contestant on a game show where the ones with the most correct answers win a new car and a vacation to Italy. We serve Him because we love Him, and the more obedient we are, the closer we will walk with Him. He has all the deep answers but is just trying to provoke our curiosity so we might become interested about the basics! With all of the teachings that Jesus was trying to explain, we can cut to the chase and conclude that He was simply telling us to let go of our lives so that we can truly live. All of our questions have an answer, and He is perfectly willing to reveal them to all who seek, but the idea is NOT that we find our answer then continue going back to our old life. We invest ALL of our life into Him so that He can reveal ALL that we need to know! *Why?* Because when we know and do His will, we can become more like Him. Think about this for a moment; would it really make a difference in the way we live for Him if He actually gave us all the answers we are seeking? I choose to agree with His divine reality and speak my destiny instead of being gathered with all the obstinate individuals that spend their lives wondering why and what could have been.

How many realize that the *no pain – no gain* saying that is used as a battle cry for physical exercise can also be applied to the spiritual realm? The concept of planning with expectation is not complicated; if you want to see a wonderful harvest, you will need to plant a lot of seed! Speaking of sowing and reaping, everyone will always INVEST into what they love. If you love to watch television, you will have the biggest and nicest one you can afford. The same is true with cars, houses, diamonds, etc. . . . We can trace our TIME and MONEY to whatever has captured our hearts - and it is connected to worship. *Really?* Yes. When it comes to being a Christian, our prayers and tithing are a huge part of walking the walk, and when we place Jesus on the bottom of our priority list, our dis-obedience becomes our most noticeable testimony. For example, those that gripe and complain in the church all the time and have negative attitudes probably do not pray or give that much. *Brother Billy, how dare you say such a thing!* Well, I can prove it. Those who intercede and stand in the gap with fervent prayer concerning the body of Christ and sacrificially give their finances, have blood, sweat, and tears invested in the spiritual realm and will not curse the ones they are praying for! *How do you know?* When we truly love God's people enough to pray for them, we have compassion and are broken in humility. We could NOT pour out the sweet fragrance of prayer and worship before the Lord's throne and then turn around and spew out poison against His body, because we have invested our faith into their miracle. You would not roll up your sleeves and lay bricks in the wall today and chisel them out tonight!

Our good words and attitudes carry blessings of LIFE and produce positive energy that edifies and brings encouragement. We also know that negative words and energy can be used to curse and destroy because they carry the power of death. *Brother Billy, you don't really believe all of that hocus pocus stuff do you?* This is nothing to debate about! It is absolute truth from the throne of God and is as real as the blood pumping through our veins. This divine principle reveals the substance and evidence that can explain the condition of everyone's life – good or bad. Walking in His wisdom involves speaking His truth, and unless we have His VISION about our mission, we not accomplish His will! It is carnal PRIDE that cancels our spiritual sensitivity and will diminish our most valuable character trait of Christ, which is love. Genuine faith and love are helping to build God's Kingdom, but giving is where the rubber meets the road. God says in *James chapter 1 and verse 22,* **"But be ye doers of the Word, and not hearers only, deceiving your own selves."** When there is very little invested, it is easy to rip up the church and tear it apart or just walk away from it, especially if it has not COST us anything. It takes FAITH to obey, HOPE to give, and LOVE to pray! If God has your bank card, there is a good chance He also has ALL of your heart. Those who faithfully support the church are taking their responsibility very seriously because they are pouring their lives and their finances into it.

If you are dedicated and committed to being a part of the bride of JESUS, you will protect, support, endure, and have patience, mercy, forgiveness, humility, and courage to stand for the body. This does not mean there are times when correction is needed, but those who are dedicated and committed to going all the way with God will always have Him and His work as their highest priority. We will learn over time that Christianity is a road that is filled with more than just good intentions. It is a life of HEARING, BELIEVING, KNOWING, and DOING! Faith confessions are the creative force that goes farther than just hoping! Amen! Faith lives what it believes and does NOT stop until it sees the manifestation! Every word that comes out of our mouths becomes either building materials for God's Kingdom or a wrecking ball of demolition. *"Death and life are in the power of the tongue: and they that love it shall eat the fruit thereof"* (Proverbs 18: 21). Can you imagine the WARFARE that is going on in the spirit realm over our words? Satan literally watched God speak the universe into existence, and he knows God's Word where the Lord says that WE have this divine creative force within us through the authority in Jesus Christ. If the devil can keep this a secret, he can prevent God's children from changing the world, and this helps us see more clearly why much of the church world has become silent. Satan is attacking pastors and teachers by trying to infuse heresy and false doctrines into the body of Christ. The failure to instruct about the power or words is inflicting anemia and fear into God's people, and its devastation is very noticeable. *"A fool's mouth is his destruction, and his lips are the snare of his soul"* (Proverbs 18: 7). Speaking God's Word, worshipping Him, and proclaiming positive confessions according to His will—all will stimulate our faith and set into motion the dreams and visions that God is giving us to accomplish! *"The words of a man's mouth are as deep waters, and the wellspring of wisdom as a flowing brook"* (Proverbs 18: 4). Somebody Praise Him! We are NOT a poor, blind, defeated, insignificant peasant crawling upon this earth! We have been given God's Word, the Holy Ghost, and the spiritual authority in the Name of Jesus to proceed and succeed! *"Even so the tongue is a little member, and boasts great things. Behold how great a matter a little fire kindleth"* (James 3:5).

Our words come from the basic learning process where the brain helps to organize letters and sounds along with developing our speech. Our problems begin when our undisciplined minds develop bad thinking habits which in turn produce negative speech. We are learning that words can be a powerful blessing or a devastating curse, and we all have been on both sides of the fence but still have much difficulty controlling our spontaneous urge to say what we think. We will never change what comes OUT until we change what is going IN! *"Whoso keepeth his mouth and his tongue, keepeth his soul from troubles"* *(Proverbs 21:23).* Christians are being convinced that the little things we are absorbing are not having an impact on the way we are thinking and the words we are speaking. This is deception. We are not realizing that we are being subtly consumed with pollution from the inside out. *How can we close the floodgates of this onslaught of corrupt knowledge?* Stop listening and singing songs about the dark side of life. Stop watching images of death and violence that steal your peace and cause you to become calloused and distant. Stop reading erotic literature that sets the imagination free to live a world of fantasy and carnality. Closely monitor and set a guard at the windows to your soul so that Christ can bring restoration and renewal into the heart. Protect the entrance to your conscience so that Jesus can have a chance to purify your mind and bring sensitivity and tenderness into your character. Let go of your plans and ideas and embrace His Word, and as you seek His absolute truth, you will have divine illumination of His great love, mercy, and compassion. As you discover His perfect will for your life, ask Him to help you, and confess by faith in your prayers that you are determined to live in total victory! God can heal and restore what you thought was ruined. If we could only obtain the revelation that changing our minds changes who we are!

The indwelling Christ and our new spirit would love to renew the brain, clean out the conscience, fire the old employees, and run the operation completely from God's point of view. However, since the *will* still has his nameplate on the door, this might not be as easy as we thought. The idea of salvation is centered on Jesus but is also connected with laying down our control, because being born again is *allowing* Christ to become our *new* Lord. Our old lord was supposed to be dethroned, and in order for Jesus to become our personal KING we must come to terms with this reality. It is ridiculous to think that we can have Jesus as our Lord and not pay any attention to His commands. Surrendering the way we have always lived is the most difficult thing we will ever do, and evolving into an overcomer will happen only if we are committed to remove our flesh from power! What many people forget is that our emotions have their own office down the hall and heavily influence how we think, which in turn controls what comes out of our mouths. Our thoughts are the offspring of how we feel, and it is our responsibility to filter and control every word before we release it. *"For by thy words thou shalt be justified, and by thy words thou shalt be condemned"* (Matthew 12:37). Until the desire to be transformed into the image of Christ becomes stronger than the desire to relax and watch life unfold on its own – we will remain the same.

"Moreover, when ye fast, be not as the hypocrites, of a sad countenance: for they disfigure their faces that they may appear unto men to fast. Verily I say unto you, they have their reward. But thou, when thou fast, anoint thine head, and wash thy face; that thou appear not unto men to fast, but unto thy Father, which sees in secret: and thy Father, which sees in secret, shall reward thee openly" (Matthew 6:16-18). Fasting is an effective purifier of the mind and soul. It takes our sleepy, distorted view of life and dumps all the puzzle pieces on the floor, then slowly clears the fog of deception and allows us to see how to put it together God's way. Have you noticed when we were younger we believed we were right, and then later we discovered that in some cases we were mistaken? This does not make us a bad person, because we were definitely sincere; it just reminds us of the fact that humans can be sincerely wrong. We perceive information through our natural eyes and interpret it through our natural minds, which can lead to error. Learning is a progression that is constantly shaping our understanding. *"Trust in the Lord with all thine heart; and lean NOT unto thine own understanding. In all thy ways acknowledge Him, and He shall direct thy paths"* (Proverbs 3:5-6). The default system is built on the deception that human understanding can be trusted as a secure truth to live by, but this lower knowledge is no more than temporal persuasions. Spiritual truth is from the spiritual realm, and the only way to know it is through God's Spirit. Mmmmm... This is a beautiful truth about holy enlightenment but so many fail to understand this principle and still remain confused about eternal truth. Of course

doing everything according to God's voice is difficult, but leaning on our own intelligence is the opposite of faithful obedience and learning how to genuinely trust Him.

Human beings are always bragging about how smart they are, but it never ceases to amaze me how stubborn we can be. It is not difficult to blame everything negative that has ever happened to us (even problems that we caused) on outside forces, because living in denial is one of the easiest things we will ever do. It is much easier to hide behind the *victim* mentality than to lay our cards on the table and face the truth. What good do we think we are accomplishing by proclaiming God as the captain of our lives but never giving Him permission to steer our ship. Most of us see ourselves in a custom personalized mirror that reflects a unique image that only we can see. This is because we do not want anyone to give us advice about how we should be handling our situations. We have discussed about fasting and how it makes our minds and spirits more sensitive to God, but we never stop to realize that when we are NOT fasting, evidently our general condition must be susceptible to being foggy and confused. (Pause and ponder). Fasting is something we seldom mention, like foot washing, because it is just too fanatical and uncomfortable. But why would we avoid something that is so crucially needed? Because we are subconsciously protecting our carnal nature! The flesh draws lines in the sand, and when given the deciding power, declares the boundaries of just how far it will go toward God. When things become uncomfortable, the flesh says I am finished! This explains why there is a church on every corner yet very few fanatical Christians. Ouch! The flesh is not threatened by a beautiful building, a comfortable pew, a peaceful song, or an uplifting devotion - it just does not want to submit to the Holy Spirit. God's grace is patiently trying to reveal to us the message of abandonment, but if surrendering our will was the *requirement* for going to church, we could unfortunately sit everyone on one pew. It is worthy to consider the fact that our *will* is the giant that is keeping us from crossing into the Promised Land, and our determination to unplug it from life-support is the only way we will ever become more than a conqueror!

With everything we are involved with in this life, it comes down to wanting spiritual sensitivity more than we want fleshly satisfaction. Do you not think it would be awesome to hold a tiny baby in our arms and *know* how powerful that little one will become in the Kingdom of God? How wonderful it would be to hear God's voice about giving someone a financial blessing or laying hands on someone and praying for a specific need or problem and see that person receive a miracle. Wouldn't it be an honor to be trusted by God to prophesy over people and be able to speak into their lives what God wants them to know? All Christians have the opportunity to become as spiritually wise and anointed, but only a handful will choose to live this level of spirituality. All can be as close to God as they want, and nothing is keeping them from it except their flesh. Oh I get it; we do not want to get close to God because we are afraid He will ask us to do something difficult or costly. Bingo! Praise God for the disciples that are walking the walk and following His voice! In *Luke Chapter 2* we find two examples of individuals that made the decision to abide in the higher levels that God intended us to live. These testimonies prove that we can see with our spirit eyes things that are hidden from our natural eyes. Mary and Joseph were bringing baby Jesus (probably no older than three months) to be dedicated at the temple according to the Law of Moses. A man named Simeon was obviously a man of prayer and fasting because that is the only way a person could develop such a powerful spiritual life. He is mentioned in *verse 25* as being **"righteous and devout with the Holy Spirit upon him."** God had spoken to him that he would not die until he had seen the face of the Messiah. On this very same day that Mary and Joseph went to the temple, he was led by the Holy Spirit to be there also, and the moment he saw the baby, he held Him and said, **"For with my eyes I have seen your salvation."** He prophesied over Jesus and blessed Him, and even though Mary and Joseph had already seen and heard the supernatural miracles about their child, they still were marveling at his words. This man's life was truly an example of what it means to abide in the awareness of God's presence as a lifestyle, and the beautiful lesson from this story reveals that this level of spiritual sensitivity is readily available for us right now.

    In *verse 36* of the same chapter, we find a prophetess named Anna who worshipped Yahweh in the temple night and day with prayers and fasting. She also was there that day and recognized baby Jesus as the Christ the Son of God and was trying to tell all who were around them about how this child would grow up and be the redeemer of God's elect. I realize that older people always go overboard when they see a baby and say things like, "this baby is really going to be something" and emotional comments like that, but this was different. Those who were watching might have thought, "Isn't that touching? A nice, sweet, old lady *(eighty four years old)* and a tiny baby" and gone on about their business. However, let us perceive that the onlookers were not in the Spirit and did not discern spiritual reality (in this particular case God was right in front of them). This reminds me of the blind Pharisees that charged Jesus with blasphemy because He declared that He was the Son of God. Yes, these religious leaders looked dignified on the outside, but Jesus said they were dead on the inside, and my question today is that if we are living the same way, what will be our consequence? Think about all that is happening right in front of us that we are not noticing. How powerful would our church services be if we were in the Spirit instead of going through the routines? Consider the divine appointments we are walking past in our everyday network because we are NOT connected with His mind or voice. How much more could we do in His Kingdom if we could clearly hear what He was speaking and the amazing things we could say and do for everyone we come in contact with. Simeon and Anna did not even have the indwelling Holy Spirit within them, and they could see spiritual realities. We have God living inside of us and have a struggle matching our socks! It is NOT God's fault that we lack discernment; it is our lack of interest to develop it.

Chapter 39

THE ANTICIPATION OF HIS GLORY

We say we want Jesus to manifest in our services, but do we fully understand what He is like and what He would do? Whatever we would do if He appeared should be nothing we are not already doing. Amen! Why would we act any differently whether we can literally see Him or not? Surely you don't suggest that just because we cannot see Him with our mortal eyes He is not there? My friends, not only is He there, but He is still busy doing exactly what He did when He walked along the roads of Galilee. If today's churches are not aware of God's presence and do not ask Him to conduct the services, then it makes one seriously wonder just who is leading the church. I have always been labeled a dreamer because I believe in miracles. I am just naïve enough to believe that when I am in the presence of His majesty that maybe God will cover our eyes as He passes by, or maybe His angels will reveal themselves flying around the sanctuary. I believe when the healing waters are stirred and hands are laid on the sick and the oppressed along with prayers that contain mountain moving faith - something wonderful is going to happen! If I did not believe in the supernatural power of God to change lives, I would need to search for the answers to why I attend church. If I did not have a high expectation that I am going to see the manifestation of God's glory every time, I would wonder if I am going just to be a member of a social club. Yes, there are occasions when I am disappointed in the programs, but I am

ALWAYS awestruck by His love and glory, and this keeps the fire of my faith unsinkable and the strength of my joy unstoppable!

Moses had such an incredible life. Let us look at what happened after he broke the tables of stone but before the Lord wrote on them the second time. In *Exodus chapter 33* we see an incredible verbal exchange as Moses was asking God to have mercy on him and the people. Then Moses asked a bold request in *verse 18:* ***"And he*** [Moses] ***said, I beseech thee, show me your glory. And He*** [God] ***said, I will make all my goodness pass before thee; and I will proclaim the name of the Lord before thee; and will be gracious to whom I will be gracious, and will show mercy on whom I will show mercy. And he*** [God] ***said, you cannot see my face: for there shall no man see me, and live. And the Lord said, behold, there is a place by me, and you must stand upon a rock: And it will come to pass, while my glory passes by, that I will put you in a cleft of the rock, and will cover you with my hand while I pass by: And I will take away my hand, and you will see my back parts: but my face will not be seen."*** So what was Moses really asking when he wanted to see God's glory? and why did he make this request? And likewise, just exactly what are we asking today when we also want to see Him? It is all about LOVE! I believe Moses was so consumed and infatuated to be at one with his Creator that he simply wanted to be as close to Him as possible. He wanted to connect with the one he was giving his complete life for! The same is true now with the Lord's remnant disciples who get lost in the wonders of His person, who thirst to know Christ more intimately, who are overwhelmed with who He is, and who want to wash His feet with tears from the deepest recesses of their beings. We simply want to see the one we are in love with.

Isaiah chapter 6, verses 1-4 mentions that either Isaiah literally witnessed the Lord in person, or he saw the Lord in a vision, but whatever the case, it builds our faith to know that God does appear to His people. ***"In the year that king Uzziah died I saw also the Lord sitting upon a throne, high and lifted up, and His train filled the temple."*** The word *train* in the Wilson's Old Testament Word Studies gives the meaning as the lower part or skirt of a garment, and it may signify here the rays of glory issuing from His lofty throne. ***"Above it stood the seraphim: each one had six wings; with two he covered his face, and with two he covered his feet, and with two he did fly. And one cried to another, and said, Holy, holy, holy, is the Lord of hosts: the*** *whole earth is full of His glory. And the post of the door moved at the voice of him that cried, and the house was filled with smoke."* Do you ever expect or desire to see God's glory when you go to church? And if you have never thought about this, may I ask what do you envision? We sing about God's power and majesty and ask Him to come into our midst, but I wonder how many really have an anticipation to embrace God's presence as Moses did. It would be interesting to hear some of the answers as to why people attend church. It is an excellent idea to write down our visions and expectations and incorporate them into our confessions and prayers. In the isolation of our secret place where we spend time in His presence is where the obsession and beauty of our intimacy is nurtured, but if we have no expectation, then where are our thoughts?

When speaking about the glory of God, without going through books of theological debates about why the word *Shekinah* is not found in the Bible, let's just say it was coined by post-biblical rabbinic scholars that discovered the meaning as a physical manifestation of God's dwelling and presence. The Jewish rabbis coined this extra-biblical expression, as a form of a Hebrew word that literally means *"He caused to dwell,"* signifying that it was a divine visitation of the habitation or dwelling of JEHOVAH on this earth. The Shekinah glory was first evident when the Israelites set out from Succoth in their escape from Egypt. There it appeared as a cloudy pillar in the day and a fiery pillar by night: *"And the Lord went before them by day in a pillar of a cloud, to lead them the way; and by night in a pillar of fire, to give them light; to go by day and night. He took not away the pillar of the cloud by day, nor the pillar of fire by night, from the people"* (Exodus 13:21-22). As we can see, apparently the visible manifestation of God's aura has always been somewhat *toned-down* because humans can survive only a filtered or *limited* amount of God's presence. As an example, we have already mentioned that Moses insisted on beholding God's glory, and we all know the story of how The Almighty hid Moses in the cleft of a rock and covered him with His hand as He passed by, and when He removed His hand, Moses could only withstand seeing Him leaving in the distance. I believe it is perfectly acceptable for us to cry out as Moses did and have an awesome spiritual experience to this degree and even more if we would seriously acknowledge Him, but a question we must consider is this: are we just as determined to live for Him as we are to see Him? Mmmmm. . . . God wants to shake our temples, fill us with His glory cloud, and lead us with the light of His holy fire, but He is searching for an individual that He can trust and is interested for all the right reasons.

The visible manifestation of God's presence was seen not only by the Israelites but ALSO by the Egyptians. In *Exodus chapter 14 and verses 24 and 25* we read, *"And it came to pass, that in the morning watch the Lord looked into the host of the Egyptians through the pillar of fire and of the cloud, and troubled the host of the Egyptians, and took off their chariot wheels, that they drove them heavily* [with difficulty]: *so that the Egyptians said, let us FLEE from the face of Israel; for the Lord fights for them against the Egyptians."* Again we recognize that just the presence of God's glory was enough to convince His enemies that He was a force to be reckoned with. In the New Testament, Jesus is God's glory, and in *Colossians chapter 2 and verse 9* we notice that, *"For in Him* [Christ] *dwelleth all the fullness of the Godhead bodily,"* which is why Jesus said to Philip, *"Anyone who has seen me has seen the Father" (John 14:9)*. In Christ, we also recognize the visible manifestation of God Himself in the second person of the Trinity. Although His glory was also veiled, Jesus along with the Holy Spirit is nonetheless the presence of God on earth now as much as He always has been, and we should be aware that Jesus within us is being observed by more people than the ones we go to church with.

Just as the divine presence of God (collectively) dwelled in a relatively plain tent called the *tabernacle* before the Temple in Jerusalem was built, so was the glory of God revealed in the relatively common man Jesus Christ who was God in the flesh. *"He is despised and rejected of men; a man of sorrows, and acquainted with grief: and we hid as it were our faces from Him; He was despised, and we esteemed* [appreciated] *Him not" (Isaiah 53:3)*. However, when we get to heaven, we will see the Father, Son, and Holy Spirit in their magnificent splendor as their glory will no longer be veiled to our natural senses. *"Beloved, now we are the sons of God, and it does not yet appear what we shall be: but we know that, when He shall appear, we shall be like Him; for we shall see Him as He is. And every man that has this hope in Him purifies himself, even as he is pure" (1 John 3:2)*. Some of the references that contribute meaning of *Shekinah* are interpreted as a thick cloud and the appearance of fire from Jehovah with awesome power. In *Exodus 24:16-17*, we notice God hovering on Mount Sinai in the cloud and fire as Moses goes up into God's presence for 40 days to receive the Ten Commandments. We also read in *Exodus chapter 40:34-38,* how God's glory cloud at times filled the tabernacle of Moses and during the day was seen residing over it. And again in *Numbers chapter 9:15-23*, we see more references explaining how the glory cloud and fire of God's presence determined the movement of the children of Israel in their journeys. Does His glory cloud still exist or have we stopped believing? Remember in *chapter 3 of Exodus* we observe Moses herding sheep and the Lord speaking to him out of a bush that is on fire but is not being consumed. In *verse 5* God tells Moses, **"And He said, draw not nigh hither** [do not come any closer]: **put off thy shoes from off thy feet, for the place whereon thou standest is holy ground."** In church we make reference to this often because we associate God's presence in the sanctuary with the reverential fear of His omniscience. In *verse 6* we read, **"Moreover He said, I am the God of thy father, the God of Abraham, the God of Isaac, and the God of Jacob. And Moses HID his face; for he was afraid to look upon God."** We are not to be afraid to approach Him, but with reverential respect we are to bow down before Him as we adore, exalt, and extol Him in awe and wonder. It is recorded that when humans have encountered angels, they have fallen to the ground on their faces in fear because of the extended radiance from God's holiness, and this should be a reminder to us about how much more we should embrace the revelation of who He is with fear and trembling.

When you come into God's sanctuary, do you expect to enter into the holy of holies? God may not have us to tie a rope around our ankles before we come into His presence, but He still requires us to reverence His holiness. Remember, we are the ones that are drawing near to Him, and in faith we should expect to reach our destination at the mercy seat and our ultimate goal should be that we might live there. To live in His presence is the priceless treasure of heaven and earth, yet many are convinced that the pleasures of this life are worth more. Others feel they are not worthy to live at the mercy seat, but Jesus has provided His blood that welcomes all who will believe. Those who are too dignified to bow before Him or embarrassed to be associated with Him will likely never experience the fullness of who He is. Since the glory of God is His habitation, why wouldn't all of His children want to experience the fullness of His person? Those who teach against the manifestation of God's Spirit, the demonstration of His miracle power, and the reality of His glory on earth have obviously never tasted nor been personally infatuated with God at all. Possessing a head-knowledge of the scriptures is NOT the same as having a personal relationship with God Himself. It is dangerous to teach against anything that involves the presence of God or the demonstration of the Holy Spirit. Let us pray for the confused that proclaim they are standing for truth while actually are deceived in the snare trap of heresy. Jesus wants us to reach out to Him and dream about Him. He desires for us to cry out to see His glory; how can we see Him or know Him any other way? It is not enough just to hear about Him, and it does not satisfy us just to read letters from Him or about Him. We want to be engulfed in His presence every moment because He is the reason we live.

Chapter 40
WORTHY IS THE LAMB

"And I beheld, and I heard the voice of many angels round about the throne and the beasts and the elders: and the number of them was ten thousand times ten thousand and thousands of thousands; saying with a LOUD voice, worthy is the Lamb that was slain to receive power, and riches, and wisdom, and strength, and honor, and glory and blessing" (Revelation 5:11-12).

The love of God allows us to see a powerful story told in *Luke chapter 19* when Jesus used a simple act of riding a colt into Jerusalem to paint a spiritual picture of one of the most important events in human history. His followers were excited with His teachings about the Kingdom of God and the supernatural manifestations they had witnessed. This small gathering in a tiny town was actually revealing Jesus as the Messiah, the Savior of the world, and a type and shadow of His future return as the triumphant King of all Kings. Let us pick up the story in *verse 32. "And they that were sent went their way, and found everything as He had said unto them. And as they were loosing the colt, the owners thereof said unto them, why do you loose the colt? And they said, the Lord has need of him. And they brought him to Jesus: and they put their garments upon the colt, and they set Jesus thereon. And as He went, they spread their clothes in the way" (verses 32-36).* Laying palm branches and their garments down on the ground as a path for Jesus as He rode into the city would be the equivalent of rolling out the *red carpet* so to speak for the arrival of a world-renowned dignitary. *Verse 37* says, **"And when He was come near, even now at the descent of the Mount of Olives, the WHOLE multitude of the disciples began to REJOICE and praise God with a LOUD voice for all the mighty works that they had seen."** Can you picture the excitement, expectation, and exuberance? They are cheering just like people do when Prince William or the President of the United States comes around to shake hands. I can see bright eyes and smiling faces because their King is coming, and they are not ashamed to shout, jump, dance, and release their enthusiasm. So why do some churches today appear unresponsive and the people seem indifferent when they have come to worship Jesus? *Has anything changed?* Absolutely NOT! He is the same as He has always been, so obviously the problem is within our hearts. What has happened to the excitement about the coming King? Where is the anticipation of His presence now? In *verse 38* we notice what they were shouting: **"Saying, blessed is the King that comes in the Name of the Lord: peace in heaven and glory in the highest."** What a perfect example of what an exhilarating worship service should be! *Psalm 118, verse 28* says, **"Thou art my God, and I will praise thee: Thou art my God, I will exalt thee."** These people were NOT ashamed to be identified with their Lord and Master. They did not care about who was watching (neighbors, bosses, storekeepers, friends, family); they were uninhibited, fearless, and overflowing with the kind of joy that all of us experienced when we first came to know Jesus. Amen!

However, as we keep reading, we notice the supposedly *wise* elders of the religious world were watching from a distance and talking negatively among themselves. *Verse 39*, "**And some of the Pharisees from among the multitude said unto Him, Master, REBUKE your disciples."** It appears these leaders were insulted and maybe even embarrassed with the commotion and all the attention this gathering was causing over an independent, radical Bible teacher. Their arrogance is causing them to become very uncomfortable just like many church leaders feel today when someone gets too emotional in worship or too fanatical in their love for Jesus. Have you ever noticed when individuals become lost in the freedom and joy of adoring God and do not care what anyone thinks about them, that many who are NOT focused on the Lord will stare and make critical judgments against them?

People who need perfect organization and cannot depart from tradition will always have a difficult time when God steps in. Many churches do NOT want the Lord to ruin what they have established. Religion leans on the mental ability to create structured programs and legalistic agendas, and there is no room for Jesus in the church, the same as there was *no room* at the Inn when He was born! These distinguished scholars thought more of their personal respect and dignity than to pray and ask God what was happening. They reasoned within the pride of their flesh that this scenario was out of order and ruled this was not in legal compliance with how worship was to be performed (besides being jealous of the new kid on the block). They did not perceive they were in the presence of the Alpha and Omega, the Creator of heaven and earth. Familiarity would not allow them to accept the reality that Jesus was the Son of the God they followed and was the author of the Bible that they had so proudly memorized.

Have you ever thought that Jesus could have played the role of a diplomat and responded to the Pharisees like this: *"Yes, you are right, this is an excitable bunch of extremists, and I do apologize for drawing so much attention to myself, and I agree that the laying down of clothes and palm branches was out of the ordinary, and I do realize it must be a bit awkward to hear them connect me with all those Messianic prophesies. Let me see if I can calm them down from acting so silly."* But of course He does nothing of the sort. Jesus knew the religious leaders were blind and did not comprehend and proceeded to declare a profound statement of truth that touches me deeply every time I think about it. Instead of trying to quench the excitement, He affirms the crowd's gestures of heartfelt respect and worship. He understood more than anyone else that the next few days were going to change the course of the world and open the bridge to heaven for all who would believe! *Verse 40* says, **"And he** [Jesus] **answered and said unto them, I tell you that, if these should hold their peace, the stones would immediately cry out."** All glory to His name forever! What an awesome vision of the power and Omniscience of The Almighty God who is worthy of all praise! Christ will be adored and exalted throughout all eternity as every knee will bow and every tongue will confess that He is Lord!

This is such a perfect example of God's unyielding sovereignty to ensure the gospel would be proclaimed throughout the entire world and to explain that our purpose in life is to live and proclaim His Kingdom gospel! How much clearer could it be that we are NOT to hold back our expressions of love and adoration, no matter what the world thinks or how the religious system criticizes us! Heaven never ceases to exalt and worship the God of infinite power and glory – and as citizens of heaven neither should we! Are there any warriors out there? Amen! May we never be influenced nor be persuaded by pride and the fear of man's persecution that would prevent us from expressing our joy to the God of our salvation! Let us SHOUT His glorious attributes from the housetops because we love Him! He is worthy of all honor, allegiance, devotion, and reverence as we will praise Him with a timeless, imperishable, and unceasing love. *"Saying, Amen: Blessing, and glory, and wisdom, and thanksgiving, and honor, and power, and might, be unto our God forever and ever amen" (Revelation 7:12).*

Do you believe that individuals who refuse to reveal their worship to God in public release their expressions in private? It seems many people have adopted the idea that being quiet is the same as reverence, but it is a deception to think that the pride of dignity is the same as keeping everything decent and in order! The true Christian life is NOT hiding in the shadows of being afraid to express our love for God, as it is impossible to disguise a remnant disciple that is ON FIRE with a passion for Jesus! We will become an unusual, peculiar people for God when we lay down our fear and BOLDLY stand for Him! Amen! Only when believers choose to lay down their pride and embarrassment and become spiritual salt and light, can God begin to use them to represent and increase His Kingdom. *"Lord, may I never be ashamed of you but join in the awareness of your constant presence as the seas and earth and sky bow before you. The mighty rushing of the wind roars with Your words of judgment, as the gentle breeze whispers Your peace. The lightning flashes Your awesome power, and the thunder echoes Your omnipotence. The trees raise their branches to the heavens as they praise You, and the waters like the voices of many choirs sing of Your endless authority and holiness. The warmness of the sun reminds us of Your eternal security, and the moon and stars like a trillion lit candles chase away the fear and darkness of the night. Help me to become bold in my love and fearless in my worship. Amen."*

I was at work one day and walked past a television in the break room that was showing a concert by a popular country music band. I stopped for a moment and was amazed at the effect this music was having on the people. They were jumping, singing, clapping, and raising their hands with such excitement and enthusiasm. I walked away thinking about how people express their love and passion for the things that mean the most to them. Then I wondered why most Christians do not act that way toward God. Could it be that people who slip quietly in and out of church may possibly act differently when they participate in something that actually thrills them? *Now brother, aren't you reading a little more into this than you should?* Well, maybe it is time to stop for a minute and think about passages like these: ***"Having a form of godliness, but denying the power thereof: from such turn away" (II Timothy3:5)***, and ***"Ever learning and never able to come to the knowledge of the truth" (verse 7)***. Our lives are filled with choices, and freewill gives us the liberty to select what is important to us. We all have priorities, but the problem in God's eyes is that many of our desires are in the wrong order. We are so attached to this world because it is the home of our flesh. Our bodies love this place (were born and raised here) and are very comfortable and spoiled living in the familiar realm of dramatized emotions, strong desires, and fickle feelings. It is the realm of default because without our hands on the spiritual steering wheel, we will naturally drift into being dominated by our human nature. It is difficult to re-learn how to live again because we are being introduced not only to Jesus as our new Master but also the transition of becoming a brand new spirit. They both exist in the spiritual dimension and are constantly calling our minds and hearts to join them. We have difficulty because God's world is enmity to our old world, which causes a continuous tug-of-war battle for control. The reason many congregations are sluggish is because the people are filled with sin, and this can cause the entire church to *camp out* just inside the entrance gate and be satisfied to stay there. Sin causes us to be ashamed, and our rebellion haunts us with embarrassment, so of course we choose to stand at a distance from God's presence. Only when we fall in love with Christ with ALL of our hearts, and He becomes the most exciting person to us in the world, will we cease to be ashamed of Him.

Chapter 41

GOD CALLING

"What shall we then say to these things? If God be for us who can be against us?" (Romans 8:31).

Jesus came to accomplish His destiny of being the sacrificial lamb that would save God's people from their sins and becoming the pathway of hope that could restore the intimate, personal relationship between God and man. If you are a remnant disciple of Christ, it does not matter what your calling or style; this is the heart of your message. If you are waiting on God to use you in His ministry, be patient and know that you are currently in training. Just because things are not happening, it does not mean that God is not arranging circumstances behind the scenes that you are not aware of. Pieces of steel that are brought out of the fire to be made into swords are not ready to use immediately. They need to be beaten, ground, polished, shined, and tested *(now that will preach).* Allow God to develop you in the secret place of prayer, fasting, study, and service so that in HIS time you will be ready when He calls. Today is the day to reach out in faith by practicing and learning how to use the gift and calling God has given to you. How much do you practice your gift? This life is a rehearsal where we implement and apply what we are experiencing in *private* so that when our heavenly Father opens the door and calls us to come forth, we are ready to do His will in the power and demonstration of His Spirit. If it is not His time and you are out of order, you will not have the blessing of His anointing, and this simply means that we are to continue in the process. If you will just wait patiently for His release, you will be endued with power from on high, and everyone will know that you are a vessel of honor. *"But they that wait upon the Lord shall renew their strength; they shall mount up with wings as eagles; they shall run and not be weary; and they shall walk and not faint"* (Isaiah 40:31). God will not send soldiers into battle unless they have been trained for front-line combat in His holy wisdom and have learned how to exercise faith and endure the many dangerous snare traps of warfare. Pray, obey, learn, watch, walk, work, and wait.

In my life there have been highs and lows, and I believe that going through mountains and valleys is perfectly normal. Every journey has a flat tire every now and then, so just listen and respond to what needs to be done so that you can get back on the road again. Sometimes the ministry can be lonely even though you are extremely busy and surrounded by people. Within the depths of our hearts, there is a confidence in knowing that only God can satisfy and fill the emotional void we feel at times. When we can sense and know He is walking with us, the path is not nearly as grueling, and this is a huge step toward developing an awareness of His presence. Of course I have felt rejection, and it is painful, but again not uncommon. No one is ever as excited about what you are doing as you are, and this does not just pertain to the ministry; it applies to whatever interest you are passionate about. With God's patience I have finally learned a very important truth about discouragement. The way people react to what you do is usually NOT personal! Those who have witnessed the gifts and talents that you have are not rejecting you because they think you are not a good person or not working toward a worthy cause. They are just NOT fascinated or even interested with the field or work you have devoted your life to. For example, those who love cars will not hesitate to buy car magazines, watch programs about cars, go to car races, museums, car shows, and maybe even own an awesome car that they adore. Is everyone infatuated with cars? No. People tend to be drawn to whatever they love, and unfortunately not many people in the world have a driving passion to become absorbed with God. So what do you do when you know you are doing God's will and the world does not even acknowledge it at all? You encourage yourself by staying close to Jesus and pouring out your heart to Him. Explain to Him how you feel and confess God's Word over yourself. Make a list of how He has blessed you, and along with positive confessions speak these out loud every day because it is your faith coming into agreement with God's will that creates and activates one of the most powerful accords in the universe. Jesus said, **"Again I say unto you, that if two of you shall agree on earth as touching anything that they shall ask, it shall be done for them of my Father which is in heaven"** *(Matthew 18:19).* You see, when you agree with God and His Word, this creates a divine principle that releases the power of God into your situation. Amen! Be careful to NOT speak negativity about your life or the work that God has called you to do, because the last thing we need is to release curses upon our own hopes and dreams. Pray fervently for all those in your network that God may provide an opportunity for you to reveal Christ to them. Do not allow bitterness and resentment to cause you to withdraw away from your mission, but rather be filled with Holy Ghost boldness to continue in your destiny. Becoming offended makes it seem like we are more concerned with a small picture of man's approval toward us, than with the big picture of God's love for the world.

I have always known there is more to life than just stumbling around like a blind man that cannot know God's will. Spiritual maturity and wisdom can be developed to follow the still small voice of God within our spirits instead of relying on the theological mind. In our search for contextual truth may we also remember the words of the great hymn, *"turn your eyes upon Jesus - look full in His wonderful face – and the things of earth will grow strangely dim – in the light of His glory and grace."* If we want to become serious about loving and obeying God, we need to consider that life comes down to a simple list of priorities. This seems elementary, doesn't it, but we need to think soberly about it for a minute. If there is anything on the list that is above God, there is a serious problem and no doubt the reason for our internal sadness and discouragement. Spiritual peace is found in the intimate relationship with Christ, and the closer you are to the Lord, the more of His power and victory you will experience. The only thing preventing us from living with Him is our decision to keep Him OFF the top of our priority list. Each person is responsible for his own list; what is on the top of your list? **"And now little children, abide in Him; that when He shall appear, we may have confidence, and not be ashamed before Him at His coming"** *(I John 2:28).*

We know that God is light and in Him is no darkness at all; however, we realize that our spiritual mission is taking place in a dark world, and reaching out to Christ through this darkness is what brings us closer to Him. Of course He is the light of the world, and He lives inside of us, but there is nothing necessarily wrong or bad with darkness or isolation in itself. When we close the doors to our secret places of isolation with Him, we find ourselves in the dark while seeking the light of His presence in our souls. There are times as we search for answers or solutions to our many problems, that it seems we are swimming in a dark sea trying to find His hand that He might pull us up to safety. Darkness and faith are connected because when we cannot see Him – it is all about TRUST. He is the highest authority, and with Him there is nothing to fear. *"These things I have spoken unto you, that in Me* [Jesus] *ye might have peace. In the world ye shall have tribulation: but be of good cheer; I have overcome the world" (John 16:33).* We learned as children to be afraid of the dark, and the world has associated the darkness with the unknown evils and dangers that will *get us* if we venture into it. When I was a young boy, my parents remodeled half of the attic which became my bedroom and a playroom, and the other half was left as storage. I was terrified of the attic, and as my dad built a partition wall and installed a door (thank God) to the *dark unknown,* this did bring me some relief. What made my anxiety worse was the fact that the rest of the family all slept downstairs on the other side of the house. I felt very isolated and often imagined that if the monsters did decide to devour me that no one could hear my screams. Anyway, from my bed I could barely see the door because my window cast just enough light for me to make out shadows. This made me very uncomfortable, but on the other hand I would rather be able to see it than not be able to keep a check on it. I remember one night I was particularly a little jittery because I kept hearing strange bumps and sounds from the other side of the door. I peeked from under the covers and saw that the door was wide open – I literally could not breathe, so I made a dash for the stairwell and nearly jumped completely down the stairs and ran into my mom and dad's room so shook up I could hardly speak! Yes, thank God, I eventually learned to face the fear by exploring the attic and came to the solid conclusion that it was just an old musty-smelling place filled with junk and spider webs. And this is exactly what we need to do with all of our *grown-up* places where we are intimidated and afraid and that cause us to be uneasy and apprehensive.

    I know people today that hate silence and do everything they can to avoid being alone with the quiet. Some individuals cannot sleep when it is still, and it is common to hear about people that need to have music or a fan running just so they can have a background noise. Others cannot walk into a room without turning on the television or be in a car without turning on the radio because they feel very uncomfortable with silence. I personally love the silence because I enjoy trying to hear the voice of God. I enjoy the peace that comes from solitude and knowing that all is well within my conscience. If we struggle to hear God speak in the quiet times, it is doubtful we can hear Him in the noisy chaos. Could it be that people do not want to hear His voice because they do not want to be reminded about the truth of their souls? Our journeys can have their dark places which have been mentioned as sometimes being like valleys of the shadow of death, but His WORD is the lamp unto our feet and the light unto our path! It does not matter where we are, we can know that He is there! If you believe God cannot handle your situation, your god is too small! If you are not finding the answers you need today and feel that the Lord has forgotten you, I can promise it has nothing to do with Him being too busy or that heaven is having an economic crisis, budget cuts, or staff downsizing. When we find Christ in the secret place and become determined to stay there until we have heard His direction for us, we will no longer feel like a castaway on a deserted island. *"I don't know"* is the most common response in the world, but not one time has God ever said it! It is true that we have plenty of questions, but He has ALL the answers, so the only thing that is preventing you from knowing all that you need to know is the lack of spending enough time with Him. Learning how to be aware of His constant presence includes forcing our minds to stay concentrated on Him, and this enables us to live in a continual state of learning. There is NO darkness too dense for God to see through clearly! There is NO problem or trial that is too complicated or hopeless that He cannot take care of! He is El-Shaddai - the God who is MORE than enough!

Our enemy wants to accuse us and say that God is tired of helping us and that He is finished with coming to our rescue. The devil works overtime to prevent us from going into our private habitations where we connect with God, because his job is all about rocking Christians to sleep and keeping their minds focused on other distractions. Maybe instead of running from the darkness we should embrace it because this can keep us alert to the deception of false security. Do you think someone that is blind could possibly have a higher level of spiritual sensitivity? *Why?* Because they are not distracted or influenced by the visual temptations of this world. If they are Christians, they are learning to turn INWARD and become more sensitive to what is happening all around them along with being more discerning to His divine reality. God is pleased when He watches His children reach out to Him in their difficulties, especially when they are trying to develop an awareness of how He is guiding and using circumstances as a part of their destiny. *What does this have to do with worship?* We should lead a lifestyle of praise even in the valleys of darkness as an overflow of our confidence that God is in total control.

Thanksgiving is being grateful and praise is exalting Him for what He has done and who He is, and as we purpose to live in this constant awareness, we realize that He is surrounding us even when we cannot sense Him or the solutions to our problems. There is a time to fight and a time to let go, a time to work and a time to rest; thus knowing when, where, and how is the divine wisdom that comes from the depths of walking in His awareness. Be encouraged. The Lord responds to the cries of His people when they truly depend on Him and follow Him in obedience and humility. There may be times when it seems you are drifting in the universe, but have peace - He knows exactly where you are and where He wants to take you. God has designed you and has great and wonderful things for you to accomplish. Have you ever heard a tiny voice whispering to you that God is tired of helping you and that He is has forgotten you? This is a lie! Listen to these promises from our God that never fails; ***"But Zion said, the Lord hath forsaken me, and my Lord hath forgotten me. Can a woman forget her sucking child, that she should not have compassion on the son of her womb? Yea, they may forget, yet I WILL NOT forget thee*** [the verb here implies a stronger meaning of being UNABLE to forget]. ***Behold, I have graven thee upon the palms of My hands; thy walls*** [our mission, welfare, and well-being] ***are continually before Me" (Isaiah 49:14-16).*** Thank you Jesus!

Let us lay our cards on the table and admit that spiritual things are NOT popular, and the deeper they are, the more people are going to do everything they can to find something else to do. Our logical thinking is always quick to point out the ideas and concepts of things like, *"When the food is delicious, the restaurant will be widely known and a packed-out success!"* But will they still be excited about how wonderful it is if the COST is more than they are willing to pay? Now hold on just a minute; maybe my common sense analogy has come up with a spiritual nugget of revelation! Could it be that people are more likely to joyfully embrace the good blessings and positive affirmations of God's Word if the PRICE does not interfere with the way they live or cause any pain? You mean that people would rather flock to church and hear a message of *chocolate cake* that proclaims everything is all right than a *Brussels sprouts* sermon that requires people to deny their flesh and surrender their wills? Imagine that; the line to sign up for sacrificing our old nature is tiny compared to the line that advertises that everyone can live a lukewarm, religious, materialistic, happy lifestyle! Maybe the rejection of our ministry has little to do with our talents and abilities but everything to do with the intense depth and truth of our message. Mmmmm...interesting. The masses have always stepped away from the call to a deeper commitment with Christ along with the lonely voices of those who *blow the trumpet* in Zion about holiness and purity. There has always been a crowd at the baby pool with hardly anyone going to the deep end, but do not be discouraged, and do not change what God has called you to do. May we be reminded that a religious spirit will influence the un-renewed mind to draw a silent, invisible line when it comes to spiritual intimacy with Jesus because the lukewarm heart only wants a taste sample – not the buffet. And of course, let us not forget that familiarity from those who know us certainly does not help with having an effective ministry. **"But Jesus said unto them, a prophet is not without honor, but in his own country, and among his own kin, and in his own house. And He could there do NO MIGHTY WORK, save that He laid His hands upon a few sick folk, and healed them"** *(Mark 6:4-5).*

Another inspiration was given to me by my wife Cheryl one night while discussing the life of loneliness and the lack of appreciation. With a very practical insight that had a profound impact on my thinking, she said that when most people read something or hear something that touches their hearts, they do not necessarily immediately contact the person who created it and thank them for a *word in due season*. The reality is that generally when Christians receive something they feel is a legitimate spiritual word from God, they presume these individuals are confident and strong enough in their calling that they do not need anyone to remind them how effective they are. For example, when you hear a song on the radio that pierces your soul, do you go home and try to contact the person who wrote it? You might go and purchase the song, but you usually do not try to personally reach the writer or singer. When you read an article in a magazine that ministers truth to your spirit and encourages you, do you write that person a letter or contact the website every time? Think of all the books you have read that touched your heart, but you never thought to contact the author. I began to think about this and realized that in my own experiences of reading and listening to others, I felt the same way and had done the same thing. It never occurred to me until recently that other ministries that feed my spirit and have a positive influence in my life need an encouraging word from ME! It seems that I have been presuming they did not need it. *Why?* Because I felt they were more spiritual than I, smarter than I am, more successful, more talented and too busy for my *peanut gallery* comments. I presumed they were getting so many other appreciations they did not need or care about mine, but if everyone thought that, how would anyone know who was being ministered to or feel encouraged to keep going? I appreciate positive feedback – and so do they!

When we begin to see the big picture of how the Lord operates, we realize that everyone deals with the same problems because we are all human. No matter how large or successful the ministry, the ones being used by God still feel insecure at times and inadequate in their labor because the enemy is always at work with his attempts to discourage and remind us that since we did not have very many *pats on our back,* then maybe what we are doing is not needed. For example, if no one comments after the minister finishes his sermon, he wonders if his contribution was a failure, when in reality it was so powerful everyone was speechless and did not know what to say. This reveals how fragile and vulnerable we are to being hurt and wounded when actually many times what we think is not true. Let us exercise by faith a new attitude of telling others how much we appreciate their ministries so that people can be encouraged and know their labors are not in vain. May we start treating those who work in God's Kingdom with respect and understanding, and in turn our willingness to be an encouragement can be passed on as a *contagious* blessing to others.

If you were in charge of a lighthouse that was built on the edge of the sea and you had not seen a ship pass by for several years, would you stop shining the light? *Why not?* Because you believe deep in your heart that someday your obedience will make a life-changing difference in someone's life! Instead of always thinking about what we can do or how we would do it better, let us take a deep breath and receive what the Lord is trying to say to us. Maybe the reason why we do not go out of our way to encourage other ministries is because we are jealous and envious of who they are, what they have done, and what they are doing. Here is a great *rocket science* revelation; we could start praying for them that God would increase their anointing and effectiveness, because this is what we are praying for ourselves! May we repent for our negative thoughts and critical judgments and lift up our heads and ask God to give us the love and interest for others who are working in the Kingdom just as we are. Sacrifice your flesh, and consider giving to others as they labor for God and are accomplishing the work that you have a vision to do. We are not competing for popularity; we are laboring for God - together! There is no place for suspicion, coveting, resentment, or jealousy in the ministry because these attitudes are sin and will drain our anointing and bring God's chastisement into our lives. Spiritual maturity realizes that it does not matter who is doing the work but rather who is being touched by the power and presence of Jesus. Let us remember the spiritual principle found in *Job chapter 42 and verse 10:* **"And the Lord turned the captivity of Job when he PRAYED for his friends: also the Lord gave Job TWICE as much as he had before."**

Chapter 42

THE POWER OF PRAISE

"Leah conceived again, and when she gave birth to a son she said, this time I WILL PRAISE THE LORD, so she named him Judah" (Genesis 29:35).

J udah comes from the Hebrew name which means praised or to praise. Judah was the fourth of 12 sons of Jacob and an ancestor of the tribe of Judah, as mentioned in the Old Testament. This particular tribe eventually formed the kingdom of Judah in the south of Israel, and its lineage includes King David and Jesus the Messiah. The connection between Judah and the Lion of the tribe of Judah can be found in the blessing given by Jacob to his son in the book of Genesis.

Every person has the choice to either praise God in any situation or rail out against the world with frustration and hopelessness. Within the power of praise is appreciating all the good things God does for us instead of taking Him for granted and living like a spoiled child. If we really believe everything He has promised in His Word, then we have nothing to worry about. *Brother, that's easy to say.* I know, but the simple things in life are usually the most powerful. Think about it for a moment. If we truly invite Him to possess our lives, this means we desire for Him to control us, and this is an awesome revelation. The next time we are facing a battle and would prefer to wave the white flag, I would like to remind us all to run through a simple test. Have you ever thought how a good indicator of whether or not we are walking in the Holy Spirit when being attacked hinges on our reaction to the assault? Being depressed with worry and embracing the dark clouds of impossibility is not only a defeated outlook but reveals our level of doubt in God's integrity! The Lord never panics about the unknown, and if we trust Him with ALL of our hearts we can know that He not only is aware of everything we are going through but also knows exactly how to fix it. When Jesus was in the boat and the storm was raging, what was He doing? Resting comfortably. *Why?* Because faith is complete confidence.

Stand back and see your situation NOT through the eyes that are connected to your brain but with the eyes of your heart, which reveals the reality of the Holy Spirit. Battles are NOT won with doubt! Triumph comes to those who sing praises to Him and who thank Him for the victory while they are still in the heat of battle. Amen! ***"By him therefore let us offer the sacrifice of praise to God CONTINUALLY, that is, the fruit of our lips giving thanks to His name"*** *(Hebrews 13:15). What does this have to with worship?* Praise is a positive confession that you are speaking forth, and it "activates" faith! When worship becomes a personal testimony, it moves God and generates the power of heaven! Be sensitive to what you are saying because you are RELEASING a manifestation of God's desire to reveal His glory! Somebody needs to praise Him right now! Speak your confession with confidence and expectation as a bold declaration that through your faith, God is injecting miracle power into your situations and enabling you to become more than a conqueror! Embrace the life-changing revelation that you are what you declare!

Adoring God is being confident that the one you are placing ALL of your trust in is really true! We cannot praise God if we do not believe that He is perfect and that He will never fail. Praise is a CONFESSION of our faith! The Lord is speaking to all of us today and asking us how in heaven's name can we possibly lead others and preach the victorious Kingdom message if we do not allow this revelation to be incorporated into our own lives? The word *hypocrite* means "actor," as in pretending to be someone you are not. Church is NOT the place for hypocrites to put on a religious show, but for battle-tested leaders that are learning to put what they are singing, praying, prophesying, and preaching about into practice. We are not humans trying to be spiritual – we are spirit beings trying to live in a human body! Trying to serve God and our flesh will result in a betrayal. Many are observing us and desperately need to see Jesus who can set them free, but if we are hesitant to praise Him

EVERYWHERE we are, then our witness is diminished and something is wrong in our hearts! Praise is the testimony of being filled with His joy and KNOWING that Christ is Lord and Savior in this life and the one to come!

Romans chapter 8 verses 15-16 says, ***"For you have not received the spirit of bondage again to fear; but you have received the Spirit of adoption, whereby we cry, Abba, Father. The Spirit itself bears witness with our spirit, that we are the children of God."*** Our heavenly Father is saying we must once and for all understand that we are NOT in bondage, but free to live boldly and walk in complete victory. The word *Abba* is another, less formal word similar to *Daddy* that communicates personal closeness. The Lord is saying we can call God our daddy because Jesus has defeated ALL fear. No longer do we need to be afraid of man or the devil, but let us rejoice in the blessings of sensitivity and discernment as HIS power gives us the victory! Fear always tries to convince us what we're not, what we can't have, and what we cannot do. Our normal reactions to fear are panic, stress, confusion, worry, anxiety, and dread because this is how our old natures are wired. We have a complete set of fleshly attributes that are connected to our emotions, and unless our minds are transformed, we will go with them every time. God knows that if our minds are not transformed and renewed in His word, we will never be overcomers. ***"For though we walk in the flesh, we do not war after the flesh: For the weapons of our warfare are not carnal, but mighty through God to the pulling down of strongholds; Casting down imaginations, and every high thing that exalts itself against the knowledge of God, and bringing into captivity every thought to the obedience of Christ"*** *(II Corinthians 10:3-5)*. The Lord is commanding us to cast down the natural thoughts of *I can't* and transfer our energies into a faith confession of ***"I CAN do all things through Christ who strengthens me."*** If we really believe that God wants us to live as triumphant overcomers in this life, then we should thank Him and PRAISE Him NOW for the victory because praise, prayer, and faith are as crucial to the spiritual warrior as guns, ammo, and a bullet-proof vest is to a combat soldier!

Comprehending how to listen and test the spirits is crucial if we desire to be led by God's voice. The Lord will always come to us in love because we are His children, and He wants to strengthen us with positive thoughts from *Romans 8:31* that says, ***"I am for you, so who can be against you?"*** What kind of Father would be cruel, impatient, harsh, critical, and negative toward His child? In *First John chapter 4 and verse 1*, we read, *"Beloved, believe* [trust] *not every spirit, but TRY* [prove] *the spirits whether they are of God: because many false prophets are gone out into the world."* Our heavenly Father reveals His strategy and then depends on us to take the first step onto the battlefield! Let us look at a very powerful story that gives us a wonderful illustration of how God expects us to react when we KNOW who He is and who we are in Him. In *II Chronicles chapter 20* the tribe of Judah is facing a powerful and ruthless army that is planning to attack them. However, the presence of the Lord is in the midst of the congregation and calls a prophet named Jehazial to step forward under the anointing. He boldly declares in *verse 15-19, "And he said, hearken ye, all Judah, and ye inhabitants of Jerusalem, and thou king Jehoshaphat, thus saith the Lord unto you, Be not afraid nor dismayed by reason of this great multitude; for the battle is NOT yours, but God's. Tomorrow go down against them: behold, they come up by the cliff of Ziz; and you shall find them at the end of the brook, before the wilderness of Jeruel. Ye shall NOT need to fight in this battle: set yourselves, stand still and see the salvation of the Lord with you, O Judah and Jerusalem: FEAR NOT, nor be dismayed; tomorrow go out against them: for the Lord will be with you. And Jehoshaphat bowed his head with his face to the ground: and all Judah and the inhabitants of Jerusalem fell before the Lord, WORSHIPPING the Lord. And the Levites, of the children of the Kohathites, and of the children of the Korhites, stood up to PRAISE the Lord God of Israel with a LOUD voice on High."* Receive this revelation today as the answer to the battle you are facing! Allow God's hope to be imbedded within your mind and heart, and stand and see the salvation of your God! When we face times of crisis, let us remember that our first response is NOT to be paralyzed with hopelessness, but to fall on our faces and worship Him! God is the same today, yesterday, and forever, and as we follow His instructions, He will intervene on our behalf because His perfect plans are always accomplished! Amen!

In *verse 20* we see the king exhorting the people to believe and have faith in God and the prophetic promise. Let us continue the story in *verses 21 and 22: "He appointed SINGERS unto the Lord, that should PRAISE the beauty of holiness, as they went out BEFORE THE ARMY, and to say, PRAISE THE LORD: for His mercy endures forever. And when they began to SING and to PRAISE, the Lord set ambushes and confusion against the children of Ammon, Moab, and mount Seir, which were come against Judah; and they were destroyed."* Praise His Holy Name! The armies began to fight each other, and as God's people watched, they were astonished to see that the enemy actually imploded with total annihilation, and there was not left one alive. Worthy is the Lamb that was slain! And let us not forget that it took three days to gather the spoils of riches and precious jewels as an added blessing for His children. This is an awesome example of the POWER of PRAISE and how God wants us to completely trust Him no matter what our circumstances look like!

God is saying when you watch all of the negativity going on in the world and you feel troubled and discouraged, pray for those who need the Lord's help and in faith SHOUT the victory in advance! When you receive a bad report and you feel the devil breathing down your neck, fall on your knees and call upon the God of your salvation and KNOW that nothing can separate you from His love! When darkness tries to flood your soul and whispers poisonous lies of despair, gloom, sadness, and depression, throw off the spirit of heaviness, put on your dancing shoes, and put on the garment of praise to prove to the devil that you BELIEVE what you know! Yes Lord! The good news of the gospel of Jesus becomes a hallelujah party when we take hold of the revelation about our identity in Christ and how the enemy actually begins to be intimidated of us when we become a pure vessel that pours out God's PRAISES! Worship is not just a celebration when we experience victories, but we also praise Him in the middle of our difficulties because our relationship is not based on when or how He reacts to our problems – it is based on how much we love Him! Performance-based religion is very shallow and does not provide true contentment or satisfaction. *"He is thy praise, and He is thy God, that hath done for thee these great and terrible things, which thine EYES have seen"* (Deuteronomy 10:21).

Of course you will not always FEEL like praising God when arrows and spears are whizzing past your nose, because the flesh will start whining to the mind, and emotions will pull the fire alarm to run and hide. However, this is the perfect time to sacrifice your *feelings* on the altar of faith and confess your confidence in God's Word! It is our responsibility to stand and fight against the dark spirits of panic and terror by embracing the Lord's joy of gladness, assurance, conviction and strength as we release it back to Him in praise! Letting go and letting God means we will NOT allow anxiety to rule and control us!

Christ identifies Himself so closely with His people that when they release praise to Him as an act of faith, He is actually incorporated into our worship and no one can stand against us because NO ONE can stand against Him! Amen! This guarantees that no matter how the circumstances turn out, we will always experience perfect victory because He made all things work together for the good to all that love God and are called according to HIS purpose. Exalting Him in Spirit and Truth is directly connected to trusting Him, and this opens the floodgates of our hearts to receive the fullness of the presence and glory of the Father's character. We must remember that when God FILLS our lives, that everything He is and all that He has includes bringing hope, peace, power, courage, miracles, revelation, prophecy, and edification to us and our storms! Somebody give Him praise and glory! Victory in Jesus will become more than a song to those who become determined to be soaked and saturated in God's covenant truth NOW! Victory is a blood covenant REALITY! *"Now therefore, our God, we thank thee and praise thy glorious name"* (I Chronicles 29:13).

PART VII

THE AWARENESS OF HIS GLORY

Chapter 43

THE BEAUTY OF DESCENDING

When we understand that something is evolving, we think of development and progression. Likewise, our spiritual evolution with Christ would be another way to explain the maturing process of our personal relationship with Him. We can visit many different types of churches and observe traditions and styles that have been passed along through the generations, and we should remain passionate about preserving truth; however it is also important to know what we believe and why we believe it. Along with absorbing knowledge, we are cautioned to watch out for a false religious dignity that attempts to blend carnality with spirituality. If we are to become remnant disciples for Christ, it is imperative that we learn how to grow in the truth of God's Word while keeping our pride *deflated,* because the more arrogant we become, the less available we are to Him. *Available to do what?* To express the innocence, sincerity, and humility that will govern the conscience to live in the delight of God's holiness. As we develop into adults, many feel the need to create their own ideas and concepts of maturity and sophistication. What we fail to realize is that just because we advance in age does not mean we are to allow the child within us to pass away. This misunderstanding of spiritual growth allows pride to be confused with spiritual maturity, and carnality with genuine innocence. We must be careful that we not allow the tenderness and excitement of our spirit to be quenched by the legalistic attitudes and guidelines of man-centered organizations. It is a common perception that how long a person has been involved with church automatically measures our spirituality, but the Christian life is NOT about seniority; it is about the evidence of being filled with God. At the heart of being born-again is the vision of starting all over and becoming as a child once again and allowing this new mentality to grow within a balanced perspective of truth. We have allowed the *increase* of our natural way of thinking to *decrease* our spiritual sensitivity, and this has led us to believe we can manage the church like we manage a grocery store. The Lord is very disappointed in the cold corporate attitudes of many people within the church that think more highly of the dignified, intellectual religious activity than the intimate fellowship between Jesus and His followers.

What does all this talk of being a child have to do with praise and worship? Pull up a chair and think with me for a minute. Children have clear consciences and do not worry about what other people think. They have not yet learned about being self-conscious or embarrassed. They respond bluntly and honestly according to how they feel. For example when they are hungry, they cry, and when they do not want to sleep, they cry, and they do not care about how loud or irritating they are! But have you ever thought about the way children react when they are standing at the door and see their daddies walking toward the house? They start laughing, hollering, stomping, and clapping - why? Because they want to be close to him: they want him to pick them up, hold them, and squeeze them. They long for the feeling of security, the bond of love, his strength and protection, as his presence brings excitement and joy.

Would it feel embarrassing to you to jump up and down and scream "daddy, daddy" when you are praising and worshipping Him? Yet, that is EXACTLY what God wants. Amen! For those who have children, there is nothing that can describe the feeling that comes from watching your children be so happy to see you! What joy it is to feel their love as they stretch out their arms and cry out your name. How much more does our heavenly Father long to see our excitement and is thrilled when we joyfully express our love for Him. I realize there is a difference between the emotional realm and the spiritual realm, but that does not mean we throw the baby out with the bathwater. Our deepest spiritual expressions toward God are intertwined in our emotions because our personalities are a part of what makes us individually unique. Allowing the *child within* to maintain a life of innocence and holiness unveils the precious image of infants sleeping safe and secure in the arms of their Fathers, and this is a lifestyle of worship.

I am reminded of my Grandmother and what a happy, bubbly personality she had. She was always filled with enthusiasm and laughed and giggled all the time. She was adventurous and always positive minded, seeing the best in everything. Even when she grew older, her charismatic spirit drew you like a magnet, and she was an example of how we are to never allow the childlike innocence within us to harden or be discarded. How I miss her enthusiasm and excitement and the sparkle of *youth* in her eyes. As we grew up, we were taught to stop running and jumping on daddy and to become more reserved and dignified. We learned to tone down our emotions and be more in control of our words and actions. We went through a process of transforming from a spontaneous and impulsive child to being more *repressed*. In our developmental stages we learned to hide our thoughts and wear a mask so that our feelings would not be exposed, which also helped to protect us from embarrassment along with understanding what is socially unacceptable. We discovered how to go through the motions and how to play mind games and adapt to situations. If left unchecked, the default system channels us into a life that is similar to a game of poker where learning how to bluff becomes crucial to our survival. When freedom and transparency are allowed to dissolve, we are left with a mechanical existence which not only has an undesirable effect on others – but also on our relationship with God. When an individual becomes born-again, it takes a while to comprehend the idea of completely trusting anyone, especially an unseen God. This is why many new Christians are leery of running with open arms and reckless abandonment to *anyone,* because we have been trained to NOT trust strangers.

Let's look at a passage of scripture in *I Corinthians 13:11*, **"When I was a child, I spoke as a child, I understood as a child, I thought as a child: but when I became a man, I put away childish things."** Some might think this means to gradually become dignified and reserved in church and in the Christian life, but actually this is referring to the differences in our ability to comprehend the depths of God today and when we will be transformed into our resurrected body in heaven. You must read *verses 10 and 12* that allow the train of thought to flow into the correct context. He is saying that we can only know in part and can only see partial images of what we will someday fully comprehend; however, within our spiritual development let us continue to realize and enjoy the depths of our relationship with Him. The Lord never intended His children to become estranged to Him in public or private. There is a huge difference between man's religious piety and having a revelation of the reverential fear of God. The enemy wants us to exchange spiritual peace for the carnal misery found in the captivity of pride and will never stop trying to make us feel that it is foolish to be joyful. In *Luke 9:26* we are reminded that **"For whosoever shall be ashamed of me and of my words, of him shall the Son of man be ashamed, when he shall come in his own glory, and in his Father's, and of the holy angels."**

Having the privilege of being involved with spiritual music has allowed me to see that praise and worship are attitudes of the heart and NOT just a place where we go or an act that we do. If we meet in a glorious amphitheater with a million dollar sound system and the music is not anointed, and the people are not in love with Jesus, it will all just be a nice concert. On the other hand, we can meet in a barn with no sound system and listen as God anoints a small child that sings *"Jesus loves me"* that can deeply touch the hearts of every listener. It's not the music that's trying to be spiritual – it's the Spirit in the music! God loves it when His people sing praises to Him, and if we are filled with God, we will sense the level of anointing that is in the music! People worship in many different ways, and the amount of divine evolution they have allowed to happen in their hearts is directly connected to how free and confident they are to express their love to Him wherever they are.

Each week I attend two unique types of church services which are somewhat similar yet contrasting. Church *ONE* is a more traditional service where I lead the music along with a full band while the congregation remains at their seats, raising their hands, reading the words of the songs on the overhead, and singing along. Church *TWO* has no one leading, no instruments, and no words; the congregation enjoys pre-recorded praise and worship songs through the sound system. They close their eyes and lift their hands and instantly connect. In these two musically distinct corporate services I have noticed some things that are interesting: Church *ONE* seems to need more encouragement to focus on the Lord. Sometimes if they feel like praising, they will respond, and sometimes they will not. In this environment there does not seem to be as strong of a spiritual expectation or craving. It is more reserved and more finicky to the menu and much more easily distracted. In today's world of contemporary worship many have become dependent on the words to the songs because that is what they have grown accustomed to, and sometimes I wonder if reading the words does not actually distract from the worship experience. The traditional idea of holding hymnals also seems to become a technical procedure that hinders the participator from entering into deeper intimacy. In church *TWO* there is no emotional preparation or anyone trying to prepare the people to praise. The ones who come are already prepared and so hungry and thirsty they are ready to enter the gates and courts of the Lord when they arrive. You can sense in the atmosphere an expectation of knowing that Jesus is available and is beckoning all to come *taste* and see that He is good. The moment the music is started, the people open up like flowers and begin to flow into God's presence. They don't care what others are doing, what the song is, or even if they have ever heard it. All that matters is connecting with God and telling Him in their own words how much they adore Him. I must include that since there is not a band or sound crew, there are no fumbles or confusion in the music or graphics, no technical problems, no frustration of band members not showing, but instead the music is smooth and peaceful and perfect every time without any distraction.

In church *ONE*, staying at your seat is the traditional custom and normal location to sing along with the music. This is fine but does tend to limit the personal freedom similar to how little children enjoy running and playing in wide open spaces. *Now brother, we need to do everything in decency and order.* I do not believe we can praise Him too much or be guilty of going over the top in our worship to the God of the universe. If we are NOT allowed to run around, jump, shout, wave flags, dance, fall on our face and weep in His presence, then maybe we need to learn the difference between legalism and liberty. In church *TWO*, there is complete freedom to worship however you desire. You can get out of your seat and walk around the sanctuary, pray for others, lie on the floor, go to the altar or anything connected to finding and enjoying the freedom to be with God. This liberty to appreciate the Lord's presence without the fear of embarrassment is very refreshing and reminds us of the simple happiness of being like a child. If we dance around the house or walk down the street singing praises to God, we can feel the release of our inhibitions, and likewise if we have a merry heart and make melody in our souls throughout the week, we will be more likely to enter into His joy in the corporate assembly.

We all come to church one of two ways; we are either primed and ready for Him, or needing for Him to stir and awaken us, but those that have learned how and made the choice to live in His presence through the week are the ones most likely to genuinely enter into His presence at church. Man's idea of normal church will no longer satisfy those who want to continue to go deeper as God's idea of *normal* church is to fill His people with His glorious love! He wants us to know His will and become the catalyst that allows His power to be made manifest within us. God's normal is signs, wonders, and miracles! Amen! God's normal is for His children to walk and release the brightness of His love and victory! The evolution of God's TRUE church is moving away from a mundane meeting of focusing on itself and is learning how to roll up its sleeves and extend Christ into the community and the world. The *river coming down* is the outpouring of the Holy Ghost to prophesy, spread the gospel, heal the broken-hearted, set the captives free and reveal the living Jesus to those who desperately need His truth. It is good to minister within the church, but how many will learn that an ever higher calling to ministry is needed beyond the church? Descending in God's Kingdom is about becoming mature enough to see that we must remain in the innocence of purity and humility, because genuine spiritual evolution is not ceasing to be a child – it's learning how to stay one. **"Verily I say unto you, except you be converted** [changed]**, and become as little children** [humble, trusting, honest, pure]**, you shall not enter into the Kingdom of heaven"** *(Matthew 18:3).*

Chapter 44
DOWNWARD MOBILITY

Staring into the gray, overcast sky, I find myself once again allowing the foggy mixture of damp and cold to influence and add to the restlessness of my emotions. The drizzling rain, the dreary, lonely feelings of quiet meditation stir thoughts within me about the time mankind has spent pondering that age-old question: *what is really our purpose?* My questions and thoughts are no different from all the other dreamers and philosophers throughout the millenniums. The majority of those I listen to in counseling also have the same need to be affirmed. We are not searching in vain for answers to impossible questions, because I believe the spiritual dimension is beckoning the seekers to wade out deeper into the realms and layers of holy wisdom; to come see, feel, and know the mysteries that are sewn within the fabric of divine reality. The truth is out there - but hidden, not because God does not want us to discover it, but He has preserved it just below the surface of our mortal existence for those who are driven and determined by faith to understand and comprehend who He is and what He wants. Our first key to breaking free is to obtain the revelation that we are living as a spiritual being within a natural environment. This higher dimension will be revealed only to the disciplined soul whose ultimate goal above all things is to become God's personal friend. These are the temples not made with hands that contain His Kingdom.

    The dimension of God is opposite from the realm where we live in many ways. I think it would be appropriate to call His dimension the right-side-up realm and where we live as the upside-down element. The Matrix concept was a fictional imagery of a world within a world, but this concept can help us to imagine that there really are TWO realms that exist within us at the same time. God wants His disciples to live a certain way according to the principles and standards of His divine reality while the default system wants to train and indoctrinate us to live according to the system of this natural world. For those who respond to the gospel of divine reality and accept Christ as their Lord, they cross-over from the default into the divine and begin the transition of mind alterations and thought transformations. As we grow in our new spiritual development, we learn that the goal of the natural realm is for the *default* humans to progress and advance higher so they can be more successful, powerful, and proud of their accomplishments. But in our new realm where we are now under God's control, His vision is for us to understand that His principles and standards are designed for the *first to be last and the last to be first*. The goals and destinies have been reversed; God's remnant disciples are called to abandon everything in this natural realm in order to comprehend and thrive within God's heavenly order, while the lost are to remain under the control of the default system and will eventually perish unless they hear and respond to the gospel of Jesus. God's people that have escaped the default system are now on a mission to rescue those who are deceived by the default system and are convinced it is the only life. Those whose eyes have been opened to this mystery are now compelled by the love of God to preach that there is a higher TRUTH within the divine reality far beyond human intelligence and earthly emotions. This band of remnant warriors will forsake the natural desire to build empires of earthly gain and instead become missionaries to this cause and students of downward mobility. This spiritual awakening and understanding is the only way anyone can be saved.

    The most important tradition found in ancient civilizations has been the passing of knowledge to the next generation for the simple reason of preserving the heritage and legacy of the past. One sign of a dissolving society is when the older leaders become satisfied, selfish, and lazy from sin or they just lose interest to teach at all. As the up and coming decision makers begin to reject traditional thinking, the original established philosophies are often set aside and replaced with new and seemingly improved concepts. Sometimes this may be the case, and other situations may not be for the better. If moral convictions that were once a normal way of life are allowed to be transformed into unfamiliar worldviews, the next generation of movers and shakers have the potential to change the complexion and of course the direction of the culture. It is easy to see that in our day and age, this is happening now. Change is good as long as it brings more of God's truth, but when mixed with false agendas and emotional opinions, it can be just as dangerous as it is helpful. A society must not become so angry and frustrated with their condition, that they accept dangerous inclinations out of desperation. This is an old *hat trick* from Satan, which falls into the category of spiritual deception with the consequences being damaging and deadly. *What does this have to do with worship?* If we fail to teach our children God's truth and do not take an active role in their spiritual development, the enemy will continue sowing tares into God's wheat field until there is a drought of God's truth. We must arise and live in the awareness of God's presence so that our young ones can SEE Jesus and know how to abide in His Word! When we lose our reasons why we believe, we have become like a ship without a compass lost in a dense fog upon the sea.

There is nothing more important for us who love Biblical wisdom than to pass the baton of spiritual life and the soul saving secrets of absolute truth to the future. We are called to preserve and demonstrate the hope and security of God's Word which has the power to transform those who choose to embrace its principles. For example, modern education is openly teaching the young minds of this age the humanistic idea that the evolution theory is uniformity; that is, it seeks to show that life in all its various forms and manifestations probably originated by causes similar to or identical with the forces and processes now prevailing. These philosophies teach the absolute supremacy and the past continuity of natural law as now observed. Uniformity says the changes now going on in our modern world have *always* been in action, and these present-day natural changes and processes are as much a part of the origin as anything that has taken place in the past. This view of nature and matter tries desperately to disprove God and His Word for the purpose of establishing a fresh world order of laws and precepts to live by. *What does all this have to do with worship?* Everything! How can we teach the next generation about worshipping the creator when the educational system is saying the Bible is filled with discrepancies? How can we as Christians serve and trust the Lord of all creation while our children are trying to decide who is telling the truth? If the Bible is a lie – there is no worship, no praying, and no personal relationship with God, which is exactly why the devil is relentlessly printing these heresies within the textbooks of our public educational system. No one knows all absolute truth except God Himself, but we must conclude there is definitely such a thing. A part of this truth that we can clearly understand is that the nature of man is evil, and as he continues to destroy the earth, even the animals will not be able to survive his greed. In turn, God is bringing judgment upon man because of his determination to sin, and is very angry to say the least with the way humans have taught the masses and treated His beautiful world. The blood of Jesus can wash away sin and can forgive anyone that receives Christ as Lord, but these errors that are being accepted as the socially accepted standards of intelligence are holding the blind in the bondage of ignorance. One absolute truth is more valuable than libraries of humanistic theories and philosophies, but until the remnant disciples of God's Kingdom take the initiative to become the light of holy love and divine wisdom, these strongholds of darkness will continue to grow.

It is sad that many have been brainwashed into the deceptions of the blind and choose to rely on fiction instead of trusting the ability of God who has already proven His validity. The Almighty holds the universe in the palm of His hand while the atheist and agnostic cannot even fathom the miracle of how a seed grows into a plant. It is with complete confidence that I proclaim that man did not evolve from a microorganism, a monkey, or any other animal form. The theories and daydreams of such thoughts are an insult to God as He has already clearly explained His miracles. Creation was not a process but rather was spoken into existence and was instantly manifested by the authority and majesty of God's Omnipotence. The liberal scholars cannot accept Biblical creation and must try to lower His identity and logically explain what He really meant in order to create Him in man's image. God is Omniscient from his nature to his Name, and He is the only one who can create from that which does not exist. Just imagine if the world embraced God and accepted Him for being who He claims to be, the arguments and opposition from the few unbelievers would be ignored. If science would bow their knees and announce the Bible as completely true and submit to His authority, this could open the door to worldwide revival! Who will acknowledge that God is the Alpha and Omega and has known everything from past, present, and future, and everything in between? ALL things were created by Him as He is the ONLY true God! For those who would attempt to belittle God's divine Omnipotence by explaining away his Word as fictional or a fabrication, may God have mercy on their souls as they are entangled and deceived with the false doctrines and foolishness of the default system.

To better understand God, man must bow down to Him with not just the physical knee but the surrender of the *will* that is in control of their hearts, and this has always been where mankind draws the line. When we are distant from God, it will come down to an attitude of haughtiness and loftiness that desires to draw our own way of living. Humans want to control their own destinies and are strongly convinced that they can, but this corrupt mindset has brought great destruction to the world since time began. Those who refuse to let go of the calloused conscience will automatically become hindrances to the progress of the Kingdom of light because they cannot comprehend what is right and wrong. They are unable to see through the distorted lenses of delusion, and in this condition are servants to the father of all lies who attempts to *brand* the minds of the impressionable into believing that being lifted UP is associated with greatness. God's kingdom, however, operates from a different standard and teaches that we descend into greatness because *less* is *more*. His way of thinking establishes the complex yet simple fact that when there is LESS of us, the MORE of Him there can be. Pomposity is an evil spirit that puffs us up and distorts our imaginations, but humility is the key to the downward mobility that we need to display in order to manifest Jesus Christ. In *Psalm 51 verse 10,* there is a verse that speaks about this mandatory attitude adjustment: ***"Create in me a clean heart, O God; and renew a right spirit within me."*** This transformation process, called salvation or *new creation reality,* consists of yielding and forcing our wills into submission, but in all honesty it has not been taught correctly; neither has it been understood by the masses. When we are *born again,* our plans and ideas must be totally surrendered to Him so that He can take His rightful place as the King of our hearts. He has a brand new set of plans and has come to rescue us from ourselves as we tear down what we know and allow Him to re-build our conscience into a new way of thinking.

If you are a student of the New Testament, you have already seen the outline of its gospel; the world hates the message of surrender, and the messenger is Jesus. Christians and non-Christians relate to Christ many different ways, and how much they accept His message depends on which Jesus they choose to tolerate. For example, most people love baby Jesus because babies are so cute and non-threatening. He is not a threat, and they love the feeling of being larger and stronger than He is.

Adults are naturally in total control of a baby, and the human conscience can rest easy in the presence of an infant. At Christmas most people are in a festive mood of cheer and good will and can go along with the story about the wise men and Bethlehem. For the masses, Jesus is harmless as long as He is kept in the manger and not allowed to grow up and express His laws and commandments. Another picture of Jesus that is widely accepted is when He fed and healed people. Our minds register this view of Jesus as a provider and supplier of our needs and we think this is great. We like the idea of someone presenting us a delicious buffet or relieving our pain, so this is a positive image that is tolerated among those who see Him as a cosmic vending machine. These are also the ones that never talk to Him or acknowledge His presence until they have a crisis. These simple-minded thoughts about Christ are easy to deal with and are about as much of God as most people want.

Where people begin to turn away from Jesus and walk away is when He is presented as Teacher and Master, which turns the tables and places him in authority and control. When the world is introduced to His anointed instructions, demands, and requirements, the room begins to thin out, as people grow uncomfortable, and rebellion begins to rise up from their human nature. To most individuals life is an amusement ride built for their enjoyment – not a life of rules and regulations. Human nature wants to stimulate every nerve and indulge in every pleasure with constant gratification and to consume it all in the spirit of excitement and lust. The people who serve this realm do not want to be told what to do in their personal thoughts and actions, and they certainly have no intention of developing spiritual discipline. They will have the last say or die trying and this comes from the ever present attitude of rebellion and the age-old battle of control between the spirit and the flesh. In fact, the more that people understand Christ and what He desires, the more they realize that He wants to completely rule their every thought and decision. This in turn places us in the crossroads of deciding just how far we are going to allow Him to intervene in our lives. Religion has always compromised, distorted, and watered down the Word of God because it is just too intrusive. The masses are being deceived with cupcake lessons in politically correct thinking and a distorted tolerance to sin, and in this light, most people are generally NOT becoming closer to God - they are drifting farther away.

Much of the religious system feeds the masses what they want to hear in order to keep up the salaries and expenses to finance their existence. The truth is that religion loves their non-threatening, *pleasure programs* but actually is opposed to the real Jesus and would never support His doctrines. The religious world seems to be powerful in pomp and ceremony, but spiritually it is shallow and powerless because it does not know God personally. The attitude toward Jesus is the same today as when they cried out for His execution - He stood before the people as an innocent man, and they hated His uncompromising word of truth! His strict holiness was enmity against the human will and was immediately rejected by humanism. Barabbas represents the flesh and the carnal mind and was offered as a free-will choice for those who gathered at this illegal trial. The authorities allowed the crowd to choose, and they selected Barabbas the same as we all have the constant decision to obey or deny our flesh. We can sum it up very simply by saying the un-renewed mind hates Jesus, and since it works hand in hand with the carnal nature, we realize exactly where the continual resistance to Jesus comes from. He is hated because He requires us to lay down our lives and take up His life. Human nature and the default system strongly believe that they have just one life and one chance to live it, and that that life is to be self-governed to do whatever it wants without God interfering. Unfortunately, those that live by this code are technically correct because they do have the legal right to trade whatever years of physical life they have for an eternity of spiritual death.

You would think that going to church and occasionally reading the Bible would allow us to understand God, but just because someone works for a company that manufactures telescopes does not necessarily mean that person knows anything about the universe. Many know about God, but very few know Him personally because such knowledge takes a lifetime of searching and learning; however, one aspect of His Spirit that we can understand rather quickly is how pride and humility have a direct effect on the *anointing dial* with any type of ministry unto the Lord. Since *James 4:6* says that God does in fact RESIST the proud, it only makes sense that pride automatically lowers our spiritual effectiveness. When we do not submit to God in what we are attempting to do, our carnal swagger exposes how confident we are to lean on our flesh and depend on our ability to *perform* without His power. A heart that is desperately needy for God welcomes the Lord into our life, but a heart that is contaminated with haughtiness is deceived and seldom effective. James goes on to say that God gives GRACE to the humble, and will open doors to His favor and increase the miracle power and blessings associated with His divine principles. God desires to demonstrate His glory through His people, but many times they are so consumed with taking curtain calls and loving the applause that they fail to acknowledge who gave them their ability. When the Bible mentions about God being jealous, it is not talking about the sin of jealousy, but rather Him wanting the attention that we are giving to something else. And we do not need to worry about sharing God's glory because in all honesty, it is NOT going to happen! We are very much like a battery operated tool, and trying to function on our own is like trying to operate without the battery.

Many of us have experienced in our Kingdom labors that when we are out of our minds excited about what we are going to do, that many times our ministry visions do not turn out the way we dreamed. And other times when we are struggling and desperately cry out for Him to help us because we feel completely inadequate, His presence and glory leaves us standing speechless. *Why?* Because there is a difference between having faith in our own abilities to accomplish what WE want to see - and knowing that it is God's power and control. It is healthy to have an expectation that He is going to be there and use us to accomplish His will, but somewhere in the mix we must remove our twisted thinking that it depends on how talented or popular we are. We try to be on guard for obvious pride, but we can be subtly deceived into thinking that we are God's person of the hour and that everyone else just needs to *get on board or get out of the way*. In the church setting, it is common for individuals to wait patiently for their chance to minister because someone else is presently in the position of what they want to do. They are convinced that if they can patiently *endure* the suffering, that God will eventually promote them into their rightful place. This may be true, but while we are standing in the shadows, we must make sure of some crucial factors that are associated with helping us move into position to be used or could possibly prolong our waiting. NUMBER 1. Are we positive this is exactly what God is telling us to do, or is it just something we know we CAN do? If we know we are called to this ministry, God will make a way, and we must not allow anyone to talk us out of it. NUMBER 2. We are NOT to be envious, jealous, resentful, bitter, or critical of those that are currently in position trying to do God's will! Amen! If we are betraying them or being negative toward them because we are on *stand-by* to take over their position, this is NOT gaining God's approval and neither is it helping us become prepared for our mission. How in the world can we expect to have God's anointing while nurturing this type of dismissive intentional behavior? A crucial pillar of the Christian life foundation is spiritual maturity, and if we are acting like a spoiled brat, the Lord is not excited about allowing us to hold any kind of titles or positions in representing His Kingdom. In fact, He is sad and disappointed in our sinful attitudes and probably will NOT open the doors for us to advance AT ALL because He knows we are NOT ready to handle the spiritual warfare and responsibilities that are a part of His ministry.

Listen, I will be the first one to say that it is difficult to understand why certain decisions are made in church. Of course there are politics and manipulations, but we must not retaliate because at the end of the day you cannot force anyone to embrace you or your ministry. It would seem that someone who coaches a baseball team would want the power-hitter to have as many "at bats" as possible, but there are also times when the team needs a base hit or a good bunt. The point is, if someone is intentionally holding you back from your calling, God will deal with it one way or another, but shame on you if you are the one that is causing God's perfect will to be delayed and are spending your precious time blaming everyone else. If we are already acting ugly and being defeated by pride BEFORE we are in position, how much more likely are we to fail when we are promoted? It is difficult to be sincere and pray for the ones that have what we want, but it is an important part of the process of taking control of our wills and bowing before God in meekness and humility. Once again, there is no substitute for the renewed mind because it allows us to take control of our thoughts, which in turn help manage who we are! And when we finally do have the opportunity to step into leadership, we still must be very sensitive to *maintain* our humility because things might appear to be satisfying at the beginning, but if we are not completely depending on Jesus, we will soon fizzle-out because we are running on the fumes of our natural proficiency. God wants to flow through us, but the vessel of honor must have a clean attitude – all the time! It is true that our callings and ministries can help bring healing to the bodies, minds, and spirits of all who hear God's Word and reach out in faith - but let us never forget that we are just the syringe. . .not the medicine nor the doctor. ***"For I say, through the grace given unto me, to every man that is among you, not to think of himself more highly than he ought to think; but to think soberly, according as God hath dealt to every man the measure of faith"*** *(Romans 12:3).*

Chapter 45
THE OVERCOMERS

"And they overcame him [the devil] **by the blood of the Lamb** *[Jesus]* **and by the word of their testimony; and they loved not their lives unto death"** *(Revelation 12:11).*

The blood of Jesus empowers His saints with the authority of His Name! Our testimony is a declaration of faith that understands who we are IN Christ and that NOTHING can stop us from accomplishing His will! The Kingdom of God is advancing – because it CANNOT be stopped! Praise Him forever! God's nature is love, and nothing can conquer love. This is not just a catch phrase but is crucially important to remember when we are walking through difficult places that are filled with discouragements and disappointments. For the remnant disciple, one of the greatest lessons to learn, and stay aware of after we have been knocked to the ground, is the determination and courage to get up and dust ourselves off and keep going. The enemy has spent the last 6000 years trying to distract men and women away from God's will, but the joy of the Lord is a fountain of strength that cannot be quenched! All of the darkness in existence cannot overcome one tiny lit candle, and all of the hate in the universe cannot outweigh one act of genuine compassion! Love IS the authority of God and will never fail, and when we learn how to encourage our own hearts, we can take another step into the maturity process of being an overcomer for Christ.

It is true there are times when we are down, and we all will have problems and situations that we must deal with in this life, but thank God that He is always there as a safe haven to give us encouragement and support that can help us through our times of troubles and sorrows. Yes, the battle is very difficult, and at times many of the soldiers may crawl and drag themselves into the sanctuary, but this is where many have never realized that the true church is actually a hospital, not a social club. The church is no place for pessimism, unbelief, or an attitude of defeat, no more than an intensive care unit is. We must be sensitive to the spirits of depression or of oppressive, critical, and judgmental attitudes that are like a contagious virus that can infect others with hopelessness and drain the atmosphere of expectation. In *I John chapter 1, verse 4* we see that joy is like a liquid in a *tank* that can run low or be filled, and it is necessary to constantly monitor our joy and protect it from being diminished. ***"And these things write we unto you, that your joy may be full."*** If the general of an army told the soldiers they did not have a chance to win the battle, the negativity would exhaust their strength and crush their faith before they even started. *So how do we stay filled with joy?* It would definitely contribute to our joy tank if we would deliberately spend more time in His presence. Nothing can take the place of simply thinking about Him and sharing our concerns and feelings with Him.

Thoughts of defeat, frustration, worry, failure, and fear are the uninvited guests in the church, and all ministry leaders are too familiar with these haunting shadows of negativity. *What does all this have to do with worship?* I believe we can agree that the spiritual strength of the individual is based on the fullness of joy within the heart. Without a strong personal relationship with God, there is limited joy, and with low joy there is a mediocre interest in worship; so we can say that the stronger our relationship with Him, the more full our joy will be, and the more He can be seen within us. As believers in the full gospel we must realize that God's idea of a normal Christian life is for us to be fearless warriors that daily operate in the realm of signs and wonders. God's Word reveals how the last days are going to unfold and how religious spirits will continue to distort the true reality of normal into an imposter normal! Nonetheless, no matter how deceptive or hypocritical the religious system becomes, Jesus will accomplish His perfect agenda with those who love Him!

When Jesus calls you to let go of the boat and walk on the water, there is nothing that can prevent your victory as long as you stay focused on His presence! Amen! Satan does not even care if we accept Christ as long as we keep Him to ourselves, because when we live as undercover agents for Jesus, we are NOT a threat to his dark domain. However, when we allow our flame to receive more oxygen from the Holy Spirit, and it turns into a raging fire, he realizes that we can be used to help recruit thousands of soldiers for the Lord's army, tear down principalities and strongholds, and do mighty miracles and wonders in Jesus' Name! It is worth the moment to consider the question: will you allow the enemy to stop you from being an overcomer? We are living in the last moments of grace, but it is also a time to become strong in our faith and personal intimacy with the Lord because our familiar and comfortable lifestyle can change very quickly, and many will be stunned to find themselves in places and situations that will NOT be comfortable to say the least. Overcomers are strong leaders that have *Special Forces* training to PRAY and OBEY in all circumstances! It will become more difficult to function in a harsh and distressing environment, but the remnant will be used to help teach and lead many into the revelation of God's absolute truth. Prepare now to be activated when the world is turned up-side down. Allow Him to fill you with the wisdom of His Word today, or you will not have the anointing or faith to stand boldly as a leader in the days ahead.

We have been given God's promises and instructions that explain how we are to react to the world's system and how to believe that He will create and provide the miracles we need. But we have become a *spoiled* generation that has never known what it means to really have a need except in a crisis which has put many of God's people into a self-induced coma of relaxation and comfort. We must not lean on our own understanding or trust in our own strength, politics, finances, or education when it comes to survival, but rather listen to God's counsel. If we are going to be provided for like Elijah at the brook and the woman with the measure of oil, we must learn how to be an encouragement not only to others, but to encourage our own hearts. If we cannot believe God to heal our sore toe today, what makes us think we will be able to believe Him for a loaf of bread in the day of famine? There is no reason to be stressed or worried about what man will do because we have been promised that direction and encouragement will be given to those who are devoted to God. ***"The Lord is near unto all them that call upon Him, to all that call upon Him in truth. He will fulfill the desire of them that fear Him: He also will hear their cry, and will save them"*** *(Psalm 18-19)*. He will lead us with the revelations of His Word, prophecies, visions, dreams, wonders, and miracles the same as He guided and provided for the children of Israel. The Lord said in *Acts chapter 2 verses 16-21,* **"But this is that which was spoken by the prophet Joel; And it will come to pass in the last days, says God, I will pour out of my Spirit upon all flesh, and your sons and your daughters will prophesy, and your young men will see visions, and your old men will dream dreams: and on my servants and on my handmaidens I will pour out in those days of my Spirit; and they will prophecy: and I will show wonders in heaven above, and signs in the earth beneath; blood, and fire, and vapor of smoke: the sun shall be turned into darkness, and the moon to blood, before that great and notable day of the Lord come: and it shall come to pass that whosoever will call on the name of the Lord will be saved."** We have our mission and God's power, but who wants to go?

The word from the Lord today is that He is trying to get our attention. He is doing everything He can to open the eyes of our hearts so that we can learn how to live for Him. Of course, the devil wants to keep these revelations a secret because he realizes this is a military strategy that can tear down his spiritual strongholds and defeat the powers of darkness, and he is on *high alert* to prevent God's overcomers from being spiritually stimulated! Remember the story found in *I Samuel chapter 30* about David and his army when they returned home to Ziklag and found the city had been burned and all of their families had been taken captive by the Amalekites. *Verse 4* says, **"Then David and all the people that were with him lifted up their voice and wept until they had no more power to weep."** But notice in the last part of *verse 6,* **"but David encouraged** [strengthened] **himself in the Lord his God."**

Those that are involved with ministering God's Kingdom will not always feel like standing strong or being electrified with an overflowing current of excitement and enthusiasm. There will be seasons of frustration and fatigue where it seems that nothing is happening and things are coming unraveled. But these are the times when we need to have a private consultation in front of the mirror and lay down God's law to our will! We have the CHOICE to believe truth or embrace the negative. The mind is like a garden, and we are the gardener. We can plant whatever we want and will harvest whatever we have sown! Our new spirit and renewed mind is ready to listen to King Jesus as He inspires us to *confess out loud* His never failing truth over ourselves, our families, and our situations. This is accomplished only when we develop a serious awareness of our thought life and how powerful our confessions can be. You see, the old nature is associated with the old way of thinking, but when our minds have been renewed in Christ, this is intended to give us better leverage when trying to wrestle our *will* into its rightful place (which is submission to Jesus). We can demand and command all we want, but until this structure of order has been established, the process will not function properly. We can take the safe path of least resistance where we just hold our shields, play defense, and do enough to get by, or we can face our fears of being uncomfortable, take a bold stand, pick up our swords, and go on the offence. This is your mission – if you decide to accept it: ***"To appoint unto them that mourn in Zion, to give them beauty for ashes, the oil of joy for mourning, the garment of PRAISE for the spirit of heaviness; that they might be called trees of righteousness, the planting of the Lord, that HE might be glorified"*** *(Isaiah 61: 3).* Will you sit around and allow discouragement to dominate your life? You are NOT insignificant - you are a catalyst that has been commissioned to arise and help others find the oil of gladness on their way to accomplishing the divine destiny Jesus has called them to live!

Soon after Jesus had resurrected, we find a beautiful passage in *John chapter 20 verses 24-31* that is a wonderful example of how much God wants to encourage us. Here is a story about the friends and family of Christ that were mourning His death when all of a sudden He appears in their midst! Of course I am sure they are awestruck and in fear until He stretches out His nail-scarred hands and reveals where He was pierced, and then they were overjoyed to see Him! He spoke peace unto them and breathed on them and filled them with the Holy Spirit because He loved them, and in our times of sadness when it seems that all is lost, He will make the extra effort to find us and prove that He is with us and that He cares about us. Thomas (also known as Didymus) was one of the twelve but was not there that night, and when he was told about Jesus visiting them, he said that until he could touch His scars, he just could not accept it. After eight days they were gathered together again, except this time Thomas was there, and Jesus appeared again. He told Thomas to reach out and touch the scars, and he did. Jesus said, ***"Be not faithless, but believing,"*** and Thomas replied, ***"my Lord and my God."*** How many times have you needed the Lord to inject faith into your doubt? When Jesus intervenes, nothing is ever the same! When He speaks to the storms, they have no choice but to obey His commands, and when He is with you on the front-line of battle, the devils and demons must bow before Him and submit to His authority! Paul and Silas were locked in prison, yet began to worship because joy is not confined to a geographic location, a mood, or an emotion – it is activated when the determination to believe God becomes stronger than the temptation to doubt Him! They made a CHOICE to praise God because they loved Him and trusted Him! The Lord knows that if you can maintain your faith, then in the name of Jesus YOU can speak to the mountains in your life, and in God's power they will be removed! ***"And ALL things, whatsoever ye shall ask in prayer, believing, ye shall receive"*** *(Matthew 21:22).*

Hopelessness is a condition of the default system that occurs when people trust only their own decisions. Human intellect and logic, impressive education, great wealth, or political power cannot save souls or bring true peace. Only God can change a mind and transform a life. I realize that church leaders must be honest and transparent with their feelings because if the *human factor* was not detected within our personalities, the ministry would seem very robotic. However, many leaders feel pressured or forced to be *bouncy happy* all the time because they want to keep everyone enthused and fear if they do not demonstrate a positive image, they will cause others to lose their zeal. Learning how to be *real* is like walking an emotional tight wire, and congregations need to remember that everyone lives in human housing. The role of a pastor is not easy and deserves more prayer and less criticism. I recently attended a meeting of pastors that were discussing the trials and challenges of ministry, and instead of being excited, I was disappointed because they were not wearing their *super-hero* capes. I listened as these veteran warriors shared their burdens and worries and as they discussed church growth and how to get people to catch their vision. As they talked about their problems with everything from excessive debt to people being unfaithful, I sensed a heaviness of negativity that was being exposed as a type of spiritual *kryptonite*. I had anticipated being inspired and was looking forward to hearing stories about miracles because I was surrounded by leaders that were filled with God's power and faith but also had become very worried about the condition and hope for the future of all churches. I felt there had been a mistake because instead of witnessing a celebration of victory with the generals, I was sitting in on a religious pity party for defeat! I was thinking to myself, that everyone knows there are problems in the church, but pastors are supposed to have the answers! In my lack of maturity and sensitivity, I had forgotten that *generals* need places to vent their frustrations and weaknesses, and a naturally safe environment would be with those who understand exactly what they are going through. **"Without counsel purposes are disappointed: but in the multitude of counselors they are established"** *(Proverbs 15:22)*. Local assemblies have teachers, counselors, associate pastors, administrators, singers, musicians, superintendents, elders, and deacons, but none of these are actually *responsible* for knowing the direction of the church because they do not literally LEAD it! Potato peelers are not always invited into the war room because this is where proven leaders can relate to each other and listen with respect and empathy about making serious decisions. Of course Christ is the head of His church, but He appoints the *under shepherd* to relay His messages and provide hands-on care for the sheep. Let us all remember that the pastor also wears the brightest bulls-eye on his back and is counting on us to surround him or her with continual intercession.

It is true, the super-natural gift and office for pastors is to know God's vision for the assembly and to lead the warriors into the battle! But what I personally failed to experience in that room was compassion for those who stand on the front lines every day. These men were letting down their guard in front of me, and as they felt secure with each other, they used this time as a place of temporary refuge away from the war, to share their hearts, experiences, and scars. It was difficult for me to adjust my thinking and discern a compassion for their struggles. They are the ones that get up in the middle of the night and kneel on cold hospital floors praying for the sick. They go into lonely nursing homes and hold the hands of people that are passing on to the next life. They are the ones that help restore order in crisis situations and have walked through many funeral homes and cemeteries. They worry about administration obligations and organizing ministries and trusting leaders to be responsible. They carry the concerns and stresses that no one else realizes because many people have shared their secret problems with the pastors and trust them to keep the secrets confidential. While none of us, including pastors, are to become overwhelmed with pressure and anxiety, let us remember that it's okay to be honest with the ones who care for our souls.

We ALL need someone we can trust to share the secrets of our hearts. **"Where no counsel is, the people fall: but in the multitude of counselors there is safety"** *(Proverbs 11:14)*. Overcomers are notorious for carrying burdens, but they also learn to leave those burdens at the foot of the cross because they are very heavy and can hinder our liberty to live in joy. May we remember that as servants of the Most High, ministers feel the same pain and heartaches that everyone does, and there is no condemnation for being sensitive. It is not an option but crucial that we all learn how to encourage ourselves and know the source of our strength. Strong leaders learn that qualities like fortitude, perseverance, and integrity are formed and activated in times of great difficulty. ***"We are troubled on every side, yet not distressed; we are perplexed, but not in despair; Persecuted, but not forsaken; cast down, but not destroyed"*** *(II Corinthians 4:8-9).*

> *"Father, I desperately need You to fill me with Your PASSION. Make me hungry and thirsty for Your presence, and help me to develop an awareness of Your voice within my heart. If I do not have Your FIRE, I will remain a fading ember and be satisfied to stay in my comfort zone. If I do not have Your love working in my conscience, I am nothing and will not be of any use to You. Break me and melt me so that I can be molded into Your image. Do a strong work in my heart that will literally CHANGE the way I think. I am weak and self-centered Lord; please give me compassion and a burden for the lost, the needy, and those who are hurting. Breathe life into me and renew a fresh enthusiasm to follow the blueprint You have drawn for me. I need Your strength and desire to become the remnant disciple You are waiting for me to be. Use me as a compassionate witness in Your fields that are white with harvest I pray. Amen."*

Chapter 46

DISCERNING THE SEASONS

"To everything there is a season, and a time to every purpose under the heaven" (Ecclesiastes 3:1).

Every minister in time will learn painfully through experience when to speak, what to say, and when being quiet is *golden*. Whether behind the pulpit, on the street corner, in a counseling session, hospital, or coffee shop, there are times we must discern what the Lord wants to say and when to keep our fleshly thoughts from babbling. We can rest assured that when God tells us it is time to speak, His wisdom will always know how to communicate because He is perfect in word, thought, and deed. In His infinite ability to know everything all at once, He perceives when hearts are open to accepting His penetrating truth or the convicting power of silence. Going beyond our emotions includes having spiritual discernment to understand that His messages are not always about comfort and peace but are strategically arranged within divine appointments to provoke and challenge as instruments of *change*. The Lord is constantly going before us to orchestrate these wonderful opportunities, but along with preparing the field for the seed, He must also get the attention of the *sower*. When God's timing is right, the simplest words can penetrate through the most solid brick walls as He is the ONLY power that can illuminate a revelation of truth that can transform a life forever. But when the messenger is NOT in tune with His presence, our words of human emotion are projected like an irritating, screeching noise that actually repels the listener and can do more negative damage than good.

What does this have to do with worship? Any leader that is involved with ministry must recognize the *green light* to proceed and the *season* of his own anointing to connect and effectively relay God's message with discernment. *What is meant by season?* Well, in *Psalm chapter 1, verse 3* we notice the writer using the analogy of a person being like a tree. **"And he shall be like a tree planted by the rivers of water** [always spiritually nourished], **that brings forth his fruit in his season** [has wisdom and discernment to operate in God's timing]; **his leaf also will not wither** [he will stay enthused, joyful, strong, and encouraged]; **and whatsoever he does will prosper** [success, integrity, respect, and blessings]."* Picking ripe fruit has everything to do with timing, so this insight has to do with making the right decisions at the right place at the right time, and all of this of course is directly connected to being led by the Holy Spirit. If sermons and songs are like medicine and problems are like illnesses, then how important is it to match up the right prescription with the right sickness? Again, learning to know God's still small voice is like understanding His diagnosis for those we are talking with no matter where we are. People have needs, and God is THE great physician who knows what is wrong and is always ready to prescribe the treatment while His servants administer anointed communication through the direction of the Holy Spirit. When there is an absence of Spirit–led sensitivity in the connection between them, the message and the messenger become like two ships passing in the night. When we become aware of God's presence, it is like becoming familiar with our spiritual GPS system that enables us to know where we are going and exactly what God wants us to do and say. **"A man has joy by the answer of his mouth: and a word spoken in due season, how good is it!"** *(Proverbs 15:23).*

It is a fact; we are NOT always on top of our game. Have you ever had times when you just felt out of sync and could not sense the anointing? These are times we need to realize that we are not helping matters by proceeding with our agenda but to slow down and try to hear what He is saying. Have you ever felt that your dreams will never come true or that your season has passed? Remember the Lord led Moses into the *wilderness* to tend sheep for forty years before He called him to lead Israel through the wilderness, and David spent much of his time as young boy alone in the fields tending sheep because these times of isolation are places where the Lord has our undivided attention. God often develops and prepares forerunners in the quiet places so they will be able to lead others through similar experiences and become better equipped to handle much larger responsibilities. It is very important to know that God honors faithfulness and if we are following His voice we are in the process of advancement. *"His lord said unto him, Well done, thou good and faithful servant; thou hast been faithful over a few things, I will make thee ruler over many things: enter thou into the joy of thy lord"* (Matthew 25:23).

In ministry it is crucial to sense when God is using individuals that are in the *season* of their anointing and be excited to witness them blessing the people. Worship leaders need to train others to lead and be aware of whom the hand of God is upon for that hour, and the same is true with pastors that may feel the duty to teach while they could just as easily call on someone else to bring the Word of the Lord. Knowing when to step aside is just as important as knowing when to step forward, and if the Spirit of God is not present at the altar, let us not beg, plead, or try to *work it up,* or attempt to make it happen! A bit of wisdom to remember: it is always much better to bring a small amount of anointed truth and have the people wanting more than to exhaust them with a dry performance until they are praying you would stop! A word of encouragement for those who are waiting for their season to come; do not feel down or disheartened by your time of silence. God is preparing you and as you submit to His authority and make yourself presentable, you can know that He is making a way for you. Always remember that delay is NOT denial and the perfect work of patience builds maturity and strong character. *I Corinthians 14:26* says, *"How is it then, brethren? When you come together, every one of you has a psalm, has a doctrine, has a tongue, has a revelation, has an interpretation. Let all things be done unto edifying."* And *verse 31* adds, *"For you may all prophesy one by one, that all may learn, and all may be comforted."*

Seasons are not to be confused with how much we can do or how good we can do it. Our feelings are very misleading because they sometimes seem like a hunch or a guess about what God is saying or desires for us to do. Spiritual seasons are special times when we *know* God's voice and are not afraid to act on it. The religious church service has a tendency to organize God completely out of the picture, which leaves very little need for spiritual discernment and is the reason why this gift is rarely mentioned. In fact, many leaders do not even think about leaving anything to a spontaneous *risk of the unknown* because it is more secure to plan ahead and prepare exactly what *they* are going to do than to listen to what *God* wants to do. The Lord has very little room to move in a service where those in charge have already mapped everything out to coordinate with their program. We do not need a Bible Scholar to figure out that this type of presentation usually makes it a human organization instead of a divine demonstration. Many complain about dead, dry services and say they long to be filled with joy and excitement. It does not necessarily mean we should dance, run, shout, and do cartwheels every time we come together either. We realize there are extremes within the realm of emotions, but all must be compelled with finding the perfect balance of God's seasons every time we come together. Incorporating a TRADITIONAL format of doing anything exactly the same every time for the sake of emotional comfort can become a religious ritual whether it be a reserved Baptist or a shouting Pentecostal. Living for God is not a generic style but a genuine response! ***"Preach the word; be instant in season, out of season; reprove, rebuke, exhort with all long-suffering and doctrine"*** ***(II Timothy 4:2).*** It is about listening and being obedient to what God is requesting and to never be intimidated or hesitant to speak truth whether it *feels* right or not. Just because people seem happy and are dancing, do not allow that to persuade you from bringing an urgent word of seriousness. Speak from God's discernment and NOT according to the way situations appear, because things may not be the way they seem. No two services are alike, and God plans it that way so that we will not try to mass produce Him or turn His sovereignty into a cookie-cutter pattern that we can take for granted. We have learned a great deal about how He operates, but let us avoid trying to control Him or reduce His presence into a religious formula.

There are also seasons of sorrow, and that is perfectly normal. Jesus was a man of sorrows, not just because He was born to be brutally murdered but also because He could feel the weight of sin and discouragement in the hearts of all mankind. We are a spiritual and human combination, and it is conventional to go from the joys of excitement and hope to be emotionally sad from the agony from human suffering. Jesus has never stopped feeling compassion for this world, and I believe His thoughts and concerns are felt and relayed through our spirits. There are seasons for fasting and interceding, and times to weep and pray, and it is time that God's remnant disciples come out of the *automatic pilot mode* of mechanical programs and get into the *real time* awareness of His mercy and kindness. Church is not a theatrical performance but an invitation from the Holy Ghost to demonstrate God's power for the hour, and until His saints cry out for the revelation to know what His Spirit has to say, they will continue in the deadness of a mundane ritual. Church should be the place to witness a spontaneous celebration of miracles and heavenly manifestations, not boring speeches or the buddy system. Those who watch the weekly *show* and are satisfied with shaking hands with strangers will be content to hold on to their pacifiers! God's remnant warriors have made the choice to abandon the *rock a bye baby* atmosphere and have learned that Jesus will INVADE the lives of those who will INVADE His throne!

Do you think being out of season has anything to do with our services being flat? Absolutely! We realize that many gather at the gates of thanksgiving but are not necessarily on the same page with His agenda because they have not dealt with some of the *walls* of sin that need to be dismantled. Not only are we held back because we have failed to repent, but this distance keeps us from knowing specifically what He wants. There have been times when I was ready to lead praise and worship and prepared my heart until it was ready to explode with *battle praise,* but before the service I felt the Holy Spirit holding me back. At first, I did not understand but eventually came to realize that I was trying to put the cart before the horse so to speak. A bound person cannot run, and shackled hearts have difficulty lifting their hands in praise. It is because they are holding on to their problems and cannot lift their hearts in freedom. They must *let go* of their secret sins and give them to the Father before they can crawl into His lap! And this includes the leadership as well as the congregation! *So what is the big deal?* This attitude is the problem - it makes the difference between death and life! Amen! Many times when we are leading the service, it is not enough just to know what to do but *when* to do it.

For example, instead of waiting until the end of the service for an altar time to deal with issues, I believe we should make a way for the people to be cleansed and delivered first! Then the people can worship and receive His engrafted Word and every blessing that He has for them throughout the entire service instead of being blindfolded and having plugs in their ears. If you knew people had been poisoned and you had the antidote that could instantly heal them, would you give it to them as quickly as possible or make them wait until after the service? Hello! Being instant in season and out is what makes the difference between meeting people's needs in church or out! Everyone desires to see powerful services, but how many will invest their time praying for the discernment of the Holy Spirit? *"The Lord God hath given me the tongue of the learned, that I should know how to speak a word in season to him that is weary: He wakens me morning by morning, he opens my ear to hear as the learned" (Isaiah 50:4).* Prayer ministries are wonderful but every child of God has been called to pray and has an equal share of the responsibilities to intercede. What is more important than hearing God's voice so that His specific will can be manifested?

The Lord's idea of His people being ministers is not just doing special deeds every now and then, but rather committing to a *lifetime* of feeding His sheep along with a sold-out determination to live in the awareness of His Spirit. Many times it is a thankless job because people seem to think there should be more of the spectacular, or more success, and no matter how hard you labor, someone will always say you could have done more. Humility allows the true servants to ride these storms of criticism and remain steady because they remember the little things, like elderly persons saying how much they appreciate what was said or done, or maybe a little girl from Sunday school drew a picture that said how much she admires and loves us. It is all right to hold our small blessings tightly because they remind us how important it is to stay faithful and strong in order to continue in our callings. *"And let us not be weary in well doing: for in due season we shall reap, if we faint not. As we have therefore opportunity, let us do good unto all men, especially unto them who are of the household of faith" (Galatians 6:9-10).* The concept of living in the awareness of God's presence is loving people, not just through a church service, or during a crisis, but developing friendships that last a lifetime. When we remove our eyes from love, we learn the art of selfishness and lose our sense of direction. Isolation has its place, but it is good to have trusted friends. *Proverbs 18: 24* says, *"A man that has friends must show himself friendly: and there is a friend that sticketh closer than a brother."*

I believe we could all agree there could be no greater friend than Jesus. Let's think for a moment and notice the qualities of a true friendship. A friend is someone who will support you and that you can trust. A true friend will not put you down or deliberately hurt your feelings. True friends are kind and have respect for you. They will love you because they choose to, not because they feel like they have to. Friends are honest with you and will tell you the truth even if you do not agree. Friends stick around and will not leave you when things get tough. They make you smile, they listen, they laugh when you laugh and cry when you cry. A brother may not be a friend, but a friend will always be a brother. You can give without love but you cannot love without giving. *"These things have I spoken unto you, that my joy might remain in you, and that your joy might be full. This is my commandment, that you love one another, as I have loved you. Greater love has no man than this that a man lay down his life for his friends. You are my friends, IF you do whatsoever I command you. From now on I call you not servants; for the servant does not know what his Lord does: but I have called you friends; for all things that I have heard of my Father I have made known to you"* (John 15:11-15).

> *"Lord, help me to become more discerning of the needs of others. Allow me to have compassion for the hearts of those who need Your wisdom and understanding. Help me to reach out to the ones who need You, and give me a passion to live a lifestyle of worship before them that they may be inspired to go deeper with You. Give me the sensitivity to hear Your voice so that You can use me in Your divine appointments. Help me to overcome my fear of rejection, and fill me with Your holy boldness! Remind me when I begin to drift away from being dependent on Your anointing. Convict my heart when pride tries to deceive me. Teach me how to become a faithful intercessor and to trust You completely in ALL things. I love You Lord. Amen."*

Chapter 47

THE UPPER ROOM

I remember years ago, an evangelist came to our church and his ministry had a profound impact on me. He laid on hands and prayed and prophesied to most everyone, not trying to promote his ministry but to take his time with the people and simply relay God's thoughts. His ministry style was a little different, but his emphasis was focused on the deeper spiritual message that God is trying to remind us how important it is to remember that the church is the people, and the people need *personal* attention. I appreciated his Kingdom message that the Lord is sounding a wake-up call to His children. A wind of *change* is blowing within the body of Christ that is stirring pastors and ministry leaders (that sincerely care about people) to develop their spiritual sensitivity. The more serious we are about listening to God's voice, the more sensitive we will be to minister to those who are hurting. Stop for a moment and take a glance around you; God is placing you and me in the perfect position to touch many who desperately need Jesus. The Lord is pouring out His Spirit into His disciples because we are the laborers and messengers that are being SENT into this last hour harvest. Jesus desires to ignite our passion, increase our anointing, and fill us with His joy as He leads His messengers to build HIS Kingdom and prepare for His return. Amen! Those who are hungry for His presence and wisdom are NOT satisfied with someone else's idea of volunteer work but are reaching out to Him with more intensity, vision, freedom, and passion to know what He is saying and how to abide in a deeper spiritual reality. The higher our level of personal intimacy with Jesus – the deeper our concern for others will be.

I personally do not see why our services cannot be glorious every time we come together, and I am convinced that God feels the same way. Why would it not be our highest priority and personal responsibility to find the key that releases His presence to fill the temple with His glory every time? Because it has everything to do with why we are NOT personally walking in the fullness of His Spirit; we are not trying very hard! I realize that *man-powered* churches will continue, but there is a remnant that is RISING, and God is empowering that group right this moment to fulfill His prophecies and accomplish His perfect plans! Somebody give Him praise and glory! His sons and daughters that love Him and have committed their lives to obeying His voice are starving to soak in His love! These extremists for Jesus have decided to drop their nets and follow Him no matter the cost because they have seen and know that this world has nothing for them while Christ is EVERYTHING! The traditional church may refuse to shelve its worn out ceremonies, but there is a royal priesthood that is breaking away to become the manifestation of every promise of God's holy Word and the representation of His glory on earth! His people who are listening to the sound of His voice can already hear the trumpets of triumph and are not only drawing near to His Kingdom message of faith, fervent prayer, and anointed worship – they are demonstrating it! He did not bring us out this far to take us back – He brought us out to take us in to the Promised Land! A land flowing with milk and honey is indicative and symptomatic of a greater good, the fertility of an awareness of His presence that is both nourishing and pleasant.

Preparing for the service is like preparing for a journey that we know will be good, but when we get going, we must listen carefully to what we are to do in order for it to be a successful trip. If we choose to do it our way, everyone leaves with a sense of mediocrity, dryness, distance, and melancholy. This feeling of heaviness is many times blamed on the leaders not being able to hear clearly what God was saying. And of course it is common for leaders to accuse the people for not being interested or not being spiritually prepared. But whoever is to blame, one thing we know for sure; it is NOT God's fault in forgetting to arrive or not desiring to appear! If miracles and blessings happen, we have a confirmation it is from God, but when it is painfully powerless and flat, we can presume it was a *human* problem. We can work on our presentations all week and arrive prepared and even have faith expectations, but not have a clue to what is going to happen. We can begin to sense what God is doing, but many times it is the split-second decisions while in the *heat of the battle* so to speak, where we find God's mind in the service. I have seen preachers change direction in the middle of the service because once they come into the anointing, they can more clearly discern His voice, and being familiar with Jesus comes from knowing Him personally.

Whatever happens, we can all agree that the more we allow Him the freedom to move, the higher percentage of needs are met. Giving Him control is the only way we can flow with His decisions, like knowing what to sing and how long to extend it, what to teach and how much, when to move in the gifts of the Spirit, who is to share in the service, and when to pray and prophesy. God definitely has a page; it is our responsibility to be on it. Another aspect that is very hard to learn is that it's not the *quantity* of our program, because a lengthy service filled with everything we can think of is not always necessarily better. Being short and straight to the point can sometimes be more effective because simplicity can pack a powerful punch! It has been said that most people have a short attention span and can retain only a small amount of content at one sitting. I personally believe that under the power of the anointing we can absorb more content, but there again it is crucial to recognize when we are anointed, when the Lord wants to do something else, or when to close. God knows every heart and how to touch each one, and what is the most effective approach, so if He whispers for us to change direction, it would be in everyone's best interest for us to obey.

I have noticed something very basic yet important about church members: they need to know that ministry leaders care about them. They are thirsty for attention and affection and want to be respected and listened to when they talk. It is a basic human need that we all love to be loved. The relationships we are developing in the church are what God wants us to continue pressing toward. As we band together in love, we will grow strong in our commitments to the church and to our personal missions. God has called each of us to represent His Kingdom of unity and love, but selfishness creates an atmosphere of coldness and false security. The church gathering was never intended to have a spectator mentality where people come in and leave without knowing each other. The growth and development of personal relationships measures the strength and spiritual vitality of a healthy assembly. It is time to change the way we do church! It is time we spend more time with one another, going to each other's houses, helping each other, working together, praying together, and learning how to be a true friend. How can we be a light to the community if we are comfortable with not having a vision for ministry? How can we have a burden to win souls if we do not even care about each other? If we truly have the revelation of love, we will love everyone, not just our family and close friends. Do we really love Jesus? Well, of course we do; what kind of silly question is that? Mmmmm...the same response that Peter had.

We sing about loving God, and hear about others loving Him and know the stories that explain how He loves us, but I believe there are many levels of understanding love, just as we learn about everything else in life. For instance, if knowing about *love* is like knowing *math*, we might be able to add and subtract but not have a clue about calculus or trigonometry. We might love our new set of wheels but have never known the depth and maturity of romantic love. It is wisdom to see that life has layers of comprehension, and each individual person can be at certain stages of perception in a particular field. In my personal development, I heard the word *love* from the time my ears could function, and as I became a teenager, my progression of understanding was still very weak. Even after I was married, I honestly believe my grasp of love was elementary to say the least. I followed my heart with as much comprehension as I had about love, and listened to my senses, but my realization was very shallow. With experience and maturity my capacity to reason has developed somewhat, and now later in life I view love as more of a spiritual revelation than an emotional goose bump. *Phileo* is the Greek word for friendship and is more of a surface affection or a physical connection of consciousness. This is not to be confused with *agape,* the Greek word for the highest form of love, which is of and from God whose very nature is love itself. Agape love is a self-sacrificing love that is even deeper than the love between married couples and cannot be counseled through psychiatric theories or associated with performance. It is the love that Jesus has for His people, and the type of love Jesus displayed when He went to the cross. It can only be appreciated, experienced, and comprehended as revelation when our heavenly Father opens the eyes of our hearts.

It is evident with such a high rate of divorce and relationship problems that most of the world's understanding about love is phileo. Many are convinced that love can be found on a dating site, but true love first begins in our personal relationship with Jesus. It is obvious why there is such a need to sow the gospel because until men and women hear God's Kingdom Word and receive Christ as their Savior, they cannot function or operate in the Holy Spirit which is the channel for embracing or manifesting any type of love. Even when we receive Christ as Lord, we must study and pray constantly in order to evolve in our understanding. When Jesus was having a last minute farewell with Peter, it was more than just a hug and salute for good luck; it was to plant a seed within Peter's heart that would *haunt* and inspire him the rest of his life. Jesus is God and knew that powerful questions can pierce the very soul of a person, triggering a spiritual avalanche of determination that can change the world. Throughout the New Testament we notice many questions Jesus asked in order to stimulate curiosity so that His words might penetrate the minds and hearts of the listener. Knowledge informs and revelation challenges, but Jesus *provoked* Peter with His words which became a Holy Ghost conviction! Listen to the account again found in *John 21:15-17, "So when they had dined, Jesus said to Simon Peter, Simon, son of Jonah, do you love me* [loyally- willing to sacrifice] *more than these? He said unto Him, yes, Lord; you know that I love you* [have affection for you]. *He said unto him - feed my sheep. He said unto him again the second time, Simon, son of Jonah, do you love me?* [Agape spiritual love]. *He said unto Him, yes, Lord; you know that I love you* [physical affection for you]. *Jesus said unto him - feed my sheep. He said unto him the third time, Simon, son of Jonah, do you love me* [are you even my friend?] *Peter was grieved* [upset, hurt], *because he said unto him the third time, do you love me. And Peter said unto Him, Lord, you know all things; you know that I love you. Jesus said unto him - feed my sheep."* What exactly does all that mean and how does it relate to worship? Actually it is the heart of worship. How can we worship in Spirit and Truth without understanding what spiritual love is? Since our love is an expression of worship and our worship is an expression of our love, the crucial aspect of this exchange is based on the depth of our cognitive perception.

This dialogue between Jesus and Peter has captured one of the most powerful correspondences between God and man. Jesus allows us to listen in on this conversation not just so we can know what He was explaining to Peter, but for the purpose of speaking to every Christian of all time! The driving force behind all of God's children being disciples and followers of Christ is walking in the Holy Spirit in obedience and submitting under the direction of the Father. Christianity is not just a set of religious conditions or a 100 question exam that will be graded on judgment day. Most people embrace the philosophy that if you are good, you will go to heaven, and if you are bad you will go to hell, but that is not all there is to it. Good works or a life of sin for that matter has nothing to do with going to heaven or hell; it is knowing Christ personally and allowing Him to be the Lord of our lives. If some are NOT saved by the blood of Jesus Christ, they are lost forever no matter what they do. If others ARE saved, they are living in the grace and righteousness that is established within the covenant relationship of God's love. When individuals receive Christ, their lives become centered on loving God and allowing that love to spill over to all people. The Lord knows the spiritual rewards for any deed will be based on the motives of love, and yet, sadly, many have given their lives to religious service in the name of tradition, doctrine, and obligation, without even having a personal relationship with Jesus. In this passage, the Lord was trying to clarify the meaning of church as an *organism* and not as an organization.

God's vision of feeding the sheep was a divine, holy revelation that was (and is) attempting to reveal the difference between going through the motions of self-righteous deeds and actually falling in love with God and His people. We are not to be like a pig farmer that throws the feed over the fence and walks away; that is not love - it is a task. Shepherds lead the sheep to the most luscious grass; they care about them dearly; they comfort them, guide them, and call each one by name. They live to care for the sheep, have a heart for them; they put medicine on them, are bonded to them; they protect them, will fight for them and die for them. Jesus used His life as His most powerful demonstration, the ultimate teaching opportunity to show us how to continue His ministry. Many have quickly read over this scripture and presumed Jesus was talking just to clergy leaders, but this is NOT the case. He is talking to every Christian because all of His people ARE ministers!

"Greater love hath no man than this, that a man lay down his life for his friends" *(John 15:13)*. The life of love is the inspiration connected to intercessory prayer and the willingness to become a living sacrifice. When we learn to love others to the point we will actually take the time to pray for them, we are in a sense laying down our lives in order that God can intervene with His miracle power. It is difficult to imagine how the Father felt as He sent His Son Jesus to ransom the lost sheep and is now trusting us to help build His Kingdom. If Peter did not understand agape love, why are we convinced that we do? There are so many *lambs* that need to be fed and taken care of and are waiting for a touch from the healer, but can we truly love others as much as we love ourselves? ***"Feed the flock of God which is among you, taking the oversight thereof, not by constraint, but willingly; not for filthy lucre, but of a ready mind. Neither as being lords over God's heritage, but being examples to the flock. And when the chief shepherd shall appear, ye shall receive a crown of glory that fadeth not away" (I Peter 5:2-4)***. He is sounding the call of urgency because there is so much to do in such a small amount of time. He has given us the combination to His vault which contains the answers, miracles, and solutions to the world's needs. Jesus is still asking: do you love Me?

Chapter 48
BE STILL AND KNOW

"Be still and KNOW that I am God: I will be exalted among the heathen, I will be exalted among the earth. The Lord of hosts is with us; the God of Jacob is our refuge. Selah" (Psalm 46:10-11).

The first disciples of Jesus lived heavily persecuted lives, and through the centuries many have suffered with pain and death. As we look back on the Christian church in America, we can see that in the beginning there were a few warriors that were engaged in the battle, but the journey was long and tiring. The army was very determined at first, but when they stopped along the way to be refreshed, the fruits of prosperity became more of a temptation to indulge than an opportunity to give. In todays, *what's-in-it-for-me* world, the army of God has become selfish and sleepy and willing to compromise instead of staying loyal to His Word. The battle cry from heaven can be heard: *"who will be strong and watch over God's flock?"* Will you live each day with the purpose to lay down your plans and pick up His staff? In these last hours, the remnant disciples are giving themselves to the work of connecting all people with Jesus! We read *Psalm 23* not with just a comfort in knowing who Christ is, but also with an awareness of our personal responsibility to live what we know. Follow me through verse one. We are to live holy and obedient unto our Lord and be content with what His blueprint allows. We are to tell all people who the Shepherd is and help teach (provide spiritual nourishment) and help them to lie down in green (truth) pastures. We have been called to pray for them and help lead them beside quiet, still waters (comfort, encourage, edify, strengthen, console) where they can find and hear God's voice. It is our mission to teach that God forgives and restores. We are to help them understand about the gift of the Lord's righteousness (justification) and how He receives all glory and honor (leading them in praise and worship). We are the ones that are to hold their hands in the valley of death, interceding and standing in the gap for their healing when our family and friends are under attack, confessing, decreeing, and agreeing in faith. We need to constantly remind everyone that God is near, and His Name and authority are above all other powers in the universe. We are to declare that Christ has our backs, that He is watching over us and assigning angels to protect us, and is working on our behalf. He is binding and loosing on earth as it is in heaven, arranging appointments and blessings that we might walk in peace with all men, even with our enemies. We are called to anoint the people with oil, praying for them, prophesying to them, supporting them, and edifying them. We do not just pat them on the back and say, *be blessed*, but are to listen and be led of the Spirit to help *supply* their needs for the gospel's sake. We rejoice with them, weep with them, and embrace them as trusted brothers and sisters that will dwell with us in the house of the Lord forever.

Jesus goes on to tell Peter that his life will end in the destruction of his flesh but no matter what happens, he must stand strong and embrace the command to follow Jesus. When the trials become severe and people turn against you in the battle – keep going forward. When the finances are gone and the lights are turned out and the doors are locked – keep walking! Keep serving; keep teaching - keep worshipping the Lord, and keep loving everyone. **"Delight thyself also in the Lord; and He shall give thee the desires of thine heart. Commit thy way unto the Lord; trust also in Him; and He shall bring it to pass"** *(Psalm 37:4-5)*. God is on the throne; He is completely in control, and He is watching over you and trying to do all that He can to help you succeed for His glory. He knows everything you are going through and realizes the obstacles and problems you are facing. He feels your discouragement and frustration and wants you to *be still and know* that His Word is perfect and never fails! You can trust Him completely with all of your heart and know that He will never let you down. **"For His anger endureth but a moment; in His favor is LIFE: weeping may endure for a night, but JOY cometh in the morning"** *(Psalm 30:5)*.

Do not give up and pull away! When the battle increases, these are not the times to trust in something else or run and hide – they are times of confirmation to push harder into His Spirit and increase the intensity of prayer and self-examination! You are victorious because Jesus is, and He lives inside of you and will see you through to the other side – IF you do not give up! Amen! Steadfast means to be loyal, committed, devoted, dedicated, dependable, and reliable! Even when the wolves circle your heart to condemn you and turn against you, confess out loud that you KNOW you have pressed toward the mark for the prize of the high calling in Christ Jesus, that nothing is impossible, that you have won the race, fulfilled your destiny, and are determined to accomplish your mission for His glory!

The Bible speaks of us being the friends of God, but if we are having a difficult time loving people, let us stop pretending to think we really love Him! The Lord gave me a song years ago that was written in first person from Jesus that said, *"if you cannot love your brother – don't say you love Me."* It is time to stop being proud of how religious we are and start examining our hearts to see how loving we are! We cannot truly love without giving, because God so loved the world that he GAVE! *Father God, open the eyes of our hearts that we might receive the revelation of Your Word through Your Holy Spirit in the name of Jesus. Amen.* Which came first - the giver or the worshipper? Well, they are so closely tied together who can separate them from each other? So do we give as an act of worship, or do we worship as an act of giving? When we receive the love of Christ into our hearts, we automatically desire to worship God and thank Him for His grace and love. Then as we progress in our learning and develop in our intimacy with Him as our Lord, we take on His nature and character which is—you guessed it - giving.

I believe if we do NOT receive the revelation of giving, we will never be able to comprehend the full meaning of worship! Likewise if we are distant and uncomfortable in His presence, we will not understand the joys of having the generosity of Christ. I cannot see how anyone could have glorious fellowship with God in worship and not have a sensitivity and awareness to other people's needs, as this would seem to contradict one another. Even praying for others requires the act of giving and sacrificing our time. Those who give of themselves in worship to God will *naturally* give of themselves to others! The problem with our deciding how much to give is that even within that statement of reasoning He knows it is still US trying to control and micromanage how we live. For example, tithing is a demand, not an option, and those who put in just what they feel they can afford are not exactly following His idea of perfect faith and obedience. Living the abundant life is not something that is passed out like candy, because it is directly conditional upon our trust in the principles of His Word. Neither can we experience the joy, freedom, peace, and fullness of His presence in worship if we are living in intentional disobedience. Our lack of faith (which is sin) can create an arrogant illusion to God's divine order, and as we attempt to write our own gospel, we begin to worship our own *version* of truth. Let us make sure we are serving and worshipping the God of the Bible and not our own concept of the way we think He is.

Worship is a product or fruit of what we feel in our hearts about a certain person or thing, and we will always give all that we have to what we love the most. We have seen and known those who were possessed with what captivated and stimulated their interest and how it seemed to consume them. Whether it is collecting, a serious hobby, or trying to accomplish something, or maybe even being infatuated with another person, these are passions that we must often consider and evaluate. It is all right to have and do things, as long as they do not have you. God wants to be the center of our focus in life and is very aware of anything else that could become an *"idol"* and hinder our personal relationship with Him. God created us, chose us, delivered us, and called us to surrender our *desires* and take up His cross because He wants ALL of our attention! Devotion and worship to anything else in this life is an insult to Him and could very well be the reason we do not have the fullness of joy. When our hearts are filled with love about something, it spills over in the form of praise and adoration, and we will naturally choose to express this inward infatuation with an outward proclamation of our convictions and emotions. For example, people who *adore* their restored classic vehicles will spend many hours tinkering with them, polishing them, boasting about them and showing them off because they are beaming with pride. Others have shaped their bodies into an impressive *shrine* of beauty and strength to the point they cannot step away from the mirror long enough to see or care about anyone else. Whatever the obsession, the point is still the same; what we love the most becomes our highest priority and will consume our attention, our thoughts, dreams, time, energy, and conversation, and we will not hesitate to stand boldly with unlimited devotion, commitment, dedication, protection, and finances in order to defend and justify our preoccupation without shame or hesitation. This is what quickly and thoroughly reveals where we hide and guard the hidden treasure of our hearts and exposes the identity of our true worship.

We have all heard how the organized church is divided into two camps of doers and talkers, and both camps are found to be completely *willing*. One camp of ten percent does all the work, and the other camp of ninety percent is completely *willing* to let them do it! As sad as this is true, we can see beneath the surface why this is so. Only the *narrow path* dwellers have actually discovered that the Christian life is based on how much we can give instead of how much we can accumulate. They have walked through the purging fires and allowed God to burn out their vanity and selfishness. They have painfully learned how to take control of their carnal natures and have been given the grace to allow God to pry their fingers loose from the influences and temptations that attempted to possess them. The *talkers* have a reasonable understanding of what God wants them to be but have never come to the point of being ready to put in place a course of action where they can execute their knowledge. This is a confusing yet perfect example of carnal Christianity and exactly what the Lord desires that we overcome.

When we realize that worship is a demonstration that identifies us with who we are as followers of Christ, we will see mercy and love as not just attributes of Jesus but a personal responsibility for us to develop. Revelation does not fall out of the sky and hit us on the head, but is more like hide and seek. Surface knowledge is like picking up walnuts after they fall on the ground, but the deeper wisdom is like mining for gold 20 feet below the ground. The mysteries that can be discovered in the spirit realm will never be revealed to us if we are constantly filling our minds with worldly distractions. It begins with a desire to know, then proceeds with diligent searching which allows God to generously illuminate a portion of truth. Then we add it to our list of revelations and continue building our understanding. With line upon line and precept upon precept we continue to pursue, study, and meditate and begin to notice the outline of a much larger picture of life than we ever imagined: and thus our views are formed. Developing the mind of Christ within our spirit allows us to see the way God sees, and of course this directly affects what we think, say, and how we act. Though we see through a glass darkly, we continue to excavate divine truth like an archeologist that spends years on site patiently and joyfully digging.

Jesus is trying to train us in this dispensation so we can rule and reign with Him in the New Holy City of Jerusalem that is coming soon! If we do not learn to sow His blessings now, we will be very disappointed with the harvest we will reap in the future. We need to realize that we cannot *out give* Him, and every dollar and every deed we hold back will haunt us someday, as it could have been used for God's glory. The greatest thing we can do for God, for others, and ourselves is to consecrate all that we have to the Lord. Amen! There are three things people can do with themselves and their possessions. They can selfishly hoard them, lavishly waste them, or sacrificially give them. Only the disciple who spends freely and gladly in obedience to God's Holy Spirit will experience the full meaning of living. The person that worships God in Spirit and chooses to trust Him in Truth will always be clothed with the garment of praise and blessing. The Lord owns it all; we are not really owners of anything, only temporary caretakers and distributors of His Kingdom. The greatest deception in the world is the idea that money can make a person happy, and a life changing revelation is that we will never have true spiritual satisfaction with our prosperity and blessings until we willingly *give* it all back to Him.

Chapter 49

AN AUDIENCE OF ONE

"O God, thou art my God; early will I seek thee; my soul thirsteth for thee, my flesh longeth for thee in a dry and thirsty land, where no water is" (Psalm 63:1).

I have been writing and singing the messages of the Lord for many years and will be the first to testify how satisfying and unique the gift has been. There have been times of great joy and also times of rejection, but spending time alone in His presence and being saturated with His love has been worth more than all of the reception and acceptance I could ever have in this world. If you have ever experienced these same feelings and responses, His hope for you today is that you might know that you have been given His gift, and if it is for no other reason than to just give God pleasure, there is no higher honor than to love Him and worship Him.

There is a passion that fuels our interests, and I would say it is fair to recognize that all of us have distinct tastes and musical styles that fit our personalities. It is strange but true that our choices of methodology even have the power to override our spiritual appreciation. For example, some people who adore country gospel would not even consider listening to Christian hip-hop or the other way around, yet both are basically saying the exact message. It is rare to find individuals who can cross-over to multiple styles and receive a blessing from each one. *If the anointing is the same in all of them, then why do some people not respect the other genres?* It is obvious; they are listening with only their natural ears. When God said, *"he that hath ears to hear, let him hear" (Matthew 11:15)*, He was referring to the inner man or the spirit man that lives within the born again Christian. When God says in *Psalm 98:4* to make a *"joyful noise,"* it is because He is listening to the heart – not just the notes or the beat. It can be understood for those who have NOT been born again to be persuaded by their natural senses because they do not have the Holy Spirit within them, but I thought the Christian was listening to a different sound from a higher dimension. Being a citizen of heaven while choosing to function as servants of our flesh can build a strong case for middle of the road carnality.

Someone who worked with my wife Cheryl once said that she could not stand the TV show, *"Touched by an Angel."* We always enjoyed the show and still watch the re-runs because of how it portrays the spiritual realm and glorifies God. This person said it *gave her the creeps,* which is a perfect representation of how the default spirit feels uncomfortable around the Holy Spirit. This explains why so many gospel tracts end up in the garbage and churches have low attendance. Aside from not appreciating the style, we know the holy presence of God is like oil and water when those who are guilty with sin come into contact with His presence. It is convicting and uncomfortable around God's throne if we are dirty, and even the outer court people have a tendency to run from anything that has the smell of heaven on it. Sometimes in our excitement and enthusiasm we become too pushy with our evangelism around those who do not want Him, and it becomes an intrusion in their personal space. We might have good intentions but have been called to proceed at the right time and develop discernment to listen with our *inner ears* for the divine appointment rather than our own agenda. God knows who is ready to receive a seed and those who will just throw it away. We would be less discouraged and see more results if we would just relax, trust him, and follow His directions. We are worshipping God and laboring for HIM – and this usually has very little to do with our emotions or ideas. Let us continue to burn the midnight oil and become better prepared as we seek HIS face and listen for His divine instructions. *"Let them praise the name of the Lord: for His name alone is excellent; His glory is above the earth and heaven" (Psalm 148:13).* In *Matthew chapter 6* we find a very comforting aspect about our personal intimacy with God that confirms His awareness of what we think and how we feel. In *verses 4, 6, and 18* we notice the phrase, *"and thy Father which sees in secret."* Years ago the Lord gave me a song called *"God knows,"* and the secret place where He *knows* is the heart of our consciences where we can follow Him even unto death because we trust that our anchor holds forever. Neither persecution nor the pain of our sacrifice can hinder our commitment because our faith is based on our personal covenant with Him. Walking in His Spirit means we have come to the place where we do not listen to our emotions or the voices of this world but are only concerned with pleasing Him.

It is hard to imagine living without electricity or seeing abandoned church buildings. Many cannot even comprehend a worship service without the videos, graphics, lights, computers, instruments, sound systems, and air conditioning that enhances our corporate assemblies. May we be careful that we do not spend more time playing with our toys than being with our first love. *What does this have to do with worship?* If we are not just as excited about praising God in our bedroom as we are in Sunday morning church – something is terribly wrong. Our prayers and praises are not something we generate to prove our holiness or devotion in public, but they are an overflow from our private intimacy and personal time of fellowship with Him. Our lives are an open worship service whether we are singing music or not, and this level of spiritual learning and knowing that hopefully we are developing now will continue when the plugs are pulled and the doors are locked. The same is true with our faith and love; those who are not investing their time wisely now when we have so many resources and opportunities to minister will struggle to stand strong when all of our comforts are stripped away. This does not mean that we cannot live in more joy than we have ever experienced before; in fact it reminds us that His presence is ALL we will ever need or could desire. Is Jesus alone enough to satisfy you? ***"But what things were gain to me, those I counted loss for Christ. Yea doubtless, and I count all things but loss for the excellency of the knowledge of Christ Jesus my Lord: for whom I have suffered the loss of all things, and do count them but dung, that I may win Christ"*** *(Philippians 3:7-8).*

We have mentioned about love being a revelation and how we eventually learn what it is and how to demonstrate it. In marriage we listen, laugh, cry, reveal our most secret thoughts, pour out our views, as we trust and come to know our soul mate deeper every day. And so it is with how we grow in our bond and adoration with our Lord. We come to Him with humility and as much sincerity as a human can have (commonly referred to as with our whole heart). We gradually learn how to practice His presence. This is a place where the chaos of the world, the fears, worries, and stresses cannot harm us because we know that God supports us and is on our side. It is a place where we do not have to perform or need to live up to an expectation because He loves us for who we are. In His presence we do not seek respect, honor, or recognition and do not have to fight for our rights, try to impress Him, or wait in line for His attention. We are never worried that He has forgotten us but simply relax and enjoy the contentment of being close to Him. In marriage we can agree that TRUST is just as important as LOVE, and it is the same with our relationship to God. *"Behold, I have graven thee upon the palms of my hands; thy walls are continually* [always in my memory] *before Me" (Isaiah 49:16)*.

One night I was visiting a church, and after the teaching they began to praise God with no time limits and no hurry to leave. In the service I was feeling the freedom and power of God's Spirit to just "soak" in His love and peace. It was so enjoyable to feel His tangible presence as I would go to the altar and talk with God, then walk around waving my arms with joy. While I was in somewhat of an intoxicated spiritual state, a wonderful lady came and handed me a small note and walked away. I looked at it with glazed eyes and it said, *"Billy, live only to please God – worship to the audience of one!"* My throat tightened, and I felt a tear fall down my cheek as I thought of how profound this message was to my heart. In ministry we have so much to think about with His Kingdom and voices that try to influence our directions, but it is so important to stay focused on the King. There is no higher purpose to serve, no greater reason to live, than to constantly seek His face and listen to His voice. *"For do I now persuade men, or God? Or do I seek to please men? For if I yet pleased men, I should not be the servant of Christ" (Galatians 1:10)*. To look into the face of the one that we love and adore Him with all of our hearts is our deepest need. This passion is the cry of our spirits to the Father who created us and called us to be with Him. Our spirits love to be as close to God as possible and never become tired of seeing His glory, soaking in His presence, serving Him, praying, learning, reading, studying, loving people, and are never bored with dreaming or thinking about Him. It is our flesh and the negative influence from the dark side that constantly gripes and complains about us going overboard with this *Jesus thing*. The nature of Christ and our human will are directly opposed to one another, and our carnality is trying as hard as it can to keep us from being an extreme fanatic for God! Yes, we are not only facing this raging battle now, but many times we forget that how faithful we were as Christian soldiers will be the focus of conversation in the judgment.

After a forest fire in Yellowstone National Park, the forest rangers began to hike up a mountain to assess the inferno's damage. One ranger found a bird literally petrified in ashes, perched like a statue on the ground at the base of a tree. Somewhat sickened by the eerie sight, one of the men knocked over the bird with a stick. When he gently struck it, three tiny chicks scurried from under their dead mother's wings. The loving mother, keenly aware of impending disaster, had carried her offspring to the base of the tree and had gathered them under her wings, instinctively knowing that the toxic smoke would rise. She could have flown to safety but had refused to abandon her babies. Then the blaze had arrived, and the heat had scorched her small body, but the mother had remained *steadfast* and had been willing to die, so those under the cover of her wings could live. When we stop and meditate about the price that Christ paid to save us, the cares and worries of this life become smaller and less significant. Jesus so loved the world that He died to save the whole of it, and would have done exactly the same if you were the only one on earth. God loves you as much as He has ever loved anyone. Think about that. You are a special being, and God designed a specific blueprint just for you, a special identity, and a one of a kind destiny! May you always remember that Jesus considers His *one-on-one* relationship with you as His highest treasure. ***"He will cover you with His feathers, and under His wings you will trust. His truth will be your shield and buckler. You will not be afraid for the terror by night; neither from the arrow that flies by day"*** *(Psalm 91:4-5).*

Jesus lived perfectly, and his life brought glory to his Father in all of His words and deeds, the same as we have been called to do. He willingly gave his body to be crushed like a rose, and the holy fragrance was so beautiful to the Father that it paid for the sins of whosoever would believe. It was not about the will of the Son, as it is neither about our wills – it is all about the will of the Father. God has a vision for each person that includes His general will and His specific will. We have been given the choice to follow this plan or create our own. How close we live in God's presence depends on how serious we are to please Him, and of course this will determine how close we will follow the outlines of our destinies. The more devoted we are to following His blueprint, the more fragrance of His presence will be released within us because when we surrender our natures and obey His will, our sacrifices become acceptable sacrificial aromas of perfect love that please Him. *"And walk in love, as Christ also has loved us, and has given himself for us an offering and a sacrifice to God for a sweet-smelling savor"* *(Ephesians 5:2).*

We are coming to the end, and I want to close with noticing again the touching story found in *John chapter 12*. This is not the time or place to discuss whether the two accounts of this story are the same or different, but the point is to reflect on the powerful love that a humble servant had for her Lord. *Verse 3* reads, *"Then Mary took a pound of ointment of spikenard, very costly, and anointed the feet of Jesus, and wiped His feet with her hair: and the house was filled with the odor of the ointment."* Judas managed the finances for the ministry of Jesus and was frustrated about how the perfume should have been sold and the money used to help the poor. But Jesus said, *"Leave her alone: against the day of my burying hath she kept this. For the poor always you have with you; but me you have not always"* *(verse 7)*. She got it right; her priorities were perfect, so she became an illustration of pure love. *Pure* and *love* are not two words that we often connect together because much of the love in this world is anything but pure. We are flawed humans and much of what we call love many times has a slightly twisted angle or ulterior motive. How disappointing it is to realize that others are using us or that we need to earn someone's love, or we learn about the cruel *exchange* games of trading love as we desperately try to be fulfilled. However, the wonder and beauty of God's love is NOT based on what we have done, how we look, or how often we can make Him happy. He loves us with a pure, holy, unconditional love which means that even in our worst moments - He loves us just the same. When we receive this revelation it leads us to TRUST Him because we know He would never forsake the one He loves. *"The Lord thy God in the midst of thee is MIGHTY; He will save, He will rejoice over thee with joy; He will rest in His love, He will joy over thee with singing."* *(Zephaniah 3:17)* The God of all creation is rejoicing over YOU and is actually singing because He loves you so much! Let us sing to Him and extol His Name over every other Name and KNOW that He is Lord and final authority over all things. *"As the hart panteth after the water brooks, so panteth my soul after thee, O God"* *(Psalm 42:1)*. The pure love of our heart is all that He has ever wanted – this is true worship.

"For where your treasure is, there will your heart be also" *(Matthew 6:21). Anybody can, everybody won't, but somebody will. What more can He do – what more can He say?* All glory, honor, and praise be unto Him forever and ever!

This song is from 1984 and is called *"Unto Thee."* I was alone in the living room praying and worshipping the Lord late one night, and tears of joy and sorrow began to overflow within me. It felt like a warm blanket of His presence came upon me as these words and melody began to come forth. I wrote them down exactly as they are here.

(Verse 1) Love spoke to my heart, and revealed an unfailing God
Who heard my cry in the midst of the storm
His mighty arm of mercy reached down and delivered my soul
O Lord you are an island that saves me from the raging sea

(Chorus) Glory, glory, unto Thee be all the glory
My fortress, my refuge
Hide me in the shadow of Your wings

(Verse 2) How can I love Thee? I offer my sacrifice
As the floodgates of thanksgiving release the river of praise
You are an ever present help in times of my distress
Holy, Thou art worthy, You are all my righteousness

(Verse 3) Darkness hid itself, the wind hushed its voice
Silence swept across the face of the deep
No thoughts have ever known, no words that can say
In sorrow my heart weeps

(Chorus) Glory, glory, unto Thee be all the glory
My fortress, my refuge
Hide me in the shadow of Your wings

Hide me in the shadow of Your wings

FINAL THOUGHTS

This is actually part fifty of the book and the number 50 represents the year of jubilee! Jubilee means that every 50th year all debts were automatically cancelled and every loan and obligation was paid in FULL. Amen! Jesus HAS paid our sin debt, and when we are *released* from the bondage of sin, we are FREE INDEED to experience the joys and excitement of being in covenant relationship with Him! Praise God - this is what the *lifestyle* of worship and living in the awareness of His presence is all about! The freedom to enjoy His abundant life causes us to be forever grateful for His love and fills us with a burning desire to express our love back to Him. Go ahead and run around the block shouting praises to our God! He is worthy of all worship and adoration! He is exalted; He is the King of Kings and the Lord of Lords! The stones will NOT need to cry out because WE WILL WORSHIP HIM! Hallelujah! *"Saying, Amen: Blessing, and glory, and wisdom, and thanksgiving, and honor, and power, and might, be unto our God for ever and ever. Amen" (Revelation 7:12).*

It is exciting to think that worship will be the center of all activity in heaven! For those who look forward to living with Jesus for all eternity, it would seem that praising and adoring Him would be a constant state of mind, but much of the time it is not. *Why?* It is simple, because most of the time, He is NOT on our minds. *How can we change this?* By changing the way we think. *But how do we do this?* It is a most difficult task to re-structure our conscience and allow God to re-wire our brains. It will come down to laying a *NEW* foundation where our *house* can be built; this bed-rock is God and His Word, and our success hinges on us being willing to abandon our wills. The amount of our heart we surrender to Him will measure how filled we are with His presence.

Since we are already living in the Spirit realm and will abide with Him forever around His throne, it would only make sense that we would be starting the celebration early by worshipping Him as a lifestyle NOW! When you examine your life today, what percentage of your heart do you feel you have given to Him? God's ultimate desire is for us to empty ourselves out so that He can fill us completely, because how can we overflow until we are full?

As we have seen throughout this book, worship is not an act that we do to prove to everyone else how spiritual we are – it is simply an honest, sincere expression of our appreciation and love for God. As we focus on developing this constant awareness of His presence, we will continue to learn how to express our passion for Christ beyond words by literally *living* for Him every moment. There are many questions related to what we do and why we do it, but the answers are always found within our intentions. We worship Christ because we love Him above all things, and this gives us the confidence to know that we cannot truly express our worship *outwardly* until we have fallen in love with Him *inwardly!* Go ahead, it's okay to shout! In this light, we CAN and MUST be consumed by Him from the inside-out so the world can SEE who Christ is IN US! When Jesus is found seated on the throne of our hearts as Lord and Master of our lives, then He alone will be the focus and adoration of our deepest spiritual intimacy and be *recognized* as the Resurrection and the Life within us!

When we draw from the wells of our souls, we tap into the deepest most *personal* resources of our beings. Within each human conscience there are hidden rooms which contain filing cabinets of secret thoughts and views that are seldom revealed or exposed. It is within these private chambers that we come to terms with what we believe and allow our trust and love to be developed. Within these hallowed halls of intimacy, God desires to have access to bring His penetrating light of truth that can transform knowledge into revelation. Our heavenly Father has an agenda, and that is to literally possess us. If we can ever become determined to harness our wills and allow Him to set-up His Kingdom within us, He can then freely take control and finish building our personal destiny that He has drawn. This can happen only when we become *tenacious* to please Him and become aware of the holy VOW we have made to Him. Let's look at the definition of *tenacious*; "Steady persistence in a course of action, especially in spite of difficulties, obstacles or discouragement. Steadfastness in doing something despite difficulty or delay in achieving success." Lord, give us passion to become tenacious for you! Amen! If the body of Christ would have the courage to drop their nets and become burdened for souls, *tenacious*, on fire, filled with the Holy Spirit, driven by love, seeking wisdom, and be serious about becoming true disciples for Christ, we would NOT even recognize this NEW Holy Ghost empowered church! This is a picture of the overcoming remnant warriors that will emerge as the glorious bride. It is prophesied by God that these witnesses will NOT fall asleep in this last hour because they have finally decided to love Him *more* than their flesh!

In closing, I want to compare the attitudes of two different Bible characters which reveal the difference of intentions and attitudes between the ones who truly love and worship God for who He is *(Spirit and Truth)*, and those who just want a one-way ticket to heaven *(I'm Ok- you're OK)*. If we love God with ALL of our minds and strength, nothing can keep us from worshipping Him. If we are just using religion to earn a reservation for Heaven's eternal luxurious playground, nothing will inspire us to adore Him now – or then! Both of these true stories expose the human conscience and identify why some people never think about worshipping God while others never stop.

Let us turn to *Luke chapter 18* and pick up on the account of how a young, wealthy man became discouraged when Jesus explained what was required to follow Him. I want us to listen carefully; **"And a certain ruler asked Him** [Jesus]**, saying, Good Master, what shall I do to inherit ETERNAL LIFE?"** *(Luke 18:18)*. If we are not sensitive, we will read over this and not discern exactly what this man was asking. It seems *eternal life* is what the masses have always been interested in, and the easy *version* of salvation has given the *broad-way* crowd just enough false security to believe that all we need to do is just understand the story of Calvary, and everything will take care of itself. Jesus continues to relay that he should obey the commandments, and the young man quickly replies that he has faithfully kept these laws and is proudly convinced he has done all that he can do. Then we notice that Jesus becomes blunt and takes the conversation to the *next level* as He interprets the divine reality of true discipleship. Jesus gets down to business and says to sell everything you have and give the money to the poor and come follow Me! There we have it - the basic fundamentals of discipleship Christianity 101; *it is not how much we know - but how much we apply*. When this highly successful businessman weighed his love for materialism and comfortable living on the scale of sacrifice, he decided that the price was too expensive and that he was NOT willing to yield his will in order to do God's will. Tragically, the love for power and control is a very common attitude among the masses that are also stumbling through life in a state of rebellion and selfishness. There are certain absolute truths we can know, and one of them is that we will never enjoy spiritual fulfillment while living in the bondage of a socially acceptable religious façade! Another sad fact is that many in this life are not even rich but still will not let go of their independence. *I Corinthians 6: 19 and 20* reminds us that we are not our own but are bought with a price – the blood of Jesus.

Let us observe the second story as we turn the page forward to *Luke chapter 19* and observe a man by the name of Zacchaeus. The Bible says he was also wealthy and a leader in his community, but notice closely what he was seeking when Jesus came into his neighborhood; ***"And he sought to see Jesus WHO HE WAS; and could not for the pressing crowd, because he was little of stature" (Luke 19:3)***. Zacchaeus ends up climbing a tree so that he can *observe the Lord,* and Jesus tells him to come down so they can go to his house. Zacchaeus testifies that he gives HALF of what he makes to the poor, and *(listen carefully)* if he makes a mistake or cheats anyone in business, he repays the mistake 4 times the amount! This clearly reveals that he is extremely honest and aware to always do what is right. What a beautiful demonstration of living in the awareness of God's presence as a lifestyle. This allows us to understand that Zacchaeus was a man of REPENTENCE - PRAYER and SPIRITUAL SENSITIVITY as Jesus continues, ***"This day is salvation come to this house, forasmuch as he also is a son of Abraham. For the Son of man is come to seek and save that which was lost"*** *(verses 9-10).*

Do you see the difference? The rich young ruler was not interested in having Jesus as his Lord or to serve Him as a lifestyle; he just wanted a legal formula that could guarantee him a front-row seat in heaven. This represents all that choose to live an individualistic, self-absorbed life that is *controlled* by the flesh and the default system. How can Jesus save people who do not think they have a problem? On the other hand, Zacchaeus knew he NEEDED God and had a passion to KNOW Jesus! He was a man that submitted, yielded, and surrendered his own plans in order to follow God's specific blueprint of his destiny. Yes, thank the Lord - He *"got it."* The Holy Spirit revealed to him this was the ONLY way to please God and make it to heaven. He is an example of those who have allowed God to pry their fingers from holding on to this world and their carnal natures, and now they are focused only on the Lamb that was slain and rose victoriously! These are the ones that are carrying their cross while singing *"Victory in Jesus, my Savior forever!"* There is no army or power in the universe that can hold back their praise to the Rose of Sharon - the Word that was made flesh! Are there any warriors out there? There is no problem so devastating that they cannot sing, *"It is well with my soul!"* There will never be a night so dark that they cannot release the light of Christ! Whether in abundance or lack, on top of the mountain or in the valley of the shadow of death, there will be a song of triumph on their lips and the oil of gladness within their souls! All of this is evident NOT because they have gathered empires of wealth and power, or have been recognized and respected in the halls of man's admiration – but because of God's great love! ***"For the which cause I also suffer these things: nevertheless I am not ashamed: For I KNOW whom I have believed, and am persuaded that He is able to keep that which I have committed unto Him against that day"*** *(II Timothy 1:12)*.

There is an old saying that declares, *"whatever is in the well will come up in the bucket,"* and if we are truly the sheep of His pasture, the expression of worship will flow out of our bellies as rivers of living water that will rise as a sweet fragrance of our endless love for Him. We will love Him NOT just for all that He can do, but for who He is. Your calling is just beginning to manifest. The Lord is stretching you and expanding your mind and heart to new and higher dimensions. All that you have done in the past is being used to prepare you for the future, and the greatest demonstrations in your ministry that will bring the most glory to God have yet to be revealed or accomplished. Amen! You have the ability to know your destiny and the opportunity to obey His will, but remember that you will never be a successful leader until you have learned how to be a willing follower. You have every freedom and opportunity to live as close to Jesus as you desire, but it is your decision how far you will travel with Him into the depths of intimacy. The Lord is gathering and preparing His remnant bride! He is coming back for a church that is pure and holy and is waiting with great expectation to welcome you into His endless joy. Cry out to the Father in fervent prayer to give you a revelation of His love and a passion to worship Him with all of your heart, and then prepare to experience the glorious wonders of heaven on earth!

"Now unto Him that is able to do exceeding abundantly above all that we ask or think, according to the power that worketh in us. Unto Him be glory in the church by Christ Jesus throughout all ages, world without end. Amen" *(Ephesians 3:20-21).*

> *"Jesus, I accept You to be my honored and cherished Lord. I choose to live in the constant awareness of Your covenant of faith, hope, and love according to the revelation of Your Word. I will listen to Your thoughts with my deepest reverence and promise to become what You died for me to be. I will stand faithfully with You in sickness and in health and will choose You above all others as long as I live. In Your holy name I vow to obey You and treasure you, to suffer for You, and be transformed completely for Your glory. From this day forward I dedicate my life to You.*
>
> *Dear love of my life, I am humbled in Your presence. I choose to pour out my heart to You until I am empty of myself. Please fill me with your holiness, your wisdom, and enable me to WALK as an ambassador for Your Kingdom. The more I learn about You, the more I realize how much I do not understand. I repent for my carnality, for I am a sinner that struggles to control my flesh. I have not been the best I can be. My mouth has spewed negativity, and I have been an enemy to your cross. Create in me a clean heart and renew a right spirit in me. I realize that I have such a long way to go. Teach me how to know the divine reality of living and growing within You. I cry out to You to re-build me – not just "remodel" me. Wash me with your blood.*
>
> *Lord it is easy to sing about Your fire, but today I sincerely ask for You to refine me and burn away everything that is not of You. Make me white and pure and so aware of Your holiness that ALL sin makes me nauseous. Give me the revelation of how to live in Your presence. Give me the desire and courage to crawl upon the altars of Your holy purging that I might be "reduced" until*

there is nothing left but You. You are a lamp unto my feet and a light unto my path. Teach me what it means to be a "light holder" for Your glory. Give me an un-yielding determination to stand without fear in the times of trials and persecutions so that I might fulfill what You died for me to be. Give me holy boldness to speak Your wisdom, and may my love be a sweet smelling fragrance unto You and all people. I purpose to adore You as a lifestyle and live in the awareness of Your presence. I am filled with anticipation and excitement as I look forward to worshipping You forever and ever. Empower me with Your anointing that breaks the yoke of bondage, and use me to bring healing and deliverance to those who are held captive to sin. It is an honor to serve as a remnant warrior and representative of Your Kingdom. I will passionately and intimately love You with all of my strength and mind, and today I humbly choose to give You the only thing you have ever wanted from me. . .my heart. I will bow down before You forever and in the holy Name of Jesus Christ I will always remain. Amen."

"Seek ye the Lord while He may be found, call ye upon Him while He is near" *(Isaiah 55:6).*

"Let everything that hath breath praise the Lord. Praise ye the Lord" *(Psalm 150:6).*

CPSIA information can be obtained
at www.ICGtesting.com
Printed in the USA
LVHW040747171222
735287LV00010B/2148